The
Greatest
Adventure Stories
Ever Told

The Greatest Adventure Stories Ever Told

Nineteen Gripping Tales

EDITED BY
LAMAR UNDERWOOD

LYONS
PRESS

Essex, Connecticut

An imprint of Globe Pequot, the trade division of
The Rowman & Littlefield Publishing Group, Inc.
4501 Forbes Blvd., Ste. 200
Lanham, MD 20706
www.rowman.com

Distributed by NATIONAL BOOK NETWORK

British Library Cataloguing in Publication Information available

Library of Congress Cataloging-in-Publication Data

ISBN 978-1-4930-8651-1 (pbk. : alk. paper)

∞™ The paper used in this publication meets the minimum requirements of
American National Standard for Information Sciences—Permanence of Paper for
Printed Library Materials, ANSI/NISO Z39.48-1992.

Contents

The
Greatest
Adventure Stories
Ever Told

Introduction

For those of us who have felt the pull of venturing past the familiar and the certain, craving the experiences and regions where risk and even danger might challenge us, the hunger for adventure is a powerful stimulus. We need to plan expeditions and outings that shake us beyond the sensations of common, everyday living. Call them whatever you like—adventures, mini-adventures. We need to go.

A person who has lived through a wilderness survival ordeal might question our use of the word "adventure" to describe an outing where our safe return was an absolute certainty. "A mere picnic," the survivalist might scoff, deeming only narrow escapes from death as being fit for the word "adventure." So much for adventure semantics.

Whether running a wild river, hiking a backcountry trail, or attaining some lonely peak, all the journeys we loosely call "adventures" have in common the sense of testing ourselves in both small and sometimes significant ways. The first such "test," if you will, starts with our wallets: Such ventures can be very expensive. Fact is, though, they don't always have to be. For example, you can book a pack-horse trip that takes you deep into the headwaters of the Yellowstone River in the Wyoming high country. Wranglers will do all the work and even cook your meals. You can also make the same trip by carrying your own backpack and hiking into the region by yourself or with a friend. Both trips can be said to be adventures. One relatively expensive, the other not expensive at all.

One interesting take on the subject of adventure comes from the noted explorer and writer Vilhjahmur Stefansson, who wrote in *My Life With the Eskimo*: "Having an adventure shows that someone is incompetent, that something has gone wrong."

For my personal taste, that view is too restricted for a great work like adventure. On the flight when Chuck Yeager broke "The Sound Barrier," nothing went wrong. Does that disqualify his epic feat from being called an "adventure story" and presented in this collection? Of course not. Not all adventures occur because a ship goes down, or an airplane crashes, or a wilderness traveler encounters unexpected difficulties. From the first explorers venturing into the blank spaces on the maps, to the present-day outdoor enthusiasts seeking personal fulfillment in the wild places still left on the planet, man has eagerly created adventures with varying degrees of boldness. The tales selected for this collection were chosen not because they relate events of particular fame or historical significance, but for the vivid and engaging power of the prose itself—for storytelling. In every case, it has been my goal as editor to bring together stories that literally lift us out of our reading chairs and make us part of the events being described—the ordeals, the disasters, the triumphs of overcoming the most challenging terrain and dangers.

Yes, when Chuck Yeager breaks "The Sound Barrier," you will be with him. You will journey down The River of Doubt in the Brazilian wilderness with Theodore Roosevelt; see the Rocky Mountain high country as the first trapper-explorers saw it; face the stormy seas of rounding Cape Horn with Francis Chichester; share Joel Kramer's journey Beyond Fear through the New Guinea mountains few white men have ever seen; and share other adventure experiences too numerous to mention here without repeating the contents page. You will find these tales so intense with feeling that reading them will make the events they describe become a part of your life.

For most of us, our carefully planned "mini adventures" will never result in days or even hours of desperate life-and-death struggles and survival ordeals. Unless we tempt fate with the kind of in-the-face challenges faced by the most intrepid sailors, mountain climbers, or whitewater river runners, we'll all come back from our outings without so much as a scare. Then, safely at home, we can face the ultimate adventures through the magic of good writing that transports us to lonely mountain crags, stormy seas, and strange forests where death lies in wait for the foolish and the unprepared.

—Lamar Underwood
March 2002

A Harrowing Journey

From *Beyond Fear*

BY JOEL P. KRAMER

Here is a trek so hazardous and grueling that I only want to take it in print, thank you very much. I am grateful though to Joel Kramer for sharing his amazing experience of crossing New Guinea by foot and by kayak, without the use of motors—a first. With companion Aaron Lippard, Kramer faced natural terrors that included crocodiles, deadly snakes, malaria-carrying mosquitoes, leeches, a variety of poisonous insects, Stone Age cannibals, rapids, and whirlpools. How's that for a wilderness agenda?

Both Kramer and Lippard are from Salt Lake City, Utah, and survived the experience, although the issue was often in doubt.

★   ★   ★   ★   ★

Aaron and I lie down beneath our shelter in the waning light of evening. I sit up and stare at the mountains from within the protection of the net. They stand pitch black against a brilliant orange sky speckled with pink clouds.

"That's the Central Divide," I say to Aaron.

"If it's not, I would sure hate to see the real one," he comments.

"Just gotta make it across . . . Then we're home free." Aaron looks up at me, then to the mountains. I can't see any detail in the gloomy, black form of rugged peaks painted across the sky.

"Home free . . . or we'll drown in rapids," he says. All is quiet. Aaron pulls himself up to the edge of the net as we study our opponent together.

"They say that's the last place on earth where cannibals and head-hunters still exist." I am whispering, as if some might be close by.

"God have mercy," Aaron prays, before lying back on his blanket. I scratch my lower legs.

"It's New Year's Eve tonight, ya know," Aaron says. I can hear him scratching as well.

"Do you itch too?" I ask.

"Around my ankles."

"Dang! What have we gotten into now? Getting off this island is my New Year's resolution." I search in the blackness for my flashlight. "It's been quite a year for me. Last year at this time I was digging a hole 18 feet in diameter, through six feet of snow in 30-below-zero temperatures, to get my tepee set up—from bitter cold to steamy jungles, grizzly bears to crocodiles. And from the depths of loneliness to the trials of hanging out with you all day." I turn my light onto my ankles to find them covered in red bumps. I examine them closer.

"I was in South Africa this time last year," Aaron remembers. I can see white tips on the new itchy sores.

"Looks like chiggers or something," I conclude. Aaron sits up. He has them all around his ankles as well.

"Must have picked them up in all the grass around here."

We scratch them together.

"Oooh, that feels good."

"Just don't rub the skin off, or you'll get a nasty infection," he warns.

"You mean *another* nasty infection," I correct him. We laugh. "It's almost worth having these sores just to have the pleasure of scratching them." I look at him. "I tell you what, if we can live through this year, what do ya say we take a vacation on the next New Year's day, or maybe we can just stay home and spend it with a beautiful woman." We're quiet for a long time.

"A beautiful woman," Aaron finally whispers. "What I wouldn't do just to talk to one."

The next thing I know, I wake up to an annoying beeping noise coming from Aaron's watch.

"Happy New Year," comes his groggy voice.

"Happy New Year." I roll over and go back to sleep.

The jungle begins to grow over the top of our shelter. The vines come twisting in as they turn into snakes embracing my legs beneath the net. I wake up, out of breath and sweaty. My body freezes when I feel something very real crawling down my leg. My hand carefully searches for my flashlight. It stops crawling. Don't move, I tell myself. It feels large, like a giant spider. It crouches on my ankle. I feel the net hanging across my right leg. I must have rolled my leg out from under the net while having the nightmare. It's going to bite me! I start to panic. Get it off! I think to myself. I clamp my eyes shut and kick my foot with a hard jerk. It doesn't come off!

"Iiiiiieeeeeeee!" I scream, feeling a bite. My leg is kicking wildly in the air. Aaron springs up beside me as I pound at my leg through the netting. I pull it back under, still crying out with the pain that now shoots up my leg.

"What! What is it!" Aaron is yelling. I get my leg under the net slapping frantically at my ankle to make sure whatever just bit me is off.

"Find a flashlight!" I yell at Aaron. I hear him searching. I feel swelling in my ankle as I grip the throbbing tissue with my hand.

"What happened?" Aaron asks again, worriedly, flashing the light on.

"Something bit me!" We look. My ankle is swelling before our eyes; two little red needle-size pricks sit side by side. "Oh Lord!" Aaron says of the sight. "What was it?"

"Something bad! It was a spider or a centipede . . . I never saw it." Aaron springs onto his knees and starts searching the netting and blankets. "It was outside. I stuck my leg out from under the net." He glares at me. "Not on purpose—I was having a bad dream." He continues his search for several minutes until he is thoroughly convinced that nothing dangerous is in the net with us. I fall back on my blanket, moaning and writhing. I rock back and forth, searching for comfort. "Well, at least I lived for a few hours in '93," I laugh nervously.

"Shut up, dude! Don't you dare leave me alone in the middle of this dang island. Just hang on and try to be calm." Aaron's voice is not so calm.

"Just keep breathing. I can't die if I keep breathing," I try to encourage myself. I know one thing for sure. If I do live, I'm in for a long night.

★   ★   ★   ★   ★

High mountains loom on the morning horizon, daring me to try. It's the beginning of the third day since the bite, which has rendered my leg useless, wasting two important days that we could have been hiking. That first night of 1993, when I was bitten, is etched in my memory as a night of severe suffering, an unending throb of pain that threatened my sanity. I was still awake when the sun rose the next morning revealing my swollen ankle, poisoned by unknown fangs. Over the past two days and nights it has become worse, wasting no time getting infected.

The mountains continue to taunt me. I want so desperately to press on. Aaron walks up to the net and glances down at our only obstacle—the large, bloated lump of infected pus and blood, as big as my fist, protruding from the side of my right ankle.

"It's not getting any better."

"No," he agrees, handing me some sago, called "sok sok" in pidgin, for breakfast. He has done well taking care of me lately.

"If it's only going to get worse, we should move on," I suggest. Aaron studies my face as I look back towards the rugged horizon. "Better now than in a few days when it could be twice as bad."

"Good idea, I mean, hey, let's get as far away from Inaru as possible before we have to carry you back."

"Inaru is gone!" I point to the southern peaks. "We have to make it over to the Lagaip. It's the fastest way out of here now, crippled or not." I grab the medical kit and start searching for the pain killers. "Stop staring at me and pass the water bottle."

"You can't get your boot on," he pleads.

"I need a stick." He looks confused. "Trust me. I have a plan—all I need is a little stick about as big around as my finger." He walks off to look for a stick while I take some pills and pull out the bottle of iodine, cotton balls, and an ace bandage.

"All right, what's the plan?" he asks, throwing me a stick.

"If I'm going to get my boot on, I need you to squeeze all the gunk out of my sore." His face reveals the same horror that I feel in the pit of my stomach.

"You're crazy!"

"Have you got any better ideas?"

"And the stick?" he questions. I place it in my mouth and clamp down. "Do you really think that's going to help?"

I pull it back out of my mouth to speak. "I don't know. They always do it in the movies." I try to muster a smile. Aaron studies my ankle. "One more thing." He looks up at me. "Once you start, don't stop until it's all out." With that, I place the stick in my mouth, put my hands under my body, and lie back on them. I talk through the stick. "Just remember, do it fast and. . . ."

I feel his hands press in without mercy. My mouth clamps shut onto the stick. I sit up, wincing in pain, as he squeezes harder; gobs of bloody pus squirt from my sore all over his hands. He looks away when I bellow out a horrible scream. I begin to tremble in unbelievable pain. I need it to end. It has to end. And then, for a moment it does, until he starts pinching from a different position. I scream until he stops. I gasp for air, opening my eyes to find the bewildered faces of the carriers looking down on me. I sit up, feeling somewhat foolish.

"You okay?" Aaron's voice is shaky. I nod that I am, though I feel dizzy and nauseated. I realize my mouth is still clamped shut, so I release the pressure. The branch is stuck, deeply embedded in my upper teeth.

"I would keep that in," Aaron suggests, lifting up the iodine. I look down to find an empty crater in the side of my ankle. He pours the iodine in, filling the hole until it overflows. I tremble with the sting's intensity, and bite back down on the stick. After several minutes, I feel some relief. I wrap my ankle up with the ace bandage and reach for my boot. After loosening the laces, I pull it onto my foot with several loud screeches. Standing up, the blood rushes down to my sore, and it begins to throb.

With the Bushy Man and carriers watching me, I try not to show my pain. Limping forward, I put as little weight as possible on my crippled ankle. I take a step onto my right foot. Pain shoots up my leg, pushing a miserable moan out of my clamped-shut mouth. I feel the eyes of the men on me. I concentrate on smiling before turning around to face them.

"Walk about," I announce.

"Iiiiieeeee!" They cry out, shaking their heads while they tisk at me.

"You won't make it anywhere like that," Aaron comments.

"Just find me a walking stick, and I'll make it to wherever we're going."

"There's where we're going," he says, pointing to the mountains that loom on the horizon of steep jungle slopes and high rocky peaks.

"Please . . . just get me a walking stick." I'm standing with my weight shifted completely onto my good foot.

★   ★   ★   ★   ★

Lord, you are my God,
And I will ever praise you.

I stop singing for a moment to pull myself another couple feet up the muddy ledge. My foot catches on a root. I look up, the sweat stinging my eyes—nothing but more jungle, more climbing. I've been in last place all day, and now I'm feeling very alone. Grabbing hold of a vine, I heave myself up, dragging my limp foot behind me. I put some weight on it, then I pull my other foot up to a root. My leg aches as I move higher.

And I will follow you all of my days,
I will learn to walk in Your ways,
And, step by step, You'll lead me,
And I will follow you all of my days.

I sing to remember why I'm climbing this mountain of suffering. This morning is the second full day of working my way, slowly and painfully to the top of the Central Divide, the climax of our expedition. I am feeling every step! This morning we repeated the process of Aaron milking my wound so I could get my boot on. The first mile out of camp was the worst. There was dizzying pain as the blood flowed down my leg and put pressure on the wound that has become more infected. Aaron has done well, doing my load of the chores. He cooks, cleans, sets up, and takes down camp so that all I have to worry about is making it to the next camp.

"Iiiiiieeeeee!" I pull up my shirt and scrape off a large leech. I have learned the hard way that moving slowly through the jungle puts me at an extreme disadvantage. My handicap gives the leeches, ants, flies, and mosquitoes more time to locate me and perform their merciless rituals of torment. I am caught between the misery of hiking and the torment of resting, the worst of both worlds. It makes sense to me now why the nationals have learned to move so quickly through their native terrain.

A vine dangles from the canopy up the ridge. It pulls tight when I get hold of it for a mighty heave, but a snap echoes and the vine drops, limp, to the ground. My hands panic in the air while the ridge slips away. The canopy becomes a streaking blur until it jerks still when my back slams hard against the ground. My sore ankle gouges against roots and rocks as I continue to tumble down the slope, my screams echo through the dense foliage. I have to stop, flashes through my mind; the bottom of the mountain is so far down it has taken me two days to get where I am. I forget the hurt for the moment and use my legs and arms to stop my out-of-control roll. With the world back in focus, I grab at a small tree to stop my slide. The tree quickly breaks from my grip, but I have slowed down enough to get hold of a vine that swings me across the ridge. Finally, I stop. Pulling my legs up to my chest, I gasp for air. Overwhelmed with pain, I cry out in hurt and frustration until enough of the throbbing subsides and I can think again. My shouts die down to moans, and I try to comfort my traumatized body with a gentle rocking motion. Finally, I sit up and slip my boot down to have a look. Blood is soaking through the ace bandage wrapped around my ankle. Ants crawl up my skin and flies prick at my back. Fury floods my heart and mind.

"Damn you!" I stand and shout to the canopy overhead, the dark shadows, the mountain. "Have you no mercy at all?" I feel something grip my shoulder and I wheel around with fright.

"You okay?" Aaron stands behind me looking concerned.

"Do I *look* okay?" I knock his hand off my shoulder and start back up the ridge. Enraged, I momentarily forget the pain as I storm up the same ridge I have already climbed. Aaron follows in silence somewhere behind. Before long, though, the pain comes back, shooting up my leg, making me even angrier. I put more weight on it. Tears flow from my eyes, and my jaw tightens. I look up into a never-ending jungle and push off three hard times in a row from my bad foot. Crying harder now, I move faster than I have in days.

"Take it easy!" Aaron is beside me now. I'm dizzy and start to sway. His hand grips my arm, and he lowers me to the ground.

"What are you doing?" His voice is confused.

"I don't care . . . I don't care anymore." I try to stand up, but he doesn't let me.

"Not until you calm down." We sit for a long time before hiking again. He swats at the flies on my back. I moan with every step; it's worse now, everything is worse. What choice do I have but to go on? Aaron hangs back for the next hour keeping me in sight. My moaning grows louder until suddenly he turns around, his face streaming with tears. He begins to cry harder as he charges me, throwing himself to the ground at my feet.

"God!" he screams in a hurt voice. "Please, please heal him!" His hand trembles on my sore ankle. He weeps out loud, his whole body shaking. "Why? Why won't you just heal him?" He cries in frustration. I reach down and place my hand on his shoulder.

"It's okay," I try to tell him, but it doesn't help. I realize my selfishness, that Aaron is more than a friend and a partner. His feelings are deeper than sympathy. I realize that everything I do, and feel, and suffer affects him. We are in this together. If I hurt, then he hurts with me! I realize the need to be strong for both of us. "It's all right, Aaron." He turns quickly around and starts back up the ridge.

My next steps don't seem to hurt as bad; it's not my ankle, but *something* has healed, something is different, something more important! I think of the ridge I am on, and suddenly know I can climb it, no matter how bad I hurt. I give thanks to God for His strength. Keeping my mouth shut, I climb for the rest of the day.

We are making our way up through a rock outcropping and come across the old woman sitting in a patch of grass. None of the other carriers seem to be around. The old woman notices our confusion and points to a large, black, gaping hole in the side of a ledge. Wild noises of beating wings and clanging metal blades striking rock ring out from the opening. I move closer, then flinch as a hurtling lump of skin and fur flies out of the blackness towards me, falling on the ground with a thud. A bat bares its teeth and hisses at me. Its wing bones are apparently shattered. Moist with blood, the broken ends of jagged bones are sticking out from the dark skin of its wing.

"Looks like it's going to be evil spirits for dinner," Aaron comments from behind. More clanging rings out from deep in the cave followed by several injured bats shooting out of the dark hole onto the grass. The old woman takes the dull end of her bush knife, and without even the slightest change of expression, begins breaking their good wings to form a squirming pile of hissing little mouths. She strikes the most likely bats on the head a few times with the broad side of the blade, being careful not to kill them. Then she begins to load them into her belum bag. The cave entrance produces about fifty bats before the Bushy Man and the others pop out onto the ridge with their eyes squinting in the sunlight.

In the search for a campsite, I fall behind again. Limping further, I notice the altimeter on Aaron's watch reads 10,000 feet. Throughout this day of climbing, the wet jungle has given way to pine trees. The wind picks up and begins to whistle; I look up at the tall pines swaying beneath a blue sky. It feels so strange to see the sky again. I take in a breath of air. The heavy humidity is gone; and the breeze is set free, whisking the dry moss that dangles from the surrounding tree limbs.

"Almost feels like the mountains back home," Aaron comments, turning around in front of me.

"Not really," I say, seeing the Bushy Man standing in a clearing waiting for us. He has come back to lead us to the camp. The air is cool, almost cold; my shirt is dry and no sweat pours across my face. I stop and wait for a moment, searching around me. No flies. No mosquitoes. Looking down, I search the ground for ants but only find a few. The thick undergrowth has vanished, leaving behind barren ground of dry dirt and rock—so much room to walk. The Bushy Man's bush knife hangs still at his side.

And then the ridge ends. I had all but given up hope that we were ever going to find the top. The wind picks up and moans an eerie sound—so ancient, so lost. Spheres of tree tops stretch out over us as we start along the crest of the ridge towards the east. How did I ever get here? I ask myself in the strangeness of this moment. Two large, rocky ledges rise up in front of us; a crack of air splits them in half. We enter the trench of solid rock and follow it until it ends in a flat area under an overhanging ledge. The smoke from a fire fills the camp. I drop to the ground from exhaustion. My ankle has been hurting so badly for so long that I have almost become used to the pain.

"I think I'm gonna like it up here," Aaron says, looking calm and safe from the usual array of attacking insects.

"Too cold for them . . . I just hope it's not too cold for us," I say.

The Bushy Man builds a cooking rack out of sticks while the others prepare a shelter on top of a small hill for Aaron and me. The overhang above the fire will be adequate for the others. The old woman starts handing wounded bats to the Bushy Man. He uses the sharp end of a vine to thread several wings before he ties the bats in place, on the rack over the fire. He ignores their tortured squeals as the flames rise up to engulf them.

Aaron decides not to watch this scene and goes to put up the net. With my now-throbbing ankle, I have no option but to stay put and watch. A heap of fifty bats now hangs over the fire, some already silent in the comfort of death, others just beginning the process. They look like "evil spirits;" their little mouths squealing in pain, revealing rows of sharp teeth. More wood is placed under them. The flames reach up, singeing the hair from their bodies. They screech, twisting and kicking on the vine as their ears curl up in the growing heat. Large blisters form and then quickly pop across the skin of their bodies and wings. I look down. If they were Birds of Paradise, then I would save them, I think to myself. Their noises of suffering finally begin to fade into the coming night.

With the absence of the gloom-and-doom jungle canopy, brilliant stretches of stars shed light on us. We are eating bat meat with men who still ponder the night-lit sky in the simplest of wonderings. I shut my eyes while I chew the dark, wild-tasting meat, trying to delete from my memory the gruesome scene of rising flames and squealing bats so strongly implanted a few hours before. The moss glows fluorescent green, performing a kind of ritual dance as the wind picks up. The air is cold, and even wrapped up tight in our blankets, the night is long and uncomfortable.

"Happy nun." I wake to find Sogamoi bent over our net.

"Nogat walkabout, Stew big pain," he announces, passing some burnt mummified bats under the netting.

"What's big pain?" Aaron asks.

"Me no suvey," Sogamoi replies. I take a bite of bat meat. It must have smoked all night, because it crumbles in my mouth like saltless jerky. Maybe it will keep for a day or so this way, I think. Aaron slips on his boots.

"I'm going to check on Stew real quick."

"Don't worry, I won't eat your bat," I tell him with a grin. Aaron returns as quickly as he leaves.

"I think you better come down." His voice is solemn. "Don't bother with your boots. We aren't going anywhere for a while."

"What is it?" I stand up, wincing with the pain shooting up from my ankle.

"I don't know. Just come down." He leads me down the small slope. Making my way down under the overhang, I realize the hurt in my foot has grown worse during the night. Stew is curled up away from the fire, his knees drawn up to his chest. He is shaking uncontrollably, with streams of sweat running down his face, even though the morning is cool. We are greatly concerned for Stew, and are stunned to hear laughter ringing out behind us. Aaron and I turn to find the rest of the men sitting in a circle enjoying one another's stories. Even Stew's wife, Agomi, sits by herself and smiles at us, seeming unconcerned.

"He's burning up with fever." Aaron has knelt down with his hand on Stew's forehead.

"Stew . . . Stew!" I shake him, but he shows no signs of comprehension; he continues severely trembling. Laughter breaks out again, eating at our distressed emotions.

"He's dying, Joel." Aaron's words quiver while tears start rolling down his colorless cheeks. Again, the laughter clashes against our fear, changing Aaron's expression to anger. Without warning, he jumps to his feet. "What is wrong with you people?" he screams. The laughter dies out. "Isn't Stew your friend?" With a red face, he turns to Agomi. "Isn't this man your husband?" His voice sounds desperate. They just stare at him. "Sogamoi, malaria, Stew gottam malaria? We twopella givem pills," he pleads in the midst of tears.

"Nogat malaria . . . big pain." Sogamoi breaks the shocked silence. He grabs his chest, "Iiiiiiieeeeee."

"Stew die?" Aaron asks. He shuts his eyes and drops his shoulders until Sogamoi understands the question.

"Me no suvey," he replies with a shrug. Aaron runs over and drops on the ground next to Stew's trembling body. "Stew! Stew!" he shouts, crying louder, but the only answer he gets is a low moan. The mountain people watch as Aaron stands and then storms up the hill to our shelter. I follow, limping my way up to the net. He sits down under the net and grabs the medical kit, pouring it out on the blankets. I look over his shoulder as he digs through the pile of worthless bandages, iodine, malaria pills, Lomotil, and stitching threads. Then, he breaks down. Holding his face in his hands, his crying turns to sobs. I crawl under the net and wait for him to finish, feeling the weight myself. Finally, he looks up.

"Have you ever watched a man die?" I ask him. He shakes his head. "Me neither." I hesitate for a moment. "These people have—it's a common part of their lives. Family, and . . . well, they just lost a friend less than a week ago."

"How can they just sit there and pretend nothing bad is happening?"

"Maybe they understand, deeply, that death is a part of life," I suggest. "How would it help Stew? How would it help them if they were depressed all day? They have to go on hunting and living, or else tomorrow they will get hungry and weak, and sickness will kill them."

"Stew was the strongest. I thought he was invincible, and now look at him. If men like him get struck down, then what chance do *we* have?" I look away, feeling his fear. He is right.

"It was the kayak, ya know . . . he carried it up here the last two days. That kayak is too heavy; everyone who carries it gets sick. Sogamoi got malaria twice when he carried it. Stew has carried it the last two days of climbing, and it looks like it is going to kill him, and for what? Twenty kina or less? It should be us, not him. And we have no medicine for him and neither do they!"

I look down at my ankle; it seems so insignificant now. "Maybe their medicine is to laugh." I pull myself back out from under the net. "Come on . . . let's go do the only thing we can."

Aaron follows me back down to Stew. I prop his head up, and we give him some pain killers with water. After gathering the men together, we lay our hands on Stew's trembling body. I pray. "There is only one Doctor in this place and one Medicine that can save our friend. Lord, our God, heal him! Thank you, Jesus. Amen."

"Amen," Aaron whispers beside me. We put one of our Gortex rain jackets on Stew and cover him with blankets before going back to the shelter to ration out rice. There isn't much food to hunt in this high country.

Surprisingly, Stew is able to sit up by morning and spends his day leaning over the fire. When his moans grow loud and more frequent, we give him some more pain killers. I find a stick for the daily "milking" of my wound, which has more gunk in it than usual. I bite down hard. As Aaron begins to squeeze, pus starts to pour from my ankle. I turn away, trying to hold my emotions in. I know the days have been rough enough, but this is too much for me. I tremble in the wake of my moans. The stick snaps in my mouth, giving way to screams as I twist back and forth on the forest floor. Finally, the squeezing stops.

"Gross!" Aaron says in disgust. I look down to find a large pile of pus next to my ankle. It's black. Dark red lines travel in webs up my leg beneath my skin. "You have blood poisoning." Without warning, he pours in the iodine, throwing me back into a twisting tremor of agony on the ground. He puts fresh bandages on, while I recover, and gives me some pills to take. "You need to go on double antibiotics until it heals up." His eyes are filling with tears again. "I have to go." He picks up the little black Bible and quickly disappears into the woods behind the net.

I begin to worry about him in the late afternoon, but Aaron finally returns. We sit in silence, watching the men coughing in the background, spitting junk out of their lungs.

"They're all getting sick."

"It's too cold up here for them. Did you figure anything out while you were gone?" He nods. "I want to hear it." He looks a little shocked.

"It might be pneumonia that Stew has. This cold, dry air is making them all sick, so I say we need to get down to the lower altitude they are used to." He fidgets with his hair while looking at the carriers sitting around the fire below us. "It took these men eighteen days to get here from their village. Carrying Stew, it will take them longer to get back, so I don't really see that as an option. We need help. Our only chance is to find missionaries somewhere downriver. We need three men to help us down to the Lagaip River. Bushy Man, Sogamoi, and Mowga can continue with us. Libi, Eabay, Bushy Man's son, Aguy, and the women can help carry Stew down the ridge, back to the Bushy Man's hut. We can give them enough food to get them there. Then they have a garden. We make it to the Lagaip as fast as possible and then try to find a missionary for help. That's the best plan I could come up with."

"It's worth a shot," I agree. Again, Aaron looks somewhat shocked at my easy acceptance of his plan. "Good luck explaining it to the men." And that's what Aaron attempted to do—all afternoon until nightfall.

Stew looks better in the morning. We say a sad goodbye to him, Aguy, Eabay, and the women. We pray for Stew one more time before continuing our climb up the finger ridge, which takes most of the morning. We had thought we were right on top of the divide, but we had only topped a finger ridge connected to the main divide. By noon, the trees have completely disappeared, replaced by rock and grass. Within half an hour, we are on top of the island—an inspiring sight. The tips of pine trees point at us from below, gently swaying in a breeze rising up the steep slope into our faces. Below the pines, the thick green canopy falls and ripples across the ridges that go on until they disappear into the distant haze. The misty Salumei gorge cuts through the ridge tops in the far distance. Finally, we can see all at once the mass of ridges that we have crossed since the breaking konda bridge.

"Shhh! Listen!" I hear voices! A hand reaches up over the lip of the ridge, the knuckles whitening as it pulls, and the old woman's worn face pops into sight. Aaron and I look at each other, puzzled. Eabay tops the ridge, followed by Aguy, Agomi, Libi, and the Bushy Man's son, who turn around and pull Stew up over the lip. He looks at me, holding a walking stick in his hand.

"Stew?" Aaron questions.

"On top," he says in a weary voice with a weak smile.

"You truly are the toughest man I have ever met." I get up and walk to the other side of the ridge while Aaron tries to find out why they didn't go down to the Bushy Man's hut like they were supposed to.

From my vantage point, it doesn't look much different on the other side of the divide, just as thick and rugged. I call for Aaron. He comes and looks silently out over the vastness.

"Why did they come with us?" I ask him.

"No idea."

"See that gorge?" I point into the distance. A gaping canyon splits the canopy and the rugged terrain in the cloud-covered distance.

"Lagaip," Aaron says.

The carriers spend a lot of time looking out over their home-terrain from this radically new angle. They have spent their lives living beneath the dark blanket of rain forest, but now they get to see their world from on high, looking down.

"Onward to Daru!" Aaron shouts when we begin our descent down the southern slope of the divide.

The slope falls away so sharply that at times our lives hang by a tree branch or a root. Everything feels insecure. I face out into empty air, and gravity forces me to go much faster than I desire. The roots and vines that I had trusted as handholds on the way up are now behind, where I can't see. I think back to the many falls I have taken while descending smaller ridges, being unable to stop myself until having landed with a painful thud next to a creek bed. The pit of my stomach tightens when I search for the end of this ridge, but it looks bottomless. The ridges fanning out to the south seem miles away.

The way down is faster, but it is much more jarring on my bad foot than the slow climb of the past several days. Within a few hours, the tops of the pine trees grow closer together, casting shadows that grow darker and darker the more we drop in elevation. The first sign of the pesky, jungle foes is a leech I pull off the side of my neck. Soon, the usual cloud of biting flies returns along with mosquitoes and ants. I want to turn around and head for the high country again.

The jungle crowds me. Its canopy, falling sharply with the steep ridge, begins to shake with powerful gusts of wind, like being underwater during a terrible storm and looking up at the angry surface. I hesitate, watching the tree tops out in front of me fiercely jerk in the wind. The storm takes us by force when dark clouds collide with the ridge. Their grayish mist engulfs us, dramatically cutting down visibility. Stew is standing behind me now; I turn around and show him how to zip up the rain jacket that I have given him to wear. I pull the hood over his head as the rain begins to penetrate the leafy roof. It is important for him to keep dry.

As we continue to hike, a thin, slippery blanket of water and mud flows along the ground under my boots. I fall, sliding and tumbling down the side of the ridge several times until, battered, annoyed, and bruised, I catch up with Aaron and the Bushy Man. Aaron is also covered in mud from recent falls. We pass the carriers and the women who have taken shelter under a rock ledge to enjoy a smoke.

After a few hours, the rain dies down. Aaron and I continue to slip and slide our way behind the Bushy Man. Aaron lets out a loud cry of agony when he strikes one of his leg sores on a branch. Even Bushy Man flinches at the sudden and horrible shout. Then he suddenly freezes mid-stride, and his hand shoots up behind him. Aaron and I stop, not daring to breathe while we search the jungle. Slowly, the Bushy Man draws an arrow onto the vine stretched deadly tight against the hardwood tips of his bow. His flat, swollen feet move silently across the mud; then he crouches, placing the bow and arrow on the ground. His legs spring straight, hurtling him through the air as he clears a log and completely disappears in the green foliage beyond. He emerges moments later with a fifteen-foot python snake which he carries by the head. It twists its tail, trying to snare a leg, but Bushy Man escapes it.

The carriers have caught up with us now. Seeing the yellow and black-colored python, Libi cuts a branch from a tree and splits three fourths of its length with his bush knife. He slides the snake's neck into the slit, clamping down the open end with his hands while using a vine to tie it shut. Then he drops the squirming serpent onto the ground. A swollen lump in its middle makes it obvious that it has recently eaten something. Aaron runs over and picks the python up. "Joel, take a picture." He hoists the snake up while I dig for the camera. I am taking the shot when everyone bursts into laughter. Looking over the camera, I see that Aaron's excited look has turned to one of misery. With the snake on the ground again, Aaron looks down at his pants.

"What happened? Did he bite you?" Then, I see a big wet stain running down his pants and start to laugh. "Looks like you got pissed on by a python." Aaron does not find any of it the least bit funny. The strong odor of snake urine stings my nostrils as he storms past me to continue the hike. The old woman fills her belum with the night's squirming dinner. Libi has adjusted the stick on the snake's head to cut off just enough air to weaken it but still keep it alive and its meat fresh.

Stew is the last to make it into camp where he collapses on the ground. Aaron gives him more pain killers, then turns his attention to the reek of the snake urine still rising off his pants. He washes them with water and dirt, and, though it helps, it doesn't kill the odor completely.

Meanwhile, the old woman spills the mostly dead python out on the ground and goes to cut firewood as dinner preparations begin. The Bushy Man's son had killed a poisonous red snake when they first found camp. Its bush-knife-hacked body lies still next to the python who is now getting massaged by the hands of Libi and the Bushy Man. The lump in the snake's belly begins to move towards its mouth. I watch in horror. Libi unties the stick around its throat once the lump is close enough. I shut my eyes, hearing the snake gagging up its victim. The slimy, semi-digested carcass of a possum lies on the jungle floor. I start to gag.

Libi ties the stick back in place over the snake's throat. This time, he clamps it down as tightly as he can, cutting off the snake's air completely. He throws the snake aside to wait for it to die. About thirty minutes later the snake goes limp. Meanwhile, the three-day-old, partly digested possum is cooked over the fire, torn apart and eaten by the mountain people. Aaron and I pass when they offer us some.

However, the snake meat is white and juicy when it comes off the fire; its flaky consistency makes it fall easily from the hundreds of ribs. It is light, without a strong flavor. There is no fat or chewy toughness to it like some of the possum and pig we have eaten. Aaron slurps at the meat, eager for more. It's not that it really tastes good; it just doesn't taste bad! The Bushy Man sucks a piece of skin into his mouth. Then Aaron asks for more. Sogamoi hands over another piece, and Aaron catches my eye in the middle of scarfing it down.

"What?" he asks. His hair sticks out in all directions; his beard wet with snake-meat juices. I smile at him.

"We have been in the jungle too long."

Soon we finish eating and go to sleep; the night is filled with coughs, hacking, and spitting. Stew groans deep into the night until Aaron gets up to give him more pain killers. Then the rising sun wakes us to another miserable day.

After hiking all morning, we finally reach the bottom of the Central Divide. It is a good feeling to have it behind us, and now the excitement of being close to the Lagaip and the downriver stretch of our expedition gives us energy for the rest of the long day's hiking, energy I didn't realize I had, especially with the lack of food. We spend the rest of the day climbing and descending the buckling ridges that we had looked down a few days before.

The night overtakes us before we can find a camp, and we end up sleeping without a net or a shelter on a bunch of rocks next to a cliff. I pull my bag up under my legs so that most of my body is lifted up by the bag, a more comfortable position than lying directly on the hard stones. Needless to say, I don't get much sleep.

The sharp rocks which have dug into my back all night wake me at sunrise. Because there isn't a camp to take down and no breakfast for anyone, we start hiking earlier than usual. A wet-leafed branch slaps me across the face, the price I pay for following too closely behind the Bushy Man who makes his way quickly through the thick jungle wall. I step into an opening and look around. Bushy Man kneels down on one knee, studying a long muddy scar across the ground, slicing a path towards the south through the dense undergrowth. The carriers react in fear, their eyes wide and apprehensive as they stumble one by one onto the trail.

"What?" I ask Sogamoi, but he quickly warns me with his hand to be quiet.

"Belong man," he whispers, pointing to the trail.

"What man?" Aaron asks, looking worried.

"Me no suvey." The men chatter amongst themselves in quiet voices that are quickly swallowed by the jungle noises blaring at us from all directions. The women are nervous as we huddle together behind the cautious Bushy Man, creeping forward down the unknown path. He is listening intently with each silent step. Questions race through my mind while everyone scans the dark jungle surrounding us. Who made this path? What kind of people have been hidden in the dense interior highlands of New Guinea since the beginning of time? The fear in the mountain people only adds to my own.

A crude fence made from split wood woven together with vines pops into view. The tension rises! Wild pig tracks mark up the mud along the outside of the fence. Inside the fence is a garden which bursts into movement when some parrots take flight, sending panic through our group. I look to the Bushy Man. He moves on down the trail, leading us over the lip of the ridge. Suddenly, several huts, built high on stilts, appear just below us. We stand perfectly still. I hold my breath. When I look down, I see a village full of people.

My eyes focus on a woman whose body is smeared with red clay. Streaks of white, black, and red paint decorate her face. My heart begins to race as I realize that she is staring back at me. The large, white, pig tusk in her nose flips back when her mouth opens wide in a scream of horror. Belum strings hanging from her hair jerk as she makes a hasty retreat. The whole village explodes into movement.

Bushy Man drops his bow and arrows on the ground. The others follow his lead. Eerie screams quickly bring my attention down to several women snatching helpless children into their arms as they flee into the forest. The men come together in the center of the village, each one armed with bows and arrows. Tall, cone-shaped hair wrapped in snake skin and tree bark sways above their heads. Fierce war cries add to the shock when the men mount arrows onto the tight vines stretched across their bows. Huddled together, they rush towards us, their sharpened boar tusks swinging from their noses. They are a mass of red bodies, black foreheads, and violent faces.

I step backwards, and Aaron slips the bag from his shoulders. There's no time to think; it's all happening fast. The men are motionless, in shock. I think of running. Lord have mercy! I pray, when I realize I can't run. They are close now; the muscles in their arms strain behind the arrows drawn deeply towards their chests. Bushy Man takes several steps forward. The warriors cry out in fierce warnings. He falls on his face like a dead man in front of their arrows. Each deadly-sharp tip points in a different direction. One is pointed at me. I close my eyes in anticipation of being shot. It doesn't come, so I look again, down the shaft of the arrow at the face of the massive man behind it. His look shows me that he indeed possesses the power to kill. The laws that protect my right to live vanish. These warriors who stand before me have obviously killed before and are ready to kill again, if necessary. These are the ones who make up the laws in this land.

Bushy Man crawls closer. Lifting his head, he directs signs of peace to the one big man who stands out from the rest, stockier and fiercer-looking than his noble warriors. A broad boar tusk pierces his nose, its whiteness standing out in harsh contrast to the blackness of his thick beard and painted forehead. He alone loosens his grip on the vine holding an arrow that had been pointed at the Bushy Man. Unlike the cone-shaped hairstyle of the others, the big man's matted hair spreads out like a mushroom decorated with eagle feathers and the colorful plumes of the Bird of Paradise, which sway in the breeze. The warriors wait in perfect stillness. Then, Bushy Man carefully slides up onto the end of a log. The big man speaks to one of his warriors who immediately creeps over, hand still on his bow, and sits on the end of the log, opposite Bushy Man.

Bushy Man speaks, and the warrior lets some tension off his bow. They begin the struggle of communication with words and signs. The longer they attempt to understand each other, the closer they get to one another, sliding across the log a little at a time. When at last, Bushy Man establishes the message of peace, the warrior greets him by snapping Bushy Man's knuckles between his fingers. The sharp tip of the arrow which had been pointing at me throughout the whole ordeal finally drops. I take a deep breath of relief. At least for the moment, we are safe.

★　★　★　★　★

The Strickland River—rocks that line the shore slip past me in a blur. I study the topo map sealed in a water-proof envelope stretched out across my lap. Finding the fork from the Lagaip, I measure the distance. It is only the middle of our second day of riding the downriver currents, and already we have covered approximately seventy miles, and can average fifty a day if we can keep up the pace. The sun is warm on my face. I feel alone.

★　★　★　★　★

The morning after the Big Man got so angry with Aaron for taking his picture, we said goodbye to the mountain people. The Big Man's reaction had been an event that nobody seemed to fully recover from. The carriers and Bushy Man acted nervous all night and by morning, they decided to leave for their side of the Centrals. I feel a cold pit in my stomach now, remembering the sad good-bye, the large smiles of Aguy, and Mowga. We gave Stew more pain killers and prayed for him one more time before shaking his hand; he seemed to have lost so much life since the first time we shook it, 18 days before on the large boulder beside the Salumei River. We had come so far since that day when Eabay held back so we could follow. The old woman and Stew's wife, Agomi, were too shy to look at us; they giggled their goodbyes while looking out into the jungle. The hardest goodbyes were the last two. I will never forget Sogamoi and the deep eyes of Bushy Man. Tears well up in my eyes. I'll never see them again.

"Jesus . . . lives here," I had said, placing my hand on Sogamoi's chest, his smile larger than life. He had reached up and put his hand on my chest. "Jesus," he repeated.

I miss him, all of them, I think to myself. The jungle has retreated high up the slopes of the peaks, reaching for the sky on either side of the river. The ridges are covered in a rich grassland that traces the paths of wind gusts rolling from slope to slope.

★　★　★　★　★

Later, the Big Man had sent three of his warriors to help us carry our gear. From the village, it took four hard days to find the Lagaip River: its currents were quick. It was quite a change to be moving faster than ever towards Daru Island, without having to exert much energy. The equivalent of a solid day's worth of hiking drifted past us in minutes.

★ ★ ★ ★ ★

We are uneasy being alone now to face whatever lies ahead. The Old Man of Koup had told us to seek out the wise men along our way, but people are scarce. And now, our trust is scarred, having so recently stared down the tips of the lost tribe's arrows, and experienced the anger of their Big Man. We have no idea who owns the gardens that sometimes line the shore, or how the people would respond to us. After all, we no longer have the wisdom of Bushy Man to save us from danger.

In seventy miles of drifting, we have only seen one group of people, and that was yesterday. Five or six men, a band of hunters or perhaps a war party, crouched on top of a boulder with bows and arrows. They had remained completely still; leaves hung from their hair and grass skirts camouflaged them against the jungle backdrop. They never moved, never waved. I didn't even see them until we neared the boulder. I was so startled, I panicked and started screaming for us to cross the river. I suppose the surprise of seeing them, their quiet ambush-like postures, the piercing stares from their leaf-covered faces, the way they held their weapons, Aaron and me all alone . . . was why I didn't trust them.

We made it several miles downriver from them before camping. Ours wasn't as pretty a shelter as the mountain people had made, but it kept the night rains off us. Our bag full of cooked kou kou intended for dinner was rotten. By morning, my empty stomach growled in protest.

★ ★ ★ ★ ★

Two hours have passed now since we forked off the Lagaip onto the Strickland River. I feel weak with hunger and helpless in my surroundings. Aaron's final words before falling asleep in last night's camp had been, "I'm afraid." Today, I am afraid with him. The river's distant shores would be a long swim if we found ourselves in trouble! The Lagaip had fought us with several class three and four rapids, not easy to maneuver in a twenty-foot sea kayak. But the Strickland River is much bigger, maybe four times the size of the La-gaip, with a swifter, unpredictable, and very powerful current. So far, the Strickland hasn't produced any rapids, but we know it's just a matter of time before she shows off her strength. Aaron and I are quiet, uneasy, sensing her nasty potential.

I look down and study the map. I see the fork and the high ridge lines that ride the horizons on either side. On the map, the grassland stretches out along either side of the river; then all lines, greens and browns, suddenly vanish into white. In a large blank area where the Strickland disappears, I read the fine black print. I have read it many times before: "Data incomplete." I look up at the ceiling of clouds hanging over our heads, said to dump between thirty and forty feet of rain on this terrain every year. With that much rain and so many clouds, it has been impossible to produce a complete map system from aerial photographs. I remember laughing about this section back home, the white splotch on the maps. In our ignorance the risk of it had struck us as funny back then. It's not the only "data incomplete" section that we have traveled through, but it is the biggest, and right on the most powerful river of our trip.

I turn around. Aaron is quiet. His lips have been sealed since we met up with the Strickland. So many questions whirl about in our minds, questions without answers, questions of waterfalls and rapids, drops in elevation and gorges. Where are the people? What are they like? It's been fifty miles since we last saw a garden! One thing is for sure, nobody is laughing now!

A low growl fills the air. The high cliff to our left suddenly falls away as we round a sharp bend. A mighty, thundering roar blasts us as the next stretch of river quickly unfolds into walls of spraying whitewater. The terrorizing scene rushes at me. The opposite shoreline is a distant blur.

"Keep her straight!" I yell. A sudden surge of cold water hurls me backward. The kayak rises to the top of a wave and turns sideways on top of a submerged boulder. I fall into a fourteen-foot-deep pit of churning power, am swallowed by the water's icy blackness. Violent, attacking torrents spin me out of control; my paddle is gone, my Teva sandals are ripped from my feet. All is thrashing, cold confusion. From somewhere the raging surface groans. I feel the magnitude of the water's power and stop my vain struggle. Helplessly spinning, I concentrate on holding my breath and wait. Finally, my lifejacket finds the surface as I gasp in air and choke on water. The current yanks me up through another wave. I catch a glimpse of Aaron struggling in the water, trying to flash me a peace sign before the white foam of another wave engulfs me. Again, I break the angry surface, searching desperately for air, coughing water out of my throat. I see the bottom of the kayak close by and swim to it, managing to barely grasp her ropes before the rapids suck us both under.

Somewhere in the darkness my knee cracks against a rock; pain shoots up my leg. I force my head between my arms for protection. The ropes burn my hands, but I don't let go. The kayak pulls me upward into bright light. As waves crash over the bottom of the overturned kayak, I search for a pocket of air to feed my starving lungs. Frantically, I pull on the ropes, using my strength and my weight, but I can't turn her back over. I am exhausted. The miserable darkness and spinning suddenly return. Then, I glimpse the surface and a moment of smooth, fast water allows me to grab the lead rope and swim for shore. The roar of the next rapid grows louder, but, the strength is gone from my arms, and the shore rocks are still far away. I can't make it! I fear. Too soon, the next rapid overtakes me.

I have to relax, I keep telling myself, clinging to the wall of the swirling kayak. A powerful desire to live overwhelms me when the surface comes back. I decide to let go and swim for shore. I can see downriver when I clear the end of the kayak. The sight of fifteen-foot waves fills me with new terror. It is the largest rapid so far. Intense fear and the sense of impending death, combine with the misery of shock and weakness as I race towards a mountain of pounding water. I quickly swim back and take my grip on the kayak. "I need a miracle, Father, . . . I need a miracle!" I pray out loud, then take several deep breaths. I hear the crash of the wave, feel a tremendous downward pull, and the kayak is now on top of me. The loud crashing of waves suddenly changes to a deep, mighty roar. I am pulled down, down, deep into violent darkness. The kayak jerks free of my grip, and I am alone. My tightly clamped eyes loosen; my legs and arms go limp. Turning over and around, amidst a power too strong to fight, my lungs begin to ache. The feeling worsens. I fight the urge to feed them water. All my hope slips away: Daru Island, friends, family, and home. The miserable feeling of drowning climaxes; my body tingles, even the desire to live becomes dull. My last glimpse of life begins to fade, buried deep beneath the muddy waters of the Strickland River.

And then, as if in a dream, darkness is flooded with light. I open my eyes to see the beauty of the sky, as my exhausted body hangs limp in the fast current. It feels strange to breathe again. Nothing seems real as I see the light green of the kayak drifting effortlessly towards a rocky shore. As I drift past boulders, I wrap my arm around one, coming to a stop. The kayak rests against the rocks in front of me, and I take hold of her ropes once again with my other hand.

I try, but I can't stand up! My hands and face tingle from lack of oxygen. Soon I manage to pull myself up onto mud where I can rest. Is this real? The rope from the kayak slightly jerks in my hand, as if trying to wake me. I roll onto my back, looking up. I feel dizzy, then sick, so I roll back over. Aaron? I think. Again, I am afraid.

Pulling myself up onto a rock, I begin to cough, nauseated. I see the wild rapids of the river and the strange stillness of the opposite shore. A sharp bend in the river sweeps in front of me. Desperately, I search for Aaron in the rage. I can't see upriver because of the waves colliding with huge boulders. Lord, please, please, save my brother! More time passes. How long has it been? I don't know. I feel strong enough to stand, but I grab at my swollen knee. I don't care about the pain. My legs tremble beneath my weight. When I still can't see upriver, an image of Aaron's floating, lifeless body flashes through my mind. Quickly, I chase it away.

Suddenly, a mass of red hair breaks the surface just in front of me, a mouth gasps loudly, tired eyes see me as they pass by. He holds one of our paddles in his hands. Aaron disappears into the rocks off shore. Relieved, I plop down on the kayak, finally enjoying the exhilaration of being alive. Several minutes pass without any sign of Aaron, however, and I start to worry again. Suddenly, his pale face, smeared with mud, pops into sight over some boulders. He crawls down towards me, the white of his shoulder protruding from a tear in his shirt.

"Let's eat," he says. Then we embrace.

"I thought I had lost you," I tell him. Quickly, he looks down.

"Let's eat the emergency rice." Aaron starts yanking on the kayak. I help him turn it over, only to find broken cords swinging free as it flips upright.

"We lost a bag," I say, reaching my hand under the spray skirt and feeling around. Another broken line is all I pull out. "Bush knife is gone." Aaron ignores me, digging like a madman into the green bag. I sit down on the soft kayak.

"We lost the bush knife," I mumble. I remember back, saying goodbye to Rudy and Jay. "Whatever you do, don't lose your bush knife," had been their wise admonition. An empty water bottle lands in front of me.

"There's a clear creek just over those boulders." Aaron's voice is shaky. I stumble up onto my good leg. He glances at my knee and then away.

"I cracked it against a rock." He doesn't respond. "We lost the bush knife, and a . . ."

"I could sure use that water." He cuts me off, lighting up the stove. My knee hurts during the climb up the boulders, but at least I can put weight on it. I pause for a moment high on a pile of rocks. Although the river turns sharply towards more deadly whitewater, the currents from the turn gently lap against the shore in front of the muddy kayak. They are what pushed us to safety, the miracle I asked for. It still doesn't seem real. Bending down, I fill the bottle, then pour some of the chilly water across my face. I look around again, moisture dripping from my beard. The thundering river rages on; images of my struggle beneath its surface flash through my mind. Shaking the water from my head, I try to forget.

"Hurry up!" Aaron shouts. He seems so different. Taking the water, he focuses on cooking. I sit down on a rock and watch his hands tremble.

"Are you all right?" I finally ask, when the rice is done.

"I'm hungry." He pours half the rice into a bowl and hands it to me. Our emergency supply of two bags has dwindled to only one and a third—all the food we have left. I take a bite. It tastes good. Aaron shovels the white, fluffy flakes into his mud-stained mouth.

I look past the spraying water, up to a fifty-foot cliff and high, rolling ridges of light, waving grass, rows of trees following creeks, dashing their way down to the river. The grass rises for miles until it clashes with a dark green line of thick jungle, blanketing steep, mountainous terrain. Bold rocky peaks hang jagged on the cloudy horizon. I lean over the kayak, searching beneath the spray skirt again and again. Finally, I sit still, in a trance. My rice grows cold. I am staring at the broken line that once held our bush knife.

"I know we're in serious trouble," Aaron admits, as if he'd just come to his senses. "I got out."

His voice startles me. I turn to look at his hollow expression. "The maps are gone and our hats," I say. Aaron feels the top of his head. I wait for him to go on.

"I made it to shore with the paddle." He points to it lying in the rocks, the long blue pole dramatically bent. "I climbed up onto a boulder and saw you and the kayak still going downriver." His voice sounds weak against the echoing rapids.

"What did you do?"

He looks straight at me, his hands still shaking. "What could I do?" He looks out across the waves, breaking themselves against boulders in front of us. "I threw myself back in."

I finish the rest of my rice in silence, as the meaning of what Aaron has just told me sinks in.

"We lost our bush knife," I tell him again, breaking the silence.

"I know," he assures me, still staring at the river.

"It was the bend . . . the current sweeping over onto the shore, that's what saved us." I see a tear roll down his cheek.

"I'll bet when God made this river, He made it with that sharp turn just for me and you," he says. I think for awhile, remembering the horror.

"I've never felt so dead as I did then, or so alive as I do now," I whisper.

"How are we going to get out of here?"

"Same way we got here." I point to the Strickland.

Having eaten the rice, we have recovered some of our strength, but our nerves are beyond repair. We dare not get back into the kayak; so for hours we push her out and around boulders, tediously working her safely through endless rapids with the ropes. With only one bend of the river behind us, we discover another obstacle. We stand in awe of a fifteen-foot-high wall of surging whitewater shooting from the bank into the river, completely blocking our path. It is a tributary rushing down from the high mountains. By the time it reaches the bottom, it has picked up tremendous momentum and is shooting its mass of water thirty feet out into the currents of the Strickland. I shudder at the amazing display of power, realizing that we have no choice. "Front or back?" I ask Aaron, who holds the bent paddle.

"How can we tell what's on the other side?" he shouts. I steady the kayak in front of us before turning around.

"Front or back?!"

"Back."

My body is weak with fear as I climb in. Coiling the front rope, I place its end in my mouth and push off from the bank. Aaron steers us out around the constant blast. The moment we are clear of it, he struggles for shore. The water in front of us is smooth as glass, then it disappears altogether. Spray gushes up in the void beyond the drop.

"Waterfall!" I scream, wheeling around in my seat. Aaron loses strength, the paddle slapping at the water with each of his exhausted strokes. I turn and launch myself out over the water, my legs and arms pounding the surface, the kayak's tow rope clenched in my teeth. Fear pushes me from behind, because I know we can't survive another swim like before. Our only chance is to get out now.

I feel rocks under my feet and start to push off of them toward the shore. The kayak swings around, the rope still tight in my teeth. Soon we are both ashore. This second scare adds to our shock.

"This isn't going to work," I say, feeling defeated. "We've been pulling two hours and haven't made half a mile. We're gonna have to walk out." My stomach wrenches at the harsh realization. Aaron hangs his head; our downriver dream is over. I dig deep into the green bag and pull out our boots and dry, crusty socks. I throw them in front of Aaron, who doesn't move.

"We had four carriers helping us before. Now, with just the two of us, we're going to have to ding some gear," he says, looking up. I agree with a nod and begin dumping the equipment out over the rocks. We throw aside a pile of all our clothing, except one change each. The sacrificial mound grows with the pole spear, a snorkel and mask, extra parachute cord, an extra compass, repair tubing for the kayak, and everything but the essentials out of the kayak-repair kit. Aaron digs into the medical kit. Bandages, lotions, creams, and powders fall with a thud onto the pile. He takes our tube of toothpaste, and I watch as he squeezes all but a third of it out on the ground. Shampoo, soap, combs, deodorants—all of it must go.

Aaron, painfully, throws aside all that we have traded for: precious treasures from the Lost Tribe, belum bags and other artifacts. He takes a piece of parachute cord and cuts it with his knife. In silence, he threads the ends through the biggest pig tusk and ties it around his neck. I pick up the camera with the telephoto lens.

"No," Aaron pleads.

"It's heavy."

"No," he repeats. So, I place it safely back into the green bag with our film. We put all the rest that we can bear to part with into my yellow L.L. Bean bag. Aaron takes his Teva sandals and places them in the discard bag.

"You'll need those." He ignores me and blows air into the yellow bag and seals it.

"If you don't have yours, then I don't want mine," he says, throwing the bag out into the current. Our hope is that somebody will discover it downriver.

The muddy corpse of our kayak lies hissing out air, deflating like our hope. "Amazing Grace will be her name," I announce before rolling her up across the uneven rocks and tying her back in place on the backpack frame. It's been only two days and 80 miles since we got her back on the river.

I put Amazing Grace up onto my back. My knee aches with every step, my body shaking beneath the weight. I begin the climb up the deep, trenched, dirt ledges that hem in the river.

Within fifty feet, Aaron collapses beneath the green bag, filled with the rest of our survival gear. I help him up, but it's not far before we both are forced to stop and rest. We look back out over the river. The waterfall turns out to be deadly rapids dropping onto overwhelmed boulders and arching down through the mist of thundering waves, dropping into a gorge hundreds of feet deep. The water funnels between narrow rock cliffs, sending us a message, ugly and clear: had we drifted another few feet, we would both be dead.

"I don't think our bag made it very far," I think out loud.

"Joel," Aaron says, staring down into the gorge. "No matter what happens . . . even the worst . . . I don't have any regrets for coming."

"Shut up!" He is shocked by my response. I look at my boots already covered in mud. "We're not dead yet!"

"Then what are we?" I don't have an answer. "We can't go downriver because of the gorge. We can't go up the side of the mountain with no bush knife. I don't know how we are going to get over that torrent we just nearly killed ourselves trying to paddle around . . . and even if we do get upriver, we haven't seen a hut or one living soul in the last fifty miles."

"We can pump up the kayak and try shooting through that gorge," I suggest.

"I'd rather starve than drown." His body shudders when he looks down into the vast chasm of angry water.

"Just wait until we start to starve, then the idea of drowning won't seem so bad." A long silence fills the air.

"I want to go to college," he tells me after a few minutes. His face is serious. "For the first time in my life, I want to go to college, get married and live in a nice house with a picket fence, and have two-point-five kids." His attempted smile is refreshing.

"Oh, come on, things aren't that bad yet." We laugh for a moment, but soon stop.

"Have you ever gone hungry?" I ask.

"No."

"Food is like gasoline: when you run out, you just don't go anymore. These packs are too heavy. I don't know if we have enough fuel with what's left of the emergency rice to even get our body weight out, much less these packs. If you ever want to get to college, then we're going to have to stash all our gear and look for help."

"Daru Island sure seems far away today, doesn't it?" Aaron is looking down on the river.

"Yes . . . it certainly does."

Sweat drips from my face, stinging my eyes. I rip my journal in half, throwing the blank half under the bundle of our gear which Aaron is tying onto a log. Our green rain gear is strapped over the top. Our desires have now changed—from crossing this island to escaping from it with our lives. To survive. That is the only goal, the only dream that we have left.

With the kayak, Amazing Grace, and the second pile of discarded equipment tied in place, we set out with only the green and blue bags. These bags hold just the essentials: the large blue tarp and the small ground tarps, the stove, the pot, the rest of our emergency rice, lighters, blankets, netting, two water bottles, malaria pills, antibiotics, Lomotil, iodine and a few bandages, our

Swiss army knife, the small snapshot camera, the film we have taken, plus five new rolls, half of our journals, a pen, and a zip-lock bag with money, passports, and airline tickets.

"Will we come back for it?" Aaron asks, his depressed trance fixed on the heap of expensive, discarded gear.

"I don't know." The river purrs far below. Behind us, the lip of the gorge is covered in tall grass.

"He brought us here." I am remembering. "I mean, I hope I didn't just wake up one morning and decide to come here with you and cross this island. Please, let it be deeper than that. The sponsorship, the money, meeting you, it's all been a process." I feel faith stirring inside of me. "Don't we remember, Aaron, the waves of the north coast and the Old Man of Koup, how scared we were through the miles of crocodile-infested rivers on the mighty Sepik, Korosmeri, Kawari, and Salumei Rivers? Don't we remember the swarms of mosquitoes, Father Don, and the Inaru missionaries?" Standing up, I turn to face him. "They were sitting down, all fifteen of them, to eat Christmas dinner, the moment we pulled up. Remember Rudy and Jay as translators with the Bosorio carriers? Remember the compassion of Sogamoi, the time we ran out of food and into the wisdom of Bushy Man? We have slept with cannibals, hiked with headhunters, and swam through waters that should have killed us." I pause. "Can't we remember all that?"

"Yeah. . . ."

"Why would He bless us through all that to let us die now? I know it, I just know it! Somehow God is going to get us out of here!"

We climb up the fifteen-foot ledge of a square boulder to eat our small, nightly portion of rice. This rock fortress is nestled on the narrow knoll of a steep hill; western skies are on fire with the sunset. The muffled Strickland mumbles from the deep gorge to the west, reminding us of the day's events. On the other side of the gorge, the grassy slopes spread themselves out under the orange sky, and on top of the grass ridges sits a massive crown made up of dark jungle and several protruding, rocky peaks. Behind us, to the east, stand more high, rugged-looking mountains. The sky behind them is much darker. To the south, the walls of the gorge open wide, forming a gaping hole in the valley floor. In the far distance, as far as I can see, are more ridges and peaks. The shine of glimmering, orange water outlines the Strickland coming out of the north, and far away, I see the black silhouette of the dividing ridge where we sat only a week before with Bushy Man and our Bosorio friends. A thick line of trees marks the northern torrent which we paddled around earlier in the day. It falls straight as an arrow from a jungle-choked canyon, far above and behind us, into the river below.

"Trapped," Aaron comments after looking around.

"I've only taken five spoonfuls of rice and it's almost all gone."

"We have powerful torrents and rivers, thick jungles and rocky peaks surrounding us on all sides." Aaron is fidgeting.

I finish my rice and drop the empty bowl off the boulder. The tarp is spread out below for us to sleep on. For the first time, we have no trees to make a shelter.

"I say we go north," I propose, checking the sky for rain clouds. It looks fairly clear.

"It could take us two weeks to get around the gorge to the south," Aaron says. I hear his stomach growling.

"Have you noticed how quiet it is?" The river far below and the jungle far above our camp produce a strange silence that feels close, drifting into a distant rumble. Aaron turns around and looks up.

"East looks like quite a climb. Can't get through that jungle without a bush knife anyway."

"No mosquitoes."

"All the water is moving too fast around here, too fast for mosquito larva and too fast for us." He looks down at the torrent we paddled around. "The north is our best bet? With a wall of water as high as this boulder, moving faster than a train . . . and beyond . . . well, after paddling fifty miles, we haven't seen one person, not even an abandoned hut or a rundown garden." He looks at me. "I just can't believe north is our best direction."

"Believe it." The dark shadows crawl up from the roots of the grasses and blacken the night.

"I never got a chance to thank you for pulling the kayak out of the river after we flipped," Aaron says.

"I didn't pull it out."

"If you would have let it go, we would be sitting here in a pair of boxers and barefoot . . . nothing else."

"I did let it go," I tell him, before climbing down to try and get some sleep.

The morning sun is hot without the protection of a canopy. Aaron and I are wearing sweat-soaked, long-sleeved shirts to protect us against grass cuts. Even something as minor as a grass cut can grow into a serious wound with all the tropical infection that floats everywhere in the humidity. We are somewhere in between ridges. The grass is several feet taller than our heads. Blindly, we push forward. We had a restless night. Hunger pains and spiders crawling on us prevented sleep, but the star-filled night had been brilliant. I looked for constellations, and when I couldn't find any, I made up my own.

Another rock catches the toe of my boot, hurling me through the wall of green until I hit the ground. I scramble to my feet; Aaron's trail of bent-over grass ends abruptly in front of me. I look about, confused. "Aaron!"

"I found some drinking water," he calls from somewhere below me. I drop down on my knees and pull the bent-over grass apart to find a cavern of empty space with Aaron lying at the bottom of it on a creek bed.

"You all right?" He rolls over and stands up, his head even with my boots.

"Hand me your water bottle," he says. He dumps out the muddy water from last night's torrent and refills it with the clear creek water. I thank him before jumping across the gap and pushing deeper through the wall of thick grass until I stumble onto a muddy vein riddled with wild boar tracks. The trail spreads the grass apart for some breathing room as it winds its way for a few hundred feet in the general direction that we are headed. Then it disappears altogether.

The grass angles steeply upwards until, finally, we reach the top of the ridge where the grass is short. Below is the line of trees protecting the turbulent waters of the torrent. We agree that our best bet of finding a way across is to go higher. So for two hours, we climb up the crest of the ridge leading us to a high plateau covered in boulders and surrounded by dark jungle. We wade through the grass, past an overhanging boulder with a large beehive to the edge of the plateau which falls sharply into the deep basin of the torrent.

Wild pigs scatter in the shadows as we slide down through thick mud under drapes of vines. The vibration of unleashed power reveals itself in a ridge of rushing water. I try to speak, but I can't even hear myself. All of my body vibrates. A gust of cool wind from the passing water blows against my sweaty face. I pick up a large branch at my feet and throw it into the torrent. Instantly, it is gone.

Aaron is shouting something. I point for us to continue up the slope. He nods in agreement. I need to go faster, but get tangled in vines. Ants bite my legs, cold wet leaves slap my face, and swarms of flies land on my sweaty shoulders. Unfortunately, I have no hat to swat them with. A sticker vine catches my unprotected hair. Aaron has fallen behind to pull leeches from his leg underneath his rain pants. A dizzy spell forces me to hug a tree covered with ants.

We continue to climb and fight, wrestle and pull, slip and get back up, get bitten but push on. Meanwhile, the torrent is losing none of its power. There are no breaks, no chances to cross. My stomach longs for food and my ears for silence; my body yearns to be delivered from the insects, to be set free from vines and enclosing undergrowth. The weakness of hunger strikes my head first with dizziness; then my hands shake and my legs get weak and wobbly. Aaron can't be doing much better since he hasn't caught up yet. I start looking for bugs, grasshoppers, anything for much-needed protein. Suddenly, a leech hooks me solid on my Adam's apple. I turn in circles, tripping over vines and crash to the ground. I pull it off and wipe my hand across the front of my neck to find it smeared with blood. Finding two rocks, I smash the leech between them, then throw its remains along with the bloody rocks into the torrent.

A large boulder stands in the middle of the blast, its peak rising above the white madness; beyond it, I can see the other side of the torrent. Aaron places his hand on my shoulder; I flinch, then point to the rock. We hike up the embankment to escape some of the noise.

"We really are trapped!" he shouts.

"I'm too weak to go any higher." He doesn't argue. "I say we find some fallen logs and build a bridge out to the top of that boulder and then across to the other side." Aaron searches my face for sanity.

"If we fall into that torrent, then . . ."

"What choice do we have!" I scream, cutting him off. I slap angrily at the ants crawling up my rain pants. "I'm going to at least try to build a bridge." I turn around to go back down.

"It won't work!" Aaron yells after me. I ignore him. I feel angry and frustrated, hungry and desperate enough to try just about anything. Aaron stares blankly as I approach the torrent with two large bamboo poles. Climbing a rocky ledge, I look down on the thrashing current beneath me. My hands tremble out of control.

I extend the first log out towards the peak of the boulder. It hits perfectly, the long slender beam hovering only inches above the rushing water. I take a breath, sliding the second bamboo beam across the first until it reaches the boulder; then I drop them beside each other and tie my end together as best I can with a vine. I push on the poles. They feel sturdy, so I stand up, taking hold of a tree branch jutting out above my head. Looking back at Aaron, I see him shaking his pale face back and forth, warning me not to try. Holding myself steady with the branch, I step out onto the beams, releasing some weight from my arms. I take another step. One more will take me away from the safety of the branch. I scoot my foot forward and press down with the weight of my body. The beam buckles in the middle and drops, touching the water. Spray shoots high into the air. I grip the branch overhead just as the poles slide out from under me. The ends of the beams drop from the boulder, then with a tremendous jerk and a blur of green, they smash into the rocky side of the water-filled trench. A loud crack rings out in the midst of the roar. An explosion of splinters spreads out into the foamy spray. Then, everything is gone.

My feet swing back onto the rock ledge. Everything in me is shaken and unsteady as I climb down, shrugging my shoulders at Aaron. He starts climbing tediously higher. I follow. Cat claw vines tear at our clothes. We grow weaker with every step. Aaron climbs away from the noisy water, coming to a stop under a clearing in the canopy. Towering mountain peaks stare down at us through the opening. Steep slopes and endless jungle rise higher than I ever thought possible. We give each other a blank stare; our little bit of hope vanishes at this awesome sight. Aaron starts forward, but I catch him by the arm.

"We're not going to make it," I tell him.

"We have to!"

"We have no bush knife and only half a bag of rice."

"What? You still want to build a bridge!" he shouts. I hang my head.

"No." I look away from the clearing towards the high ridges. "But to cross those mountains is just as unrealistic as crossing this torrent!" He sits down in frustration and throws his arms up above his head.

"We have to do something!" His face is turning red as he screams. "We can't just sit here!"

"No! What we have to do is relax, use our heads, and think!" I take off up the side of the ridge, angrily wrestling with vines. I feel trapped and claustrophobic as I rush forward. I need to see the sky, escape the ants. I need food. I'm out of breath and near the point of collapse, but my panic pushes me up, cursing vines, pulling. Dew falls from leaves, drenching my hair. I see the light of the edge, then blue. My eyes squint in the brightness. I wade into the grass, climb a boulder and sit down. The torrent is far away now, and the mountains are obscured by the wall of jungle. My head drops onto my knees, and sweat runs from my face, streaking my rain pants. I catch my breath and remain still. Sometime later, I sense Aaron near me.

"I know the way out," I announce. I point towards the Strickland. He shakes his head, respectfully.

"I'm not going through that gorge."

"Neither am I."

"What then?"

"We swim across, then hike upriver on the other side." He fidgets, uncomfortable with my suggestion. "If we want to get out of here, we are going to have to swim across our biggest fear."

"And if we don't make it across before the rapids?"

"You know the answer to that." I jump down from the rock.

★ ★ ★ ★ ★

The grumbling Strickland grates my nerves. The last of the rice hasn't been enough to fill our emptiness. In front of us, the grassy ridge falls sharply, and further on, the cruel waters of our foe lie in wait. My eyes are heavy from a long, sleepless night spent under a beehive. This morning a bee's sting woke me, bringing me out of another haunting nightmare about drowning. Aaron is not behind me anymore. He has chosen his own way down to the river bank. But I don't feel much like a leader anyway—more like an animal, intent on survival. I nearly kill myself sliding down the steep, dirt bank. A four-foot monitor lizard stirs below me. I visualize eating him raw, but he disappears down a hole.

"My way was easier," comes Aaron's voice from behind me. I guess he decided to follow after all. Kneeling down, I blow air into the blue bag and seal it tight. "How are we going to do this?" Aaron asks. I start towards the torrent, its wind blowing my hair as it shoots out across the river. I turn to the river, slipping the bag strap around my neck.

"Joel!" Aaron calls out, but I don't want to talk anymore, or listen to the river's power, or see the water drop downriver. If I have to do something, if there's no choice, I'd rather just go! I run to the edge of the river, launching myself from a boulder. Adrenaline rushes. My legs and arms burst into action as I drop into the cold water. The only thing I see is the other shore. Kicking and pulling with all my strength, I feel the strap cut into my neck. Fear pushes me towards the far shore. The rapids grow louder, closer, but fighting for every breath, I never take my eyes from the rocky bank until I climb the rocks.

Aaron waits on the other side. After several minutes, he dives in and swims with panicked strokes. By the time he makes it across, just down from me, his energy is gone. I wait for him to recover enough to walk to me.

It takes all morning just to make it to the first rapid where Amazing Grace had flipped yesterday. It is over six miles of straight whitewater between where we first fell out, to the sharp bend in the river that saved our lives. This has been engraved in our memories as the longest and most horrifying swim of our lives.

Sometimes the river sweeps the shore, forcing us high across piles of driftwood and numerous boulders. In the late afternoon, the river sinks, revealing a dark strip of black sand. Several hours ago, we were forced to swim back across the river. Even without threatening whitewater, the swim took its toll on our energy.

We walk on in a drained daze of hunger, around endless bends, searching for something to eat, insects, a beached fish, anything. My face is hot and sunburned; my head dizzy. Dark clouds flash with lightning in the distance as the river starts to rise.

"Joel! Come here!" Aaron shouts. He is kneeling in the sand. Some hope has found its way into his eyes. He points to tracks in the sand—the imprint of a human foot—then two fresh sets, side by side, one small, the other large. They lead upriver!

Escape from the Blackfeet

From *Mountain Man*

BY VARDIS FISHER

Vardis Fisher's *Mountain Man* sits on a shelf in my modest library directly alongside A. B. Guthrie Jr.'s *The Big Sky*. Both are the ultimate classics in fiction dealing with the mountain men hunters and trappers and the Rocky Mountain fur trade during the 1840s.

   Mountain Man is the story of Sam Minard, a giant of a man in both physical stature and character. His encounters with the dreaded Pied Noir, the Blackfeet, fill the book with dramatic situations of incredible force. Fisher's prose spares no detail in the action, but also paints the nature and landscape of the region with vivid sensitivity.

   Mountain Man was one of the sources of material for the popular film *Jeremiah Johnson* with Robert Redford.

   In this excerpt from *Mountain Man*, Sam finds himself in a predicament of the sort that "rubbed out" many of his trapper peers. His only chance for survival is to make a seemingly impossible escape and find his way through the frozen wilderness to the cabin of a homesteader named Kate, whom he had befriended earlier.

   Good reading about the days of the mountain men and their adventures in the Rockies just doesn't get any better than this.

★   ★   ★   ★   ★

At the big bend of the Musselshell he took from a cache the keg of rum, the kettle, and a few other things, and then sat on the bay and looked west and south, wondering if he should take the safer way over the Teton Pass or the more dangerous way by Three Forks. Storm determined it. It was snowing this morning, and all the signs said it

34

would be an early and a long hard winter. If he went by the pass it would take twice as long and he might find himself snowbound up against the Tetons or the southern Bitterroots. By far the easier route was by Three Forks, where John Colter had made his incredible run to freedom; where the Indian girl who went west with Lewis and Clark had been captured as a child; and where beaver were thickest in all the Western land. It was there also that more than one trapper had fallen under the arrows or bullets of the Blackfeet.

It was a foolhardy decision but mountain men were foolhardy men.

For a hundred and fifty miles, with snow falling on him most of the way, he went up the river, and then followed a creek through a mountain pass. He was leaving a trail that a blind Indian could follow. Straight ahead now was the Missouri; on coming to it he went up it to the Three Forks, the junction of the Gallatin, Madison, and Jefferson rivers. He knew this area fairly well. Lewis and Clark had gone up the Jefferson River, which came down from the west, but Sam planned to go southwest and cut across to a group of hot springs in dense forest. The snow was almost a foot deep now and still falling, but he had seen no tracks of redmen, only of wild beasts, and he had no sense of danger. Just the same he hastened out of the Three Forks area, eager to lose his path in forested mountains. He might have made it if pity had not overthrown prudence. He had gone up the Beaverhead, past a mountainous mass on his left, and hot springs that would be known as the Potosi, and had then ridden straight west to a group of hot springs deep in magnificent forest, when suddenly he came in view of a mountain tragedy that stopped him.

Two great bulls of the wapiti or elk family had been fighting and had got their horns locked, and a pack of wolves was circling them, while turkey buzzards sat in treetops, looking down. Sam saw at once that it had been a terrific fight; the earth was torn and the brush trampled over half an acre. The two bulls looked evenly matched, each with a handsome set of antlers, and beautifully muscled shoulders and neck. Sam had sometimes wondered why the Creator had put such an immense growth of bone on the head of elk and moose; their antlers were about all their necks could carry, much less handle on a run through heavy timber, or in a fight with another bull. It was not an uncommon thing to find bulls dead with horns entangled in dense underbrush, or interlocked, as now. These two had their rumps up in the air to the full length of their hind legs but both were on their knees and unable to move their heads at all. Any moment the wolves would have moved in to hamstring them and bring them down, and feast in their bellies while they still breathed. If Sam had found one bull dead and the other bugling over him he would have thought it all right, but to find two magnificent warriors unable to continue their fight, who deeply wanted to, was such an ironic miscarriage of the divine plan that he was outraged. He would set them free if he could, so they could resume their fight.

Sam looked round him and listened. Thinking that he was many miles from danger, he secured his horses to a tree, hung his rifle from the saddle-horn, and walked about a hundred feet to the bulls. He went close to them to study the interlocking of the antlers. The astonishing thing about it was that bulls were able to do it; Sam had heard men say that they had taken two antlered heads and tried for hours to get the horns inextricably locked. These two sets were so firmly and securely the prisoners of one another that it looked to Sam as if he would have to cut through two or three bones to set them free. He had no saw but he had a hatchet. While considering the matter he walked around the two beasts, studying them with the practiced eye of one who knew the good points of a fighter. Yes indeed, they were well matched; he thought there was not thirty pounds' difference in their weight; their antlers had the same number of points and in clay banks had been honed to the same sharpness. They had been in a great battle, all right; their eyes were bloodshot, their chin whiskers were clotted with the stuff that fury had blown from their nostrils, and both had been savagely raked along ribs and flank. What a handsome pair they were! Sam patted them on thier quivering hams and said, "Old fellers, I kallate I'll have to chop some of your horns off. It'll hurt just enough to make you fight better." He again studied the antlers. So absorbed by the drama that he had been thinking only of the two warriors, he glanced over toward the horses where his hatchet was and turned rigid, his eyes opening wide with amazement.

Seven Blackfeet braves had slipped soundlessly out of the forest and seven rifles were aimed at Sam's chest. Seven hideously painted redmen were holding the rifles, their black eyes glittering and gleaming with triumph and anticipation, for they were thinking of rum and ransom and the acclaim of the Blackfeet nation. Why in God's name, Sam wondered, hadn't he smelled them? It was because the odors of elk and battle had filled his nostrils. In the instant when he saw the seven guns aimed at his heart, at a distance of eighty feet, Sam had also seen a horde of red devils around his horses. He knew that if he moved toward the revolvers at his belt seven guns would explode.

Slowly he raised his hands.

He had turned gray with anger and chagrin. This was the first time in his adult life that he had been taken completely by surprise. A Blackfeet warrior over six feet tall, broad and well-muscled, with the headdress of a subchief, now lowered his gun and came forward. He came up to Sam, and gloating black eyes looked into enraged blue-gray eyes, as red hands took the knife from its sheath and unbuckled the revolver belt. Guns and knife were tossed behind him. The chief then hawked phlegm up his throat, and putting his face no more than twelve inches from Sam's and looking straight into his eyes, he exploded the mouthful into Sam's face. A tremor ran through the whiteman from head to feet. In that moment he could have killed the chief but in the next he would have fallen under the guns. Other warriors now came over from the horses, all painted for battle. They began to dance around their captive, in the writhing snakelike movements of which the red people were masters. Sam thought there were about sixty of them. He stood immobile, the saliva and mucus dripping from his brows and beard, his eyes cold with hate; he was fixing the chief's height and face in his mind, for he was already looking forward to vengeance.

After a few moments the chief put aside his dignity and joined the dance. It seemed that all these warriors had rifles and long knives and tomahawks. In a victorious writhing snake dance they went round and round Sam, their black eyes flashing their contempt at him; and Sam looked at them and considered his plight. Now and then one gave shrieks of delight and redoubled his frenzies; or one, and then a second and a third, would pause and aim their guns at Sam, or raise knife or tomahawk as though to hurl it. Sam stood with arms folded across his chest. In the way he looked at them he tried to express his scorn but these shrieking writhing killers were children, for whom the only contempt was their own. Not one of them had paid the slightest attention to the bulls with locked horns, or cared with what agonies or humiliation they died.

When at last the Indians made preparations to take their prisoner and depart they still paid no attention to the bulls. With loud angry curses and then with signs Sam made them conscious of the two beasts; and they spat with contempt and said, with signs, that they had plenty of meat and would leave these to the wolves. Their insolence filled Sam with fresh rage. He was now less concerned for himself than for two helpless fighters who had a right to another chance—who in any case were too brave and too noble to die with wolves chewing into their bellies and with buzzards sitting on their horns. Speaking in tones that rang with anger and with angry signs, Sam told the chief that he should shoot the two bulls or chop a part of their horns off, or he should crawl off like a sick old woman and die with the rabbits. After appearing to give the matter some thought the chief went to the beasts and looked at their horns. He shouted then to his warriors and several of them ran over to him; he spoke again, and they put muzzles at the base of the skulls and fired. The two bulls sank to the earth, locked together in death.

Sam had been hoping that the Indians would break open the keg of rum and drink it here but the wily chief had other plans. One plan was to humiliate and degrade the whiteman until he was delivered to the vengeance of the Crows. He would not be delivered with all possible dispatch; he would be taken north to the principal Blackfeet village, where the squaws could shriek round him and hurl dung and urine on him, and with the voices of ravens and magpies caw and gaggle and screech at him; and where the children, emulating their elders in ferocities and obscenities, could smear him with every foul thing they could find and shoot arrows through his hair, as he stood thonged and bound to a tree. Such thoughts were going through Sam's mind. He expected all that red cunning and ingenuity could devise, though he imagined that they would not seriously wound him, or starve him until he could not walk, if they expected to collect a huge ransom. It would be childlike contempts and indignities all day and all night.

These had begun when the chief exploded in his face. As soon as they had him manacled with stout leather ropes the other warriors vied with one another in heaping abuse and insult upon him. With leather thongs soaked in the hot waters of a spring they bound his hands together; and around the leather between his wrists was tied the end of a leather rope thirty feet long. A huge brave took the other end of the rope and made it secure to his saddle. Mounting his horse, he jerked the rope tight, and with pure devilment kept jerking it, after taking his position in the line. About half the warriors went ahead of Sam, about half behind, with the chief at the rear, riding Sam's bay and leading the packhorse. Now and then one of the redmen, eager to torment the captive, would leave his position in the line; and breaking off a green chokecherry branch, he would slash stinging blows across Sam's defenseless face. With blood running from brow or cheek Sam would look hard at the painted face, hoping to fix it in memory and telling himself that these were the fiends who had slaughtered the defenseless family of the mother on the Musselshell. He had the face of the chief in memory; the red varmint had a scar about three inches long above the left eyebrow, and another scar just under the left chin. If with God's help he could ever free himself he would hunt down that face. In some such manner as this, he supposed, they had taken Jesus to the hill; but Jesus had carried a great burden, under which he had fallen again and again; and when he fell they spat on him and kicked him and cursed him. The one who had slashed at Sam's face had been rebuked by the chief, but his boldness had given ideas to other braves; and hour after hour as Sam moved through heavy snowstorm one man after another dropped out of line to hawk and spit on him or hurl snow in his face or make murderous gestures at him.

After a while the braves seemed to understand that it was all right to show their contempt if they did not wound him; and so by turns they hawked and spat and shrieked, or hurled snow, mud, and pine cones at his face. In their black eyes was a clear picture of what they wanted to do with him, for they knew not only that he was the Crow-killer but that he was the one who had scalped the four Blackfeet warriors and impaled their skulls on the stakes around the cabin.

It was the snowfall that worried Sam more than the insults. This storm looked like the real thing. If winter was already setting in and there was to be three or four feet of snow in the mountains in the next week or two, as there sometimes was this far north, what good would escape do him, with the snow too deep to wade through? It would be a dim future for him if it kept snowing, and they meanwhile weakened him with starvation and cold.

Why the red people so loved to torture their helpless captives was a riddle to all the mountain men. Sam thought it was because they were children. A lot of white children tortured things. Windy Bill said he could tell stories from childhood that would curdle the blood of a wolf. Sam had never heard of a whiteman who tortured a captive. Once when a wounded redman was singing his death song Sam had seen Tomahawk Jack pick up a stone to knock the helpless Indian on the head, and had heard Mick Boone let off a howl of rage as he struck the stone from Jack's hand. "Shoot him decentlike, if you wanta!" Mick had roared. "He ain't no coyote." Sam had once seen a whiteman kick a wounded Indian in the belly and head; he had seen another scalp a redman while he was alive and conscious; but deliberate torture for torture's sake he thought he had never seen. Torture for the redmen was as normal as beating their wives. The wolf ate his victim alive but he was not aware of that. The blowfly hatched its eggs in the open wounds of helpless beasts, and maggots swarmed through the guts of an animal before its pain-filled eyes closed in death. The shrike impaled on thorns the live babies of lark and thrush. The weasel and the stoat were ruthless killers. A horde of mosquitoes as thick as fog would suck so much blood from a deer or an elk that it would die of enervation; and sage ticks, bloated with blood until they were as large as a child's thumb, sometimes so completely covered an old beast that it seemed to be only a hair bag of huge gray warts. But the red people tortured for the pure hellish joy of seeing a helpless thing suffer unspeakable agonies. It was chiefly for this reason that mountain men loathed them, and killed them with as little emotion as they killed mosquitoes.

If he could have done it Sam would have struck all these warriors dead and ridden away with never a thought for them. As it was, his mind was on escape and vengeance. These redmen knew, all the red people knew, that if ever a mountain man was affronted, when helpless, and treated with derision, contempt, mockery, and filth, the mountain men would come together to avenge the wrong, and that the vengeance would be swift, merciless, and devastating. Sam had no doubt that this chief knew it. There could be only one thought in his mind, that this captive would never escape from the Blackfeet or from the Crows, and that mountain men would never know what became of him. The chief would take his captive to his people, so that they could gloat over him and see with their own eyes that he was not invincible after all—that he had been captured by the Bloods, mightiest of warriors, boldest and most fearless and most feared, and most envied of all fighting men on earth. Sam thought that he might be slapped, spat on, kicked, knocked down, but not severely injured; that some of the squaws might squat over him; that children might drag their filthy fingers through his hair and beard and pluck at his eyelids and threaten his privates; and that dogs of the village might howl into the heavens their eagerness to attack him. He would be given, once a day, a quart of foul soup, with ants and beetles and crickets in it, for the red people knew that some of their food made white people gag, and this kind they took delight in forcing on white captives. For as long as he was a prisoner that would be his fate. Then four hundred warriors in full war paint and regalia would march off with him in the direction of the Crow nation. On arriving at the border between the two nations they would encamp and kill a hundred buffalo, and feast and sing and dance, while scouts went forth to tell the old chief that his enemy was bound and helpless. For days the wiliest and craftiest old men in the two nations would haggle and dispute over the size of the ransom. The Bloods would demand many kegs of rum, many rifles, a ton of ammunition, at least four hundred of their finest horses, and piles of their beaded buckskin. The Crows would give no more than a tithe of what was demanded. The Bloods knew that. They would ask for a hundred, hoping for fifty, prepared to settle for twenty, even for ten, plus the privilege of watching the torture of Sam Minard.

Well, if it kept snowing this way they could not take him to the Crows before late spring. If he was not able to escape he would have a long winter of starvation and cold and insults. Sam did not for a moment intend to be delivered to the Crows. He did not believe that the Creator would allow a man to be taken and tortured and killed for no reason but that he had sought vengeance for the murder of his wife and child. The holy book said that God claimed vengeance as His own. In Sam's book of life it was a law that man best served the divine plan who made a supreme effort to help himself.

Sam intended his effort to be supreme. Now and then, while trudging along, he looked down at the elkskin that bound his wrists. If he got a good chance he could chew it in two but he knew that when he was not marching his hands would be bound behind him. To sever tough leather rope when his hands were behind him would be impossible, unless he could abrade it against something hard and sharp, such as stone, a split bone, or wood. During the nights he would have one guard, or possibly two. He would have to eat what they gave him to eat, no matter what it was, and preserve his strength as well as he could. He would do his best to sleep a good part of each night. He would act as if resigned to his fate. If only they would make camp and open the rum!

The day of his capture they moved without pause until almost midnight. All day long a heavy snow fell. While walking in the deep wide trail made by those ahead of him Sam tried to look through the storm to mountains roundabout. By branches on trees he knew they were going north. He supposed that this war party would traverse mountain valleys and passes west of the Missouri until they came to the big bend, where, he had heard, they had a large village on Sun River, and another over on the Marias. They might take him all the way to Canada but he doubted that they would, for if they did it would be a long journey to the Crows. By the time dusk fell he thought he had been walking about five hours. He was hungry. When his bound hands reached down to get snow for his thirst the savage on the horse ahead of him would jerk at the rope and try to shake the snow out of his hands. He was a mean critter, that one. Sam would clench the snow in his palms to hold it but the moment he moved hands toward his mouth the watchful redskin would jerk at the rope with all his might. Sam said aloud to him, "I reckon I better fix your face in my mind, for somewhere, someday, we might have a huggin match." When a third or a fourth time the Indian jerked the rope Sam in sudden rage swung his arms to the right and far back, hoping to break the Indian's grasp on the other end. But the other end was tied round the saddlehorn. To punish Sam, the Indian kept jerking at the rope, and rage in Sam grew to such violence that it took all his will to restrain a forward rush to seize and strangle his foe. I'd best calm down, he thought; for if he got weak and fell he would be dragged along like a dead coyote. His time would come: he refused to think of alternatives: his time would come, somewhere, and he would hear bones crack in this Indian's neck, and he would see the black eyes pop out of the skull, as though pushed from behind.

When at last at midnight the party made camp Sam was tied to a tree and put under guard. Snow was still falling. The snow where he was to stand, sit, or lie during the remainder of the night was about eighteen inches deep, a third of it new snow. If the storm broke away it would be a bitter night. He did not expect them to give him a blanket or a robe; he would be surprised if they gave him food. They would want to weaken him some. He would sit or lie by the tree all night, with the storm covering him over, and at daylight he would march again. The man assigned to guard him had a large robe (it looked to Sam like one of his own), on a part of which he sat, with the remainder up over his shoulders and head like a great furry cape. He had a rifle across his lap and a long knife at his waist. Under his fur tent he sat, immobile, sheltered, warm, his black eyes never leaving Sam's face, save now and then to glance at his hands. Sam wondered if this would be his only guard. If so, and if the man dozed, Sam could chew at the bonds. He knew that it would take his strong teeth an hour or two to chew through the tough wet leather, and he knew that two or three minutes would likely be all the time he would have. About fifty feet beyond him and the guard the party had pitched camp and built fires, but Sam could see no sign of rum-drinking. Possibly they would not drink until they came to the village.

About an hour after the first fire was built he saw a warrior coming toward him with something in his hands. As the redman drew near Sam saw that it was one of his own tin cups or one just like it, and that the cup was steaming. The Indian proffered the cup and Sam took it, knowing that this was his supper; and after the Indian had gone away he looked into the cup and sniffed at its steam. He didn't know what was in the cup but his grim humor imagined that it was a stew of coprophagous insects. There was almost a pint of it. All through the soup he could see what looked like hairs and small bugs, but with both hands he put the cup to his mouth and gulped the contents. Two or three small pieces of half-cooked flesh he chewed. Ten feet from him the guard ate his supper, his eyes fixed most of the time on Sam. Sam set the tin cup aside. With snow he washed the beard around his mouth.

Under him he felt the wetness of melting snow; his rump and thighs itched in wet leather. If he had to march day after day in deep snowpaths and eat only this thin slop he would need sleep, but how could a man sleep with melting snow under and over him? Before morning he would be chilled through. One thing was now plain to him: when a man faced torture and death he was forced to do some thinking. Looking up through the lovely swirling flakes, he told himself that if the Creator was all-mighty there was justice in the world; and if that were so, there would be justice here, for him. He suspected that this was a childish thought but it comforted him. It comforted him to reach emotionally across the wintry desolation to the shack where Kate sat, talking to her children, with the snow falling white on her gray hair. While thinking of her, alone and half frozen and facing a bitter winter, there came a flash of recognition that made him pause in his breathing: in this war party were some of the braves who had slaughtered her family. The brute who had jerked the rope was one of them. They knew they had in their power the man who had set the four Blackfeet heads on the stakes. What a struggle must be convulsing their wild savage souls, as they wavered between avarice and blood lust! How they would have loved to drink the whiteman's firewater, while with insane shrieks they hacked his flesh off in little gobbets and filled his wounds with the big red ants!

Having now, it seemed to him, seen his plight in clear terms, Sam faced the question whether greed or blood lust would win. He saw now all the more reason why his escape, if he were to make one, should be as early as possible. It would be fatal for him if they took him to one of the larger villages, because there the squaws would tear the floor out of hell and blood lust would win. He studied the guard before him, praying that the villain would fall asleep. This hope was dashed when about two in the morning two fresh guards came to relieve him. The crafty chief was taking no chances.

Of the two savages who now sat and faced him Sam could have said only that they had black hair and eyes. Each had a rifle across his lap, a knife at his waist. Sam knew there could be no escape this night. In two hours other guards would relieve these two, and at the first gray of daylight he would march again. He probably would have to walk from daylight till dark, with no more than a cup or two of stinking soup to nourish him. The only thing to do was to try to sleep.

He pushed his legs out and lay back, his face turned to the golden bark of a yellow pine tree. He closed his eyes. Even if he could not sleep with snow melting under and over him he could relax and doze and that would be good. He thought an hour had passed when he felt a presence close to him. He smelled it. He smelled an Indian strong with the Blackfeet odor but he did not open his eyes and stare, as a greenhorn would have done. If a savage had come over, eager to thrust a knife into him, he would need in his black heart only the most trivial excuse. He could say to his chief that the paleface had opened his eyes and leapt at him, and in self-defense he had struck. Telling himself as a warning that the redman was emotional, high-strung, impulsive, Sam allowed nothing in his face and posture to change, as a guard, drawn knife in hand, bent over him and studied his face. In his mind Sam had the picture. He could have leapt with his incredible speed and even with bound hands he could have broken the man's neck, but that would only have brought on slow torture and death. There was nothing to do but pretend to sleep and trust in a Being whose first law was justice. . . .

Sam would have said that the redskin bent over him for at least five minutes. Then the rancid odor went away. But even then Sam did not open his eyes or stir. The snow had been melting on his eyelids and face, and his eyes and face were wet. About four o'clock he actually sank into sleep, and slept until he heard the first movements at daylight. Chilled through and half frozen, he struggled to his feet and tried to shake moisture from his leather clothing. It was plain to him now that if he were going to make an effort to escape it would have to be in the next twenty-four hours.

He sank to the snow by the tree and waited.

★　★　★　★　★

His breakfast was another cup of soup. He thought the scraps of meat in it were dog or owl or crow. Today, as yesterday, the redmen were all mounted, with the chief on Sam's bay. Again Sam had to walk. This day and this night were like the former day and night. He had no chance to escape. His wily captors put the rope twice around the leather that bound his wrists, and both ends around the tree and over to the guards. His second night was ten miserable chilled hours under storm and guards.

The third day and night repeated the first and second, and Sam knew that after two or three more days like these he would be too weak to escape, or to want to. He would make a move, even if it was desperate and useless. After camp was pitched the chief came to Sam where he was tied to a fir tree and looked into his eyes. The redskin had on fresh war paint and more rancid grease on his hair; nothing about him looked human, not even his eyes, for in his hideous face his eyes could have been those of a beast. There was in them no trace of the human or the civilized—they were the hard glittering eyes of an animal looking at its prey. Sam thought the falcon must look like that when it moved to dive and strike.

He had not expected the Indian to hit him, and when, with startling swiftness, the blow fell across his cheek, Sam's eyes opened wide with astonishment. Then he looked steadily at the creature before him, telling himself that if he escaped he would never rest until he had tracked this coward down. He again made note of the man's shape, height, weight, the length of his hair, the scars, and the exact appearance of his teeth when his lips parted to snarl. Sam had no notion of why the fool had come over to strike him; years ago he had given up trying to understand the Indian male. Some infernal evil was busy in this man's mind and heart.

The chief turned to shout and there hastened over a brave who, like his boss, smelled of rancid grease and redbank war paint. The chief spoke to the brave as he came up, and at once this man stepped so close to Sam that his face was only fourteen inches from Sam's face. He looked into Sam's eyes and made an ugly sound. Sam knew it was an expression of contempt. The warrior then said, "Brave, uggh!" and again hawked the contempt up. Sam was startled; he had not known that any man in this party spoke English. "Yuh brave?" the redskin asked, and turned to spit a part of his contempt. Sam stared at the fellow, wondering if he was a half-breed. With signs and broken English the warrior told Sam that for the chief he was a coward and a sick old dog. He was an old coyote covered over with scabs and wood ticks. When the chief slapped him he had challenged him to a fight, but here the paleface stood, cowering and trembling. Were there any brave men among the palefaces?

Sam was silent. He knew that this was an Indian trick but he didn't know the reason for it. It was a preposterous lie to say that the chief would fight him, with fists, knives, or guns, or with any weapon. It was a trick. Was it some plan to cripple him, so that he could not possibly escape—to hamstring him or blind him? Sam looked up into the storm and waited for what was to come.

In his crippled English the warrior was now telling Sam that they were going to ransom him to the Crows. What the Crows would do to him he tried to suggest by stripping fir needles and pretending that they were gobbets of flesh, and by pretending with a finger to slice his nose, lips, tongue, genitals, until they were all gone. He indicated that the joints of fingers and toes would be broken, one by one; with a piece of hooked wire each eye would be pulled out of its socket; and with a string tied around each eyeball he would be led through the village, while the squaws sliced off his buttocks and tossed them to the dogs.

What purpose the creature had in mind with his catalogue of horrors Sam did not know. All the while the redskin talked and gestured, with glittering of his black eyes and guttural gloatings of joy, Sam's mind was busy. He now suspected that this band of warriors had been begging the chief to turn the prisoner over to them, and their share of the rum, so that they could torture and drink and celebrate. The animal before him had worked himself into such a frenzy of maiming and blood-letting that Sam was afraid the frenzy might prove contagious. He decided to speak. He would not speak as a normal man or in a normal voice. He would speak as The Terror, as the man of all mountain men most feared by the red people, and as a great leader and chief.

His first sound was a thunderous roar from his deep chest, and it came with such a shattering explosion that the astounded and terrified redskin almost fell backwards. The chief retreated with him and there they stood, two braves with their black eyes popped out, as Sam flung his mighty arms toward the sky and trumpeted his disdain in his deepest and most dreadful voice. "Almighty God up there in Your kingdom, look down on Your son, for he will be gone beaver before he will stand such insults! These cowards have about used up my patience! I will stand no more of it!" Now, with a deliberate effort to astound and abash them, he swiftly puffed his cheeks in and out, to make the heavy golden beard dance and quiver over most of his face; he bugged and rolled his eyes, and they shone and gleamed like polished granite; and flinging both arms heavenward, he cried in a voice that could have been heard two miles away, "Almighty Father, I wasn't born to be slapped around and spit on and the first thing I know I'll open up this red nigger and pull his liver out and choke him with it! Look down, and give me the strength of Samson!" He then burst into a crazy-man wild hallooing and exulting that sent the two Indians and the guards into further retreat, and brought into view all those in camp.

The redmen, drunk or sober, could raise an infernal racket, but such a trumpet-tongued deafening uproar of bombination and reverberation they had never heard; and while they all stared as though hypnotized the golden-bearded giant began to jump up and down and contort himself like a monster in convulsions, his voice rising to a shrieking caterwauling that set the dogs to howling and the horses to whinnying. His fires fed by enormous anger and contempt for these ill-smelling creatures who had him in their power, Sam simply turned himself loose and bellowed and howled out of him the emotions that had been filling him to bursting. All the while he was thinking of such things as Beethoven's sonatas in C major and F minor, and his own act he put on with such a shattering crescendo that even he felt a little unnerved by it. These unspeakable creatures had even taken from him his tobacco, his harp, and the lock of hair from the head of his wife; and they had fondled his revolvers and pointed them at him, and with his knife had made movements at his throat. They opened his baggage in plain sight of him and with shrieks of delight had held up to view one thing and another—his moccasins, skins, flour, coffee, cloth—until he had got so utterly filled with anger for their insolence and contempt and stinking soup that he could only unleash his whole being to the Almighty in a war song of menace and challenge, and get it out of him so that he could again breathe naturally. For a full five minutes he kept it up, his thunderous overture to the infinite; and then, covered with sweat, he stepped back and stood against the tree, arms folded on his chest with his bound hands under his chin, his eyes looking at them. Fifty-eight pairs of black eyes were looking at him. Such a tempest of rage and challenge they had never heard from man or beast and would never hear again.

It was the chief who approached Sam. He came within ten feet of him and stood like a man who thought this bearded giant might explode, as the infernal spirit regions in Colter's hell exploded. After studying Sam a full minute he summoned the brave who spoke English. But Sam had the offensive and he intended to keep it; he could tell that these superstitious children were not sure now whether he was man or some kind of god. So, with prodigious gestures of menace and challenge, and a great roaring into the sky, Sam made them understand that he would fight any five of them in a fight to the death, all of them to come against him as one man, in full view of the Blackfeet people and a hundred mountain men; and after he had slain the five, the hundred mountain men would fight the whole Blackfeet nation, the thousand of them or ten thousand, or as many as the leaves on trees and the berries on bushes. He knew that his challenge would not be accepted, or even considered; but he had in mind a plan. He went on to say that if they were no braver than sick squaws crawling in the sagebrush, or dying coyotes with their heads in holes—if they were no more than rabbits, if they were a nation of magpies with broken wings, they should take him to the Sparrowhawks and get the thing over with. But if big ransom was what they wanted—tobacco and rum and guns and beads and bullets and coffee and sugar—they should ransom him to the mountain men, who would pay much more; and after he was set free they could capture him again and sell him again. But whatever they did, they would all die like puking coyotes in their vomit if they forgot for a moment that he was a great chief and a mighty one, who wore fifty eagle feathers in his headpiece; and he was to be treated with dignity and honors; and if he was not, all the mountain men would march against them and hunt them down to the last crippled dog.

To further confuse and addle their wits he burst into tremendous song. As before, the redmen seemed hypnotized as Sam smote his breast and shot his arms skyward and poured out of his lungs the furious majesties of impatience and anger. As suddenly as he had begun he stopped, and then roared at the pidgin brave, telling him to come forward if he were not a coward hiding under a stinkbush. The man advanced, slowly and with absurd caution, as if expecting Sam to blow him off the scene. Sam told him that he, Samson John Minard, was a chief, and a bigger and more important chief than the contemptible eater of crickets who had slapped his face. Sam said to tell him that he would raise his hair and pull his scent bag off if he didn't treat him the way a chief should be treated. "Go, you quivering coyote, and tell him! Tell him

Chief Samson is to be put in a tent, as befits a great one, and given his pipe and tobacco." Sam knew he would get no tobacco: once the smokers of kinnikinic and cedar bark and willow got hold of whiteman's tobacco they sucked it into their lungs day and night until it was gone. But he saw that he had aroused some of the warriors to clamorous proposals, and that the chief was talking things over with them. After a few minutes the brave told Sam that a tent would be prepared for him and he would have a robe to lie on.

A half hour later several braves came over, and untying the rope from the tree, led Sam like a beast to the tent. There he exploded in another deliberate tantrum; flinging his bound arms wildly, he said they would take the tether rope off his wrists, for did they think he was a horse to be hobbled and staked out? Hadn't they among their fifty-eight one who was warrior enough to guard an unarmed prisoner? This taunt bore results. The chief had Sam taken into one of the larger tepees, and put as guard over him one, he was told, who had made a coup when only a boy, and had more Flathead and Crow scalps than Sam had fingers and toes. Sam then repeated his proposal, in words and signs, that they should ransom him to the mountain men, and then see if they were brave enough to capture him a second time, for a second ransom.

When first made, this proposal had fired the greed of some of the warriors. Their passions had caught flame like tall dry prairie grass, as they foresaw innumerable kegs of rum and piles of tobacco. As children with little sense of the realities, they had no doubt that they could capture him a second time, or many times; and if there was to be so much firewater in the future why not drink what they had just captured? This was what Sam had hoped for. Once thirst possessed their senses there could be no prevailing against them. The chief knew that, but he was eager as any to unstop the rum and pour the liquid fire down his throat. He gave orders, and men rushed into the forest to find dead wood; other braves made ready three elk, which had been killed that afternoon. As Sam watched the preparations he tried to look sleepy and very hopeless. Five gallons might not lay them all out senseless but it was strong rum; forty pints for fifty-eight would average almost eleven ounces to the man. That ought to be enough.

The rope had been untied from the leather that bound Sam's wrists, and he had been given a small thin robe that had lost most of its hair. On this in the tent he sat and planned and waited. The brave who had been sent in to guard him was taller and heavier than most Indians: Sam thought he stood an inch or two above six feet and weighed more than two hundred pounds. He supposed that the chief had chosen one of his boldest and most dependable men, and one of the most savage, for this critter hadn't sat a full minute when

with Sam's Bowie he made passes across his throat. He took from his lap a
tomahawk and made movements with it to show Sam how he would split his
skull. His face expressionless, Sam watched the grim pantomime; inside he was
thinking: If my plan works, you dog-eater, you and me will be huggin before
this night is over.

Sam was weighing his chances in every way he could conceive of. The
tent was about ten feet across and about eight feet high where it was anchored
to the center pole. If he were to move fast inside it, Sam told himself, he would
have to bend over, for if his head struck the tent the Indians outside might see
the movement. The guard sat on a heavy robe. As he faced Sam he was just to
the left of the flap, which had been thrown open and back. There were three
big fires blazing outside; the voices were shrill. The firelight cast flickering illu-
minations over the guard's face and gave a horrifying appearance of evil to his
war paint. His right hand clasped the handle of the knife, his left the handle of
the tomahawk. He had no gun. He was alert but tense; he had to turn his head
now and then to peer out. Sam knew the man was burning with infernal thirst
and was wondering if he would share the rum or be forgotten. Oh, they would
bring him a chunk of roasted elk but would they bring him the water that
turned a man into fire? If only he were the one who spoke some English, Sam
could have talked to him and tried to make a frenzy of his resentment and impatience. As it was, he did nothing and said nothing; it would be best to look
sleepy and tired. Sam was sitting straight across from the guard; their faces were
only about six feet apart, their moccasined feet only about two. Sam's face was
in shadow; he knew that the guard could not see him clearly, but Sam could
see the emotions convulsing the guard's face. That Injun's belly was burning for
rum. If they forgot him he would be mad enough to grease hell with war paint
before this night was over.

The guard made no move that Sam's lidded eyes did not see. During
the first hour he had turned to look out at least once every ten minutes; he was
then looking out every five minutes; and at the end of an hour and a half he
was looking out every minute or less, and the way he moved showed that he
was itching with resentment and suspicion and that his thirst was like hell's
own. Nothing, Sam told himself, was more likely to make a guard think his
prisoner secure than a boiling passion that took his mind off him and returned
it and took it off again. Alcohol could do it; a female could do it. Alcohol, it
now seemed to Sam, was the redman's curse, and woman the whiteman's. . . .

Just itch all over, Sam thought, his bound hands in plain view on his
lap, his head sunk as though he were half gone in fatigue and sleep. Just itch,
you bastard, and keep looking. Sam had never felt more brilliantly alert, as

though all his senses and mind and emotions shone in the full blaze of noon sunlight. Never had his eyes been sharper. Just git yourself a thirst like that in hell, Sam was saying inside; and over and over calculated the risks and his chances. He figured that he had been sitting with the guard about two hours. For nearly an hour he had smelled the roasting flesh. He knew that tripods of green trees had been set up and that hanging from them were the carcasses, slowly roasting in flames and smoke. Redmen when hungry never waited for flesh to cook but almost at once began to hack off bloody gobbets; and by the time their hunger was appeased there wasn't much left but bone and gristle. Before long now these Indians would be drinking. Sam had hoped they would drink before they ate. Once they started drinking they would have pictures of mountain men bringing them whole rivers and lakes of rum, to ransom the Crow-killer, so that a second time they could capture him, for more lakes and rivers. What dreams children dreamed!

There now came to the door of the tent a face whose war paint had been smeared over with fresh blood. In this brave's hands was a piece of pine bark, on which rested a pound or two of hot elk meat. The guard set the meat by him and began to gesticulate, and to talk in a high shrill voice ill-becoming a bold brave warrior; Sam knew that he was asking why he had not been fetched a cup of spirit water. The two braves gestured and yelled at one another, and the one who had brought the meat then went away. Sam did not move or lift the lids on his eyes, for he knew that his moment was drawing near. Very gently he tried to ease his cramps and relax his muscles.

In only a few moments the Indian returned with a tin cup in his hand. Sam knew that in the cup was rum. The guard eagerly took the cup and sniffed, and he was so enchanted that he laid the knife on his lap, and seizing the cup with both hands, put the rim to his lips. Sam's gaze was on the other Indian; he was praying that the fellow would go away. He had hoped that the guard would be alone with him when he drank and that his first gulp would be so large it would strangle him. Sam was to say later that both his prayers were answered. The Indian in the tepee doorway, eager to get back to the drinking and feasting, did vanish; and the blockhead with the cup of rum did take such a huge mouthful that the fiery spirits choked him. He suddenly tightened all over and was fumbling to set the cup down when Sam moved with the swiftness that had become legendary. In an instant his powerful hands were on the redman's throat. Everything that he did now had been thought through, over and over, so that there would be no false move or wasted moment. As hands seized the throat a knee came with terrific force into the man's diaphragm, paralyzing his whole torso. In the next instant Sam released the throat and his right hand seized the knife. He twisted his right hand around until he could put the blade to the leather and sever it, and the moment that was done, the left hand was back to the throat to be sure it made no sounds, and the right hand was gathering the robe, tomahawk, and piece of elk meat. He then slipped under the back of the tent into the gray-white night.

In a flash he was gone across the pale snow and into the trees.

★　★　★　★　★

It was snowing hard. During the hours when he sat waiting for his chance Sam had known that he would need the Almighty's help if he were to outrun the pursuit of fifty-eight hell-fiends, and the bitter cold and deep snows of winter. His instincts told him that he was going east but he was not sure of it. During this day's march he had seen a range of mountains west of him, another north, and another east, and he had thought the range on the east was the Continental Divide. If it was, the Missouri River was only forty or fifty miles east of it, and from there across the desolation to Kate was a hundred and fifty or two hundred miles.

During his many hours of thinking and planning he had recognized that it would be folly to go south, over the trail up which they had come, or west to the Flatheads. His captors would expect him to take one of these routes. They would not expect him to go north into Blood and Piegan land, or to be fool enough to try to cross the Divide after heavy snows had come. Earlier in the day the war party had crossed a river but he did not know what river it was. He had never been through this country. He had heard that there were several rivers in this area, all of which came down from the Divide and flowed west. Up one of these rivers looked to him like the only possible way to freedom.

After he had trotted swiftly for four or five miles he stopped to listen. He could hear no sounds. He put the piece of meat to his nostrils, for he was as famished as a wolf. While sitting and waiting he had wondered if he ought to take one of the guard's thighs, but he was a sentimental man and he thought he would rather starve than eat human flesh. He had calculated all the risks and had decided that in starvation lay his greatest danger. He could hope to get his hands on little except roots along streams, berries still clinging to bushes, a fool hen possibly, a fish now and then in a shallow pool, rose hips, marrow in old bones; or, if very lucky, a deer or an antelope stuck in deep snow.

He was glad that it was snowing hard. He was singing inside at the thought of being free. He thanked God for both and he thanked Him for rum. He hoped that rum and rage would make fifty-seven warriors so drunk that they would fall down and freeze to death. He thought he had heard bones snap in the guard's neck. If they found him dead all hell would break loose; they would run round and round and the dogs would be baying at their heels. But Sam doubted that they would take his trail before morning. They would think he had gone back down the path to the Three Forks and that they could catch him in a day or two; or they would think he had headed for his in-laws and would get stuck in deep snow. If it were to snow all night they might not be able to tell by morning which way he had taken. But the dogs would know.

There was a cold wind down from the mountains. He listened again and thought he heard faint shrieks, and dogs barking, but he could not be sure. His direction now was due north and two hours before daylight he came to a river. Taking off his moccasins and leather leggins he waded into the shallow stream and turned up it, to the east, walking as rapidly as he could, in water only ankle-deep or sometimes to his crotch. It was cold but for a while it did not seem cold; his blood was hot from exertion, his soul singing, his hopes high. He had yanked off the guard's medicine bag and was amazed to find in it his mouth harp. It was as if a brother had joined him, or Beethoven's ugly face up in the sky had smiled. When first captured he would not have given a buck-skin whang for his life; but now, with God's help, he was a free man again, and he would remain free and alive, even if he had to live on tree bark. The redmen might follow his path to the river but there they would lose it, and two or three of them might go upriver but most of them would go downriver. He could not, like John Colter, find an acre of driftwood and lie under it for half a day and most of a night; he could only hoard his strength and keep going. Some of the river stones cut his feet but he remembered that John's feet had been filled with cactus thorns; he was starved but he told himself that Colter had lived on hips and roots; Hugh Glass with maggots swarming in his wounds had crawled for a hundred miles; and a man named Scott, starved and sick unto death, had dragged himself forward for sixty miles. And yonder Kate sat in the cold and sang. A man could do it if he had to. He recalled other tales of hero-ism and fortitude, to warm and cheer him as he struggled up the river.

Sam was not feeling sorry for himself. He was not that kind. He was not telling himself that he would perish. He was only warming himself with the feats of brave free men, his kind of men. Afraid that he was moving only about three miles an hour in his tortuous journey up the river, he looked round him but there was no other way. Until daylight he would keep moving and perhaps for an hour after daylight, for he thought it would take the red-men half the morning to find his path and follow it to the river. He would find some snuggery back under the bank—an old beaver house or a wash under an overhanging earth ledge or a pile of driftwood; and he would hole up until night came again. He could catch a few hours' sleep, if he lay on his belly, for in that position his snoring, Lotus had told him, was light. He would eat half the elk meat and all the rose hips he could find; and when darkness came he would be gone again.

What he found was a high-water eddy underwash, under a grove of large aspen; the spring torrents had raised the river four or five feet above its present level, and the high water swirling round and round in the eddy had cut away the earth back under the trees. Sam crawled for thirty feet and after putting on his leggins and moccasins and wrapping the robe around him he cut off morsels of flesh and chewed them thoroughly. Never had elk tasted so good. Looking out the way he had come, he could see only a hint of daylight. If Indians were to wade up the river, as he had done, it was possible that they would spot his hideaway and crouch low to look back under. But they would never wade far in a river. They would think he had made a raft and gone downriver, toward his in-laws, and by the time they discovered their error he would be over the Divide.

All day until dusk he rested and slept a little and heard no Indians and saw nothing alive but one hawk. All day the snow fell. All night he took his slow way up the river. By midnight he had reached the foothills; by morning he was fighting white water. An hour after daylight he had found no hiding place, but in shallow pools he had caught a few small trout, a part of which he ate for breakfast, with a handful of rose pods. He was still struggling upward on bruised and bleeding feet when about noon he saw a cavern back in a ledge of stone. Its mouth was close to the river, with a wide shelf of spilled stones at the entrance. Leaving the river, he climbed up across talus to look in. The cavern was far deeper than he had expected, so deep in fact that his gaze went blind back in the gloom. He smelled wild-beast odors, and the odors of dove, bat, and swallow. After entering the cave he stood under a ceiling thirty feet high and looked round him. At one side he saw a smaller cave that also ran back into gloom; this he explored to find a spot where he could lie down. The animal smells in the smaller cave were overpowering. They were so heavy and so saturated with mustiness and dusts that he could feel them in his nostrils.

Returning to the mouth of the cavern, he stood by a brown stone wall to give him protective coloring and looked back down the river. The falling snow was only a thin mist now, the kind that makes way for freezing cold; he could see far down the river's meandering course and across the valley. There was no smoke from Indian fires anywhere. He went down to the river for a water-washed stone on which to lay his meat and fish. Then, sitting in the cavern mouth, he cut off about three ounces of meat and ate it, and two fish no larger than his finger. Along the riverbanks he had gathered about a quart of rose hips. How a man could live and walk for a week on nothing but these, as some men were said to have done, he could not imagine.

While looking round him he sneezed. The echoes of it startled him, for they were remarkably loud and clear. Impressed by the cavern's acoustics, he spoke, saying, "Hot biscuits," and sang a few bars of an old ballad. The echoing astonished and then alarmed him. It was somewhat like music from a great organ, rolling through vaulted chambers, with ceilings high and low. He burst into a Mozart theme, and the echoes rolling away from him into the far dark recesses sounded to him like an orchestra playing. He wondered if he was losing his mind. After he had found a spot where he could lie and try to sleep he thought of the Rocky Mountains caverns he had explored, and of the strange sculpturing that water, wind, and time had made underground. "Almighty God—" he said, and liked so well the amplified and golden-toned echo that he uttered other words. "Dear Lotus, dear son—Lotus!" he said more loudly, and from all around him back in the stone mountains the word came back to him like an organ tone.

Sam was not a man who usually felt gooseflesh in moments of danger but he had been enfeebled by hunger and want of sleep. Gooseflesh spread over him in the moment when he smelled the danger; turning swiftly to a sitting position, tomahawk in one hand and knife in the other, he saw ambling toward him not more than fifty feet away a grizzly so large that it seemed almost to fill the cavern. In a flash Sam knew that the reverberating echoes had disturbed the monster's slumber, somewhere back in the gloom, and it had come to give battle to its enemy. That it intended to give battle Sam knew the instant he saw it. The next moment he was on his feet, advancing, the hatchet ready to strike and the knife to plunge. He marched right up to the beast and smote the prow of the nose a crushing blow with the head of the axe. In an instant his arm came back and he struck again, and this time the blow fell across the sensitive nostrils. The big furry fellow said *woof-woof* and began to back off, with Sam after him, hoping for grizzly steaks; but almost at once the beast vanished, and there was only the whimpering plaintive sound of a frightened child, as the shuffling fur ball hastened back to its winter bed.

Pale from fright and weakness and breathing hard, Sam watched it disappear. He felt for a moment that he was being tested with more than he could bear. Hungry, weary to the depths of his marrow, and numbed through with cold, he would now have to leave the cavern and go. There might be a whole pack of grizzlies back in the dark; and even if there were not, the whimpering one would nurse his injuries and come forth again. Over by the entrance Sam stood a few moments, looking out. He knew by the nimbus around the winter sun that the weather was going to change. After seven days of deep storm the temperature would fall; sometimes in this area it went to thirty, forty, even to fifty below. Sometimes there were blizzards that not even the wolves and hawks could endure. There was cold that split trees open with the sound of gunfire; that froze broad rivers from bank to bank and almost to their bottoms; and the snow so hard that even the giant moose with its sharp hoofs could walk on it. It was cold that welded a man's hand to the steel of gun or knife, if he was fool enough to touch it.

After searching the valley for sign of Indians and seeing none Sam looked up the river gorge to the continental backbone. After he had crossed the Divide the rivers would be flowing east instead of west, and he would be going down instead of climbing. With the robe flung across his left shoulder, the food enfolded by a piece of it and tucked up under an armpit, the hatchet in his left hand and the knife in his right, he scrambled down to the water's edge; sat and took off moccasins and leggins and trousers; and thrust wounded feet into the icy waters. Then he waded upstream. He guessed he might as well eat the remainder of the elk and the three small fish, and keep going and keep going. After he had gone a mile or two he peeled the outer bark off a spruce and licked the juice of the cambium. It was resinous and bitter. Hank Cady had said that lessen a man has something better he kin live on it if he hafta. The cambium itself Sam found unchewable, and so peeled off strips of it and licked the juice, as he had licked fruit juices off his hands as a child. While licking the juice he looked round him, wondering if there was anything else on this mountain that a man could eat. During the long miles up this river he had seen no birds, except a hawk or two and one duck; no sign of grouse or sage hen, no sign of deer or elk trail. On the mountain slopes above him he could see no snowpaths. The untramped, unmarked snow on either side of the river was about three feet deep. He wondered if it would be less exhausting to plow through it than to fight his way up over slippery boulders, in water from a foot to three feet deep. Wading in river waters up a mountain canyon was the most fatiguing toil he had ever known; he was sure he was not covering more than two miles an hour but he kept at it, doggedly, all day long, pausing only when night closed round him.

He then searched both banks, hoping to find a shelter in which he could sleep. But he found only an arbor, under a dense tangle of berry vines and mountain laurel, over which the snow had formed a roof; he crawled back under it, out of sight. After putting on his clothes he wrapped the robe around him, and lying on his left side facing the river, he put two fish on leaves a few inches from his face, hatchet and knife within reach, and in a few minutes was sound asleep. His first dream was of his wife; they were somewhere in buffalo land, and while she gathered berries and mushrooms he cooked steaks and made hot biscuits. It was a cold night and he slept cold, but for eight hours he did not awaken. It was the first solid rest he had had in a week.

When at daylight he stirred it took him a few moments to understand where he was. Then, like Jedediah Smith, he gave thanks to God; dwelt for a few minutes on the bones of his wife and child, yonder in the winter, and on a mother sitting in a pile of bedding looking out at an empty white world; and then ate the two fish. Yes, it had turned colder. On the eastern side of the Divide would be the wild storm-winds down from Canada; there he would need more than a mouthful of frozen fish to keep him going. But he felt cheerful this morning and he told himself that he was as strong as a bull moose. He thought he was safe from the Blackfeet now. Ahead of him lay an ordeal that might be the most difficult he would ever endure, but he would struggle through it, day after day, all the way across the white winter loneliness, until he came at last to Kate's door.

"Keep a fire for me, and a light," he said, and faced into the sharp winds from the north.

The Fiend of the Cooperage

BY ARTHUR CONAN DOYLE

It hardly comes as a surprise to say that the talented creator of Sherlock Holmes, the most memorable sleuth in English literature, was a man who knew how to tell a great story. But, as Holmes might have said, there's more to Conan Doyle than meets the eye. Here, he comes up with an incredible tale set in the jungles far from London. In it, you will meet an adversary that would have put shivers down the spine of even the great Sherlock.

*　*　*　*　*

It was no easy matter to bring the *Gamecock* up to the island, for the river had swept down so much silt that the banks extended for many miles out into the Atlantic. The coast was hardly to be seen when the first white curl of the breakers warned us of our danger, and from there onwards we made our way very carefully under mainsail and jib, keeping the broken water well to the left, as is indicated on the chart. More than once her bottom touched the sand (we were drawing something under six feet at the time), but we had always way enough and luck enough to carry us through. Finally the water shoaled, very rapidly, but they had sent a canoe from the factory, and the Krooboy pilot brought us within two hundred yards of the island. Here we dropped our anchor, for the gestures of the negro indicated that we could not hope to get any farther. The blue of the sea had changed to the brown of the river, and, even under the shelter of the island, the current was singing and swirling round our bows. The stream appeared to be in spate, for it was over the roots of the palm trees, and everywhere upon its muddy greasy surface we could see logs of wood and debris of all sorts which had been carried down by the flood.

When I had assured myself that we swung securely at our moorings, I thought it best to begin watering at once, for the place looked as if it reeked with fever. The heavy river, the muddy, shining banks, the bright poisonous green of the jungle, the moist steam in the air, they were all so many danger signals to one who could read them. I sent the longboat off, therefore, with two large hogsheads, which should be sufficient to last us until we made St Paul de Loanda. For my own part I took the dinghy and rowed for the island, for I could see the Union Jack fluttering above the palms to mark the position of Armitage and Wilson's trading station.

When I had cleared the grove, I could see the place, a long, low, white-washed building, with a deep veranda in front, and an immense pile of palm-oil barrels heaped upon either flank of it. A row of surf boats and canoes lay along the beach, and a single small jetty projected into the river. Two men in white suits with red cummerbunds round their waists were waiting upon the end of it to receive me. One was a large portly fellow with a greyish beard. The other was slender and tall, with a pale pinched face, which was half-concealed by a great mushroom-shaped hat.

'Very glad to see you,' said the latter, cordially. 'I am Walker, the agent of Armitage and Wilson. Let me introduce Dr Severall of the same company. It is not often we see a private yacht in these parts.'

'She's the *Gamecock*,' I explained. 'I'm owner and captain—Meldrum is the name.'

'Exploring?' he asked.

'I'm a lepidopterist—a butterfly-catcher. I've been doing the west coast from Senegal downwards.'

'Good sport?' asked the Doctor, turning a slow yellow-shot eye upon me.

'I have forty cases full. We came in here to water, and also to see what you have in my line.'

These introductions and explanations had filled up the time whilst my two Krooboys were making the dinghy fast. Then I walked down the jetty with one of my new acquaintances upon either side, each plying me with questions, for they had seen no white man for months.

'What do we do?' said the Doctor, when I had begun asking questions in my turn. 'Our business keeps us pretty busy, and in our leisure time we talk politics.'

'Yes, by the special mercy of Providence Severall is a rank Radical, and I am a good stiff Unionist, and we talk Home Rule for two solid hours every evening.'

'And drink quinine cocktails,' said the Doctor. 'We're both pretty well salted now, but our normal temperature was about 103 last year. I shouldn't, as an impartial adviser, recommend you to stay here very long unless you are collecting bacilli as well as butterflies. The mouth of the Ogowai River will never develop into a health resort.'

There is nothing finer than the way in which these outlying pickets of civilization distil a grim humour out of their desolate situation, and turn not only a bold, but a laughing face upon the chances which their lives may bring. Everywhere from Sierra Leone downwards I had found the same reeking swamps, the same isolated fever-racked communities, and the same bad jokes. There is something approaching to the divine in that power of man to rise above his conditions and to use his mind for the purpose of mocking at the memories of his body.

'Dinner will be ready in about half an hour, Captain Meldrum,' said the Doctor. 'Walker has gone in to see about it; he's the housekeeper this week. Meanwhile, if you like, we'll stroll round and I'll show you the sights of the island.'

The sun had already sunk beneath the line of palm trees, and the great arch of the heaven above our head was like the inside of a huge shell, shimmering with dainty pinks and delicate iridescence. No one who has not lived in a land where the weight and heat of a napkin become intolerable upon the knees can imagine the blessed relief which the coolness of evening brings along with it. In this sweeter and purer air the Doctor and I walked round the little island, he pointing out the stores, and explaining the routine of his work.

'There's a certain romance about the place,' said he, in answer to some remark of mine about the dullness of their lives. 'We are living here just upon the edge of the great unknown. Up there,' he continued, pointing to the north-east, 'Du Chaillu penetrated, and found the home of the gorilla. That is the Gaboon country—the land of the great apes. In this direction,' pointing to the south-east, 'no one has been very far. The land which is drained by this river is practically unknown to Europeans. Every log which is carried past us by the current has come from an undiscovered country. I've often wished that I was a better botanist when I have seen the singular orchids and curious-looking plants which have been cast up on the eastern end of the island.'

The place which the Doctor indicated was a sloping brown beach, freely littered with the flotsam of the stream. At each end was a curved point, like a little natural breakwater, so that a small shallow bay was left between. This was full of floating vegetation, with a single huge splintered tree lying stranded in the middle of it, the current rippling against its high black side.

'These are all from up country,' said the Doctor. 'They get caught in our little bay, and then when some extra freshet comes they are washed out again and carried out to sea.'

'What is the tree?' I asked.

'Oh, some kind of teak, I should imagine, but pretty rotten by the look of it. We get all sorts of big hardwood trees floating past here, to say nothing of the palms. Just come in here, will you?'

He led the way into a long building with an immense quantity of barrel staves and iron hoops littered about in it.

'This is our cooperage,' said he. 'We have the staves sent out in bundles, and we put them together ourselves. Now, you don't see anything particularly sinister about this building, do you?'

I looked round at the high corrugated iron roof, the white wooden walls, and the earthen floor. In one corner lay a mattress and a blanket.

'I see nothing very alarming,' said I.

'And yet there's something out of the common, too,' he remarked. 'You see that bed? Well, I intend to sleep there tonight. I don't want to buck, but I think it's a bit of a test for nerve.'

'Why?'

'Oh, there have been some funny goings on. You were talking about the monotony of our lives, but I assure you that they are sometimes quite as exciting as we wish them to be. You'd better come back to the house now, for after sundown we begin to get the fever-fog up from the marshes. There, you can see it coming across the river.'

I looked and saw long tentacles of white vapour writhing out from among the thick green underwood and crawling at us over the broad swirling surface of the brown river. At the same time the air turned suddenly dank and cold.

'There's the dinner gong,' said the Doctor. 'If this matter interests you I'll tell you about it afterwards.'

It did interest me very much, for there was something earnest and subdued in his manner as he stood in the empty cooperage, which appealed very forcibly to my imagination. He was a big, bluff, hearty man, this Doctor, and yet I had detected a curious expression in his eyes as he glanced about him— an expression which I would not describe as one of fear, but rather that of a man who is alert and on his guard.

'By the way,' said I, as we returned to the house, 'you have shown me the huts of a good many of your native assistants, but I have not seen any of the natives themselves.'

'They sleep in the hulk over yonder,' the Doctor answered, pointing over to one of the banks.

'Indeed. I should not have thought in that case they would need the huts.'

'Oh, they used the huts until quite recently. We've put them on the hulk until they recover their confidence a little. They were all half mad with fright, so we let them go, and nobody sleeps on the island except Walker and myself.'

'What frightened them?' I asked.

'Well, that brings us back to the same story. I suppose Walker has no objection to your hearing all about it. I don't know why we should make any secret about it, though it is certainly a pretty bad business.'

He made no further allusion to it during the excellent dinner which had been prepared in my honour. It appeared that no sooner had the little white topsail of the *Gamecock* shown round Cape Lopez than these kind fellows had begun to prepare their famous pepper-pot—which is the pungent stew peculiar to the West Coast—and to boil their yams and sweet potatoes. We sat down to as good a native dinner as one could wish, served by a smart Sierra Leone waiting boy. I was just remarking to myself that he at least had not shared in the general flight, when, having laid the dessert and wine upon the table, he raised his hand to his turban.

'Anything else I do, Massa Walker?' he asked.

'No, I think that is all right, Moussa,' my host answered. 'I am not feeling very well tonight, though, and I should much prefer if you would stay on the island.'

I saw a struggle between his fears and his duty upon the swarthy face of the African. His skin had turned of that livid purplish tint which stands for pallor in a negro, and his eyes looked furtively about him.

'No, no, Massa Walker,' he cried, at last, 'you better come to the hulk with me, sah. Look after you much better in the hulk, sah!'

'That won't do, Moussa. White men don't run away from the posts where they are placed.'

Again I saw the passionate struggle in the negro's face, and again his fears prevailed.

'No use, Massa Walker, sah!' he cried. 'S'elp me, I can't do it. If it was yesterday or if it was tomorrow, but this is the third night, sah, an' it's more than I can face.'

Walker shrugged his shoulders.

'Off with you then!' said he. 'When the mail-boat comes you can get back to Sierra Leone, for I'll have no servant who deserts me when I need him most. I suppose this is all mystery to you, or has the Doctor told you, Captain Meldrum?'

'I showed Captain Meldrum the cooperage, but I did not tell him any-thing,' said Dr Severall. 'You're looking bad, Walker,' he added, glancing at his companion. 'You have a strong touch coming on you.'

'Yes, I've had the shivers all day, and now my head is like a cannon-ball. I took ten grains of quinine, and my ears are singing like a kettle. But I want to sleep with you in the cooperage tonight.'

'No, no, my dear chap. I won't hear of such a thing. You must get to bed at once, and I am sure Meldrum will excuse you. I shall sleep in the cooperage, and I promise you that I'll be round with your medicine before breakfast.'

It was evident that Walker had been struck by one of those sudden and violent attacks of remittent fever which are the curse of the West Coast. His sallow cheeks were flushed and his eyes shining with fever, and suddenly as he sat there he began to croon out a song in the high-pitched voice of delirium.

'Come, come, we must get you to bed, old chap,' said the Doctor, and with my aid he led his friend into his bedroom. There we undressed him and presently, after taking a strong sedative, he settled down into a deep slumber.

'He's right for the night,' said the Doctor, as we sat down and filled our glasses once more. 'Sometimes it is my turn and sometimes his, but, fortunately, we have never been down together. I should have been sorry to be out of it tonight, for I have a little mystery to unravel. I told you that I intended to sleep in the cooperage.'

'Yes, you said so.'

'When I said sleep I meant watch, for there will be no sleep for me. We've had such a scare here that no native will stay after sundown, and I mean to find out tonight what the cause of it all may be. It has always been the cus-tom for a native watchman to sleep in the cooperage, to prevent the barrel hoops being stolen. Well, six days ago the fellow who slept there disappeared, and we have never seen a trace of him since. It was certainly singular, for no canoe had been taken, and these waters are too full of crocodiles for any man to swim to shore. What became of the fellow, or how he could have left the island is a complete mystery. Walker and I were merely surprised, but the blacks were badly scared and queer Voodoo tales began to get about amongst them. But the real stampede broke out three nights ago, when the new watchman in the cooperage also disappeared.'

'What became of him?' I asked.

'Well, we not only don't know, but we can't even give a guess which would fit the facts. The niggers swear there is a fiend in the cooperage who claims a man every third night. They wouldn't stay in the island—nothing could persuade them. Even Moussa, who is a faithful boy enough, would, as you have seen, leave his master in a fever rather than remain for the night. If we are to continue to run this place we must reassure our niggers, and I don't know any better way of doing it than by putting in a night there myself. This is the third night, you see, so I suppose the thing is due, whatever it may be.'

'Have you no clue?' I asked. 'Was there no mark of violence, no blood-stain, no footprints, nothing to give a hint as to what kind of danger you may have to meet?'

'Absolutely nothing. The man was gone and that was all. Last time it was old Ali, who has been wharf-tender here since the place was started. He was always as steady as a rock, and nothing but foul play would take him from his work.'

'Well,' said I, 'I really don't think that this is a one-man job. Your friend is full of laudanum, and come what might he can be of no assistance to you. You must let me stay and put in a night with you at the cooperage.'

'Well, now, that's very good of you, Meldrum,' said he heartily, shaking my hand across the table. 'It's not a thing that I should have ventured to pro-pose, for it is asking a good deal of a casual visitor, but if you really mean it—'

'Certainly I mean it. If you will excuse me a moment, I will hail the *Gamecock* and let them know that they need not expect me.'

As we came back from the other end of the little jetty we were both struck by the appearance of the night. A huge blue-black pile of clouds had built itself up upon the landward side, and the wind came from it in little hot pants, which beat upon our faces like the draught from a blast furnace. Under the jetty the river was swirling and hissing, tossing like white spurts of spray over the planking.

'Confound it!' said Dr Severall. 'We are likely to have a flood on the top of all our troubles. That rise in the river means heavy rain up-country, and when it once begins you never know how far it will go. We've had the island nearly covered before now. Well, we'll just go and see that Walker is comfort-able, and then if you like we'll settle down in our quarters.'

The sick man was sunk in a profound slumber, and we left him with some crushed limes in a glass beside him in case he should awake with the thirst of fever upon him. Then we made our way through the unnatural gloom thrown by that menacing cloud. The river had risen so high that the little bay which I have described at the end of the island had become almost obliterated through the submerging of its flanking peninsula. The great raft of driftwood, with the huge black tree in the middle, was swaying up and down in the swollen current.

'That's one good thing a flood will do for us,' said the Doctor. 'It car-ries away all the vegetable stuff which is brought down on to the east end of the island. It came down with the freshet the other day, and here it will stay until a flood sweeps it out into the main stream. Well, here's our room, and here are some books and here is my tobacco pouch, and we must try and put in the night as best we may.'

By the light of our single lantern the great lonely room looked very gaunt and dreary. Save for the piles of staves and heaps of hoops there was absolutely nothing in it, with the exception of the mattress for the Doctor, which had been laid in the corner. We made a couple of seats and a table out of the staves, and settled down together for a long vigil. Severall had brought a revolver for me and was himself armed with a double-barrelled shotgun. We loaded our weapons and laid them cocked within reach of our hands. The little circle of light and the black shadows arching over us were so melancholy that he went off to the house, and returned with two candles. One side of the cooperage was pierced, however, by several open windows, and it was only by screening our lights behind staves that we could prevent them from being extinguished.

The Doctor, who appeared to be a man of iron nerves, had settled down to a book, but I observed that every now and then he laid it upon his knee, and took an earnest look all round him. For my part, although I tried once or twice to read, I found it impossible to concentrate my thoughts upon the book. They would always wander back to this great empty silent room, and to the sinister mystery which overshadowed it. I racked my brains for some possible theory which would explain the disappearance of these two men. There was the black fact that they were gone, and not the least tittle of evidence as to why or whither. And here we were waiting in the same place—waiting without an idea as to what we were waiting for. I was right in saying that it was not a one-man job. It was trying enough as it was, but no force upon earth would have kept me there without a comrade.

What an endless, tedious night it was! Outside we heard the lapping and gurgling of the great river, and the soughing of the rising wind. Within, save for our breathing, the turning of the Doctor's pages, and the high, shrill ping of an occasional mosquito, there was a heavy silence. Once my heart sprang into my mouth as Severall's book suddenly fell to the ground and he sprang to his feet with his eyes on one of the windows.

'Did you see anything, Meldrum?'

'No, did you?'

'Well, I had a vague sense of movement outside that window.' He caught up his gun and approached it. 'No, there's nothing to be seen, and yet I could have sworn that something passed slowly across it.'

'A palm leaf, perhaps,' said I, for the wind was growing stronger every instant.

'Very likely,' said he, and settled down to his book again, but his eyes were for ever darting little suspicious glances up at the window. I watched it also, but all was quiet outside.

And then suddenly our thoughts were turned into a new direction by the bursting of the storm. A blinding flash was followed by a clap which shook the building. Again and again came the vivid white glare with thunder at the same instant, like the flash and roar of a monstrous piece of artillery. And then down came the tropical rain, crashing and rattling on the corrugated iron roofing of the cooperage. The big hollow room boomed like a drum. From the darkness arose a strange mixture of noises, a gurgling, splashing, tinkling, bubbling, washing, dripping—every liquid sound that nature can produce from the thrashing and swishing of the rain to the deep steady boom of the river. Hour after hour the uproar grew louder and more sustained.

'My word,' said Severall, 'we are going to have the father of all the floods this time. Well, here's the dawn coming at last and that is a blessing. We've about exploded the third night superstition, anyhow.'

A grey light was stealing through the room, and there was the day upon us in an instant. The rain had eased off, but the coffee-coloured river was roaring past like a waterfall. Its power made me fear for the anchor of the *Gamecock*.

'I must get aboard,' said I. 'If she drags she'll never be able to beat up the river again.'

'The island is as good as a breakwater,' the Doctor answered. 'I can give you a cup of coffee if you will come up to the house.'

I was chilled and miserable, so the suggestion was a welcome one. We left the ill-omened cooperage with its mystery still unsolved, and we splashed our way up to the house.

'There's the spirit lamp,' said Severall. 'If you would just put a light to it, I will see how Walker feels this morning.'

He left me, but was back in an instant with a dreadful face.

'He's gone!' he cried hoarsely.

The words sent a thrill of horror through me. I stood with the lamp in my hand, glaring at him.

'Yes, he's gone!' he repeated. 'Come and look!'

I followed him without a word, and the first thing that I saw as I entered the bedroom was Walker himself lying huddled on his bed in the grey flannel sleeping suit in which I had helped to dress him on the night before.

'Not dead, surely!' I gasped.

The Doctor was terribly agitated. His hands were shaking like leaves in the wind.

'He's been dead some hours.'

'Was it fever?'

'Fever? Look at his foot!'

I glanced down and a cry of horror burst from my lips. One foot was not merely dislocated, but was turned completely round in a most grotesque contortion.

'Good God!' I cried. 'What can have done this?'

Severall had laid his hand upon the dead man's chest.

'Feel here,' he whispered.

I placed my hand at the same spot. There was no resistance. The body was absolutely soft and limp. It was like pressing a sawdust doll.

'The breast-bone is gone,' said Severall in the same awed whisper. 'He's broken to bits. Thank God that he had the laudanum. You can see by his face that he died in his sleep.'

'But who can have done this?'

'I've had about as much as I can stand,' said the Doctor, wiping his forehead. 'I don't know that I'm a greater coward than my neighbours, but this gets beyond me. If you're going out to the *Gamecock*—'

'Come on!' said I, and off we started. If we did not run it was because each of us wished to keep up the last shadow of his self-respect before the other. It was dangerous in a light canoe on that swollen river, but we never paused to give the matter a thought. He bailing and I paddling we kept her above water, and gained the deck of the yacht. There, with two hundred yards of water between us and this cursed island we felt that we were our own men once more.

'We'll go back in an hour or so,' said he. 'But we need have a little time to steady ourselves. I wouldn't have had the niggers see me as I was just now for a year's salary.'

'I've told the steward to prepare breakfast. Then we shall go back,' said I. 'But in God's name, Dr Severall, what do you make of it all?'

'It beats me—beats me clean. I've heard of Voodoo devilry, and I've laughed at it with the others. But that poor old Walker, a decent, God-fearing, nineteenth-century, Primrose-League Englishman should go under like this without a whole bone in his body—it's given me a shake, I won't deny it. But look there, Meldrum, is that hand of yours mad or drunk, or what is it?'

Old Patterson, the oldest man of my crew, and as steady as the Pyramids, had been stationed in the bows with a boat-hook to fend off the drifting logs which came sweeping down with the current. Now he stood with crooked knees, glaring out in front of him, and one forefinger stabbing furiously at the air.

'Look at it!' he yelled. 'Look at it!'

And at the same instant we saw it.

A huge black tree-trunk was coming down the river, its broad glistening back just lapped by the water. And in front of it—about three feet in front—arching upwards like the figure-head of a ship, there hung a dreadful face, swaying slowly from side to side. It was flattened, malignant, as large as a small beer-barrel, of a faded fungoid colour, but the neck which supported it was mottled with a dull yellow and black. As it flew past the *Gamecock* in the swirl of the waters I saw two immense coils roll up out of some great hollow in the tree, and the villainous head rose suddenly to the height of eight or ten feet, looking with dull, skin-covered eyes at the yacht. An instant later the tree had shot past us and was plunging with its horrible passenger towards the Atlantic.

'What was it?' I cried.

'It is our fiend of the cooperage,' said Dr Severall, and he had become in an instant the same bluff, self-confident man that he had been before. 'Yes, that is the devil who has been haunting our island. It is the great python of the Gaboon.'

I thought of the stories which I had heard all down the coast of the monstrous constrictors of the interior, of their periodical appetite, and of the murderous effects of their deadly squeeze. Then it all took shape in my mind. There had been a freshet the week before. It had brought down this huge hollow tree with its hideous occupant. Who knows from what far distant tropical forest it may have come! It had been stranded on the little east bay of the island. The cooperage had been the nearest house. Twice with the return of its appetite it had carried off the watchman. Last night it had doubtless come again, when Severall had thought he saw something move at the window, but our lights had driven it away. It had writhed onwards and had slain poor Walker in his sleep.

'Why did it not carry him off?' I asked.

'The thunder and lightning must have scared the brute away. There's your steward, Meldrum. The sooner we have breakfast and get back to the island the better, or some of those niggers might think that we had been frightened.'

Yeager

From *The Right Stuff*

BY TOM WOLFE

Strap yourself in. You're headed for part of the wild blue yonder where no man has ever gone and lived to tell about it. Tom Wolfe is providing the engine, Chuck Yeager will be doing the flying, and a demon called "The Sound Barrier" is waiting above the clouds.

★   ★   ★   ★   ★

Anyone who travels very much on airlines in the United States soon gets to know the voice of *the airline pilot* . . . coming over the intercom . . . with a particular drawl, a particular folksiness, a particular down-home calmness that is so exaggerated it begins to parody itself (nevertheless!—it's reassuring) . . . the voice that tells you, as the airliner is caught in thunderheads and goes bolting up and down a thousand feet at a single gulp, to check your seat belts because "it might get a little choppy" . . . the voice that tells you (on a flight from Phoenix preparing for its final approach into Kennedy Airport, New York, just after dawn): "Now, folks, uh . . . this is the captain . . . ummmm . . . We've got a little ol' red light up here on the control panel that's tryin' to tell us that the *landin'* gears're not . . . uh . . . *lockin'* into position when we lower 'em . . . Now . . . *I* don't believe that little ol' red light knows what it's *talkin'* about—I believe it's that little ol' red *light* that iddn' workin' right" . . . faint chuckle, long pause, as if to say, *I'm not even sure all this is really worth going into—still, it may amuse you* . . . "But . . . I guess to play it by the rules, we oughta *hum*or that little ol' light . . . so we're gonna take her down to about, oh, two or three hundred feet over the runway at Kennedy, and the folks down there on the ground are gonna see if they caint give us a *visual* inspection of those ol' landin' gears"—with which he is obviously on intimate ol'-buddy

6 8

terms, as with every other working part of this mighty ship—"and if I'm right . . . they're gonna tell us everything is copacetic all the way aroun' an' we'll jes take her on in" . . . and, after a couple of low passes over the field, the voice returns: "Well, folks, those folks down there on the ground—it must be too early for 'em or somethin'—I 'spect they still got the *sleep*ers in their eyes . . . 'cause they say they caint tell if those ol' landin' gears are all the way down or not . . . But, you know, up here in the cockpit we're convinced they're all the way down, so we're jes gonna take her on in . . . And oh" . . . (*I almost forgot*) . . . "while we take a little swing out over the ocean an' empty some of that surplus fuel we're not gonna be needin' anymore—that's what you might be seein' comin' out of the wings—our lovely little ladies . . . if they'll be so kind . . . they're gonna go up and down the aisles and show you how we do what we call 'assumin' the position' " . . . another faint chuckle (*We do this so often, and it's so much fun, we even have a funny little name for it*) . . . and the stewardesses, a bit grimmer, by the looks of them, than *that voice,* start telling the passengers to take their glasses off and take the ballpoint pens and other sharp objects out of their pockets, and they show them *the position,* with the head lowered . . . while down on the field at Kennedy the little yellow emergency trucks start roaring across the field—and even though in your pounding heart and your sweating palms and your broiling brainpan you *know* this is a critical moment in your life, you still can't quite bring yourself to be*lieve* it, because if it were . . . how could *the captain,* the man who knows the actual situation most intimately . . . how could he keep on drawlin' and chucklin' and driftin' and lollygaggin' in that particular voice of his—

Well!—who doesn't know that voice! And who can forget it!—even after he is proved right and the emergency is over.

That particular voice may sound vaguely Southern or Southwestern, but it is specifically Appalachian in origin. It originated in the mountains of West Virginia, in the coal country, in Lincoln County, so far up in the hollows that, as the saying went, "they had to pipe in daylight." In the late 1940's and early 1950s this up-hollow voice drifted down from on high, from over the high desert of California, down, down, down, from the upper reaches of the Brotherhood into all phases of American aviation. It was amazing. It was *Pygmalion* in reverse. Military pilots and then, soon, airline pilots, pilots from Maine and Massachusetts and the Dakotas and Oregon and everywhere else, began to talk in that poker-hollow West Virginia drawl, or as close to it as they could bend their native accents. It was the drawl of the most righteous of all the possessors of the right stuff: Chuck Yeager.

Yeager had started out as the equivalent, in the Second World War, of the legendary Frank Luke of the 27th Aero Squadron in the First. Which is to say, he was the boondocker, the boy from the back country, with only a high-school education, no credentials, no cachet or polish of any sort, who took off the feed-store overalls and put on a uniform and climbed into an airplane and lit up the skies over Europe.

Yeager grew up in Hamlin, West Virginia, a town on the Mud River not far from Nitro, Hurricane Whirlwind, Salt Rock, Mud, Sod, Crum, Leet, Dollie, Ruth, and Alum Creek. His father was a gas driller (drilling for natural gas in the coalfields), his older brother was a gas driller, and he would have been a gas driller had he not enlisted in the Army Air Force in 1941 at the age of eighteen. In 1943, at twenty, he became a flight officer, i.e., a non-com who was allowed to fly, and went to England to fly fighter planes over France and Germany. Even in the tumult of the war Yeager was somewhat puzzling to a lot of other pilots. He was a short, wiry, but muscular little guy with dark curly hair and a tough-looking face that seemed (to strangers) to be saying: "You best not be lookin' me in the eye, you peckerwood, or I'll put four more holes in your nose." But that wasn't what was puzzling. What was puzzling was the way Yeager talked. He seemed to talk with some older forms of English elocution, syntax, and conjugation that had been preserved uphollow in the Appalachians. There were people up there who never said they disapproved of anything, they said: "I don't hold with it." In the present tense they were willing to *help* out, like anyone else; but in the past tense they only *holped*. "H'it weren't nothin' I hold with, but I holped him out with it, anyways."

In his first eight missions, at the age of twenty, Yeager shot down two German fighters. On his ninth he was shot down over German-occupied French territory, suffering flak wounds; he bailed out, was picked up by the French underground, which smuggled him across the Pyrenees into Spain disguised as a peasant. In Spain he was jailed briefly, then released, whereupon he made it back to England and returned to combat during the Allied invasion of France. On October 12, 1944, Yeager took on and shot down five German fighter planes in succession. On November 6, flying a propeller-driven P-51 Mustang, he shot down one of the new jet fighters the Germans had developed, the Messerschmitt-262, and damaged two more, and on November 20 he shot down four FW-190s. It was a true Frank Luke-style display of warrior fury and personal prowess. By the end of the war he had thirteen and a half kills. He was twenty-two years old.

In 1946 and 1947 Yeager was trained as a test pilot at Wright Field in Dayton. He amazed his instructors with his ability at stunt-team flying, not to mention the unofficial business of hassling. That plus his up-hollow drawl had everybody saying, "He's a natural-born stick 'n' rudder man." Nevertheless, there was something extraordinary about it when a man so young, with so little experience in flight test, was selected to go to Muroc Field in California for the X-1 project.

Muroc was up in the high elevations of the Mojave Desert. It looked like some fossil landscape that had long since been left behind by the rest of terrestrial evolution. It was full of huge dry lake beds, the biggest being Rogers Lake. Other than sagebrush the only vegetation was Joshua trees, twisted freaks of the plant world that looked like a cross between cactus and Japanese bonsai. They had a dark petrified green color and horribly crippled branches. At dusk the Joshua trees stood out in silhouette on the fossil wasteland like some arthritic nightmare. In the summer the temperature went up to 110 degrees as a matter of course, and the dry lake beds were covered in sand, and there would be windstorms and sandstorms right out of a Foreign Legion movie. At night it would drop to near freezing, and in December it would start raining, and the dry lakes would fill up with a few inches of water, and some sort of putrid pre-historic shrimps would work their way up from out of the ooze, and sea gulls would come flying in a hundred miles or more from the ocean, over the mountains, to gobble up these squirming little throwbacks. A person had to see it to believe it: flocks of sea gulls wheeling around in the air out in the middle of the high desert in the dead of winter and grazing on antediluvian crus-taceans in the primordial ooze.

When the wind blew the few inches of water back and forth across the lake beds, they became absolutely smooth and level. And when the water evaporated in the spring, and the sun baked the ground hard, the lake beds be-came the greatest natural landing fields ever discovered, and also the biggest, with miles of room for error. That was highly desirable, given the nature of the enterprise at Muroc.

Besides the wind, sand, tumbleweed, and Joshua trees, there was noth-ing at Muroc except for two quonset-style hangars, side by side, a couple of gasoline pumps, a single concrete runway, a few tarpaper shacks, and some tents. The officers stayed in the shacks marked "barracks," and lesser souls stayed in the tents and froze all night and fried all day. Every road into the property had a guardhouse on it manned by soldiers. The enterprise the Army had undertaken in this godforsaken place was the development of supersonic jet and rocket planes.

At the end of the war the Army had discovered that the Germans not only had the world's first jet fighter but also a rocket plane that had gone 596 miles an hour in tests. Just after the war a British jet, the Gloster Meteor, jumped the official world speed record from 469 to 606 in a single day. The next great plateau would be Mach 1, the speed of sound, and the Army Air Force considered it crucial to achieve it first.

The speed of sound, Mach 1, was known (thanks to the work of the physicist Ernst Mach) to vary at different altitudes, temperatures, and wind speeds. On a calm 60-degree day at sea level it was about 760 miles an hour, while at 40,000 feet, where the temperature would be at least sixty below, it was about 660 miles an hour. Evil and baffling things happened in the transonic zone, which began at about .7 Mach. Wind tunnels choked out at such velocities. Pilots who approached the speed of sound in dives reported that the controls would lock or "freeze" or even alter their normal functions. Pilots had crashed and died because they couldn't budge the stick. Just last year Geoffrey de Havilland, son of the famous British aircraft designer and builder, had tried to take one of his father's DH 108s to Mach 1. The ship started buffeting and then disintegrated, and he was killed. This led engineers to speculate that the g-forces became infinite at Mach 1, causing the aircraft to implode. They started talking about "the sonic wall" and "the sound barrier."

So this was the task that a handful of pilots, engineers, and mechanics had at Muroc. The place was utterly primitive, nothing but bare bones, bleached tarpaulins, and corrugated tin rippling in the heat with caloric waves; and for an ambitious young pilot it was perfect. Muroc seemed like an outpost on the dome of the world, open only to a righteous few, closed off to the rest of humanity, including even the Army Air Force brass of command control, which was at Wright Field. The commanding officer at Muroc was only a colonel, and his superiors at Wright did not relish junkets to the Muroc rat shacks in the first place. But to pilots this prehistoric throwback of an airfield became . . . shrimp heaven! the rat-shack plains of Olympus!

Low Rent Septic Tank Perfection . . . yes; and not excluding those traditional essentials for the blissful hot young pilot: Flying & Drinking and Drinking & Driving.

Just beyond the base, to the southwest, there was a rickety wind-blown 1930's-style establishment called Pancho's Fly Inn, owned, run, and bartended by a woman named Pancho Barnes. Pancho Barnes wore tight white sweaters and tight pants, after the mode of Barbara Stanwyck in *Double Indemnity*. She was only forty-one when Yeager arrived at Muroc, but her face was so weather-beaten, had so many hard miles on it, that she looked older, especially to the young pilots at the base. She also shocked the pants off them with her vulcanized tongue. Everybody she didn't like was an old bastard or a sonofabitch. People she liked were old bastards and sonsabitches, too. "I tol' 'at ol' bastard to get 'is ass on over here and I'd g'im a drink." But Pancho Barnes was anything but Low Rent. She was the granddaughter of the man who designed the old Mount Lowe cable-car system, Thaddeus S. C. Lowe. Her maiden name was Florence Leontine Lowe. She was brought up in San Marino, which adjoined Pasadena and was one of Los Angeles' wealthiest suburbs, and her first husband—she was married four times—was the pastor of the Pasadena Episcopal Church, the Rev. C. Rankin Barnes. Mrs. Barnes seemed to have few of the conventional community interests of a Pasadena matron. In the late 1920's, by boat and plane, she ran guns for Mexican revolutionaries and picked up the nickname Pancho. In 1930 she broke Amelia Earhart's airspeed record for women. Then she barnstormed around the country as the featured performer of "Pancho Barnes's Mystery Circus of the Air." She always greeted her public in jodhpurs and riding boots, a flight jacket, a white scarf, and a white sweater that showed off her terrific Barbara Stanwyck chest. Pancho's desert Fly Inn had an airstrip, a swimming pool, a dude ranch corral, plenty of acreage for horseback riding, a big old guest house for the lodgers, and a connecting building that was the bar and restaurant. In the barroom the floors, the tables, the chairs, the walls, the beams, the bar were of the sort known as extremely weather-beaten, and the screen doors kept banging. Nobody putting together such a place for a movie about flying in the old days would ever dare make it as dilapidated and generally go-to-hell as it actually was. Behind the bar were many pictures of airplanes and pilots, lavishly autographed and inscribed, badly framed and crookedly hung. There was an old piano that had been dried out and cracked to the point of hopeless desiccation. On a good night a huddle of drunken aviators could be heard trying to bang, slosh, and navigate their way through old Cole Porter tunes. On average nights the tunes were not that good to start with. When the screen door banged and a man walked through the door into the saloon, every eye in the place checked him out. If he wasn't known as somebody who had something to do with flying at Muroc, he would be eyed like some lame goddamned mouseshit sheepherder from *Shane.*

The plane the Air Force wanted to break the sound barrier with was called the X-1. The Bell Aircraft Corporation had built it under an Army contract. The core of the ship was a rocket of the type first developed by a young Navy inventor, Robert Truax, during the war. The fuselage was shaped like a 50-caliber bullet—an object that was known to go supersonic smoothly. Military pilots seldom drew major test assignments; they went to highly paid civilians working for the aircraft corporations. The prime pilot for the X-1 was a man whom Bell regarded as the best of the breed. This man looked like a movie star. He looked like a pilot from out of *Hell's Angels.* And on top of everything else there was his name: Slick Goodlin.

The idea in testing the X-1 was to nurse it carefully into the transonic zone, up to seven-tenths, eight-tenths, nine-tenths the speed of sound (.7 Mach, .8 Mach, .9 Mach) before attempting the speed of sound itself, Mach 1, even though Bell and the Army already knew the X-1 had the rocket power to go to Mach 1 and beyond, if there *was* any *beyond*. The consensus of aviators and engineers, after Geoffrey de Havilland's death, was that the speed of sound was an absolute, like the firmness of the earth. The sound barrier was a farm you could buy in the sky. So Slick Goodlin began to probe the transonic zone in the X-1, going up to .8 Mach. Every time he came down he'd have a riveting tale to tell. The buffeting, it was so fierce—and the listeners, their imaginations aflame, could practically see poor Geoffrey de Havilland disintegrating in midair. And the goddamned aerodynamics—and the listeners got a picture of a man in ballroom pumps skidding across a sheet of ice, pursued by bears. A controversy arose over just how much bonus Slick Goodlin should receive for assaulting the dread Mach 1 itself. Bonuses for contract test pilots were not unusual; but the figure of $150,000 was now bruited about. The Army balked, and Yeager got the job. He took it for $283 a month, or $3,396 a year; which is to say, his regular Army captain's pay.

The only trouble they had with Yeager was in holding him back. On his first powered flight in the X-1 he immediately executed an unauthorized zero-g roll with a full load of rocket fuel, then stood the ship on its tail and went up to .85 Mach in a vertical climb, also unauthorized. On subsequent flights, at speeds between .85 Mach and .9 Mach, Yeager ran into most known airfoil problems—loss of elevator, aileron, and rudder control, heavy trim pressures, Dutch rolls, pitching and buffeting, the lot—yet was convinced, after edging over .9 Mach, that this would all get better, not worse, as you reached Mach 1. The attempt to push beyond Mach 1—"breaking the sound barrier"—was set for October 14, 1947. Not being an engineer, Yeager didn't believe the "barrier" existed.

October 14 was a Tuesday. On Sunday evening, October 12, Chuck Yeager dropped in at Pancho's, along with his wife. She was a brunette named Glennis, whom he had met in California while he was in training, and she was such a number, so striking, he had the inscription "Glamorous Glennis" written on the nose of his P-51 in Europe and, just a few weeks back, on the X-1 itself. Yeager didn't go to Pancho's and knock back a few because two days later the big test was coming up. Nor did he knock back a few because it was the weekend. No, he knocked back a few because night had come and he was a pilot at Muroc. In keeping with the military tradition of Flying & Drinking, that was what you did, for no other reason than that the sun had gone down. You went to Pancho's and knocked back a few and listened to the screen doors banging and to other aviators torturing the piano and the nation's repertoire of Familiar Favorites and to lonesome mouse-turd strangers wandering in through the banging doors and to Pancho classifying the whole bunch of them as old bastards and miserable peckerwoods. That was what you did if you were a pilot at Muroc and the sun went down.

So about eleven Yeager got the idea that it would be a hell of a kick if he and Glennis saddled up a couple of Pancho's dude-ranch horses and went for a romp, a little rat race, in the moonlight. This was in keeping with the military tradition of Flying & Drinking and Drinking & Driving, except that this was prehistoric Muroc and you rode horses. So Yeager and his wife set off on a little proficiency run at full gallop through the desert in the moonlight amid the arthritic silhouettes of the Joshua trees. Then they start racing back to the corral, with Yeager in the lead and heading for the gateway. Given the pre-vailing conditions, it being nighttime, at Pancho's, and his head being filled with a black sandstorm of many badly bawled songs and vulcanized oaths, he sees too late that the gate has been closed. Like many a hard-driving midnight pilot before him, he does not realize that he is not equally gifted in the control of all forms of locomotion. He and the horse hit the gate, and he goes flying off and lands on his right side. His side hurts like hell.

The next day, Monday, his side still hurts like hell. It hurts every time he moves. It hurts every time he breathes deep. It hurts every time he moves his right arm. He knows that if he goes to a doctor at Muroc or says anything to anybody even remotely connected with his superiors, he will be scrubbed from the flight on Tuesday. They might even go so far as to put some other miserable peckerwood in his place. So he gets on his motorcycle, an old junker that Pancho had given him, and rides over to see a doctor in the town of Rosa-mond, near where he lives. Every time the goddamned motorcycle hits a pebble in the road, his side hurts like a sonofabitch. The doctor in Rosamond informs him he has two broken ribs and he tapes them up and tells him that if he'll just keep his right arm immobilized for a couple of weeks and avoid any physical exertion or sudden movements, he should be all right.

Yeager gets up before daybreak on Tuesday morning—which is sup-posed to be the day he tries to break the sound barrier—and his ribs still hurt like a sonofabitch. He gets his wife to drive him over to the field, and he has to keep his right arm pinned down to his side to keep his ribs from hurting so much. At dawn, on the day of a flight, you could hear the X-1 screaming long before you got there. The fuel for the X-1 was alcohol and liquid oxygen,

oxygen converted from a gas to a liquid by lowering its temperature to 297 degrees below zero. And when the lox, as it was called, rolled out of the hoses and into the belly of the X-1, it started boiling off and the X-1 started steaming and screaming like a teakettle. There's quite a crowd on hand, by Muroc standards . . . perhaps nine or ten souls. They're still fueling the X-1 with the lox, and the beast is wailing.

The X-1 looked like a fat orange swallow with white markings. But it was really just a length of pipe with four rocket chambers in it. It had a tiny cockpit and a needle nose, two little straight blades (only three and a half inches thick at the thickest part) for wings, and a tail assembly set up high to avoid the "sonic wash" from the wings. Even though his side was throbbing and his right arm felt practically useless, Yeager figured he could grit his teeth and get through the flight—except for one specific move he had to make. In the rocket launches, the X-1, which held only two and a half minutes' worth of fuel, was carried up to twenty-six thousand feet underneath the wings of a B-29. At seven thousand feet, Yeager was to climb down a ladder from the bomb bay of the B-29 to the open doorway of the X-1, hook up to the oxygen system and the radio microphone and earphones, and put his crash helmet on and prepare for the launch, which would come at twenty-five thousand feet. This helmet was a homemade number. There had never been any such thing as a crash helmet before. Throughout the war pilots had used the old skin-tight leather helmet-and-goggles. But the X-1 had a way of throwing the pilot around so violently that there was danger of getting knocked out against the walls of the cockpit. So Yeager had bought a big leather football helmet—there were no plastic ones at the time—and he butchered it with a hunting knife until he carved the right kind of holes in it, so that it would fit down over his regular flying helmet and the earphones and the oxygen rig. Anyway, then his flight engineer, Jack Ridley, would climb down the ladder, out in the breeze, and shove into place the cockpit door, which had to be lowered out of the belly of the B-29 on a chain. Then Yeager had to push a handle to lock the door airtight. Since the X-1's cockpit was minute, you had to push the handle with your right hand. It took quite a shove. There was no way you could move into position to get enough leverage with your left hand.

Out in the hangar Yeager makes a few test shoves on the sly, and the pain is so incredible he realizes that there is no way a man with two broken ribs is going to get the door closed. It is time to confide in somebody, and the logical man is Jack Ridley. Ridley is not only the flight engineer but a pilot himself and a good old boy from Oklahoma to boot. He will understand about Flying & Drinking and Drinking & Driving through the goddamned Joshua trees. So Yeager takes Ridley off to the side in the tin hangar and says: Jack, I got me a little ol' problem here. Over at Pancho's the other night I sorta . . . dinged my goddamned ribs. Ridley says, Whattya mean . . . *dinged?* Yeager says, Well, I guess you might say I damned near like to . . . *broke* a coupla the sonsabitches. Whereupon Yeager sketches out the problem he foresees.

Not for nothing is Ridley the engineer on this project. He has an inspiration. He tells a janitor named Sam to cut him about nine inches off a broom handle. When nobody's looking, he slips the broomstick into the cockpit of the X-1 and gives Yeager a little advice and counsel.

So with that added bit of supersonic flight gear Yeager went aloft.

At seven thousand feet he climbed down the ladder into the X-1's cockpit, clipped on his hoses and lines, and managed to pull the pumpkin football helmet over his head. Then Ridley came down the ladder and lowered the door into place. As Ridley had instructed, Yeager now took the nine inches of broomstick and slipped it between the handle and the door. This gave him just enough mechanical advantage to reach over with his left hand and whang the thing shut. So he whanged the door shut with Ridley's broomstick and was ready to fly.

At 26,000 feet the B-29 went into a shallow dive, then pulled up and released Yeager and the X-1 as if it were a bomb. Like a bomb it dropped and shot forward (at the speed of the mother ship) at the same time. Yeager had been launched straight into the sun. It seemed to be no more than six feet in front of him, filling up the sky and blinding him. But he managed to get his bearings and set off the four rocket chambers one after the other. He then experienced something that became known as the ultimate sensation in flying: "booming and zooming." The surge of the rockets was so tremendous, forced him back into his seat so violently, he could hardly move his hands forward the few inches necessary to reach the controls. The X-1 seemed to shoot straight up in an absolutely perpendicular trajectory, as if determined to snap the hold of gravity via the most direct route possible. In fact, he was only climbing at the 45-degree angle called for in the flight plan. At about .87 Mach the buffeting started.

On the ground the engineers could no longer see Yeager. They could only hear . . . that poker-hollow West Virginia drawl.

"Had a mild buffet there . . . jes the usual instability . . ."

Jes the usual instability?

Then the X-1 reached the speed of .96 Mach, and that incredible caint-hardlyin' aw-shuckin' drawl said:

"Say, Ridley . . . make a note here, will ya?" (*if you ain't got nothin' better to do*) ". . . elevator effectiveness *re*-gained."

Just as Yeager had predicted, as the X-1 approached Mach 1, the stability improved. Yeager had his eyes pinned on the machometer. The needle reached .96, fluctuated, and went off the scale.

And on the ground they heard . . . that voice:

"Say, Ridley . . . make another note, will ya?" (*if you ain't too bored yet*) ". . . there's somethin' wrong with this ol' machometer . . ." (faint chuckle) ". . . it's gone kinda screwy on me . . ."

And in that moment, on the ground, they heard a boom rock over the desert floor—just as the physicist Theodore von Kármán had predicted many years before.

Then they heard Ridley back in the B-29: "If it is, Chuck, we'll fix it. Personally I think you're seeing things."

Then they heard Yeager's poker-hollow drawl again:

"Well, I guess I am, Jack . . . And I'm still goin' upstairs like a bat."

The X-1 had gone through "the sonic wall" without so much as a bump. As the speed topped out at Mach 1.05, Yeager had the sensation of shooting straight through the top of the sky. The sky turned a deep purple and all at once the stars and the moon came out—and the sun shone at the same time. He had reached a layer of the upper atmosphere where the air was too thin to contain reflecting dust particles. He was simply looking out into space. As the X-1 nosed over at the top of the climb, Yeager now had seven minutes of . . . Pilot Heaven . . . ahead of him. He was going faster than any man in history, and it was almost silent up here, since he had exhausted his rocket fuel, and he was so high in such a vast space that there was no sensation of motion. He was master of the sky. His was a king's solitude, unique and inviolate, above the dome of the world. It would take him seven minutes to glide back down and land at Muroc. He spent the time doing victory rolls and wing-over-wing aerobatics while Rogers Lake and the High Sierras spun around below.

On the ground they had understood the code as soon as they heard Yeager's little exchange with Ridley. The project was secret, but the radio exchanges could be picked up by anyone within range. The business of the "screwy machometer" was Yeager's deadpan way of announcing that the X-1's instruments indicated Mach 1. As soon as he landed, they checked out the X-1's automatic recording instruments. Without any doubt the ship had gone supersonic. They immediately called the brass at Wright Field to break the tremendous news. Within two hours Wright Field called back and gave some firm orders. A top security lid was being put on the morning's events. That the press was not to be informed went without saying. But neither was anyone else, anyone at all, to be told. Word of the flight was not to go beyond the flight line. And even among the people directly involved—who were there and knew about it, anyway—there was to be no celebrating. Just what was on the minds of the brass at Wright is hard to say. Much of it, no doubt, was a simple holdover from wartime, when every breakthrough of possible strategic importance was kept under wraps. That was what you did—you shut up about them. Another possibility was that the chiefs at Wright had never quite known what to make of Muroc. There was some sort of weird ribald aerial tarpaper mad-monk squadron up on the roof of the desert out there . . .

In any case, by mid-afternoon Yeager's tremendous feat had become a piece of thunder with no reverberation. A strange and implausible stillness settled over the event. Well . . . there was not supposed to be any celebration, but come nightfall . . . Yeager and Ridley and some of the others ambled over to Pancho's. After all, it was the end of the day, and they were pilots. So they knocked back a few. And they had to let Pancho in on the secret, because Pancho had said she'd serve a free steak dinner to any pilot who could fly supersonic and walk in here to tell about it, and they had to see the look on *her* face. So Pancho served Yeager a big steak dinner and said they were a buncha miserable peckerwoods all the same, and the desert cooled off and the wind came up and the screen doors banged and they drank some more and bawled some songs over the cackling dry piano and the stars and the moon came out and Pancho screamed oaths no one had ever heard before and Yeager and Ridley roared and the old weather-beaten bar boomed and the autographed pictures of a hundred dead pilots shook and clattered on the frame wires and the faces of the living fell apart in the reflections, and by and by they all left and stumbled and staggered and yelped and bayed for glory before the arthritic silhouettes of the Joshua trees. Shit!—there was no one to tell except for Pancho and the goddamned Joshua trees!

Over the next five months Yeager flew supersonic in the X-1 more than a dozen times, but still the Air Force insisted on keeping the story secret. *Aviation Week* published a report of the flights late in December (without mentioning Yeager's name) provoking a minor debate in the press over whether or not *Aviation Week* had violated national security—and *still* the Air Force refused to publicize the achievement until June of 1948. Only then was Yeager's name released. He received only a fraction of the publicity that would have been his had he been presented to the world immediately, on October 14,

1947, as the man who "broke the sound barrier." This dragged-out process had curious effects.

In 1952 a British movie called *Breaking the Sound Barrier,* starring Ralph Richardson, was released in the United States, and its promoters got the bright idea of inviting the man who had actually done it, Major Charles E. Yeager of the U.S. Air Force, to the American premiere. So the Air Force goes along with it and Yeager turns up for the festivities. When he watches the movie, he's stunned. He can't believe what he's seeing. Far from being based on the exploits of Charles E. Yeager, *Breaking the Sound Barrier* was inspired by the death of Geoffrey de Havilland in his father's DH 108. At the end of the movie a British pilot solves the mystery of "the barrier" by *reversing the controls* at the critical moment during a power dive. The buffeting is tearing his ship to pieces, and every rational process in his head is telling him to *pull back* on the stick to keep from crashing—and he *pushes it down* instead . . . and zips right through Mach 1 as smooth as a bird, regaining full control!

Breaking the Sound Barrier happened to be one of the most engrossing movies about flying ever made. It seemed superbly realistic, and people came away from it sure of two things: it was an Englishman who had broken the sound barrier, and he had done it by reversing the controls in the transonic zone.

Well, after the showing they bring out Yeager to meet the press, and he doesn't know where in the hell to start. To him the whole goddamned picture is outrageous. He doesn't want to get mad, because this thing has been set up by Air Force P.R. But he is not happy. In as calm a way as he can word it on the spur of the moment, he informs one and all that the picture is an utter shuck from start to finish. The promoters respond, a bit huffily, that this picture is not, after all, a documentary. Yeager figures, well, anyway, that settles that. But as the weeks go by, he discovers an incredible thing happening. He keeps running into people who think he's the first *American* to break the sound barrier . . . and that he learned how to *reverse the controls* and zip through from the Englishman who did it first. The last straw comes when he gets a call from the Secretary of the Air Force.

"Chuck," he says, "do you mind if I ask you something? Is it true that you broke the sound barrier by reversing the controls?"

Yeager is stunned by this. The Secretary—*the Secretary!*—of the U.S. Air Force!

"No, sir," he says, "that is . . . not correct. Anyone who reversed the controls going transonic would be dead."

Yeager and the rocket pilots who soon joined him at Muroc had a hard time dealing with publicity. On the one hand, they hated the process. It meant talking to reporters and other fruit flies who always hovered, eager for the juice . . . and invariably got the facts screwed up . . . *But that wasn't really the problem, was it!* The real problem was that reporters violated the invisible walls of the fraternity. They blurted out questions and spoke boorish words about . . . all the unspoken things!—about fear and bravery (they would say the words!) and how you *felt* at such-and-such a moment! It was obscene! They presumed a knowledge and an intimacy they did not have and had no right to. Some aviation writer would sidle up and say, "I hear Jenkins augered in. That's too bad." *Augered in!*—a phrase that belonged exclusively to the fraternity!—coming from the lips of this *ant* who was *left behind* the moment Jenkins made his first step up the pyramid long, long ago. It was repulsive! But on the other hand . . . one's healthy pilot ego loved the glory—wallowed in it!—lapped it up!—no doubt about it! The Pilot Ego—ego didn't come any bigger! The boys wouldn't have minded the following. They wouldn't have minded appearing once a year on a balcony over a huge square in which half the world is assembled. They wave. The world roars its approval, its applause, and breaks into a sustained thirty-minute storm of cheers and tears (moved by my righteous stuff!). And then it's over. All that remains is for the wife to paste the clippings in the scrapbook.

A little adulation on the order of the Pope's; that's all the True Brothers at the top of the pyramid really wanted.

The Sentinel

From *Expedition to Earth*

BY ARTHUR C. CLARKE

When the subject of exploration adventure comes up, conquering the blank spaces on the map, one tale that certainly qualifies as a must-read is Arthur C. Clarke's short story "The Sentinel," first published in the *Avon Science Fiction and Fantasy Reader* way back in 1951. As throughout his distinguished writing career, the "blank spaces" on Arthur Clarke's map are not deserts and jungles and mountains ranges—none of this earth's anyway. His subject is the Cosmos, the moon and beyond.

"The Sentinel" has quite a distinguished history. It was the major source for the idea behind the late Stanley Kubrick's classic film *2001: A Space Odyssey.* Clarke collaborated with Kubrick on the screenplay.

To me this is the ultimate "We Are Not Alone"-type story and, like many of Clarke's tales, transcends the genre of science fiction.

★ ★ ★ ★ ★

The next time you see the full moon high in the south, look carefully at its right-hand edge and let your eye travel upward along the curve of the disk. Round about two o'clock you will notice a small, dark oval: anyone with normal eyesight can find it quite easily. It is the great walled plain, one of the finest on the Moon, known as the Mare Crisium—the Sea of Crises. Three hundred miles in diameter, and almost completely surrounded by a ring of magnificent mountains, it had never been explored until we entered it in the late summer of 1996.

Our expedition was a large one. We had two heavy freighters which had flown our supplies and equipment from the main lunar base in the Mare Serenitatis, five hundred miles away. There were also three small rockets which were intended for short-range transport over regions which our surface vehicles couldn't cross. Luckily, most of the Mare Crisium is very flat. There are none of the great crevasses so common and so dangerous elsewhere, and very few craters or mountains of any size. As far as we could tell, our powerful caterpillar tractors would have no difficulty in taking us wherever we wished to go.

I was geologist—or selenologist, if you want to be pedantic—in charge of the group exploring the southern region of the Mare. We had crossed a hundred miles of it in a week, skirting the foothills of the mountains along the shore of what was once the ancient sea, some thousand million years before. When life was beginning on Earth, it was already dying here. The waters were retreating down the flanks of those stupendous cliffs, retreating into the empty heart of the Moon. Over the land which we were crossing, the tideless ocean had once been half a mile deep, and now the only trace of moisture was the hoarfrost one could sometimes find in caves which the searing sunlight never penetrated.

We had begun our journey early in the slow lunar dawn, and still had almost a week of Earth-time before nightfall. Half a dozen times a day we would leave our vehicle and go outside in the space-suits to hunt for interesting minerals, or to place markers for the guidance of future travelers. It was an uneventful routine. There is nothing hazardous or even particularly exciting about lunar exploration. We could live comfortably for a month in our pressurized tractors, and if we ran into trouble we could always radio for help and sit tight until one of the spaceships came to our rescue.

I said just now that there was nothing exciting about lunar exploration, but of course that isn't true. One could never grow tired of those incredible mountains, so much more rugged than the gentle hills of Earth. We never knew, as we rounded the capes and promontories of that vanished sea, what new splendors would be revealed to us. The whole southern curve of the Mare Crisium is a vast delta where a score of rivers once found their way into the ocean, fed perhaps by the torrential rains that must have lashed the mountains in the brief volcanic age when the Moon was young. Each of these ancient valleys was an invitation, challenging us to climb into the unknown uplands beyond. But we had a hundred miles still to cover, and could only look longingly at the heights which others must scale.

We kept Earth-time aboard the tractor, and precisely at 22.00 hours the final radio message would be sent out to Base and we would close down for the day. Outside, the rocks would still be burning beneath the almost vertical sun, but to us it was night until we awoke again eight hours later. Then one of us would prepare breakfast, there would be a great buzzing of electric razors, and someone would switch on the short-wave radio from Earth. Indeed, when the smell of frying sausages began to fill the cabin, it was sometimes hard to believe that we were not back on our own world—everything was so normal and homely, apart from the feeling of decreased weight and the unnatural slowness with which objects fell.

It was my turn to prepare breakfast in the corner of the main cabin that served as a galley. I can remember that moment quite vividly after all these years, for the radio had just played one of my favorite melodies, the old Welsh air, "David of the White Rock." Our driver was already outside in his spacesuit, inspecting our caterpillar treads. My assistant, Louis Garnett, was up forward in the control position, making some belated entries in yesterday's log.

As I stood by the frying pan waiting, like any terrestrial housewife, for the sausages to brown, I let my gaze wander idly over the mountain walls which covered the whole of the southern horizon, marching out of sight to east and west below the curve of the Moon. They seemed only a mile or two from the tractor, but I knew that the nearest was twenty miles away. On the Moon, of course, there is no loss of detail with distance—none of that almost imperceptible haziness which softens and sometimes transfigures all far-off things on Earth.

Those mountains were ten thousand feet high, and they climbed steeply out of the plain as if ages ago some subterranean eruption had smashed them skyward through the molten crust. The base of even the nearest was hidden from sight by the steeply curving surface of the plain, for the Moon is a very little world, and from where I was standing the horizon was only two miles away.

I lifted my eyes toward the peaks which no man had ever climbed, the peaks which, before the coming of terrestrial life, had watched the retreating oceans sink sullenly into their graves, taking with them the hope and the morning promise of a world. The sunlight was beating against those ramparts with a glare that hurt the eyes, yet only a little way above them the stars were shining steadily in a sky blacker than a winter midnight on Earth.

I was turning away when my eye caught a metallic glitter high on the ridge of a great promontory thrusting out into the sea thirty miles to the west. It was a dimensionless point of light, as if a star had been clawed from the sky by one of those cruel peaks, and I imagined that some smooth rock surface was catching the sunlight and heliographing it straight into my eyes. Such things were not uncommon. When the Moon is in her second quarter, observers on Earth can sometimes see the great ranges in the Oceanus Procellarum burning with a blue-white iridescence as the sunlight flashes from their slopes and leaps again from world to world. But I was curious to know what kind of rock could be shining so brightly up there, and I climbed into the observation turret and swung our four-inch telescope round to the west.

I could see just enough to tantalize me. Clear and sharp in the field of vision, the mountain peaks seemed only half a mile away, but whatever was catching the sunlight was still too small to be resolved. Yet it seemed to have an elusive symmetry, and the summit upon which it rested was curiously flat. I stared for a long time at that glittering enigma, straining my eyes into space, until presently a smell of burning from the galley told me that our breakfast sausage had made their quarter-million mile journey in vain.

All that morning we argued our way across the Mare Crisium while the western mountains reared higher in the sky. Even when we were out prospecting in the space-suits, the discussion would continue over the radio. It was absolutely certain, my companions argued, that there had never been any form of intelligent life on the Moon. The only living things that had ever existed there were a few primitive plants and their slightly less degenerate ancestors. I knew that as well as anyone, but there are times when a scientist must not be afraid to make a fool of himself.

"Listen," I said at last, "I'm going up there, if only for my own peace of mind. That mountain's less than twelve thousand feet high—that's only two thousand under Earth gravity—and I can make the trip in twenty hours at the outside. I've always wanted to go up into those hills, anyway, and this gives me an excellent excuse."

"If you don't break your neck," said Garnett, "you'll be the laughing-stock of the expedition when we get back to Base. That mountain will probably be called Wilson's Folly from now on."

"I won't break my neck," I said firmly. "Who was the first man to climb Pico and Helicon?"

"But weren't you rather younger in those days?" asked Louis gently.

"That," I said with great dignity, "is as good a reason as any for going."

We went to bed early that night, after driving the tractor to within half a mile of the promontory. Garnett was coming with me in the morning; he was a good climber, and had often been with me on such exploits before. Our driver was only too glad to be left in charge of the machine.

At first sight, those cliffs seemed completely unscalable, but to anyone with a good head for heights, climbing is easy on a world where all weights are only a sixth of their normal value. The real danger in lunar mountaineering lies in overconfidence; a six-hundred-foot drop on the Moon can kill you just as thoroughly as a hundred-foot fall on Earth.

We made our first halt on a wide ledge about four thousand feet above the plain. Climbing had not been very difficult, but my limbs were stiff with the unaccustomed effort, and I was glad of the rest. We could still see the trac-tor as a tiny metal insect far down at the foot of the cliff, and we reported our progress to the driver before starting on the next ascent.

Inside our suits it was comfortably cold, for the refrigeration units were fighting the fierce sun and carrying away the body-heat of our exertions. We seldom spoke to each other, except to pass climbing instructions and to discuss our best plan of ascent. I do not know what Garnett was thinking, probably that this was the craziest goose-chase he had ever embarked upon. I more than half agreed with him, but the joy of climbing, the knowledge that no man had ever gone this way before and exhilaration of the steadily widen-ing landscape gave me all the reward I needed.

I don't think I was particularly excited when I saw in front of us the wall of rock I had first inspected through the telescope from thirty miles away. It would level off about fifty feet above our heads, and there on the plateau would be the thing that had lured me over these barren wastes. It was, almost certainly, nothing more than a boulder splintered ages ago by a falling meteor, and with its cleavage planes still fresh and bright in this incorruptible, un-changing silence.

There were no hand-holds on the rock face, and we had to use a grapnel. My tired arms seemed to gain new strength as I swung the three-pronged metal anchor round my head and sent it sailing up toward the stars. The first time it broke loose and came falling slowly back when we pulled the rope. On the third attempt, the prongs gripped firmly and our combined weights could not shift it.

Garnett looked at me anxiously. I could tell that he wanted to go first, but I smiled back at him through the glass of my helmet and shook my head. Slowly, taking my time, I began the final ascent.

Even with my space-suit, I weighed only forty pounds here, so I pulled myself up hand over hand without bothering to use my feet. At the rim I paused and waved to my companion, then I scrambled over the edge and stood upright, staring ahead of me.

You must understand that until this very moment I had been almost completely convinced that there could be nothing strange or unusual for me to find here. Almost, but not quite; it was that haunting doubt that had driven me forward. Well, it was a doubt no longer, but the haunting had scarcely begun.

I was standing on a plateau perhaps a hundred feet across. It had once been smooth—too smooth to be natural—but falling meteors had pitted and scored its surface through immeasurable eons. It had been leveled to support a glittering, roughly pyramidal structure, twice as high as a man, that was set in the rock like a gigantic, many-faceted jewel.

Probably no emotion at all filled my mind in those first few seconds. Then I felt a great lifting of my heart, and a strange, inexpressible joy. For I loved the Moon, and now I knew that the creeping moss of Aristarchus and Eratosthenes was not the only life she had brought forth in her youth. The old, discredited dream of the first explorers was true. There had, after all, been a lunar civilization—and I was the first to find it. That I had come perhaps a hundred million years too late did not distress me; it was enough to have come at all.

My mind was beginning to function normally, to analyze and to ask questions. Was this a building, a shrine—or something for which my language had no name? If a building, then why was it erected in so uniquely inaccessible a spot? I wondered if it might be a temple, and I could picture the adepts of some strange priesthood calling on their gods to preserve them as the life of the Moon ebbed with the dying oceans, and calling on their gods in vain.

I took a dozen steps forward to examine the thing more closely, but some sense of caution kept me from going too near. I knew a little of archaeology, and tried to guess the cultural level of the civilization that must have smoothed this mountain and raised the glittering mirror surfaces that still dazzled my eyes.

The Egyptians could have done it, I thought, if their workmen had possessed whatever strange materials these far more ancient architects had used. Because of the thing's smallness, it did not occur to me that I might be looking at the handiwork of a race more advanced than my own. The idea that the Moon had possessed intelligence at all was still almost too tremendous to grasp, and my pride would not let me take the final, humiliating plunge.

And then I noticed something that set the scalp crawling at the back of my neck—something so trivial and so innocent that many would never have noticed it at all. I have said that the plateau was scarred by meteors; it was also coated inches-deep with the cosmic dust that is always filtering down upon the surface of any world where there are no winds to disturb it. Yet the dust and the meteor scratches ended quite abruptly in a wide circle enclosing the little pyramid, as though an invisible wall was protecting it from the ravages of time and that slow but ceaseless bombardment from space.

There was someone shouting in my earphones, and I realized that Garnett had been calling me for some time. I walked unsteadily to the edge of the cliff and signaled him to join me, not trusting myself to speak. Then I went back toward that circle in the dust. I picked up a fragment of splintered rock and tossed it gently toward the shining enigma. If the pebble had vanished at that invisible barrier I should not have been surprised, but it seemed to hit a smooth, hemispherical surface and slide gently to the ground.

I knew then that I was looking at nothing that could be matched in the antiquity of my own race. This was not a building, but a machine, protecting itself with forces that had challenged Eternity. Those forces, whatever they might be, were still operating, and perhaps I had already come too close. I thought of all the radiations man had trapped and tamed in the past century. For all I knew, I might be as irrevocably doomed as if I had stepped into the deadly, silent aura of an unshielded atomic pile.

I remember turning then toward Garnett, who had joined me and was now standing motionless at my side. He seemed quite oblivious to me, so I did not disturb him but walked to the edge of the cliff in an effort to marshal my thoughts. There below me lay the Mare Crisium—Sea of Crises, indeed—strange and weird to most men, but reassuringly familiar to me. I lifted my eyes toward the crescent Earth, lying in her cradle of stars, and I wondered what her clouds had covered when these unknown builders had finished their work. Was it the steaming jungle of the Carboniferous, the bleak shoreline over which the first amphibians must crawl to conquer the land—or, earlier still, the long loneliness before the coming of life?

Do not ask me why I did not guess the truth sooner—the truth that seems so obvious now. In the first excitement of my discovery, I had assumed without question that this crystalline apparition had been built by some race belonging to the Moon's remote past, but suddenly, and with overwhelming force, the belief came to me that it was as alien to the Moon as I myself.

In twenty years we had found no trace of life but a few degenerate plants. No lunar civilization, whatever its doom, could have left but a single token of its existence.

I looked at the shining pyramid again, and the more remote it seemed from anything that had to do with the Moon. And suddenly I felt myself shaking with a foolish, hysterical laughter, brought on by excitement and overexertion: for I had imagined that the little pyramid was speaking to me and was saying: "Sorry, I'm a stranger here myself."

It has taken us twenty years to crack that invisible shield and to reach the machine inside those crystal walls. What we could not understand, we broke at last with the savage might of atomic power and now I have seen the fragments of the lovely, glittering thing I found up there on the mountain.

They are meaningless. The mechanisms—if indeed they are mechanisms—of the pyramid belong to a technology that lies far beyond our horizon, perhaps to the technology of paraphysical forces.

The mystery haunts us all the more now that the other planets have been reached and we know that only Earth has ever been the home of intelligent life in our Universe. Nor could any lost civilization of our own world have built that machine, for the thickness of the meteoric dust on the plateau has enabled us to measure its age. It was set there upon its mountain before life had emerged from the seas of Earth.

When our world was half its present age, *something* from the stars swept through the Solar System, left this token of its passage, and went again upon its way. Until we destroyed it, that machine was still fulfilling the purpose of its builders; and as to that purpose, here is my guess.

Nearly a hundred thousand million stars are turning in the circle of the Milky Way, and long ago other races on the worlds of other suns must have scaled and passed the heights that we have reached. Think of such civilizations, far back in time against the fading afterglow of Creation, masters of a universe so young that life as yet had come only to a handful of worlds. Theirs would have been a loneliness we cannot imagine, the loneliness of gods looking out across infinity and finding none to share their thoughts.

They must have searched the star-clusters as we have searched the planets. Everywhere there would be worlds, but they would be empty or peopled with crawling, mindless things. Such was our own Earth, the smoke of the great volcanoes still staining the skies, when that first ship of the peoples of the dawn came sliding in from the abyss beyond Pluto. It passed the frozen outer worlds, knowing that life could play no part in their destinies. It came to rest among the inner planets, warming themselves around the fire of the Sun and waiting for their stories to begin.

Those wanderers must have looked on Earth, circling safely in the narrow zone between fire and ice, and must have guessed that it was the favorite of the Sun's children. Here, in the distant future, would be intelligence; but there were countless stars before them still, and they might never come this way again.

So they left a sentinel, one of millions they have scattered throughout the Universe, watching over all worlds with the promise of life. It was a beacon that down the ages has been patiently signaling the fact that no one had discovered it.

Perhaps you understand now why that crystal pyramid was set upon the Moon instead of on the Earth. Its builders were not concerned with races still struggling up from savagery. They would be interested in our civilization only if we proved our fitness to survive—by crossing space and so escaping from the Earth, our cradle. That is the challenge that all intelligent races must meet, sooner or later. It is a double challenge, for it depends in turn upon the conquest of atomic energy and the last choice between life and death.

Once we had passed that crisis, it was only a matter of time before we found the pyramid and forced it open. Now its signals have ceased, and those whose duty it is will be turning their minds upon Earth. Perhaps they wish to help our infant civilization. But they must be very, very old, and the old are often insanely jealous of the young.

I can never look now at the Milky Way without wondering from which of those banked clouds of stars the emissaries are coming. If you will pardon so commonplace a simile, we have set off the fire-alarm and have nothing to do but to wait.

I do not think we will have to wait for long.

The Worst Journey in the World

From *The Worst Journey in the World*

BY APSLEY CHERRY-GARRARD

Apsley Cherry-Garrard was a member of the Antarctic search party that in November, 1912 discovered the bodies of Robert Falcon Scott and his companions in the remnants of the snow-covered tent where they had perished of exhaustion and starvation. Englishman Scott and his men had failed in their attempt to be the first to reach the South Pole (Norwegian explorer Roald Admundsen had beaten them), then met their doom undertaking the 800-mile trek back to the expedition's permanent base in the McMurdo Sound area.

Even though it was undertaken in what was summer in the Antarctic, Scott's journey was a terrible ordeal of pushing along on skis while manhauling their sledges of supplies. Eventually, the survivors of the trek huddled in their tent, unable to go a step further in the terrible storms that had hounded them since their retreat from the Pole began. Ironically, a depot cache of fuel and food was only a few miles away.

Apsley Cherry-Garrard, a young volunteer for the Scott expedition that had begun in 1910, was not with the final Scott party but made a separate Antarctic trek with three men that rivals the Scott experience for hardships endured, but ended without the loss of life. Cherry-Garrard's *The Worst Journey in the World* is an account not only of his own experience, but of Scott's experiences as well. Using Scott's journals found in the tent with the bodies, Cherry-Garrard describes what happened to Scott and his companions on their terrible retreat from the Pole. The text of this excerpt from the book picks up the action on January 19, after Scott, Wilson, Bowers, and Oates had made the overwhelmingly bitter discovery that the Norwegians had beaten them to the Pole. Now, defeated, they have begun their second battle: To return to the safety of the expedition base camp 800 miles away.

No matter whether you're reading about Cherry-Garrard's personal ordeal, or his account of what Scott and his men endured, *The Worst Journey in the World* ranks as a classic in survival literature.

★   ★   ★   ★   ★

All the joy had gone from their sledging. They were hungry, they were cold, the pulling was heavy, and two of them were not fit. As long ago as 14 January Scott wrote that Oates was feeling the cold and fatigue more than the others[23] and again he refers to the matter on 20 January.[24] On 19 January Wilson wrote: 'We get our hairy faces and mouths dreadfully iced up on the march, and often one's hands very cold indeed holding ski-sticks. Evans, who cut his knuckle some days ago at the last depot, has a lot of pus in it tonight.' January 20: 'Evans has got 4 or 5 of his finger-tips badly blistered by the cold. Titus also his nose and cheeks - al[so] Evans and Bowers.' January 28: 'Evans has a number of badly blistered finger-ends which he got at the Pole. Titus' big toe is turning blue-black.' January 31: 'Evans' finger-nails all coming off, very raw and sore.' February 4: 'Evans is feeling the cold a lot, always getting frost-bitten. Titus' toes are blackening, and his nose and cheeks are dead yellow. Dressing Evans' fingers every other day with boric vaseline: they are quite sweet still.' February 5: 'Evans' fingers suppurating. Nose very bad [hard] and rotten-looking.'[25]

Scott was getting alarmed about Evans, who 'has dislodged two finger-nails tonight; his hands are really bad, and, to my surprise, he shows signs of losing heart over it. He hasn't been cheerful since the accident.'[26] 'The party is not improving in condition, especially Evans, who is becoming rather dull and incapable.' 'Evans' nose is almost as bad as his fingers. He is a good deal crocked up.'[27]

Bowers's diary, quoted above, finished on 25 January, on which day they picked up their One and a Half Degree Depot. 'I shall sleep much better with our provision bag full again,' wrote Scott that night. 'Bowers got another rating sight tonight—it was wonderful how he managed to observe in such a

---

23. *Scott's Last Expedition,* vol. i, p. 541.
24. ibid., p. 549.
25. Wilson.
26. *Scott's Last Expedition,* vol. i, p. 557.
27. ibid., pp. 560, 561.

horribly cold wind.' They marched 16 miles the next day, but got off the out-ward track, which was crooked. On 27 January they did 14 miles on a 'very bad surface of deep-cut sastrugi all day, until late in the afternoon when we began to get out of them.'[28] 'By Jove, this is tremendous labour,' said Scott.

They were getting into the better surfaces again: 15.7 miles for 28 January, 'a fine day and a good march on very decent surface.'[29] On 29 January Bowers wrote his last full day's diary:

> Our record march today. With a good breeze and improving surface we were soon in among the double tracks where the supporting party left us. Then we picked up the memorable camp where I transferred to the advance party. How glad I was to change over. The camp was much drifted up and immense sastrugi were everywhere, S.S.E. in direction and S.E. We did 10.4 miles before lunch. I was breaking back on sledge and controlling; it was beastly cold and my hands were perished. In the afternoon I put on my dogskin mitts and was far more comfortable. A stiff breeze with drift continues: temperature −25°. Thank God our days of having to face it are over. We completed 19.5 miles [22 statute] this evening, and so are only 29 miles from our precious [Three Degree] Depot. It will be bad luck indeed if we do not get there in a march and a half anyhow.[30]

Nineteen miles again on 30 January, but during the previous day's march Wilson had strained a tendon in his leg. 'I got a nasty bruise on the Tib[ialis] ant[icus] which gave me great pain all the afternoon.' 'My left leg exceedingly painful all day, so I gave Birdie my ski and hobbled alongside the sledge on foot. The whole of the Tibialis anticus is swollen and tight, and full of teno synovitis, and the skin red and oedematous over the skin. But we made a very fine march with the help of a brisk breeze.' January 31:

> Again walking by the sledge with swollen leg but not nearly so painful. We had 5.8 miles to go to reach our Three Degree Depot. Picked this up with a week's provision and a line from Evans, and then for lunch an extra biscuit each, making 4 for lunch and 1/10 whack of butter extra as well. Afternoon we passed cairn where Birdie's ski had been left. These we picked up and came on till 7:30 p.m. when the wind which had been very light all day dropped, and with temp. −20° it felt delightfully warm and sunny and clear. We have

---

28. Wilson.
29. ibid.
30. Bowers.

$\frac{1}{10}$ extra pemmican in the hoosh now also. My leg pretty swollen again tonight.[31]

They travelled 13.5 miles that day, and 15.7 on the next. 'My leg much more comfortable, gave me no pain, and I was able to pull all day, holding on to the sledge. Still some oedema. We came down a hundred feet or so today on a fairly steep gradient.'[32]

They were now approaching the crevassed surfaces and the ice-falls which mark the entrance to the Beardmore Glacier, and 2 February was marked by another accident, this time to Scott.

On a very slippery surface I came an awful 'purler' on my shoulder. It is hor-ribly sore tonight and another sick person added to our tent—three out of five injured, and the most troublesome surfaces to come. We shall be lucky if we get through without serious injury. Wilson's leg is better, but might easily get bad again, and Evans' fingers. . . . We have managed to get off 17 miles. The extra food is certainly helping us, but we are getting pretty hungry. The weather is already a trifle warmer, the altitude lower and only 80 miles or so to Mount Darwin. It is time we were off the summit—Pray God another four days will see us pretty well clear of it. Our bags are getting very wet and we ought to have more sleep.[33]

They had been spending some time in finding the old tracks. But they had a good landfall for the depot at the top of the glacier and on 3 February they decided to push on due north, and to worry no more for the present about tracks and cairns. They did 16 miles that day. Wilson's diary runs:

Sunny and breezy again. Came down a series of slopes, and finished the day going up one. Enormous deep-cut sastrugi and drifts and shiny egg-shell sur-face. Wind all S.E.E.ly. Today at about 11 p.m. we got our first sight again of mountain peaks on our eastern horizon . . . . We crossed the outmost line of crevassed ridge top today, the first on our return.

February 4. 18 miles. Clear cloudless blue sky, surface drift. During forenoon we came down gradual descent including 2 or 3 irregular terrace slopes, on crest of one of which were a good many crevasses. Southernmost were just big enough for Scott and Evans to fall in to their waists, and very deceptively covered up. They ran east and west. Those nearer the crest were

---

31. Wilson.
32. ibid.
33. *Scott's Last Expedition,* vol. i, p. 559.

the ordinary broad street-like crevasses, well lidded. In the afternoon we again came to a crest, before descending, with street crevasses, and one we crossed had a huge hole where the lid had fallen in, big enough for a horse and cart to go down. We have a great number of mountain tops on our right and south of our beam as we go due north now. We are now camped just below a great crevassed mound, on a mountain top evidently.

February 5. 18.2 miles. We had a difficult day, getting in amongst a frightful chaos of broad chasm-like crevasses. We kept too far east and had to wind in and out amongst them and cross a multitude of bridges. We then bore west a bit and got on better all the afternoon and got round a good deal of the upper disturbances of the falls here.

[Scott wrote: 'We are camped in a very disturbed region, but the wind has fallen very light here, and our camp is comfortable for the first time for many weeks.'34]

February 6. 15 miles. We again had a forenoon of trying to cut corners. Got in amongst great chasms running E. and W. and had to come out again. We then again kept west and downhill over tremendous sastrugi, with a slight breeze, very cold. In afternoon, continued bearing more and more towards Mount Darwin: we got round one of the main lines of ice-fall and looked back up to it. . . . Very cold march: many crevasses: I walking by the sledge on foot found a good many: the others all on ski.

February 7. 15.5 miles. Clear day again and we made a tedious march in the forenoon along a flat or two, and down a long slope: and then in the afternoon we had a very fresh breeze, and very fast run down long slopes covered with big sastrugi. It was a strenuous job steering and checking behind by the sledge. We reached the Upper Glacier Depot by 7.30 p.m. and found everything right.35

This was the end of the plateau: the beginning of the glacier. Their hard time should be over so far as the weather was concerned. Wilson notes how fine the land looked as they approached it: 'The colour of the Dominion Range rock is in the main all brown madder or dark reddish chocolate, but there are numerous bands of yellow rock scattered amongst it. I think it is composed of dolerite and sandstone as on the W. side.'36

The condition of the party was of course giving anxiety: how much it is impossible to say. A good deal was to be hoped from the warm weather ahead. Scott and Bowers were probably the fittest men. Scott's shoulder soon

---

34. ibid., p. 561.
35. Wilson.
36. ibid.

mended and 'Bowers is splendid, full of energy and bustle all the time'[37] Wilson was feeling the cold more than either of them now. His leg was not yet well enough to wear ski. Oates had suffered from a cold foot for some time. Evans, however, was the only man whom Scott seems to have been worried about. 'His cuts and wounds suppurate, his nose looks very bad, and altogether he shows considerable signs of being played out.' . . . 'Well, we have come through our seven weeks' ice-cap journey and most of us are fit, but I think another week might have had a very bad effect on P.O. Evans, who is going steadily down-hill.'[38] They had all been having extra food which had helped them much, though they complained of hunger and want of sleep. Directly they got into the warmer weather on the glacier their food satisfied them, 'but we must march to keep on the full ration, and we want rest, yet we shall pull through all right, D.V. We are by no means worn out.'[39]

There are no germs in the Antarctic, save for a few isolated specimens which almost certainly come down from civilization in the upper air currents. You can sleep all night in a wet bag and clothing, and sledge all day in a mail of ice, and you will not catch a cold nor get any aches. You can get deficiency diseases, like scurvy, for inland this is a deficiency country, without vitamins. You can also get poisoned if you allow your food to remain thawed out too long, and if you do not cover the provisions in a depot with enough snow the sun will get at them, even though the air temperature is far below freezing. But it is not easy to become diseased.

On the other hand, once something does go wrong it is the deuce and all to get it right: especially cuts. And the isolation of the polar traveller may place him in most difficult circumstances. There are no ambulances and hospitals, and a man on a sledge is a very serious weight. Practically any man who undertakes big polar journeys must face the possibility of having to commit suicide to save his companions, and the difficulty of this must not be over-rated, for it is in some ways more desirable to die than to live, if things are bad enough: we got to that stage on the Winter Journey. I remember discussing this question with Bowers, who had a scheme of doing himself in with a pick-axe if necessity arose, though how he could have accomplished it I don't know: or, as he said, there might be a crevasse and at any rate there was the medical case. I was horrified at the time: I had never faced the thing out with myself like that.

37. *Scott's Last Expedition,* vol. i, p. 561.
38. ibid., pp. 562, 563.
39. ibid., p. 566.

They left the Upper Glacier Depot under Mount Darwin on 8 February. This day they collected the most important of those geological specimens to which, at Wilson's special request, they clung to the end, and which were mostly collected by him. Mount Darwin and Buckley Island, which are really the tops of high mountains, stick out of the ice at the top of the glacier, and the course ran near to both of them, but not actually up against them. Shackleton found coal on Buckley Island, and it was clear that the place was of great geological importance, for it was one of the only places in the Antarctic where fossils could be found, so far as we knew. The ice-falls stretched away as far as you could see towards the mountains which bound the glacier on either side, and as you looked upwards towards Buckley Island they were like a long breaking wave. One of the great difficulties about the Beardmore was that you saw the ice-falls as you went up, and avoided them, but coming down you knew nothing of their whereabouts until you fell into the middle of pressure and crevasses, and then it was almost impossible to say whether you should go right or left to get out.

Evans was unable to pull this day, and was detached from the sledge, but this was not necessarily a very serious sign: Shackleton on his return journey was not able to pull at this place. Wilson wrote as follows:

February 8, Mt. Buckley Cliffs. A very busy day. We had a very cold forenoon march, blowing like blazes from the S. Birdie detached and went on ski to Mt. Darwin and collected some dolerite, the only rock he could see on the Nunatak, which was the nearest. We got into a sort of crusted surface where the snow broke through nearly to our knees and the sledge-runner also. I thought at first we were all on a thinly bridged crevasse. We then came on east a bit, and gradually got worse and worse going over an ice-fall, having great trouble to prevent sledge taking charge, but eventually got down and then made N.W. or N. into the land, and camped right by the moraine under the great sandstone cliffs of Mt. Buckley, out of the wind and quite warm again: it was a wonderful change. After lunch we all geologized on till supper, and I was very late turning in, examining the moraine after supper. Socks, all strewn over the rocks, dried splendidly. Magnificent Beacon sandstone cliffs. Masses of limestone in the moraine, and dolerite crags in various places. Coal seams at all heights in the sandstone cliffs, and lumps of weathered coal with fossil vegetable. Had a regular field-day and got some splendid things in the short time.

February 9, Moraine visit. We made our way along down the moraine, and at the end of Mt. Buckley [I] unhitched and had half an hour over the rocks and again got some good things written up in sketch-book. We then left the moraine and made a very good march on rough blue ice all day with very small and scarce scraps of névé, on one of which we camped for the night with a rather overcast foggy sky, which cleared to bright sun in the night. We are all thoroughly enjoying temps. of +10° or thereabouts now, with no wind instead of the summit winds which are incessant with temp. −20°.

February 10. ?16m. We made a very good forenoon march from 10 to 2.45 towards the Cloudmaker. Weather overcast gradually obscured everything in snowfall fog, starting with crystals of large size. . . . We had to camp after 2½ hours' afternoon march as it got too thick to see anything and we were going downhill on blue ice. . .[40]

The next day in bad lights and on a bad surface they fell into the same pressure which both the other returning parties experienced. Like them they were in the middle of it before they realized.

Then came the fatal decision to steer east. We went on for 6 hours, hoping to do a good distance, which I suppose we did, but for the last hour or two we pressed on into a regular trap. Getting on to a good surface we did not reduce our lunch meal, and thought all going well, but half an hour after lunch we got into worst ice mess I have ever been in. For three hours we plunged on on ski, first thinking we were too much to the right, then too much to the left; meanwhile the disturbance got worse and my spirits received a very rude shock. There were times when it seemed almost impossible to find a way out of the awful turmoil in which we found ourselves.

. . . The turmoil changed in character, irregular crevassed surface giving way to huge chasms, closely packed and most difficult to cross. It was very heavy work, but we had grown desperate. We won through at 10 p.m., and I write after 12 hours on the march . . .[41]

Wilson continues the story:

February 12. We had a good night just outside the ice-falls and disturbances, and a small breakfast of tea, thin hoosh and biscuit, and began the forenoon

40. Wilson.
41. *Scott's Last Expedition,* vol. i, p. 567.

by a decent bit of travelling on rubbly blue ice in crampons: then plunged into an ice-fall and wandered about in it for hours and hours.

February 13. We had one biscuit and some tea after a night's sleep on very hard and irregular blue ice amongst the ice-fall crevasses. No snow on the tent, only ski, etc. Got away at 10 a.m. and by 2 p.m. found the depot, having had a good march over hard rough blue ice. Only ½ hour in the disturbance of yesterday. The weather was very thick, snowing and overcast, could only just see the points of bearing for depot. However, we got there, tired and hungry, and camped and had hoosh and tea and 3 biscuits each. Then away again with our three and a half days' food from this red flag depot and off down by the Cloudmaker moraine. We travelled about 4 hours on hard blue ice, and I was allowed to geologize the last hour down the two outer lines of boulders. The outer one all dolerite and quartz rocks, the inner all dolerite and sandstone. . . . We camped on the inner line of boulders, weather clearing all the afternoon.[42]

Meanwhile both Wilson and Bowers had been badly snow-blind, though Wilson does not mention it in his diary; and this night Scott says Evans had no power to assist with camping work. A good march followed on 14 February, but

there is no getting away from the fact that we are not pulling strong. Probably none of us: Wilson's leg still troubles him and he doesn't like to trust himself on ski; but the worse case is Evans, who is giving us serious anxiety. This morning he suddenly disclosed a huge blister on his foot. It delayed us on the march, when he had to have his crampon readjusted. Sometimes I feel he is going from bad to worse, but I trust he will pick up again when we come to steady work on ski like this afternoon. He is hungry and so is Wilson. We can't risk opening out our food again, and as cook at present I am serving something under full allowance. We are inclined to get slack and slow with our camping arrangement, and small delays increase. I have talked of the matter tonight and hope for improvement. We cannot do distance without the hours.[43]

There was something wrong with this party: more wrong, I mean, than was justified by the tremendous journey they had already experienced.

---

42. Wilson.
43. *Scott's Last Expedition,* vol. i, pp. 570–71.

Except for the blizzard at the bottom of the Beardmore and the surfaces near the Pole it had been little worse than they expected. Evans, however, who was considered by Scott to be the strongest man of the party, had already collapsed, and it is admitted that the rest of the party was becoming far from strong. There seems to be an unknown factor here somewhere.

Wilson's diary continues:

February 15. 13¾ *m. geog.* I got on ski again first time since damaging my leg and was on them all day for 9 hours. It was a bit painful and swelled by the evening, and every night I put on snow poultice. We are not yet abreast of Mt. Kyffin, and much discussion how far we are from the Lower Glacier Depot, probably 18 to 20 m.: and we have to reduce food again, only one biscuit tonight with a thin hoosh of pemmican. Tomorrow we have to make one day's food which remains last over the two. The weather became heavily over-cast during the afternoon and then began to snow, and though we got in our 4 hours' march it was with difficulty, and we only made a bit over 5 miles. However, we are nearer the depot tonight.

February 16. 12½ *m. geog.* Got a good start in fair weather after one biscuit and a thin breakfast, and made 7½ m. in the forenoon. Again the weather be-came overcast and we lunched almost at our old bearing on Kyffin of lunch Dec. 15. All the afternoon the weather became thick and thicker and after 3½ hours Evans collapsed, sick and giddy, and unable to walk even by the sledge on ski, so we camped. Can see no land at all anywhere, but we must be getting pretty near the Pillar Rock. Evans' collapse has much to do with the fact that he has never been sick in his life and is now helpless with his hands frost-bitten. We had thin meals for lunch and supper.

February 17. The weather cleared and we got away for a clear run to the depot and had gone a good part of the way when Evans found his ski shoes coming off. He was allowed to readjust and continue to pull, but it happened again, and then again, so he was told to unhitch, get them right, and follow on and catch us up. He lagged far behind till lunch, and when we camped we had lunch, and then went back for him as he had not come up. He had fallen and had his hands frost-bitten, and we then returned for the sledge, and brought it, and fetched him in on it as he was rapidly losing the use of his legs. He was comatose when we got him into the tent, and he died without recovering consciousness that night about 10 p.m. We had a short rest for an hour or two in our bags that night, then had a meal and came on through the pressure ridges about 4 miles farther down and reached our Lower Glacier Depot. Here we camped at last, had a good meal and slept a good night's rest which we badly needed. Our depot was all right.[44]

A very terrible day. . . . On discussing the symptoms we think he began to get weaker just before we reached the Pole, and that his downward path was accelerated first by the shock of his frost-bitten fingers, and later by falls during rough travelling on the glacier, further by his loss of all confidence in himself. Wilson thinks it certain he must have injured his brain by a fall. It is a terrible thing to lose a companion in this way, but calm reflection shows that there could not have been a better ending to the terrible anxieties of the past week. Discussion of the situation at lunch yesterday shows us what a desperate pass we were in with a sick man on our hands at such a distance from home.[45]

★   ★   ★   ★   ★

Stevenson has written of a traveller whose wife slumbered by his side what time his spirit re-adventured forth in memory of days gone by. He was quite happy about it, and I suppose his travels had been peaceful, for days and nights such as these men spent coming down the Beardmore will give you nightmare after nightmare, and wake you shrieking—years after.

Of course they were shaken and weakened. But the conditions they had faced, and the time they had been out, do not in my opinion account entirely for their weakness nor for Evans's collapse, which may have had something to do with the fact that he was the biggest, heaviest and most muscular man in the party. I do not believe that this is a life for such men, who are expected to pull their weight and to support and drive a larger machine than their companions, and at the same time to eat no extra food. If, as seems likely, the ration these men were eating was not enough to support the work they were doing, then it is clear that the heaviest man will feel the deficiency sooner and more severely than others who are smaller than he. Evans must have had a most terrible time: I think it is clear from the diaries that he had suffered very greatly without complaint. At home he would have been nursed in bed: here he must march (he was pulling the day he died) until he was crawling on his frost-bitten hands and knees in the snow—horrible: most horrible perhaps for those who found him so, and sat in the tent and watched him die. I am told that simple concussion does not kill as suddenly as this: probably some clot had moved in his brain.

---

44. Wilson.
45. *Scott's Last Expedition*, vol. i, p. 573.

For one reason and another they took very nearly as long to come down the glacier with a featherweight sledge as we had taken to go up it with full loads. Seven days' food were allowed from the Upper to the Lower Glacier Depot. Bowers told me that he thought this was running it fine. But the two supporting parties got through all right, though they both tumbled into the horrible pressure above the Cloudmaker. The Last Return Party took 7½ days: the Polar Party 10 days: the latter had been 25½ days longer on the plateau than the former. Owing to their slow progress down the glacier the Polar Party went on short rations for the first and last time until they camped on 19 March: with the exception of these days they had either their full, or more than their full ration until that date.

Until they reached the Barrier on their return journey the weather can be described neither as abnormal nor as unexpected. There were 300 statute miles (260 geo.) to be covered to One Ton Depot, and 150 statute miles (130 geo.) more from One Ton to Hut Point. They had just picked up one week's food for five men: between the Beardmore and One Ton were three more depots each with one week's food for five men. They were four men: their way was across the main body of the Barrier out of sight of land, and away from any immediate influence of the comparatively warm sea ahead of them. Nothing was known of the weather conditions in the middle of the Barrier at this time of year, and no one suspected that March conditions there were very cold. Shackleton turned homeward on 10 January: reached his Bluff Depot on 23 February, and Hut Point on 28 February.

Wilson's diary continues:

> *February 18.* We had only five hours' sleep. We had butter and biscuit and tea when we woke up at 2 p.m., then came over the Gap entrance to the pony-slaughter camp, visiting a rock moraine of Mt. Hope on the way.
>
> *February 19.* Late in getting away after making up new 10-foot sledge and digging out pony meat. We made 5½ m. on a very heavy surface indeed.[1]

This bad surface is the feature of their first homeward marches on the Barrier. From now onwards they complain always of the terrible surfaces, but a certain amount of the heavy pulling must be ascribed to their own weakness. In the low temperatures which occurred later bad surfaces were to be expected: but now the temperatures were not really low, about zero to $-17°$: fine

---

1. Wilson.

clear days for the most part and, a thing to be noticed, little wind. They wanted wind, which would probably be behind them from the south. 'Oh! for a little wind,' Scott writes. 'E. Evans evidently had plenty.' He was already very anxious.

> If this goes on we shall have a bad time, but I sincerely trust it is only the re-sult of this windless area close to the coast and that, as we are making steadily outwards, we shall shortly escape it. It is perhaps premature [19 Feb.] to be anxious about covering distance. In all other respects things are improving. We have our sleeping-bags spread on the sledge and they are drying, but, above all, we have our full measure of food again. Tonight we had a sort of stew fry of pemmican and horseflesh, and voted it the best hoosh we had ever had on a sledge journey. The absence of poor Evans is a help to the commis-sariat, but if he had been here in a fit state we might have got along faster. I wonder what is in store for us, with some little alarm at the lateness of the season.

And on 20 February, when they made 7 miles, 'At present our sledge and ski leave deeply ploughed tracks which can be seen winding for miles be-hind. It is distressing, but as usual trials are forgotten when we camp, and good food is our lot. Pray God we get better travelling as we are not so fit as we were, and the season is advancing apace.' And on 21 February, 'We never won a march of 8½ miles with greater difficulty, but we can't go on like this.'[2]

A breeze suddenly came away from S.S.E., force 4 to 6, at 11 a.m. on 22 February, and they hoisted the sail on the sledge they had just picked up. They immediately lost the tracks they were following, and failed to find the cairns and camp remains which they should have picked up if they had been on the right course, which was difficult here owing to the thick weather we had on the outward march. Bowers was sure they were too near the land and they steered out, but still failed to pick up the line on which their depots and their lives depended. Scott was convinced they were outside, not inside the line. The next morning Bowers took a round of angles, and they came to the conclusion, on slender evidence, that they were still too near the land. They had an unhappy march still off the tracks, 'but just as we decided to lunch, Bowers' wonderful sharp eyes detected an old double lunch cairn, the theodo-lite telescope confirmed it, and our spirits rose accordingly.'[3] Then Wilson had

---

2. *Scott's Last Expedition,* vol. i, pp. 575–6.
3. ibid., p. 577.

another 'bad attack of snow-glare: could hardly keep a chink of eye open in goggles to see the course. Fat pony hoosh.'[4] This day they reached the Lower Barrier Depot.

They were in evil case, but they would have been all right, these men, if the cold had not come down upon them, a bolt quite literally from the blue of a clear sky: unexpected, unforetold and fatal. The cold itself was not so tremendous until you realize that they had been out four months, that they had fought their way up the biggest glacier in the world in feet of soft snow, that they had spent seven weeks under plateau conditions or rarefied air, big winds and low temperatures, and they had watched one of their companions die— not in a bed, in a hospital or ambulance, nor suddenly, but slowly, night by night and day by day, with his hands frost-bitten and his brain going, until they must have wondered, each man in his heart, whether in such case a human being could be left to die, that four men might live. He died a natural death and they went out on to the Barrier.

Given such conditions as were expected, and the conditions for which preparation had been made, they would have come home alive and well. Some men say the weather was abnormal: there is some evidence that it was. The fact remains that the temperature dropped into the minus thirties by day and the minus forties by night. The fact also remains that there was a great lack of southerly winds, and in consequence the air near the surface was not being mixed: excessive radiation took place, and a layer of cold air formed near the ground. Crystals also formed on the surface of the snow and the wind was not enough to sweep them away. As the temperature dropped so the surface for the runners of the sledges became worse, as I explained elsewhere. They were pulling as it were through sand.

In the face of the difficulties which beset them their marches were magnificent: 11½ miles on 25 February and again on the following day: 12.2 miles on 27 February, and 11½ miles again on 28 and 29 February. If they could have kept this up they would have come through without a doubt. But I think it was about now that they suspected, and then were sure, that they could not pull through. Scott's diary, written at lunch, 2 March, is as follows:

> Misfortunes rarely come singly. We marched to the [Middle Barrier] depot fairly easily yesterday afternoon, and since that have suffered three distinct blows which have placed us in a bad position. First, we found a shortage of oil; with most rigid economy it can scarce carry us to the next depot on this

---

4. Wilson

surface [71 miles away]. Second, Titus Oates disclosed his feet, the toes show-ing very bad indeed, evidently bitten by the late temperatures. The third blow came in the night, when the wind, which we had hailed with some joy, brought dark overcast weather. It fell below −40° in the night, and this morning it took 1½ hours to get our foot-gear on, but we got away before eight. We lost cairn and tracks together and made as steady as we could N. by W., but have seen nothing. Worse was to come—the surface is simply awful. In spite of strong wind and full sail we have only done 5½ miles. We are in *very* Queer Street, since there is no doubt we cannot do the extra marches and feel the cold horribly.[6]

They did nearly ten miles that day, but on 3 March they had a terrible time. 'God help us,' wrote Scott, 'we can't keep up this pulling, that is certain. Amongst ourselves we are unendingly cheerful, but what each man feels in his heart I can only guess. Putting on foot-gear in the morning is getting slower and slower, therefore every day more dangerous.'

The following extracts are taken from Scott's diary.

March 4. Lunch. We are in a very tight place indeed, but none of us despondent *yet,* or at least we preserve every semblance of good cheer, but one's heart sinks as the sledge stops dead at some sastrugi behind which the surface sand lies thickly heaped. For the moment the temperature is in the −20°—an improve-ment which makes us much more comfortable, but a colder snap is bound to come again soon. I fear that Oates at least will weather such an event very poorly. Providence to our aid! We can expect little from man now except the possibility of extra food at the next depot. It will be real bad if we get there and find the same shortage of oil. Shall we get there? Such a short distance it would have appeared to us on the summit! I don't know what I should do if Wilson and Bowers weren't so determinedly cheerful over things.

Monday, March 5. Lunch. Regret to say going from bad to worse. We got a slant of wind yesterday afternoon, and going on 5 hours we converted our wretched morning run of 3½ miles into something over 9. We went to bed on a cup of cocoa and pemmican solid with the chill off. . . . The result is telling on all, but mainly on Oates, whose feet are in a wretched condition. One swelled up tremendously last night and he is very lame this morning. We started march on tea and pemmican as last night—we pretend to prefer the pemmican this way. Marched for 5 hours this morning over a slightly better

6. *Scott's Last Expedition,* vol. i, pp. 582, 583.

surface covered with high moundy sastrugi. Sledge capsized twice; we pulled on foot, covering 5½ miles. We are two pony marches and 4 miles from our depot. Our fuel dreadfully low and the poor Soldier nearly done. It is pathetic enough because we can do nothing for him; more hot food might do a little, but only a little, I fear. We none of us expected these terribly low temperatures, and of the rest of us, Wilson is feeling them most; mainly, I fear, from his self-sacrificing devotion in doctoring Oates' feet. We cannot help each other, each has enough to do to take care of himself. We get cold on the march when the trudging is heavy, and the wind pierces our worn garments. The others, all of them, are unendingly cheerful when in the tent. We mean to see the game through with a proper spirit, but it's tough work to be pulling harder than we ever pulled in our lives for long hours, and to feel that the progress is so slow. One can only say 'God help us!' and plod on our weary way, cold and very miserable, though outwardly cheerful. We talk of all sorts of subjects in the tent, not much of food now, since we decided to take the risk of running a full ration. We simply couldn't go hungry at this time.

Tuesday, March 6. Lunch. We did a little better with help of wind yesterday afternoon, finishing 9½ miles for the day, and 27 miles from depot. But this morning things have been awful. It was warm in the night and for the first time during the journey I overslept myself by more than an hour; then we were slow with foot-gear; then, pulling with all our might (for our lives) we could scarcely advance at rate of a mile an hour; Then it grew thick and three times we had to get out of harness to search for tracks. The result is something less than 3½ miles for the forenoon. The sun is shining now and wind gone. Poor Oates is unable to pull, sits on the sledge when we are track-searching— he is wonderfully plucky, as his feet must be giving him great pain. He makes no complaint, but his spirits only come up in spurts now, and he grows more silent in the tent. We are making a spirit lamp to try and replace the primus when our oil is exhausted. . . .

Wednesday, March 7. A little worse, I fear. One of Oates' feet *very* bad this morning; he is wonderfully brave. We still talk of what we will do together at home.

We only made 6½ miles yesterday. This morning in 4½ hours we did just over 4 miles. We are 16 miles from our depot. If we only find the correct proportion of food there and this surface continues, we may get to the next depot [Mt. Hooper, 72 miles farther] but not to One Ton Camp. We hope against hope that the dogs have been to Mt. Hooper; then we might pull through. If there is a shortage of oil we can have little hope. One feels that for poor Oates the crisis is near, but none of us are improving, though we are wonderfully fit considering the really excessive work we are doing. We are only kept going by good food. No wind this morning till a chill northerly air came ahead. Sun bright and cairns showing up well. I should like to keep the track to the end.

Thursday, March 8. Lunch. Worse and worse in morning; poor Oates' left foot can never last out, and time over foot-gear something awful. Have to wait in night foot-gear for nearly an hour before I start changing, and then am generally first to be ready. Wilson's feet giving trouble now, but this mainly because he gives so much help to others. We did 4½ miles this morning and are now 8½ miles from the depot—a ridiculously small distance to feel in difficulties, yet on this surface we know we cannot equal half our marches, and that for that effort we expend nearly double the energy. The great question is: What shall we find at the depot? If the dogs have visited it we may get along a good distance, but if there is another short allowance of fuel, God help us indeed. We are in a very bad way, I fear, in any case.

Saturday, March 10. Things steadily downhill. Oates' foot worse. He has rare pluck and must know that he can never get through. He asked Wilson if he had a chance this morning, and of course Bill had to say he didn't know. In point of fact he has none. Apart from him, if he went under now, I doubt whether we could get through. With great care we might have a dog's chance, but no more. The weather conditions are awful, and our gear gets steadily more icy and difficult to manage . . .

Yesterday we marched up the depot, Mt. Hooper. Cold comfort. Shortage on our allowance all round. I don't know that any one is to blame. The dogs which would have been our salvation have evidently failed. Meares had a bad trip home I suppose.

This morning it was calm when we breakfasted, but the wind came from the W.N.W. as we broke camp. It rapidly grew in strength. After travelling for half an hour I saw that none of us could go on facing such conditions. We were forced to camp and are spending the rest of the day in a comfortless blizzard camp, wind quite foul.

Sunday, March 11. Titus Oates is very near the end, one feels. What we or he will do, God only knows. We discussed the matter after breakfast; he is a brave fine fellow and understands the situation, but he practically asked for advice. Nothing could be said but to urge him to march as long as he could. One satisfactory result to the discussion: I practically ordered Wilson to hand over the means of ending our troubles to us, so that any one of us may know how to do so. Wilson had no choice between doing so and our ransacking the medicine case. We have 30 opium tabloids apiece and he is left with a tube of morphine. So far the tragical side of our story.

The sky completely overcast when we started this morning. We could see nothing, lost the tracks, and doubtless have been swaying a good deal since— 3.1 miles for the forenoon—terribly heavy dragging—expected it. Know that 6 miles is about the limit of our endurance now, if we get no help from wind or surfaces. We have 7 days' food and should be about 55 miles from One Ton Camp tonight, 6 × 7 = 42, leaving us 13 miles short of our distance, even if things get no worse. Meanwhile the season rapidly advances.

Monday, March 12. We did 6.9 miles yesterday, under our necessary average. Things are left much the same, Oates not pulling much, and now with hands as well as feet pretty well useless. We did 4 miles this morning in 4 hours 20 min.—we may hope for 3 this afternoon, 7 × 6 = 42. We shall be 47 miles from the depot. I doubt if we can possibly do it. The surface remains awful, the cold intense, and our physical condition running down. God help us! Not a breath of favourable wind for more than a week, and apparently liable to head winds at any moment.

Wednesday, March 14. No doubt about the going downhill, but everything going wrong for us. Yesterday we woke to a strong northerly wind with temp. −37°. Couldn't face it, so remained in camp til 2, then did 5¼ miles. Wanted to march later, but party feeling the cold badly as the breeze (N.) never took off entirely, and as the sun sank the temp. fell. Long time getting supper in dark.

This morning started with southerly breeze, set sail and passed another cairn at good speed; half-way, however, the wind shifted to W. by S. or W.S.W., blew through our wind-clothes and into our mitts. Poor Wilson horribly cold, could [not] get off ski for some time. Bowers and I practically made camp, and when we got into the tent at last we were all deadly cold. Then temp. now midday down −43° and the wind strong. We *must* go on, but now the making of every camp must be more difficult and dangerous. It must be near the end, but a pretty merciful end. Poor Oates got it again in the foot. I shudder to think what it will be like tomorrow. It is only with greatest pains rest of us keep off frost-bites. No idea there could be temperatures like this at this time of year with such winds. Truly awful outside the tent. Must fight it out to the last biscuit; but can't reduce rations.

Friday, March 16, or Saturday, 17. Lost track of dates, but think the last correct. Tragedy all along the line. At lunch, the day before yesterday, poor Titus Oates said he couldn't go on; he proposed we should leave him in his sleeping-bag. That we could not do, and we induced him to come on, on the afternoon march. In spite of its awful nature for him he struggled on and we made a few miles. At night he was worse and we knew the end had come.

Should this be found I want these facts recorded. Oates' last thoughts were of his mother, but immediately before he took pride in thinking that his regiment would be pleased with the bold way in which he met his death. We can testify to his bravery. He has borne intense suffering for weeks without complaint, and to the very last was able and willing to discuss outside subjects. He did not—would not—give up hope till the very end. He was a brave soul. This was the end. He slept through the night before last, hoping not to wake; but he woke in the morning—yesterday. It was blowing a blizzard. He said, 'I am just going outside and may be some time.' He went out into the blizzard and we have not seen him since.

I take this opportunity of saying that we have stuck to our sick companions to the last. In case of Edgar Evans, when absolutely out of food and he lay insensible, the safety of the remainder seemed to demand his abandonment, but Providence mercifully removed him at this critical moment. He died a natural death, and we did not leave him till two hours after his death. We knew that poor Oates was walking to his death, but though we tried to dissuade him, we knew it was the act of a brave man and an English gentleman. We all hope to meet the end with a similar spirit, and assuredly the end is not far.

I can only write at lunch and then only occasionally. The cold is intense, −40° at midday. My companions are unendingly cheerful, but we are all on the verge of serious frost-bites, and though we constantly talk of fetching through I don't think any one of us believes it in his heart.

We are cold on the march now, and at all times except meals. Yesterday we had to lay up for a blizzard and today we move dreadfully slowly. We are at No. 14 Pony Camp, only two pony marches from One Ton Depot. We leave here our theodolite, a camera, and Oates' sleeping-bags. Diaries, etc., and geological specimens carried at Wilson's special request, will be found with us or on our sledge.

Sunday, March 18. Today, lunch, we are 21 miles from the depot. Ill fortune presses, but better may come. We have had more wind and drift from ahead yesterday; had to stop marching; wind N.W., force 4, temp. −35°. No human being could face it, and we are worn out *nearly.*

My right foot has gone, nearly all the toes—two days ago I was proud possessor of best feet. . . . Bowers takes first place in condition, but there is not much to choose after all. The others are still confident of getting through—or pretend to be—I don't know! We have the last *half* fill of oil in our primus and a very small quantity of spirit—this alone between us and thirst. The wind is fair for the moment, and that is perhaps a fact to help. The mileage would have seemed ridiculously small on our outward journey.

Monday, March 19. Lunch. We camped with difficulty last night and were dreadfully cold till after our supper of cold pemmican and biscuit and a half pannikin of cocoa cooked over the spirit. Then, contrary to expectation, we got warm and all slept well. Today we started in the usual dragging manner. Sledge dreadfully heavy. We are 15½ miles from the depot and ought to get there in three days. What progress! We have two days' food but barely a day's fuel. All our feet are getting bad—Wilson's best, my right foot worse, left all right. There is no chance to nurse one's feet till we can get hot food into us. Amputation is the least I can hope for now, but will the trouble spread? That is the serious question. The weather doesn't give us a chance—the wind from N. to N.W. and −40° temp. today.

Wednesday, March 21. Got within 11 miles of depot Monday night; had to lay up all yesterday in severe blizzard. Today forlorn hope, Wilson and Bowers going to depot for fuel.

22 and 23. Blizzard bad as ever—Wilson and Bowers unable to start— tomorrow last chance—no fuel and only one or two of food left—must be near the end. Have decided it shall be natural—we shall march for the depot with or without our effects and die in our tracks.

Thursday, March 29. Since the 21st we have had a continuous gale from W.S.W. and S.W. We had fuel to make two cups of tea apiece and bare food for two days on the 20th. Every day we have been ready to start for our depot *11 miles* away, but outside the door of the tent it remains a scene of whirling drift. I do not think we can hope for any better things now. We shall stick it out to the end, but we are getting weaker, of course, and the end cannot be far.

It seems a pity, but I do not think I can write more.

R. SCOTT

Last entry. For God's sake, look after our people.

The following extracts are from letters written by Scott:

To Mrs E. A. Wilson

MY DEAR MRS WILSON. If this letter reaches you, Bill and I will have gone out together. We are very near it now and I should like you to know how splendid he was at the end—everlastingly cheerful and ready to sacrifice himself for others, never a word of blame to me for leading him into this mess. He is not suffering, luckily, at least only minor discomforts.

His eyes have a comfortable blue look of hope and his mind is peaceful with the satisfaction of his faith in regarding himself as part of the great scheme of the Almighty. I can do no more to comfort you than to tell you that he died as he lived, a brave, true man—the best of comrades and staunchest of friends.

My whole heart goes out to you in pity. Yours,

R. SCOTT

To Mrs Bowers

MY DEAR MRS BOWERS. I am afraid this will reach you after one of the heaviest blows of your life.

I write when we are very near the end of our journey, and I am finishing it in company with two gallant, noble gentlemen. One of these is your son. He had come to be one of my closest and soundest friends, and I appreciate his wonderful upright nature, his ability and energy. As the troubles have thickened his dauntless spirit ever shone brighter and he has remained cheerful, hopeful and indomitable to the end . . .

To Sir J. M. Barrie

MY DEAR BARRIE. We are pegging out in a very comfortless spot. Hoping this letter may be found and sent to you, I write a word of farewell . . . Good-bye. I am not at all afraid of the end, but sad to miss many a humble pleasure which I had planned for the future on our long marches. I may not have proved a great explorer, but we have done the greatest march ever made and come very near to great success. Good-bye, my dear friend. Yours ever,

R. SCOTT

We are in a desperate state, feet frozen, etc. No fuel and a long way from food, but it would do your heart good to be in our tent, to hear our songs and the cheery conversation as to what we will do when we get to Hut Point.

Later. We are very near the end, but have not and will not lose our good cheer. We have four days of storm in our tent and nowhere's food or fuel. We did intend to finish ourselves when things proved like this, but we have decided to die naturally in the tracks.[7]

The following extracts are from letters written to other friends:

. . . I want to tell you that I was *not* too old for this job. It was the younger men that went under first. . . . After all we are setting a good example to our countrymen, if not by getting into a tight place, by facing it like men when we were there. We could have come through had we neglected the sick.

Wilson, the best fellow that ever stepped, has sacrificed himself again and again to the sick men of the party . . .

. . . Our journey has been the biggest on record, and nothing but the most exceptional hard luck at the end would have caused us to fail to return.

What lots and lots I could tell you of this journey. How much better has it been than lounging in too great comfort at home.

Message to the Public

The causes of the disaster are not due to faulty organization, but to misfortune in all risks which had to be undertaken.

---

7. *Scott's Last Expedition,* vol. i, pp. 584–99.

1. The loss of pony transport in March 1911 obliged me to start later than I had intended, and obliged the limits of stuff transported to be narrowed.
2. The weather throughout the outward journey, and especially the long gale in 83°S., stopped us.
3. The soft snow in lower reaches of glacier again reduced pace.

We fought these untoward events with a will and conquered, but it cut into our provision reserve.

Every detail of our food supplies, clothing and depots made on the interior ice-sheet and over that long stretch of 700 miles to the Pole and back, worked to perfection. The advance party would have returned to the glacier in fine form and with surplus of food, but for the astonishing failure of the man whom we had least expected to fail. Edgar Evans was thought the strongest man of the party.

The Beardmore Glacier is not difficult in fine weather, but on our return we did not get a single completely fine day; this with a sick companion enormously increased our anxieties.

As I have said elsewhere, we got into frightfully rough ice and Edgar Evans received a concussion of the brain—he died a natural death, but left us a shaken party with the season unduly advanced.

But all the facts above enumerated were as nothing to the surprise which awaited us on the Barrier. I maintain that our arrangements for returning were quite adequate, and that no one in the world would have expected the temperatures and surfaces which we encountered at this time of the year. On the summit in lat. 85°–°86 we had −20°, −30°. On the Barrier in lat. 82°, 10,000 feet lower, we had −30° in the day, −47° at night pretty regularly, with continuous head-wind during our day marches. It is clear that these circumstances come on very suddenly, and our wreck is certainly due to this sudden advent of severe weather, which does not seem to have any satisfactory cause. I do not think human beings ever came through such a month as we have come through, and we should have got through in spite of the weather but for the sickening of a second companion, Captain Oates, and a shortage of fuel in our depots for which I cannot account, and finally, but for the storm which has fallen on us within 11 miles of the depot at which we hoped to secure our final supplies. Surely misfortune could scarcely have exceeded this last blow. We arrived within 11 miles of our old One Ton Camp with fuel for one last meal and food for two days. For four days we have been unable to leave the tent—the gale howling about us. We are weak, writing is difficult, but for my own sake I do not regret this journey, which has shown that Englishmen can endure hardships, help one another, and meet death with as great a fortitude as ever in the past. We took risks, we knew we took them; things have come out against us, and therefore we have no cause for complaint, but bow to the will of Providence, determined still to do our best to the last. But if we have been willing to give our lives to this enterprise, which is for the honour of our country, I appeal to our countrymen to see that those who depend on us are properly cared for.

Had we lived, I should have had a tale to tell of the hardihood, endurance, and courage of my companions which would have stirred the heart of every Englishman. These rough notes and our dead bodies must tell the tale, but surely, surely a great rich country like ours will see that those who are dependent on us are properly provided for. R. SCOTT.[8]

---

8. *Scott's Last Expedition,* vol. i, pp. 605–7.

From the Little Colorado to the Foot of the Grand Canyon

From *Exploration of the Colorado River and Its Tributaries*

BY JOHN WESLEY POWELL

By the time John Wesley Powell took on the daunting task of running the Green and Colorado Rivers in 1869, he had already had about as much adventure as most men would want in a lifetime. Born in New York in 1834, Powell served as an aide to General Ulysses S. Grant and lost an arm at the Battle of Shiloh. He was a professor of geology after the Civil War, and following the completion of the Union-Pacific Railroad through the West, he turned his attention to this region of exciting geological and exploration possibilities.

Powell's journeys in wooden boats with nine other men took him into places where no white man had ever made a footprint, including the Grand Canyon. Dangers and hardships were great, but nothing could hold back this intrepid explorer with a thirst for discovery—and the courage to back it up.

★　★　★　★　★

August 13.—We are now ready to start on our way down the Great Unknown. Our boats, tied to a common stake, chafe each other as they are tossed by the fretful river. They ride high and buoyant, for their loads are lighter than we could desire. We have but a month's rations remaining. The flour has been resifted through the mosquito-net sieve; the spoiled bacon has been dried and the worst of it boiled; the few pounds of dried apples have been spread in the sun and reshrunken to their normal bulk. The sugar has all melted and gone on its way down the river. But we have a large sack of coffee. The lightening of the boats has this advantage: they will ride the waves better and we shall have but little to carry when we make a portage.

We are three quarters of a mile in the depths of the earth, and the great river shrinks into insignificance as it dashes its angry waves against the walls and cliffs that rise to the world above; the waves are but puny ripples, and we but pigmies, running up and down the sands or lost among the boulders.

We have an unknown distance yet to run, an unknown river to explore. What falls there are, we know not; what rocks beset the channel, we know not; what walls rise over the river, we know not. Ah, well! we may conjecture many things. The men talk as cheerfully as ever; jests are bandied about freely this morning; but to me the cheer is somber and the jests are ghastly.

With some eagerness and some anxiety and some misgiving we enter the canyon below and are carried along by the swift water through walls which rise from its very edge. They have the same structure that we noticed yesterday—tiers of irregular shelves below, and, above these, steep slopes to the foot of marble cliffs. We run six miles in a little more than half an hour and emerge into a more open portion of the canyon, where high hills and ledges of rock intervene between the river and the distant walls. Just at the head of this open place the river runs across a dike; that is, a fissure in the rocks, open to depths below, was filled with eruptive matter, and this on cooling was harder than the rocks through which the crevice was made, and when these were washed away the harder volcanic matter remained as a wall, and the river has cut a gateway through it several hundred feet high and as many wide. As it crosses the wall, there is a fall below and a bad rapid, filled with boulders of trap; so we stop to make a portage. Then on we go, gliding by hills and ledges, with distant walls in view; sweeping past sharp angles of rock; stopping at a few points to examine rapids, which we find can be run, until we have made another five miles, when we land for dinner.

Then we let down with lines over a long rapid and start again. Once more the walls close in, and we find ourselves in a narrow gorge, the water again filling the channel and being very swift. With great care and constant watchfulness we proceed, making about four miles this afternoon, and camp in a cave.

August 14.—At daybreak we walk down the bank of the river, on a little sandy beach, to take a view of a new feature in the canyon. Heretofore hard rocks have given us bad river; soft rocks, smooth water; and a series of rocks harder than any we have experienced sets in. The river enters the gneiss! We can see but a little way into the granite gorge, but it looks threatening.

After breakfast we enter on the waves. At the very introduction it inspires awe. The canyon is narrower than we have ever before seen it: the water is swifter; there are but few broken rocks in the channel; but the walls are set, on either side, with pinnacles and crags; and sharp, angular buttresses, bristling with wind- and wave-polished spires, extend far out into the river.

Ledges of rock jut into the stream, their tops sometimes just below the surface, sometimes rising a few or many feet above; and island ledges and island pinnacles and island towers break the swift course of the stream into chutes and eddies and whirlpools. We soon reach a place where a creek comes in from the left, and, just below, the channel is choked with boulders, which have washed down this lateral canyon and formed a dam, over which there is a fall of 30 or 40 feet; but on the boulders foothold can be had, and we make a portage. Three more such dams are found. Over one we make a portage; at the other two are chutes through which we can run.

As we proceed the granite rises higher, until nearly a thousand feet of the lower part of the walls are composed of this rock.

About eleven o'clock we hear a great roar ahead, and approach it very cautiously. The sound grows louder and louder as we run, and at last we find ourselves above a long, broken fall, with ledges and pinnacles of rock obstructing the river. There is a descent of perhaps 75 or 80 feet in a third of a mile, and the rushing waters break into great waves on the rocks, and lash themselves into a mad, white foam. We can land just above, but there is no foothold on either side by which we can make a portage. It is nearly a thousand feet to the top of the granite; so it will be impossible to carry our boats around, though we can climb to the summit up a side gulch and, passing along a mile or two, descend to the river. This we find on examination; but such a portage would be impracticable for us, and we must run the rapid or abandon the river. There is no hesitation. We step into our boats, push off, and away we go, first on smooth but swift water, then we strike a glassy wave and ride to its top, down again into the trough, up again on a higher wave, and down and up on waves higher and still higher until we strike one just as it curls back, and a breaker rolls over our little boat. Still on we speed, shooting past projecting rocks, till the little boat is caught in a whirlpool and spun round several times. At last we pull out again into the stream. And now the other boats have passed us. The open compartment of the *Emma Dean* is filled with water and every breaker rolls over us. Hurled back from a rock, now on this side, now on that, we are carried into an eddy, in which we struggle for a few minutes, and are then out again, the breakers still rolling over us. Our boat is unmanageable, but she cannot sink, and we drift down another hundred yards through breakers—how, we scarcely know. We find the other boats have turned into an eddy at the foot of the fall and are waiting to catch us as we come, for the men have seen that our boat is swamped. They push out as we come near and pull us in against the wall. Our boat bailed, on we go again.

The walls now are more than a mile in height—a vertical distance difficult to appreciate. Stand on the south steps of the Treasury building in Washington and look down Pennsylvania Avenue to the Capitol; measure this distance overhead, and imagine cliffs to extend to that altitude, and you will understand what is meant; or stand at Canal Street in New York and look up Broadway to Grace Church, and you have about the distance; or stand at Lake Street bridge in Chicago and look down to the Central Depot, and you have it again.

A thousand feet of this is up through granite crags; then steep slopes and perpendicular cliffs rise one above another to the summit. The gorge is black and narrow below, red and gray and flaring above, with crags and angular projections on the walls, which, cut in many places by side canyons, seem to be a vast wilderness of rocks. Down in these grand, gloomy depths we glide, ever listening, for the mad waters keep up their roar; ever watching, ever peering ahead, for the narrow canyon is winding and the river is closed in so that we can see but a few hundred yards, and what there may be below we know not; so we listen for falls and watch for rocks, stopping now and then in the bay of a recess to admire the gigantic scenery; and ever as we go there is some new pinnacle or tower, some crag or peak, some distant view of the upper plateau, some strangely shaped rock, or some deep, narrow side canyon.

Then we come to another broken fall, which appears more difficult than the one we ran this morning. A small creek comes in on the right, and the first fall of the water is over boulders, which have been carried down by this lateral stream. We land at its mouth and stop for an hour or two to examine the fall. It seems possible to let down with lines, at least a part of the way, from point to point, along the righthand wall. So we make a portage over the first rocks and find footing on some boulders below. Then we let down one of the boats to the end of her line, when she reaches a corner of the projecting rock, to which one of the men clings and steadies her while I examine an eddy below. I think we can pass the other boats down by us and catch them in the eddy. This is soon done, and the men in the boats in the eddy pull us to their side. On the shore of this little eddy there is about two feet of gravel beach above the water. Standing on this beach, some of the men take the line of the little boat and let it drift down against another projecting angle. Here is a little shelf, on which a man from my boat climbs, and a shorter line is passed to him, and he fastens the boat to the side of the cliff; then the second one is let down, bringing the line of the third. When the second boat is tied up, the two men standing on the beach above spring into the last boat, which is pulled up alongside of ours; then we let down the boats for 25 or 30 yards by walking along the shelf, landing them again in the mouth of a side canyon. Just below this there is another pile of boulders, over which we make another portage. From the foot of these rocks we can climb to another shelf, 40 or 50 feet above the water.

On this bench we camp for the night. It is raining hard, and we have no shelter, but find a few sticks which have lodged in the rocks, and kindle a fire and have supper. We sit on the rocks all night, wrapped in our *ponchos,* getting what sleep we can.

August 15.—This morning we find we can let down for 300 or 400 yards, and it is managed in this way: we pass along the wall by climbing from projecting point to point, sometimes near the water's edge, at other places 50 or 60 feet above, and hold the boat with a line while two men remain aboard and prevent her from being dashed against the rocks and keep the line from getting caught on the wall. In two hours we have brought them all down, as far as it is possible, in this way. A few yards below, the river strikes with great violence against a projecting rock and our boats are pulled up in a little bay above. The little boat is held by the bow obliquely up the stream. We jump in and pull out only a few strokes, and sweep clear of the dangerous rock. The other boats follow in the same manner and the rapid is passed.

It is not easy to describe the labor of such navigation. We must prevent the waves from dashing the boats against the cliffs. Sometimes, where the river is swift, we must put a bight of rope about a rock, to prevent the boat from being snatched from us by a wave; but where the plunge is too great or the chute too swift, we must let her leap and catch her below or the undertow will drag her under the falling water and sink her. Where we wish to run her out a little way from shore through a channel between rocks, we first throw in little sticks of driftwood and watch their course, to see where we must steer so that she will pass the channel in safety. And so we hold, and let go, and pull, and lift, and ward—among rocks, around rocks, and over rocks.

And now we go on through this solemn, mysterious way. The river is very deep, the canyon very narrow, and still obstructed, so that there is no steady flow of the stream; but the waters reel and roll and boil, and we are scarcely able to determine where we can go. Now the boat is carried to the right, perhaps close to the wall; again, she is shot into the stream, and perhaps is dragged over to the other side, where, caught in a whirlpool, she spins about. We can neither land nor run as we please. The boats are entirely unmanageable; no order in their running can be preserved; now one, now another, is ahead, each crew laboring for its own preservation. In such a place we come to another rapid. Two of the boats run it perforce. One succeeds in landing, but there is no foothold by which to make a portage and she is pushed out again into the stream. The next minute a great reflex wave fills the open compartment; she is water-logged, and drifts unmanageable. Breaker after breaker rolls over her and one capsizes her. The men are thrown out; but they cling to the boat, and she drifts down some distance alongside of us and we are able to catch her. She is soon bailed out and the men are aboard once more; but the oars are lost, and so a pair from the *Emma Dean* is spared. Then for two miles we find smooth water.

Clouds are playing in the canyon to-day. Sometimes they roll down in great masses, filling the gorge with gloom; sometimes they hang aloft from wall to wall and cover the canyon with a roof of impending storm, and we can peer long distances up and down this canyon corridor, with its cloud-roof overhead, its walls of black granite, and its river bright with the sheen of broken waters. Then a gust of wind sweeps down a side gulch and, making a rift in the clouds, reveals the blue heavens, and a stream of sunlight pours in. Then the clouds drift away into the distance, and hang around crags and peaks and pinnacles and towers and walls, and cover them with a mantle that lifts from time to time and sets them all in sharp relief. Then baby clouds creep out of side canyons, glide around points, and creep back again into more distant gorges. Then clouds arrange in strata across the canyon, with intervening vista views to cliffs and rocks beyond. The clouds are children of the heavens, and when they play among the rocks they lift them to the region above.

It rains! Rapidly little rills are formed above, and these soon grow into brooks, and the brooks grow into creeks and tumble over the walls in innumerable cascades, adding their wild music to the roar of the river. When the rain ceases the rills, brooks, and creeks run dry. The waters that fall during a rain on these steep rocks are gathered at once into the river; they could scarcely be poured in more suddenly if some vast spout ran from the clouds to the stream itself. When a storm bursts over the canyon a side gulch is dangerous, for a sudden flood may come, and the inpouring waters will raise the river so as to hide the rocks.

Early in the afternoon we discover a stream entering from the north—a clear, beautiful creek, coming down through a gorgeous red canyon. We land and camp on a sand beach above its mouth, under a great, overspreading tree with willow-shaped leaves.

August 16.—We must dry our rations again to-day and make oars.

The Colorado is never a clear stream, but for the past three or four days it has been raining much of the time, and the floods poured over the walls have brought down great quantities of mud, making it exceedingly turbid now. The little affluent which we have discovered here is a clear, beautiful creek, or river, as it would be termed in this western country, where streams are not abundant. We have named one stream, away above, in honor of the great chief of the "Bad Angels," and as this is in beautiful contrast to that, we conclude to name it "Bright Angel."

Early in the morning the whole party starts up to explore the Bright Angel River, with the special purpose of seeking timber from which to make oars. A couple of miles above we find a large pine log, which has been floated down from the plateau, probably from an altitude of more than 6,000 feet, but not many miles back. On its way it must have passed over many cataracts and falls, for it bears scars in evidence of the rough usage which it has received. The men roll it on skids, and the work of sawing oars is commenced.

This stream heads away back under a line of abrupt cliffs that terminates the plateau, and tumbles down more than 4,000 feet in the first mile or two of its course; then runs through a deep, narrow canyon until it reaches the river.

Late in the afternoon I return and go up a little gulch just above this creek, about 200 yards from camp, and discover the ruins of two or three old houses, which were originally of stone laid in mortar. Only the foundations are left, but irregular blocks, of which the houses were constructed, lie scattered about. In one room I find an old mealing-stone, deeply worn, as if it had been much used. A great deal of pottery is strewn around, and old trails, which in some places are deeply worn into the rocks, are seen.

It is ever a source of wonder to us why these ancient people sought such inaccessible places for their homes. They were, doubtless, an agricultural race, but there are no lands here of any considerable extent that they could have cultivated. To the west of Oraibi, one of the towns in the Province of Tusayan, in northern Arizona, the inhabitants have actually built little terraces along the face of the cliff where a spring gushes out, and thus made their sites for gardens. It is possible that the ancient inhabitants of this place made their agricultural lands in the same way. But why should they seek such spots? Surely the country was not so crowded with peoples to demand the utilization of so barren a region. The only solution suggested of the problem is this: We know that for a century or two after the settlement of Mexico many expeditions were sent into the country now comprising Arizona and New Mexico, for the purpose of bringing the town-building people under the dominion of the Spanish government. Many of their villages were destroyed, and the inhabitants fled to regions at that time unknown; and there are traditions among the people who inhabit the pueblos that still remain that the canyons were these unknown lands. It may be these buildings were erected at that time; sure it is that they have a much more modern appearance than the ruins scattered over Nevada, Utah, Colorado, Arizona, and New Mexico. Those old Spanish conquerors had a monstrous greed for gold and a wonderful lust for saving souls. Treasures they must have, if not on earth, why, then, in heaven; and when they failed to find heathen temples bedecked with silver, they propitiated Heaven by seizing the heathen themselves. There is yet extant a copy of a record made by a heathen artist to express his conception of the demands of the conquerors. In one part of the picture we have a lake, and near by stands a priest pouring water on the head of a native. On the other side, a poor Indian has a cord about his throat. Lines run from these two groups to a central figure, a man with beard and full Spanish panoply. The interpretation of the picture-writing is this: "Be baptized as this saved heathen, or be hanged as that damned heathen." Doubtless, some of these people preferred another alternative, and rather than be baptized or hanged they chose to imprison themselves within these canyon walls.

August 17.—Our rations are still spoiling; the bacon is so badly injured that we are compelled to throw it away. By an accident, this morning, the saleratus was lost overboard. We have now only musty flour sufficient for ten days and a few dried apples, but plenty of coffee. We must make all haste possible. If we meet with difficulties such as we have encountered in the canyon above, we may be compelled to give up the expedition and try to reach the Mormon settlements to the north. Our hopes are that the worst places are passed, but our barometers are all so much injured as to be useless, and so we have lost our reckoning in altitude, and know not how much descent the river has yet to make.

The stream is still wild and rapid and rolls through a narrow channel. We make but slow progress, often landing against a wall and climbing around some point to see the river below. Although very anxious to advance, we are determined to run with great caution, lest by another accident we lose our remaining supplies. How precious that little flour has become! We divide it among the boats and carefully store it away, so that it can be lost only by the loss of the boat itself.

We make ten miles and a half, and camp among the rocks on the right. We have had rain from time to time all day, and have been thoroughly drenched and chilled; but between showers the sun shines with great power and the mercury in our thermometers stands at 115°, so that we have rapid changes from great extremes, which are very disagreeable. It is especially cold in the rain to-night. The little canvas we have is rotten and useless; the rubber *ponchos* with which we started from Green River City have all been lost; more than half the party are without hats, not one of us has an entire suit of clothes, and we have not a blanket apiece. So we gather driftwood and build a fire; but after supper the rain, coming down in torrents, extinguished it, and we sit up all night on the rocks, shivering, and are more exhausted by the night's discomfort than by the day's toil.

August 18.—The day is employed in making portages and we advance but two miles on our journey. Still it rains.

While the men are at work making portages I climb up the granite to its summit and go away back over the rust-colored sandstones and greenish-yellow shales to the foot of the marble wall. I climb so high that the men and boats are lost in the black depths below and the dashing river is a rippling brook, and still there is more canyon above than below. All about me are interesting geologic records. The book is open and I can read as I run. All about me are grand views, too, for the clouds are playing again in the gorges. But somehow I think of the nine days' rations and the bad river, and the lesson of the rocks and the glory of the scene are but half conceived.

I push on to an angle, where I hope to get a view of the country beyond, to see if possible what the prospect may be of our soon running through this plateau, or at least of meeting with some geologic change that will let us out of the granite; but, arriving at the point, I can see below only a labyrinth of black gorges.

August 19.—Rain again this morning. We are in our granite prison still, and the time until noon is occupied in making a long, bad portage.

After dinner, in running a rapid the pioneer boat is upset by a wave. We are some distance in advance of the larger boats. The river is rough and swift and we are unable to land, but cling to the boat and are carried down stream over another rapid. The men in the boats above see our trouble, but they are caught in whirlpools and are spinning about in eddies, and it seems a long time before they come to our relief. At last they do come; our boat is turned right side up and bailed out; the oars, which fortunately have floated along in company with us, are gathered up, and on we go, without even landing. The clouds break away and we have sunshine again.

Soon we find a little beach with just room enough to land. Here we camp, but there is no wood. Across the river and a little way above, we see some driftwood lodged in the rocks. So we bring two boat loads over, build a huge fire, and spread everything to dry. It is the first cheerful night we have had for a week—a warm, drying fire in the midst of the camp, and a few bright stars in our patch of heavens overhead.

August 20.—The characteristics of the canyon change this morning. The river is broader, the walls more sloping, and composed of black slates that stand on edge. These nearly vertical slates are washed out in places—that is, the softer beds are washed out between the harder, which are left standing. In this way curious little alcoves are formed, in which are quiet bays of water, but on a much smaller scale than the great bays and buttresses of Marble Canyon.

The river is still rapid and we stop to let down with lines several times, but make greater progress, as we run ten miles. We camp on the right bank. Here, on a terrace of trap, we discover another group of ruins. There was evidently quite a village on this rock. Again we find mealing-stones and much broken pottery, and up on a little natural shelf in the rock back of the ruins we find a globular basket that would hold perhaps a third of a bushel. It is badly broken, and as I attempt to take it up it falls to pieces. There are many beautiful flint chips, also, as if this had been the home of an old arrow-maker.

August 21.—We start early this morning, cheered by the prospect of a fine day and encouraged also by the good run made yesterday. A quarter of a mile below camp the river turns abruptly to the left, and between camp and that point is very swift, running down in a long, broken chute and piling up against the foot of the cliff, where it turns to the left. We try to pull across, so as to go down on the other side, but the waters are swift and it seems impossible for us to escape the rock below; but, in pulling across, the bow of the boat is turned to the farther shore, so that we are swept broadside down and are prevented by the rebounding waters from striking against the wall. We toss about for a few seconds in these billows and are then carried past the danger. Below, the river turns again to the right, the canyon is very narrow, and we see in advance but a short distance. The water, too, is very swift, and there is no landing-place. From around this curve there comes a mad roar, and down we are carried with a dizzying velocity to the head of another rapid. On either side high over our heads there are overhanging granite walls, and the sharp bends cut off our view, so that a few minutes will carry us into unknown waters. Away we go on one long, winding chute. I stand on deck, supporting myself with a strap fastened on either side of the gunwale. The boat glides rapidly where the water is smooth, then, striking a wave, she leaps and bounds like a thing of life, and we have a wild, exhilarating ride of ten miles, which we make in less than an hour. The excitement is so great that we forget the danger until we hear the roar of a great fall below; then we back on our oars and are carried slowly toward its head and succeed in landing just above and find that we have to make another portage. At this we are engaged until some time after dinner.

Just here we run out of the granite. Ten miles in less than half a day, and limestone walls below. Good cheer returns; we forget the storms and the gloom and the cloud-covered canyons and the black granite and the raging river, and push our boats from shore in great glee.

Though we are out of the granite, the river is still swift, and we wheel about a point again to the right, and turn, so as to head back in the direction from which we came; this brings the granite in sight again, with its narrow gorge and black crags; but we meet with no more great falls or rapids. Still, we run cautiously and stop from time to time to examine some places which look bad. Yet we make ten miles this afternoon; twenty miles in all to-day.

August 22.—We come to rapids again this morning and are occupied several hours in passing them, letting the boats down from rock to rock with lines for nearly half a mile, and then have to make a long portage. While the men are engaged in this I climb the wall on the northeast to a height of about 2,500 feet, where I can obtain a good view of a long stretch of canyon below. Its course is to the southwest. The walls seem to rise very abruptly for 2,500 or 3,000 feet, and then there is a gently sloping terrace on each side for two or three miles, when we again find cliffs, 1,500 or 2,000 feet high. From the brink of these the plateau stretches back to the north and south for a long distance. Away down the canyon on the right wall I can see a group of mountains, some of which appear to stand on the brink of the canyon. The effect of the terrace is to give the appearance of a narrow winding valley with high walls on either side and a deep, dark, meandering gorge down its middle. It is impossible from this point of view to determine whether or not we have granite at the bottom; but from geologic considerations, I conclude that we shall have marble walls below.

After my return to the boats we run another mile and camp for the night. We have made but little over seven miles to-day, and a part of our flour has been soaked in the river again.

August 23.—Our way to-day is again through marble walls. Now and then we pass for a short distance through patches of granite, like hills thrust up into the limestone. At one of these places we have to make another portage, and, taking advantage of the delay, I go up a little stream to the north, wading it all the way, sometimes having to plunge in to my neck, in other places being compelled to swim across little basins that have been excavated at the foot of the falls. Along its course are many cascades and springs, gushing out from the rocks on either side. Sometimes a cottonwood tree grows over the water. I come to one beautiful fall, of more than 150 feet, and climb around it to the right on the broken rocks. Still going up, the canyon is found to narrow very much, being but 15 or 20 feet wide; yet the walls rise on either side many hundreds of feet, perhaps thousands; I can hardly tell.

In some places the stream has not excavated its channel down vertically through the rocks, but has cut obliquely, so that one wall overhangs the other. In other places it is cut vertically above and obliquely below, or obliquely above and vertically below, so that it is impossible to see out overhead. But I can go no farther; the time which I estimated it would take to make the portage has almost expired, and I start back on a round trot, wading in the creek where I must and plunging through basins. The men are waiting for me, and away we go on the river.

Just after dinner we pass a stream on the right, which leaps into the Colorado by a direct fall of more than 100 feet, forming a beautiful cascade. There is a bed of very hard rock above, 30 or 40 feet in thickness, and there are much softer beds below. The hard beds above project many yards beyond the softer, which are washed out, forming a deep cave behind the fall, and the stream pours through a narrow crevice above into a deep pool below. Around on the rocks in the cavelike chamber are set beautiful ferns, with delicate fronds and enameled stalks. The frondlets have their points turned down to form spore cases. It has very much the appearance of the maidenhair fern, but is much larger. This delicate foliage covers the rocks all about the fountain, and gives the chamber great beauty. But we have little time to spend in admiration; so on we go.

We make fine progress this afternoon, carried along by a swift river, shooting over the rapids and finding no serious obstructions. The canyon walls for 2,500 or 3,000 feet are very regular, rising almost perpendicularly, but here and there set with narrow steps, and occasionally we can see away above the broad terrace to distant cliffs.

We camp to-night in a marble cave, and find on looking at our reckoning that we have run 22 miles.

August 24.—The canyon is wider to-day. The walls rise to a vertical height of nearly 3,000 feet. In many places the river runs under a cliff in great curves, forming amphitheaters half-dome shaped.

Though the river is rapid, we meet with no serious obstructions and run 20 miles. How anxious we are to make up our reckoning every time we stop, now that our diet is confined to plenty of coffee, a very little spoiled flour, and very few dried apples! It has come to be a race for a dinner. Still, we make such fine progress that all hands are in good cheer, but not a moment of daylight is lost.

August 25.—We make 12 miles this morning, when we come to monuments of lava standing in the river,—low rocks mostly, but some of them shafts more than a hundred feet high. Going on down three or four miles, we find them increasing in number. Great quantities of cooled lava and many cinder cones are seen on either side; and then we come to an abrupt cataract. Just over the fall on the right wall a cinder cone, or extinct volcano, with a well-defined crater, stands on the very brink of the canyon. This, doubtless, is the one we saw two or three days ago. From this volcano vast floods of lava have been poured down into the river, and a stream of molten rock has run up the canyon three or four miles and down we know not how far. Just where it poured over the canyon wall is the fall. The whole north side as far as we can see is lined with the black basalt, and high up on the opposite wall are patches of the same material, resting on the benches and filling old alcoves and caves, giving the wall a spotted appearance.

The rocks are broken in two along a line which here crosses the river, and the beds we have seen while coming down the canyon for the last 30 miles have dropped 800 feet on the lower side of the line, forming what geologists call a "fault." The volcanic cone stands directly over the fissure thus formed. On the left side of the river, opposite, mammoth springs burst out of this crevice, 100 or 200 feet above the river, pouring in a stream quite equal in volume to the Colorado Chiquito.

This stream seems to be loaded with carbonate of lime, and the water, evaporating, leaves an incrustation on the rocks; and this process has been continued for a long time, for extensive deposits are noticed in which are basins with bubbling springs. The water is salty.

We have to make a portage here, which is completed in about three hours; then on we go.

We have no difficulty as we float along, and I am able to observe the wonderful phenomena connected with this flood of lava. The canyon was doubtless filled to a height of 1,200 or 1,500 feet, perhaps by more than one flood. This would dam the water back; and in cutting through this great lava bed, a new channel has been formed, sometimes on one side, sometimes on the other. The cooled lava, being of firmer texture than the rocks of which the walls are composed, remains in some places; in others a narrow channel has been cut, leaving a line of basalt on either side. It is possible that the lava cooled faster on the sides against the walls and that the center ran out; but of this we can only conjecture. There are other places where almost the whole of the lava is gone, only patches of it being seen where it has caught on the walls. As we float down we can see that it ran out into side canyons. In some places this basalt has a fine, columnar structure, often in concentric prisms, and masses of these concentric columns have coalesced. In some places, when the flow occurred the canyon was probably about the same depth that it is now, for we can see where the basalt has rolled out on the sands, and—what seems curious to me—the sands are not melted or metamorphosed to any appreciable extent. In places the bed of the river is of sandstone or limestone, in other places of lava, showing that it has all been cut out again where the sandstones and limestones appear; but there is a little yet left where the bed is of lava.

What a conflict of water and fire there must have been here! Just imagine a river of molten rock running down into a river of melted snow. What a seething and boiling of the waters; what clouds of steam rolled into the heavens!

Thirty-five miles to-day. Hurrah!

August 26.—The canyon walls are steadily becoming higher as we advance. They are still bold and nearly vertical up to the terrace. We still see evidence of the eruption discovered yesterday, but the thickness of the basalt is decreasing as we go down stream; yet it has been reinforced at points by streams that have come down from volcanoes standing on the terrace above, but which we cannot see from the river below.

Since we left the Colorado Chiquito we have seen no evidences that the tribe of Indians inhabiting the plateaus on either side ever come down to the river; but about eleven o'clock to-day we discover an Indian garden at the foot of the wall on the right, just where a little stream with a narrow flood plain comes down through a side canyon. Along the valley the Indians have planted corn, using for irrigation the water which bursts out in springs at the foot of the cliff. The corn is looking quite well, but it is not sufficiently ad-vanced to give us roasting ears; but there are some nice green squashes. We carry ten or a dozen of these on board our boats and hurriedly leave, not will-ing to be caught in the robbery, yet excusing ourselves by pleading our great want. We run down a short distance to where we feel certain no Indian can follow, and what a kettle of squash sauce we make! True, we have no salt with which to season it, but it makes a fine addition to our unleavened bread and coffee. Never was fruit so sweet as these stolen squashes.

After dinner we push on again and make fine time, finding many rapids, but none so bad that we cannot run them with safety; and when we stop, just at dusk, and foot up our reckoning, we find we have run 35 miles again. A few days like this, and we are out of prison.

We have a royal supper—unleavened bread, green squash sauce, and strong coffee. We have been for a few days on half rations, but now have no stint of roast squash.

August 27.—This morning the river takes a more southerly direction. The dip of the rocks is to the north and we are running rapidly into lower formations. Unless our course changes we shall very soon run again into the granite. This gives some anxiety. Now and then the river turns to the west and excites hopes that are soon destroyed by another turn to the south. About nine o'clock we come to the dreaded rock. It is with no little misgiving that we see the river enter these black, hard walls. At its very entrance we have to make a portage; then let down with lines past some ugly rocks. We run a mile or two farther, and then the rapids below can be seen.

About eleven o'clock we come to a place in the river which seems much worse than any we have yet met in all its course. A little creek comes down from the left. We land first on the right and clamber up over the granite pinnacles for a mile or two, but can see no way by which to let down, and to run it would be sure destruction. After dinner we cross to examine on the left. High above the river we can walk along on the top of the granite, which is broken off at the edge and set with crags and pinnacles, so that it is very difficult to get a view of the river at all. In my eagerness to reach a point where I can see the roaring fall below, I go too far on the wall, and can neither advance nor retreat. I stand with one foot on a little projecting rock and cling with my hand fixed in a little crevice. Finding I am caught here, suspended 400 feet above the river, into which I must fall if my footing fails, I call for help. The men come and pass me a line, but I cannot let go of the rock long enough to take hold of it. Then they bring two or three of the largest oars. All this takes time which seems very precious to me; but at last they arrive. The blade of one of the oars is pushed into a little crevice in the rock beyond me in such a manner that they can hold me pressed against the wall. Then another is fixed in such a way that I can step on it; and thus I am extricated.

Still another hour is spent in examining the river from this side, but no good view of it is obtained; so now we return to the side that was first examined, and the afternoon is spent in clambering among the crags and pinnacles and carefully scanning the river again. We find that the lateral streams have washed boulders into the river, so as to form a dam, over which the water makes a broken fall of 18 or 20 feet; then there is a rapid, beset with rocks, for 200 or 300 yards, while on the other side, points of the wall project into the river. Below, there is a second fall; how great, we cannot tell. Then there is a rapid, filled with huge rocks, for 100 or 200 yards. At the bottom of it, from the right wall, a great rock projects quite halfway across the river. It has a sloping surface extending up stream, and the water, coming down with all the momentum gained in the falls and rapids above, rolls up this inclined plane many feet, and tumbles over to the left. I decide that it is possible to let down over the first fall, then run near the right cliff to a point just above the second, where we can pull out into a little chute, and, having run over that in safety, if we pull with all our power across the stream, we may avoid the great rock below. On my return to the boat I announce to the men that we are to run it in the morning. Then we cross the river and go into camp for the night on some rocks in the mouth of the little side canyon.

After supper Captain Howland asks to have a talk with me. We walk up the little creek a short distance, and I soon find that his object is to remonstrate against my determination to proceed. He thinks that we had better abandon the river here. Talking with him, I learn that he, his brother, and William Dunn have determined to go no farther in the boats. So we return to camp. Nothing is said to the other men.

For the last two days our course has not been plotted. I sit down and do this now, for the purpose of finding where we are by dead reckoning. It is a clear night, and I take out the sextant to make observation for latitude, and I find that the astronomic determination agrees very nearly with that of the plot—quite as closely as might be expected from a meridian observation on a planet. In a direct line, we must be about 45 miles from the mouth of the Rio Virgen. If we can reach that point, we know that there are settlements up that river about 20 miles. This 45 miles in a direct line will probably be 80 or 90 by the meandering line of the river. But then we know that there is comparatively open country for many miles above the mouth of the Virgen, which is our point of destination.

As soon as I determine all this, I spread my plot on the sand and wake Howland, who is sleeping down by the river, and show him where I suppose we are, and where several Mormon settlements are situated.

We have another short talk about the morrow, and he lies down again; but for me there is no sleep. All night long I pace up and down a little path, on a few yards of sand beach, along by the river. Is it wise to go on? I go to the boats again to look at our rations. I feel satisfied that we can get over the danger immediately before us; what there may be below I know not. From our outlook yesterday on the cliffs, the canyon seemed to make another great bend to the south, and this, from our experience heretofore, means more and higher granite walls. I am not sure that we can climb out of the canyon here, and, if at the top of the wall, I know enough of the country to be certain that it is a desert of rock and sand between this and the nearest Mormon town, which, on the most direct line, must be 75 miles away. True, the late rains have been favorable to us, should we go out, for the probabilities are that we shall find water still standing in holes; and at one time I almost conclude to leave the river. But for years I have been contemplating this trip. To leave the exploration unfinished, to say that there is a part of the canyon which I cannot explore, having already nearly accomplished it, is more than I am willing to acknowledge, and I determine to go on.

I wake my brother and tell him of Howland's determination, and he promises to stay with me; then I call up Hawkins, the cook, and he makes a like promise; then Sumner and Bradley and Hall, and they all agree to go on.

August 28.—At last daylight comes and we have breakfast without a word being said about the future. The meal is as solemn as a funeral. After breakfast I ask the three men if they still think it best to leave us. The elder Howland thinks it is, and Dunn agrees with him. The younger Howland tries to persuade them to go on with the party; failing in which, he decides to go with his brother.

Then we cross the river. The small boat is very much disabled and un-seaworthy. With the loss of hands, consequent on the departure of the three men, we shall not be able to run all of the boats; so I decide to leave my *Emma Dean.*

Two rifles and a shotgun are given to the men who are going out. I ask them to help themselves to the rations and take what they think to be a fair share. This they refuse to do, saying they have no fear but that they can get something to eat; but Billy, the cook, has a pan of biscuits prepared for dinner, and these he leaves on a rock.

Before starting, we take from the boat our barometers, fossils, the min-erals, and some ammunition and leave them on the rocks. We are going over this place as light as possible. The three men help us lift our boats over a rock 25 or 30 feet high and let them down again over the first fall, and now we are all ready to start. The last thing before leaving, I write a letter to my wife and I give it to Howland. Sumner gives him his watch, directing that it be sent to his sister should he not be heard from again. The records of the expedition have been kept in duplicate. One set of these is given to Howland; and now we are ready. For the last time they entreat us not to go on, and tell us that it is mad-ness to set out in this place; that we can never get safely through it; and, further, that the river turns again to the south into the granite, and a few miles of such rapids and falls will exhaust our entire stock of rations, and then it will be too late to climb out. Some tears are shed; it is rather a solemn parting; each party thinks the other is taking the dangerous course.

My old boat left, I go on board of the *Maid of the Canyon.* The three men climb a crag that overhangs the river to watch us off. The *Maid of the Canyon* pushes out. We glide rapidly along the foot of the wall, just grazing one great rock, then pull out a little into the chute of the second fall and plunge over it. The open compartment is filled when we strike the first wave below, but we cut through it, and then the men pull with all their power toward the left wall and swing clear of the dangerous rock below all right. We are scarcely a minute in running it, and find that, although it looked bad from above, we have passed many places that were worse.

The other boat follows without more difficulty. We land at the first practicable point below, and fire our guns, as a signal to the men above that we have come over in safety. Here we remain a couple of hours, hoping that they will take the smaller boat and follow us. We are behind a curve in the canyon and cannot see up to where we left them, and so we wait until their coming seems hopeless, and then push on.

And now we have a succession of rapids and falls until noon, all of which we run in safety. Just after dinner we come to another bad place. A little stream comes in from the left, and below there is a fall, and still below another fall. Above, the river tumbles down, over and among the rocks, in whirlpools and great waves, and the waters are lashed into mad, white foam. We run along the left, above this, and soon see that we cannot get down on this side, but it seems possible to let down on the other. We pull up stream again for 200 or 300 yards and cross. Now there is a bed of basalt on this northern side of the canyon, with a bold escarpment that seems to be a hundred feet high. We can climb it and walk along its summit to a point where we are just at the head of the fall. Here the basalt is broken down again, so it seems to us, and I direct the men to take a line to the top of the cliff and let the boats down along the wall. One man remains in the boat to keep her clear of the rocks and prevent her line from being caught on the projecting angles. I climb the cliff and pass along to a point just over the fall and descend by broken rocks, and find that the break of the fall is above the break of the wall, so that we cannot land, and that still below the river is very bad, and that there is no possibility of a portage. Without waiting further to examine and determine what shall be done, I hasten back to the top of the cliff to stop the boats from coming down. When I arrive I find the men have let one of them down to the head of the fall. She is in swift water and they are not able to pull her back; nor are they able to go on with the line, as it is not long enough to reach the higher part of the cliff which is just before them; so they take a bight around a crag. I send two men back for the other line. The boat is in very swift water, and Bradley is standing in the open compartment, holding out his oar to prevent her from striking against the foot of the cliff. Now she shoots out into the stream and up as far as the line will permit, and then, wheeling, drives headlong against the rock, and then out and back again, now straining on the line, now striking against the rock. As soon as the second line is brought, we pass it down to him; but his attention is all taken up with his own situation, and he does not see that we are passing him the line. I stand on a projecting rock, waving my hat to gain his attention, for my voice is drowned by the roaring of the falls. Just at this moment I see him take his knife from its sheath and step forward to cut the line. He has evidently decided that it is better to go over with the boat as it is than to wait for her to be broken to pieces. As he leans over, the boat sheers again into the stream, the stem-post breaks away and she is loose. With perfect composure Bradley seizes the great scull oar, places it in the stern rowlock, and pulls with all his power (and he is an athlete) to turn the bow of the boat down stream, for he wishes to go bow down, rather than to drift broadside on. One, two strokes he makes, and a third just as she goes over, and the boat is fairly turned, and she goes down almost beyond our sight, though we are more than a hundred feet above the river. Then she comes up again on a great wave, and down and up, then around behind some great rocks, and is lost in the mad, white foam below. We stand frozen with fear, for we see no boat. Bradley is gone! so it seems. But now, away below, we see something coming out of the waves. It is evidently a boat. A moment more, and we see Bradley standing on deck, swinging his hat to show that he is all right. But he is in a whirlpool. We have the stem-post of his boat attached to the line. How badly she may be disabled we know not. I direct Sumner and Powell to pass along the cliff and see if they can reach him from below. Hawkins, Hall, and myself run to the other boat, jump aboard, push out, and away we go over the falls. A wave rolls over us and our boat is unmanageable. Another great wave strikes us, and the boat rolls over, and tumbles and tosses, I know not how. All I know is that Bradley is picking us up. We soon have all right again, and row to the cliff and wait until Sumner and Powell can come. After a difficult climb they reach us. We run two or three miles farther and turn again to the northwest, continuing until night, when we have run out of the granite once more.

August 29.—We start very early this morning. The river still continues swift, but we have no serious difficulty, and at twelve o'clock emerge from the Grand Canyon of the Colorado. We are in a valley now, and low mountains are seen in the distance, coming to the river below. We recognize this as the Grand Wash.

A few years ago a party of Mormons set out from St. George, Utah, taking with them a boat, and came down to the Grand Wash, where they divided, a portion of the party crossing the river to explore the San Francisco Mountains. Three men—Hamblin, Miller, and Crosby—taking the boat, went on down the river to Callville, landing a few miles below the mouth of the

Rio Virgen. We have their manuscript journal with us, and so the stream is comparatively well known.

To-night we camp on the left bank, in a mesquite thicket.

The relief from danger and the joy of success are great. When he who has been chained by wounds to a hospital cot until his canvas tent seems like a dungeon cell, until the groans of those who lie about tortured with probe and knife are piled up, a weight of horror on his ears that he cannot throw off, cannot forget, and until the stench of festering wounds and anaesthetic drugs has filled the air with its loathsome burthen,—when he at last goes out into the open field, what a world he sees! How beautiful the sky, how bright the sunshine, what "floods of delirious music" pour from the throats of birds, how sweet the fragrance of earth and tree and blossom! The first hour of convalescent freedom seems rich recompense for all pain and gloom and terror.

Something like these are the feelings we experience to-night. Ever before us has been an unknown danger, heavier than immediate peril. Every waking hour passed in the Grand Canyon has been one of toil. We have watched with deep solicitude the steady disappearance of our scant supply of rations, and from time to time have seen the river snatch a portion of the little left, while we were a-hungered. And danger and toil were endured in those gloomy depths, where oft-times clouds hid the sky by day and but a narrow zone of stars could be seen at night. Only during the few hours of deep sleep, consequent on hard labor, has the roar of the waters been hushed. Now the danger is over, now the toil has ceased, now the gloom has disappeared, now the firmament is bounded only by the horizon, and what a vast expanse of constellations can be seen!

The river rolls by us in silent majesty; the quiet of the camp is sweet; our joy is almost ecstasy. We sit till long after midnight talking of the Grand Canyon, talking of home, but talking chiefly of the three men who left us. Are they wandering in those depths, unable to find a way out? Are they searching over the desert lands above for water? Or are they nearing the settlements?

Across the Pacific by Raft

From *Kon-Tiki*

BY THOR HEYERDAHL

When native Norwegian Thor Heyerdahl and his bride went to live on the remote Pacific island called Fatu-Hiva in the primitive Marquesas in 1936, he had no idea that he was in the fledging stages of what would become one of the most interesting and famous sea voyages of all time. Listening to the native tribal elders, Heyerdahl learned of the legends passed on for generations that told how ancient white men had first come to the islands. In recent centuries, the first Europeans to reach the islands were astonished to find some of the natives had fair skin and were bearded. These people, preached the elders, were from a race of people who had come to the islands back in the times of the gods Tiki and Hutu Matua. They had come sailing across the sea "from a mountainous land in the east which was scorched by the sun."

Being of an open-minded scientific bent, Heyerdahl did not discount such tales; he embraced them. Over the years he researched the possibility that ancient men had indeed sailed from the "sun scorched" coasts of Peru, picked up the Humboldt Current, and been swept to the Marquesas and the Tuamotu Archipelago in the distant reaches of the Pacific. The result of all this was the launching of the Kon-Tiki raft, made of nine huge balsa wood logs lashed together, a square sail, and a small "cabin" made of banana leaves to accommodate Heyerdahl and his fellow voyagers. The five-man crew set sail from Callao, Peru, on April 28, 1947, hoping for a journey that would duplicate the route of the ancients.

Whether the expedition proved anything or not, Heyerdahl's hypothesis that the currents would take the craft to the pacific island worked. Kon-Tiki made landfall on the island of Puka Puka in Polynesia on August 7.

In this excerpt from the book we join the raft just past what Heyerdahl figured to be the halfway point.

★ ★ ★ ★ ★

When the sea was not too rough, we were often out in the little rubber dinghy taking photographs. I shall not forget the first time the sea was so calm that two men felt like putting the balloon-like little thing into the water and going for a row. They had hardly got clear of the raft when they dropped the little oars and sat roaring with laughter. And, as the swell lifted them away and they disappeared and reappeared among the seas, they laughed so loud every time they caught a glimpse of us that their voices rang out over the desolate Pacific. We looked around us with mixed feelings and saw nothing comic but our own hirsute faces; but as the two in the dinghy should be accustomed to those by now, we began to have a lurking suspicion that they had suddenly gone mad. Sunstroke, perhaps. The two fellows could hardly scramble back on board the *Kon-Tiki* for sheer laughter and, gasping, with tears in their eyes they begged us just to go and see for ourselves.

Two of us jumped down into the dancing rubber dinghy and were caught by a sea which lifted us clear. Immediately we sat down with a bump and roared with laughter. We had to scramble back on the raft as quickly as possible and calm the last two who had not been out yet, for they thought we had all gone stark staring mad.

It was ourselves and our proud vessel which made such a completely hopeless, lunatic impression on us the first time we saw the whole thing at a distance. We had never before had an outside view of ourselves in the open sea. The logs of timber disappeared behind the smallest waves, and, when we saw anything at all, it was the low cabin with the wide doorway and the bristly roof of leaves that bobbed up from among the seas. The raft looked exactly like an old Norwegian hayloft lying helpless, drifting about in the open sea—a warped hayloft full of sunburned bearded ruffians. If anyone had come paddling after us at sea in a bathtub, we should have felt the same spontaneous urge to laughter. Even an ordinary swell rolled halfway up the cabin wall and looked as if it would pour in unhindered through the wide open door in which the bearded fellows lay gaping. But then the crazy craft came up to the surface again, and the vagabonds lay there as dry, shaggy, and intact as before. If a higher sea came racing by, cabin and sail and the whole mast might disappear behind the mountain of water, but just as certainly the cabin with its vagabonds would be there again next moment. The situation looked bad, and we could not realize that things had gone so well on board the zany craft.

Next time we rowed out to have a good laugh at ourselves we nearly had a disaster. The wind and sea were higher than we supposed, and the *Kon-Tiki* was cleaving a path for herself over the swell much more quickly than we realized. We in the dinghy had to row for our lives out in the open sea in an attempt to regain the unmanageable raft, which could not stop and wait and could not possibly turn around and come back. Even when the boys on board the *Kon-Tiki* got the sail down, the wind got such a grip on the bamboo cabin that the raft drifted away to westward as fast as we could splash after her in the dancing rubber dinghy with its tiny toy oars. There was only one thought in the head of every man—we must not be separated. Those were horrible minutes we spent out on the sea before we got hold of the runaway raft and crawled on board to the others, home again.

From that day it was strictly forbidden to go out in the rubber dinghy without having a long line made fast to the bow, so that those who remained on board could haul the dinghy in if necessary. We never went far away from the raft, thereafter, except when the wind was light and the Pacific curving itself in a gentle swell. But we had these conditions when the raft was halfway to Polynesia and the ocean, all dominating, arched itself round the globe toward every point of the compass. Then we could safely leave the *Kon-Tiki* and row away into the blue space between sky and sea.

When we saw the silhouette of our craft grow smaller and smaller in the distance, and the big sail at last shrunken to a vague black square on the horizon, a sensation of loneliness sometimes crept over us. The sea curved away under us as blue upon blue as the sky above, and where they met all the blue flowed together and became one. It almost seemed as if we were suspended in space. All our world was empty and blue; there was no fixed point in it but the tropical sun, golden and warm, which burned our necks. Then the distant sail of the lonely raft drew us to it like a magnetic point on the horizon. We rowed back and crept on board with a feeling that we had come home again to our own world—on board and yet on firm, safe ground. And inside the bamboo cabin we found shade and the scent of bamboos and withered palm leaves. The sunny blue purity outside was now served to us in a suitably large dose through the open cabin wall. So we were accustomed to it and so it was good for a time, till the great clear blue tempted us out again.

It was most remarkable what a psychological effect the shaky bamboo cabin had on our minds. It measured eight by fourteen feet, and to diminish the pressure of wind and sea it was built low so that we could not stand upright under the ridge of the roof. Walls and roof were made of strong bamboo canes, lashed together and guyed, and covered with a tough wickerwork of split bamboos. The green and yellow bars, with fringes of foliage hanging down from the roof, were restful to the eye as a white cabin wall never could have been, and, despite the fact that the bamboo wall on the starboard side was open for one third of its length and roof and walls let in sun and moon, this primitive lair gave us a greater feeling of security than white-painted bulkheads and closed portholes would have given in the same circumstances.

We tried to find an explanation for this curious fact and came to the following conclusion. Our consciousness was totally unaccustomed to associating a palm-covered bamboo dwelling with sea travel. There was no natural harmony between the great rolling ocean and the drafty palm hut which was floating about among the seas. Therefore, either the hut would seem entirely out of place in among the waves, or the waves would seem entirely out of place round the hut wall. So long as we kept on board, the bamboo hut and its jungle scent were plain reality, and the tossing seas seemed rather visionary. But from the rubber boat, waves and hut exchanged roles.

The fact that the balsa logs always rode the seas like a gull, and let the water right through aft if a wave broke on board, gave us an unshakable confidence in the dry part in the middle of the raft where the cabin was. The longer the voyage lasted, the safer we felt in our cozy lair, and we looked at the white-crested waves that danced past outside our doorway as if they were an impressive movie, conveying no menace to us at all. Even though the gaping wall was only five feet from the unprotected edge of the raft and only a foot and a half above the water line, yet we felt as if we had traveled many miles away from the sea and occupied a jungle dwelling remote from the sea's perils once we had crawled inside the door. There we could lie on our backs and look up at the curious roof which twisted about like boughs in the wind, enjoying the jungle smell of raw wood, bamboos, and withered palm leaves.

Sometimes, too, we went out in the rubber boat to look at ourselves by night. Coal-black seas towered up on all sides, and a glittering myriad of tropical stars drew a faint reflection from plankton in the water. The world was simple—stars in the darkness. Whether it was 1947 B.C. or A.D. suddenly became of no significance. We lived, and that we felt with alert intensity. We realized that life had been full for men before the technical age also—in fact, fuller and richer in many ways than the life of modern man. Time and evolution somehow ceased to exist; all that was real and that mattered were the same today as they had always been and would always be. We were swallowed up in the absolute common measure of history—endless unbroken darkness under a swarm of stars.

Before us in the night the *Kon-Tiki* rose out of the seas to sink down again behind black masses of water that towered between her and us. In the moonlight there was a fantastic atmosphere about the raft. Stout, shining wooden logs fringed with seaweed, the square pitch-black outline of a Viking sail, a bristly bamboo hut with the yellow light of a paraffin lamp aft—the whole suggested a picture from a fairytale rather than an actual reality. Now and then the raft disappeared completely behind the black seas; then she rose again and stood out sharp in silhouette against the stars, while glittering water poured from the logs.

When we saw the atmosphere about the solitary raft, we could well see in our mind's eye the whole flotilla of such vessels, spread in fan formation beyond the horizon to increase the chances of finding land, when the first men made their way across this sea. The Inca Tupak Yupanqui, who had brought under his rule both Peru and Ecuador, sailed across the sea with an armada of many thousand men on balsa rafts, just before the Spaniards came, to search for islands which rumor had told of out in the Pacific. He found two islands, which some think were the Galapagos, and after eight months' absence he and his numerous paddlers succeeded in toiling their way back to Ecuador. Kon-Tiki and his followers had certainly sailed in a similar formation several hundred years before but, having discovered the Polynesian islands, they had no reason for trying to struggle back.

When we jumped on board the raft again, we often sat down in a circle round the paraffin lamp on the bamboo deck and talked of the seafarers from Peru who had had all these same experiences fifteen hundred years before us. The lamp flung huge shadows of bearded men on the sail, and we thought of the white men with the beards from Peru whom we could follow in mythology and architecture all the way from Mexico to Central America and into the northwestern area of South America as far as Peru. Here this mysterious civilization disappeared, as by the stroke of a magic wand, before the coming of the Incas and reappeared just as suddenly out on the solitary islands in the west which we were now approaching. Were the wandering teachers men of an early civilized race from across the Atlantic, who in times long past, in the same simple manner, had come over with the westerly ocean current and the trade wind from the area of the Canary Islands to the Gulf of Mexico? That was indeed a far shorter distance than the one we were covering, and we no longer believed in the sea as a completely isolating factor.

Many observers have maintained, for weighty reasons, that the great Indian civilizations, from the Aztecs in Mexico to the Incas in Peru, were inspired by sporadic intruders from over the seas in the east, while all the American Indians in general are Asiatic hunting and fishing peoples who in the course of twenty thousand years or more trickled into America from Siberia. It is certainly striking that there is not a trace of gradual development in the high civilizations which once stretched from Mexico to Peru. The deeper the archaeologists dig, the higher the culture, until a definite point is reached at which the old civilizations have clearly arisen without any foundation in the midst of primitive cultures.

And the civilizations have arisen where the current comes in from the Atlantic, in the midst of the desert and jungle regions of Central and South America, instead of in the more temperate regions where civilizations, in both old and modern times, have had easier conditions for their development.

The same cultural distribution is seen in the South Sea islands. It is the island nearest to Peru, Easter Island, which bears the deepest traces of civilization, although the insignificant little island is dry and barren and is the farthest from Asia of all the islands in the Pacific.

When we had completed half our voyage, we had sailed just the distance from Peru to Easter Island and had the legendary island due south of us. We had left land at a chance point in the middle of the coast of Peru to imitate an average raft putting to sea. If we had left the land farther south, nearer Kon-Tiki's ruined city Tiahuanaco, we should have got the same wind but a weaker current, both of which would have carried us in the direction of Easter Island.

When we passed 110° west, we were within the Polynesian ocean area, inasmuch as the Polynesian Easter Island was now nearer Peru than we were. We were on a line with the first outpost of the South Sea islands, the center of the oldest island civilization. And when at night our glowing road guide, the sun, climbed down from the sky and disappeared beyond the sea in the west with his whole spectrum of colors, the gentle trade wind blew life into the stories of the strange mystery of Easter Island. While the night sky smothered all concept of time, we sat and talked and bearded giants' heads were again thrown upon the sail.

But far down south, on Easter Island, stood yet larger giants' heads cut in stone, with bearded chins and white men's features, brooding over the secret of centuries.

Thus they stood when the first Europeans discovered the island in 1722, and thus they had stood twenty-two Polynesian generations earlier, when, according to native tradition, the present inhabitants landed in great canoes and exterminated all men among an earlier population found on the island. The primitive newcomers had arrived from the islands farther west, but the Easter Island traditions claim that the earliest inhabitants, and the true discoverers of the island, had come from a distant land *toward the rising sun.* There is no land in this direction but South America. With the early extermination of the unknown local architects the giant stone heads on Easter Island have become one of the foremost symbols of the insoluble mysteries of antiquity. Here and there on the slopes of the treeless island their huge figures have risen to the sky, stone colossi splendidly carved in the shape of men and set up as a single block as high as a normal building of three or four floors. How had the men of old been able to shape, transport, and erect such gigantic stone colossi? As if the problem was not big enough, they had further succeeded in balancing an extra giant block of red stone like a colossal wig on the top of several of the heads, thirty-six feet above the ground. What did it all mean, and what kind of mechanical knowledge had the vanished architects who had mastered problems great enough for the foremost engineers of today?

If we put all the pieces together, the mystery of Easter Island is perhaps not insoluble after all, seen against a background of raftsmen from Peru. The old civilization has left on this island traces which the tooth of time has not been able to destroy.

Easter Island is the top of an ancient extinct volcano. Paved roads laid down by the old civilized inhabitants lead to well-preserved landing places on the coast and show that the water level round the island was exactly the same then as it is today. This is no remains of a sunken continent but a tiny desolate island, which was as small and solitary when it was a vivid cultural center as it is today.

In the eastern corner of this wedge-shaped island lies one of the extinct craters of the Easter Island volcano, and down in the crater lies the sculptors' amazing quarry and workshop. It lies there exactly as the old artists and architects left it hundreds of years ago, when they fled in haste to the eastern extremity of the island where, according to tradition, there was a furious battle which made the present Polynesians victors and rulers of the island, whereas all grown men among the aboriginals were slain and burned in a ditch. The sudden interruption of the artists' work gives a clear cross section of an ordinary working day in the Easter Island crater. The sculptors' stone axes, hard as flint, lie strewn about their working places and show that this advanced people was as ignorant of iron as Kon-Tiki's sculptors were when they were driven in flight from Peru, leaving behind them similar gigantic stone statues on the Andes plateau. In both places the quarry can be found where the legendary white people with beards hewed blocks of stone thirty feet long or more right out of the mountainside with the help of axes of still harder stone. And in both places the gigantic blocks, weighing many tons, were transported for many miles over rough ground before being set up on end as enormous human figures, or raised on top of one another to form mysterious terraces and walls.

Many huge unfinished figures still lie where they were begun, in their niches in the crater wall on Easter Island, and show how the work was carried on in different stages. The largest human figure, which was almost completed when the builders had to flee, was sixty-six feet long; if it had been finished and set up, the head of this stone colossus would have been level with the top of an eight-floor building. Every separate figure was hewn out of a single connected block of stone, and the working niches for sculptors round the lying stone figures show that not many men were at work at the same time on each figure. Lying on their backs with their arms bent and their hands placed on their stomachs, exactly like the stone colossi in South America, the Easter Island figures were completed in every minute detail before they were removed from the workshop and transported to their destinations round about on the island. In the last stage inside the quarry the giant was attached to the cliff side by only a narrow ridge under his back; then this too was hewn away, the giant meanwhile being supported by boulders.

Large quantities of these figures were just dragged down to the bottom of the crater and set up on the slope there. But a number of the largest colossi were transported up and over the wall of the crater, and for many miles round over difficult country, before being set up on a stone platform and having an extra stone colossus of red tuff placed on their heads. This transport in itself may appear to be a complete mystery, but we cannot deny that it took place or that the architects who disappeared from Peru left in the Andes Mountains stone colossi of equal size, which show that they were absolute experts in this line. Even if the monoliths are largest and most numerous on Easter Island, and the sculptors there had acquired an individual style, the same vanished civilization erected similar giant statues in human shape on many of the other Pacific islands, but only on those nearest to America, and everywhere the monoliths were brought to their final site from out-of-the-way quarries. In the Marquesas, I heard legends of how the gigantic stones were maneuvered, and, as these corresponded exactly to the natives' stories of the transport of the stone pillars to the huge portal on Tongatabu, it can be assumed that the same people employed the same method with the columns on Easter Island.

The sculptors' work in the pit took a long time but required only a few experts. The work of transport each time a statue was completed was more quickly done but, on the other hand, required large numbers of men. Little Easter Island was then both rich in fish and thoroughly cultivated, with large plantations of Peruvian sweet potatoes, and experts believe that the island in its great days could have supported a population of seven or eight thousand. About a thousand men were quite enough to haul the huge statues up and over the steep crater wall, while five hundred were sufficient to drag them on further across the island.

Wearproof cables were plaited from bast and vegetable fibers, and, using wooden frames, the multitude dragged the stone colossus over logs and small boulders made slippery with taro roots. That old civilized peoples were masters in making ropes and cables is well known from the South Sea islands and still more from Peru, where the first Europeans found suspension bridges a hundred yards long laid across torrents and gorges by means of plaited cables as thick as a man's waist.

When the stone colossus had arrived at its chosen site and was to be set up on end, the next problem arose. The crowd built a temporary inclined plane of stone and sand and pulled the giant up the less steep side, legs first. When the statue reached the top, it shot over a sharp edge and slid straight down so that the footpiece landed in a ready-dug hole. As the complete inclined plane still stood there, rubbing against the back of the giant's head, they rolled up an extra cylinder of stone and placed it on the top of his head; then the whole temporary plane was removed. Ready-built inclined planes like this stand in several places on Easter Island, waiting for huge figures which have never come. The technique was admirable but in no way mysterious if we cease to underestimate the intelligence of men in ancient times and the amount of time and manpower which they had at their command.

But why did they make these statues? And why was it necessary to go off to another quarry four miles away from the crater workshop to find a special kind of red stone to place on the figure's head? Both in South America and in the Marquesas Islands the whole statue was often of this red stone, and the natives went great distances to get it. Red headdresses for persons of high rank were an important feature both in Polynesia and in Peru.

Let us see first whom the statues represented. When the first Europeans visited the island, they saw mysterious "white men" on shore and, in contrast to what is usual among peoples of this kind, they found men with long flowing beards, the descendants of women and children belonging to the first race on the island, who had been spared by the invaders. The natives themselves declared that some of their ancestors had been white, while others had been brown. They calculated precisely that the last-named had immigrated from elsewhere in Polynesia twenty-two generations before, while the first had come from eastward in large vessels as much as fifty-seven generations back (i.e., ca. 400–500 A.D.). The race which came from the east were given the name "long-ears," because they lengthened their ears artificially by hanging weights on the lobes so that they hung down to their shoulders. These were the mysterious "long-ears" who were killed when the "short-ears" came to the island, and all the stone figures on Easter Island had large ears hanging down to their shoulders, as the sculptors themselves had had.

Now the Ica legends in Peru say that the sun-king Kon-Tiki ruled over a white people with beards who were called by the Incas "big-ears," because they had their ears artificially lengthened so that they reached down to their shoulders. The Incas emphasized that it was Kon-Tiki's "big-ears" who had erected the abandoned giant statues in the Andes Mountains before they were exterminated or driven out by the Incas themselves in the battle on an island in Lake Titicaca.

To sum up: Kon-Tiki's white "big-ears" disappeared from Peru westward with ample experience of working on colossal stone statues, and Tiki's white "long-ears" came to Easter Island from eastward skilled in exactly the same art, which they at once took up in full perfection so that not the smallest trace can be found on Easter Island of any development leading up to the masterpieces on the island.

There is often a greater resemblance between the great stone statues in South America and those on certain South Sea islands than there is between the monoliths on the different South Sea islands compared with one another. In the Marquesas Islands and Tahiti such statues were known under the generic name *Tiki,* and they represented ancestors honored in the islands' history who, after their death, had been ranked as gods. And therein undoubtedly may be found the explanation of the curious red stone caps on the Easter Island figures. At the time of the European explorations there existed on all the islands in Polynesia scattered individuals and whole families with reddish hair and fair skins, and the islanders themselves declared that it was these who were descended from the first white people on the islands. On certain islands religious festivals were held, the participators in which colored their skins white and their hair red to resemble their earliest ancestors. At annual ceremonies on Easter Island the chief person of the festival had all his hair cut off so that his head might be painted red. And the colossal red-stone caps on the giant statues on Easter Island were carved in the shape which was typical of the local hair style; they had a round knot on the top, just as the men had their hair tied in a little traditional topknot in the middle of the head.

The statues on Easter Island had long ears because the sculptors themselves had lengthened ears. They had specially chosen red stones as wigs because the sculptors themselves had reddish hair. They had their chins carved pointed and projecting, because the sculptors themselves grew beards. They had the typical physiognomy of the white race with a straight and narrow nose and thin sharp lips, because the sculptors themselves did not belong to the Indonesian race. And when the statues had huge heads and tiny legs, with their hands laid in position on their stomachs, it was because it was just in this way the people were accustomed to make giant statues in South America. The sole decoration of the Easter Island figures is a belt which was always carved round the figure's stomach. The same symbolic belt is found on every single statue in Kon-Tiki's ancient ruins by Lake Titicaca. It is the legendary emblem of the sun-god, the rainbow belt. There was a myth on the island of Mangareva according to which the sun-god had taken off the rainbow which was his magic belt and climbed down it from the sky on to Mangareva to people the island with his white-skinned children. The sun was once regarded as the oldest original ancestor in all these islands, as well as in Peru.

We used to sit on deck under the starry sky and retell Easter Island's strange history, even though our own raft was carrying us straight into the heart of Polynesia so that we should see nothing of that remote island but its name on the map. But so full is Easter Island of traces from the east that even its name can serve as a pointer.

"Easter Island" appears on the map because some chance Dutchman "discovered" the island one Easter Sunday. And we have forgotten that the natives themselves, who already lived there, had more instructive and significant names for their home. This island has no less than three names in Polynesian.

One name is *Te-Pito-te-Henua*, which means "navel of the islands." This poetical name clearly places Easter Island in a special position in regard to the other islands farther westward and is the oldest designation for Easter Island according to the Polynesians themselves. On the eastern side of the island, near the traditional landing place of the first "long-ears," is a carefully tooled sphere of stone which is called the "golden navel" and is in turn regarded as the navel of Easter Island itself. When the poetical Polynesian ancestors carved the island navel on the east coast and selected the island nearest Peru as the navel of their myriad islands further west, it had a symbolic meaning. And when we know that Polynesian tradition refers to the discovery of their islands as the "birth" of their islands, then it is more than suggested that Easter Island of all places was considered the "navel," symbolic of the islands' birthmark and as the connecting link with their original motherland.

Easter Island's second name is Rapa Nui which means "Great Rapa," while Rapa Iti or "Little Rapa" is another island of the same size which lies a very long way west of Easter Island. Now it is the natural practice of all peoples to call their first home "Great—" while the next is called "New—" or "Little—" even if the places are of the same size. And on Little Rapa the natives have quite correctly maintained traditions that the first inhabitants of the island came from Great Rapa, Easter Island, to the eastward, nearest to America. This points directly to an original immigration from the east.

The third and last name of this key island is *Mata-Kite-Rani,* which means "the eye (which) looks (toward) heaven." At first glance this is puzzling, for the relatively low Easter Island does not look toward heaven any more than the other loftier islands—for example, Tahiti, the Marquesas, or Hawaii. But *Rani,* heaven, had a double meaning to the Polynesians. It was also their ancestors' original homeland, the holy land of the sun-god, Tiki's forsaken mountain kingdom. And it is very significant that they should have called just their easternmost island, of all the thousands of islands in the ocean, "the eye which looks toward heaven." It is all the more striking seeing that the kindred name *Mata-Rani,* which means in Polynesian "the eye of heaven," is an old Peruvian place name, that of a spot on the Pacific coast of Peru opposite Easter Island and right at the foot of Kon-Tiki's old ruined city in the Andes.

The fascination of Easter Island provided us with plenty of subjects of conversation as we sat on deck under the starry sky, feeling ourselves to be participators in the whole prehistoric adventure. We almost felt as if we had done nothing else since Tiki's days but sail about the seas under sun and stars searching for land.

We no longer had the same respect for waves and sea. We knew them and their relationship to us on the raft. Even the shark had become a part of the everyday picture; we knew it and its usual reactions. We no longer thought of the hand harpoon, and we did not even move away from the side of the raft, if a shark came up alongside. On the contrary, we were more likely to try and grasp its back fin as it glided unperturbed along the logs. This finally developed into a quite new form of sport—tug of war with shark without a line.

We began quite modestly. We caught all too easily more dolphins than we could eat. To keep a popular form of amusement going without wasting food, we hit on comic fishing without a hook for the mutual entertainment of the dolphins and ourselves. We fastened unused flying fish to a string and drew them over the surface of the water. The dolphins shot up to the surface and seized the fish, and then we tugged, each in our own direction, and had a fine circus performance, for if one dolphin let go another came in its place. We had fun, and the dolphins got the fish in the end.

Then we started the same game with the sharks. We had either a bit of fish on the end of a rope or often a bag with scraps from dinner, which we let out on a line. Instead of turning on its back, the shark pushed its snout above the water and swam forward with jaws wide to swallow the morsel. We could not help pulling on the rope just as the shark was going to close its jaws again, and the cheated animal swam on with an unspeakably foolish, patient expression and opened its jaws again for the offal, which jumped out of its mouth every time it tried to swallow it. It ended by the shark's coming right up to the logs and jumping up like a begging dog for the food which hung dangling in a bag above its nose. It was just like feeding a gaping hippopotamus in a zoological gardens, and one day at the end of July, after three months on board the raft, the following entry was made in the diary:

—*We made friends with the shark which followed us today. At dinner we fed it with scraps which we poured right down into its open jaws. It has the effect of a half fierce, half good-natured and friendly dog when it swims alongside us. It cannot be denied that sharks can seem quite pleasant so long as we do not get into their jaws ourselves. At least we find it amusing to have them about us, except when we are bathing.*

One day a bamboo stick, with a bag of sharks' food tied to a string, was lying ready for use on the edge of the raft when a sea came and washed it overboard. The bamboo stick was already lying afloat a couple of hundred yards astern of the raft, when it suddenly rose upright in the water and came rushing after the raft by itself, as if it intended to put itself nicely back in its place again. When the fishing rod came swaying nearer us, we saw a ten-foot shark swimming right under it, while the bamboo stick stuck up out of the waves like a periscope. The shark had swallowed the food bag without biting off the line. The fishing rod soon overtook us, passed us quite quietly, and vanished ahead.

But, even if we gradually came to look upon the shark with quite other eyes, our respect for the five or six rows of razor-sharp teeth which lay in ambush in the huge jaws never disappeared.

One day Knut had an involuntary swim in company with a shark. No one was ever allowed to swim away from the raft, both on account of the raft's drift and because of sharks. But one day it was extra quiet and we had just pulled on board such sharks as had been following us, so permission was given for a quick dip in the sea. Knut plunged in and had gone quite a long way before he came up to the surface to crawl back. At that moment we saw from the mast a shadow bigger than himself coming up behind him, deeper down. We shouted warnings as quietly as we could so as not to create a panic, and Knut heaved himself toward the side of the raft. But the shadow below belonged to a still better swimmer, which shot up from the depths and gained on Knut. They reached the raft at the same time. While Knut was clambering on board, a six-foot shark glided past right under his stomach and stopped beside the raft. We gave it a dainty dolphin's head to thank it for not having snapped.

Generally it is smell more than sight which excites the sharks' voracity. We have sat with our legs in the water to test them, and they have swum toward us till they were two or three feet away, only quietly to turn their tails toward us again. But, if the water was in the least bloodstained, as it was when we had been cleaning fish, the sharks' fins came to life and they would suddenly collect like bluebottles from a long way off. If we flung out shark's guts, they simply went mad and dashed about in a blind frenzy. They savagely devoured the liver of their own kind and then, if we put a foot into the sea, they came for it like rockets and even dug their teeth into the logs where the foot had been. The mood of a shark may vary immensely, the animal being completely at the mercy of its own emotions.

The last stage in our encounter with sharks was that we began to pull their tails. Pulling animals' tails is held to be an inferior form of sport, but that may be because no one has tried it on a shark. For it was, in truth, a lively form of sport.

To get hold of a shark by the tail we first had to give it a real tidbit. It was ready to stick its head high out of the water to get it. Usually it had its food served dangling in a bag. For, if one has fed a shark directly by hand once, it is no longer amusing. If one feeds dogs or tame bears by hand, they set their teeth into the meat and tear and worry it till they get a bit off or until they get the whole piece for themselves. But, if one holds out a large dolphin at a safe distance from the shark's head, the shark comes up and smacks his jaws together, and, without one's having felt the slightest tug, half the dolphin is suddenly gone and one is left sitting with a tail in one's hand. We found it a hard job to cut the dolphin in two with knives, but in a fraction of a second the shark, moving its triangular saw teeth quickly sideways, had chopped off the backbone and everything else like a sausage machine.

When the shark turned quietly to go under again, its tail flickered up above the surface and was easy to grasp. The shark's skin was just like sandpaper to hold on to, and inside the upper point of its tail there was an indentation which might have been made solely to allow of a good grip. If we once got a firm grasp there, there was no chance of our grip's not holding. Then we had to give a jerk, before the shark could collect itself, and get as much as possible of the tail pulled in tight over the logs. For a second or two the shark realized nothing, but then it began to wriggle and struggle in a spiritless manner with the fore part of its body, for without the help of its tail a shark cannot get up any speed. The other fins are only apparatus for balancing and steering. After a few desperate jerks, during which we had to keep a tight hold of the tail, the surprised shark became quite crestfallen and apathetic, and, as the loose stomach began to sink down toward the head, the shark at last became completely paralyzed.

When the shark had become quiet and, as it were, hung stiff awaiting developments, it was time for us to haul in with all our might. We seldom got more than half the heavy fish up out of the water; then the shark too woke up and did the rest itself. With violent jerks it swung its head round and up on to the logs, and then we had to tug with all our might and jump well out of the way, and that pretty quickly, if we wanted to save our legs. For now the shark was in no kindly mood. Jerking itself round in great leaps, it thrashed at the bamboo wall, using its tail as a sledge hammer. Now it no longer spared its iron muscles. The huge jaws were opened wide, and the rows of teeth bit and snapped in the air for anything they could reach. It might happen that the war dance ended in the shark's more or less involuntarily tumbling overboard and disappearing for good after its shameful humiliation, but most often the shark flung itself about at random on the logs aft, till we got a running noose round the root of its tail or till it had ceased to gnash its devilish teeth forever.

The parrot was quite thrilled when we had a shark on deck. It came scurrying out of the bamboo cabin and climbed up the wall at frantic speed till it found itself a good, safe lookout post on the palm-leaf roof, and there it sat shaking its head or fluttered to and fro along the ridge, shrieking with excitement. It had at an early date become an excellent sailor and was always bubbling over with humor and laughter. We reckoned ourselves as seven on board—six of us and the green parrot. The crab Johannes had, after all, to reconcile itself to being regarded as a cold-blooded appendage. At night the parrot crept into its cage under the roof of the bamboo cabin, but in the daytime it strutted about the deck or hung on to guy ropes and stays and did the most fascinating acrobatic exercises.

At the start of the voyage we had turnbuckles on the stays of the mast but they wore the ropes, so we replaced them by ordinary running knots. When the stays stretched and grew slack from sun and wind, all hands had to turn to and brace up the mast, so that its mangrove wood, as heavy as iron, should not bump against and cut into the ropes till they fell down. While we were hauling and pulling, at the most critical moment the parrot began to call out with its cracked voice: "Haul! Haul! Ho, ho, ho, ho, ha ha ha!" And if it made us laugh, it laughed till it shook at its own cleverness and swung round and round on the stays.

At first the parrot was the bane of our radio operators. They might be sitting happily absorbed in the radio corner with their magic earphones on and perhaps in contact with a radio "ham" in Oklahoma. Then their earphones would suddenly go dead, and they could not get a sound however much they coaxed the wires and turned the knobs. The parrot had been busy and bitten off the wire of the aerial. This was specially tempting in the early days, when the wire was sent up with a little balloon. But one day the parrot became seriously ill. It sat in its cage and moped and touched no food for two days, while its droppings glittered with golden scraps of aerial. Then the radio operators repented of their angry words and the parrot of its misdeeds, and from that day Torstein and Knut were its chosen friends and the parrot would never sleep anywhere but in the radio corner. The parrot's mother tongue was Spanish when it first came on board; Bengt declared it took to talking Spanish with a Norwegian accent long before it began to imitate Torstein's favorite ejaculations in full-blooded Norwegian.

We enjoyed the parrot's humor and brilliant colors for two months, till a big sea came on board from astern while it was on its way down the stay from the masthead. When we discovered that the parrot had gone overboard, it was too late. We did not see it. And the *Kon-Tiki* could not be turned or stopped; if anything went overboard from the raft, we had no chance of turning back for it—numerous experiences had shown that.

The loss of the parrot had a depressing effect on our spirits the first evening; we knew that exactly the same thing would happen to ourselves if we fell overboard on a solitary night watch. We tightened up on all the safety regulations, brought into use new life lines for the night watch, and frightened one another out of believing that we were safe because things had gone well in the first two months. One careless step, one thoughtless movement, could send us where the green parrot had gone, even in broad daylight.

We had several times observed the large white shells of cuttlefish eggs, lying floating like ostrich eggs or white skulls on the blue swell. On one solitary occasion we saw a squid lying wriggling underneath. We observed the snow-white balls floating on a level with ourselves and thought at first that it would be an easy matter to row out in the dinghy and get them. We thought the same that time when the rope of the plankton net broke so that the cloth net was left behind alone, floating in our wake. Each time we launched the dinghy, with a rope attached, to row back and pick up the floating object. But we saw to our surprise that the wind and sea held the dinghy off and that the line from the *Kon-Tiki* had so violent a braking effect in the water that we could never row right back to a point we had already left. We might get within a few yards of what we wanted to pick up, but then the whole line was out and the *Kon-Tiki* was pulling us away westward. "Once overboard always overboard" was a lesson that was gradually branded into our consciousness on board. If we wanted to go with the rest, we must hang on till the *Kon-Tiki* ran her bow against land on the other side.

The parrot left a blank in the radio corner, but, when the tropical sun shone out over the Pacific next day, we soon became reconciled to his loss. We hauled in many sharks the next few days, and we constantly found black curved parrots' beaks, or so we thought, among tunnies' heads and other curiosities in the shark's belly. But on closer examination the black beaks always proved to belong to assimilated cuttlefish.

The two radio operators had had a tough job in their corner since the first day they came on board. The very first day, in the Humboldt Current, sea water trickled even from the battery cases so that they had to cover the sensitive radio corner with canvas to save what could be saved in the high seas. And then they had the problem of fitting a long enough aerial on the little raft. They tried to send the aerial up with a kite, but in a gust of wind the kite simply plunged down into a wave crest and disappeared. Then they tried to send it up with a balloon, but the tropical sun burned holes in the balloon so that it collapsed and sank into the sea. And then they had the trouble with the parrot. In addition to all this, we were a fortnight in the Humboldt Current before we came out of a dead zone of the Andes in which the short wave was as dumb and lifeless as the air in an empty soapbox.

But then one night the short wave suddenly broke through, and Torstein's call signal was heard by a chance radio amateur in Los Angeles who was sitting fiddling with his transmitter to establish contact with another amateur in Sweden. The man asked what kind of set we had and, when he got a satisfactory answer to his question, he asked Torstein who he was and where he lived. When he heard that Torstein's abode was a bamboo cabin on a raft in the Pacific, there were several peculiar clickings until Torstein supplied more details. When the man on the air had pulled himself together, he told us that his name was Hal and his wife's name Anna and that she was Swedish by birth and would let our families know we were alive and well.

It was a strange thought for us that evening that a total stranger called Hal, a chance moving-picture operator far away among the swarming population of Los Angeles, was the only person in the world but ourselves who knew where we were and that we were well. From that night onward Hal, alias Harold Kempel, and his friend Frank Cuevas took it in turns to sit up every night and listen for signals from the raft, and Herman received grateful telegrams from the head of the U.S. Weather Bureau for his two daily code reports from an area for which there were extremely few reports and no statistics. Later Knut and Torstein established contact with other radio amateurs almost every night, and these passed on greetings to Norway through a radio "ham" named Egil Berg at Notodden.

When we were just a few days out in mid-ocean, there was too much salt water for the radio corner, and the station stopped working altogether. The operators stood on their heads day and night with screws and soldering irons, and all our distant radio fans thought the raft's days were ended. But then one night the signals LI 2 B burst out into the ether, and in a moment the radio corner was buzzing like a wasp's nest as several hundred American operators seized their keys simultaneously and replied to the call.

Indeed one always felt as if one were sitting down on a wasp's nest if one strayed into the radio operators' domain. It was damp with sea water, which forced its way up along the woodwork everywhere, and, even if there was a piece of raw rubber on the balsa log where the operator sat, one got electric shocks both in the hinder parts and in the finger tips if one touched the Morse key. And, if one of us outsiders tried to steal a pencil from the well-equipped corner, either his hair stood straight up on his head or he drew long sparks from the stump of the pencil. Only Torstein and Knut and the parrot would wriggle their way about in that corner unscathed, and we put up a sheet of cardboard to mark the danger zone for the rest of us.

Late one night Knut was sitting tinkering by lamplight in the radio corner when he suddenly shook me by the leg and said he had been talking to a fellow who lived just outside Oslo and was called Christian Amundsen. This was a bit of an amateur record, for the little short-wave transmitter on board the raft with its 13,990 kilocycles per second did not send out more than 6 watts, about the same strength as a small electric torch. This was August 2, and we had sailed more than sixty degrees round the earth, so that Oslo was at the opposite end of the globe. King Haakon was seventy-five years old the day after, and we sent him a message of congratulations direct from the raft; the day after that Christian was again audible and sent us a reply from the King, wishing us continued good luck and success on our voyage.

Another episode we remember as an unusual contrast to the rest of the life on the raft. We had two cameras on board, and Erik had with him a parcel of materials for developing photographs on the voyage, so that we could take duplicate snapshots of things that had not come out well. After the whale shark's visit he could contain himself no longer, and one evening he mixed the chemicals and water carefully in exact accordance with the instructions and developed two films. The negatives looked like long-distance photographs—nothing but obscure spots and wrinkles. The film was ruined. We telegraphed to our contacts for advice, but our message was picked up by a radio amateur near Hollywood. He telephoned a laboratory and soon afterward he broke in and told us that our developer was too warm; we must not use water above 60° or the negative would be wrinkled.

We thanked him for his advice and ascertained that the very lowest temperature in our surroundings was that of the ocean current itself, which was nearly 80°. Now Herman was a refrigerating engineer, and I told him by way of a joke to get the temperature of the water down to 60°. He asked to have the use of the little bottle of carbonic acid belonging to the already inflated rubber dinghy, and after some hocus-pocus in a kettle covered with a sleeping bag and a woolen vest suddenly there was snow on Herman's stubbly beard, and he came in with a big lump of white ice in the kettle.

Erik developed afresh with splendid results.

Even though the ghost words carried through the air by short waves were an unknown luxury in Kon-Tiki's early days, the long ocean waves beneath us were the same as of old and they carried the balsa raft steadily westward as they did then, fifteen hundred years ago.

The weather became a little more unsettled, with scattered rain squalls, after we had entered the area nearer the South Sea islands and the trade wind had changed its direction. It had blown steadily and surely from the southeast until we were a good way over in the Equatorial Current; then it had veered round more and more toward due east. We reached our most northerly position on June 10 with latitude 6° 19′ south. We were then so close up to the Equator that it looked as if we should sail above even the most northerly islands of the Marquesas group and disappear completely in the sea without finding land. But then the trade wind swung round farther, from east to northeast, and drove us in a curve down toward the latitude of the world of islands.

It often happened that wind and sea remained unchanged for days on end, and then we clean forgot whose steering watch it was except at night, when the watch was alone on deck. For, if sea and wind were steady, the steering oar was lashed fast and the Kon-Tiki sail remained filled without our attending to it. Then the night watch could sit quietly in the cabin door and look at the stars. If the constellations changed their position in the sky, it was time for him to go out and see whether it was the steering oar or the wind that had shifted.

It was incredible how easy it was to steer by the stars when we had seen them marching across the vault of the sky for weeks on end. Indeed, there was not much else to look at at night. We knew where we could expect to see the different constellations night after night, and, when we came up toward the Equator, the Great Bear rose so clear of the horizon in the north that we were anxious lest we should catch a glimpse of the Pole Star, which appears when one comes from southward and crosses the Equator. But as the northeasterly trade wind set in, the Great Bear sank again.

The old Polynesians were great navigators. They took bearings by the sun by day and the stars by night. Their knowledge of the heavenly bodies was astonishing. They knew that the earth was round, and they had names for such abstruse conceptions as the Equator and the northern and southern tropics. In Hawaii they cut charts of the ocean on the shells of round bottle gourds, and on certain other islands they made detailed maps of plaited boughs to which shells were attached to mark the islands, while the twigs marked particular currents. The Polynesians knew five planets, which they called wandering stars, and distinguished them from the fixed stars, for which they had nearly two hundred different names. A good navigator in old Polynesia knew well in what part of the sky the different stars would rise and where they would be at different times of the night and at different times of the year. They knew which stars culminated over the different islands, and there were cases in which an island was named after a star which culminated over it night after night and year after year.

Apart from the fact that the starry sky lay like a glittering giant compass revolving from east to west, they understood that the different stars right over their heads always showed them how far north or south they were. When the Polynesians had explored and brought under their sway their present domain, which is the whole of the sea nearest to America, they maintained traffic between some of the islands for many generations to come. Historical traditions relate that, when the chiefs from Tahiti visited Hawaii, which lay more than 2,000 sea miles farther north and several degrees farther west, the helmsman steered first due north by sun and stars, till the stars right above their heads told them that they were on the latitude of Hawaii. Then they turned at a right angle and steered due west till they came so near that birds and clouds told them where the group of islands lay.

Whence had the Polynesians obtained their vast astronomical knowledge and their calendar, which was calculated with astonishing thoroughness? Certainly not from Melanesian or Malayan peoples to the westward. But the same old vanished civilized race, the "white and bearded men," who had taught Aztecs, Mayas, and Incas their amazing culture in America, had evolved a curiously similar calendar and a similar astronomical knowledge which Europe in those times could not match. In Polynesia, as in Peru, the calendar year had been so arranged as to begin on the particular day of the year when the constellation of the Pleiades first appeared above the horizon, and in both areas this constellation was considered the patron of agriculture.

In Peru, where the continent slopes down toward the Pacific, there stand to this day in the desert sand the ruins of an astronomical observatory of great antiquity, a relic of the same mysterious civilized people which carved stone colossi, erected pyramids, cultivated sweet potatoes and bottle gourds, and began their year with the rising of the Pleiades. Kon-Tiki knew the movement of the stars when he set sail upon the Pacific Ocean.

On July 2 our night watch could no longer sit in peace studying the night sky. We had a strong wind and nasty sea after several days of light northeasterly breeze. Late in the night we had brilliant moonlight and a quite fresh sailing wind. We measured our speed by counting the seconds we took to pass a chip, flung out ahead on one side of us, and found that we were establishing a speed record. While our average speed was from twelve to eighteen "chips," in the jargon current on board, we were now for a time down to "six chips," and the phosphorescence swirled in a regular wake astern of the raft.

Four men lay snoring in the bamboo cabin while Torstein sat clicking with the Morse key and I was on steering watch. Just before midnight I caught sight of a quite unusual sea which came breaking astern of us right across the whole of my disturbed field of vision. Behind it I could see here and there the foaming crests of two more huge seas like the first, following hard on its heels. If we ourselves had not just passed the place, I should have been convinced that what I saw was high surf flung up over a dangerous shoal. I gave a warning shout, as the first sea came like a long wall sweeping after us in the moonlight, and wrenched the raft into position to take what was coming.

When the first sea reached us, the raft flung her stern up sideways and rose up over the wave back which had just broken, so that it hissed and boiled all along the crest. We rode through the welter of boiling foam which poured along both sides of the raft, while the heavy sea itself rolled by under us. The bow flung itself up last as the wave passed, and we slid, stern first, down into a broad trough of the waves. Immediately after the next wall of water came on and rose up, while we were again lifted hurriedly into the air and the clear water masses broke over us aft as we shot over the edge. As a result the raft was flung right broadside on to the seas, and it was impossible to wrench her round quickly enough.

The next sea came on and rose out of the stripes of foam like a glittering wall which began to fall along its upper edge just as it reached us. When it plunged down, I saw nothing else to do but hang on as tight as I could to a projecting bamboo pole of the cabin roof; there I held my breath while I felt that we were flung sky-high and everything round me carried away in roaring whirlpools of foam. In a second we and the *Kon-Tiki* were above water again and gliding quietly down a gentle wave back on the other side. Then the seas were normal again. The three great wave walls raced on before us, and astern in the moonlight a string of coconuts lay bobbing in the water.

The last wave had given the cabin a violent blow, so that Torstein was flung head over heels into the radio corner and the others woke, scared by the noise, while the water gushed up between the logs and in through the wall. On the port side of the foredeck the bamboo wickerwork was blown open like a small crater, and the diving basket had been knocked flat up in the bow, but everything else was as it had been. Where the three big seas came from, we have never been able to explain with certainty, unless they were due to disturbances on the sea bottom, which are not so uncommon in these regions.

Two days later we had our first storm. It started by the trade wind dying away completely, and the feathery, white trade-wind clouds, which were drifting over our heads up in the topmost blue, being suddenly invaded by a thick black cloud bank which rolled up over the horizon from southward. Then there came gusts of wind from the most unexpected directions, so that it was impossible for the steering watch to keep control. As quickly as we got our stern turned to the new direction of the wind, so that the sail bellied out stiff and safe, just as quickly the gusts came at us from another quarter, squeezed the proud bulge out of the sail, and made it swing round and thrash about to the peril of both crew and cargo. But then the wind suddenly set in to blow straight from the quarter whence the bad weather came, and, as the black clouds rolled over us, the breeze increased to a fresh wind which worked itself up into a real storm.

In the course of an incredibly short time the seas round about us were flung up to a height of fifteen feet, while single crests were hissing twenty and twenty-five feet above the trough of the sea, so that we had them on a level with our masthead when we ourselves were down in the trough. All hands had to scramble about on deck bent double, while the wind shook the bamboo wall and whistled and howled in all the rigging.

To protect the radio corner we stretched canvas over the rear wall and port side of the cabin. All loose cargo was lashed securely, and the sail was hauled down and made fast around the bamboo yard. When the sky clouded over, the sea grew dark and threatening, and in every direction it was whitecrested with breaking waves. Long tracks of dead foam lay like stripes to windward down the backs of the long seas; and everywhere, where the wave ridges had broken and plunged down, green patches like wounds lay frothing for a long time in the blue-black sea. The crests blew away as they broke, and the spray stood like salt rain over the sea. When the tropical rain poured over us in horizontal squalls and whipped the surface of the sea, invisible all round us, the water that ran from our hair and beards tasted brackish, while we crawled about the deck naked and frozen, seeing that all the gear was in order to weather the storm.

When the storm rushed up over the horizon and gathered about us for the first time, strained anticipation and anxiety were discernible in our looks. But when it was upon us in earnest, and the *Kon-Tiki* took everything that came her way with ease and buoyancy, the storm became an exciting form of sport, and we all delighted in the fury round about us which the balsa raft mastered so adroitly, always seeing that she herself lay on the wave tops like a cork, while all the main weight of the raging water was always a few inches beneath. The sea had much in common with the mountains in such weather. It was like being out in the wilds in a storm, up on the highest mountain plateaus, naked and gray. Even though we were right in the heart of the tropics, when the raft glided up and down over the smoking waste of sea we always thought of racing downhill among snowdrifts and rock faces.

The steering watch had to keep its eyes open in such weather. When the steepest seas passed under the forward half of the raft, the logs aft rose right out of the water, but the next second they plunged down again to climb up over the next crest. Each time the seas came so close upon one another that the hindmost reached us while the first was still holding the bow in the air. Then the solid sheets of water thundered in over the steering watch in a terrifying welter, but next second the stern went up and the flood disappeared as through the prongs of a fork.

We calculated that in an ordinary calm sea, where there were usually seven seconds between the highest waves, we took in about two hundred tons of water astern in twenty-four hours. But we hardly noticed it because it just flowed in quietly round the bare legs of the steering watch and as quietly disappeared again between the logs. But in a heavy storm more than ten thousand tons of water poured on board astern in the course of twenty-four hours, seeing that loads varying from a few gallons to two or three cubic yards, and occasionally much more, flowed on board every five seconds. It sometimes broke on board with a deafening thunderclap, so that the helmsman stood in water up to his waist and felt as if he were forcing his way against the current in a swift river. The raft seemed to stand trembling for a moment, but then the cruel load that weighed her down astern disappeared overboard again in great cascades.

Herman was out all the time with his anemometer measuring the squalls of gale force, which lasted for twenty-four hours. Then they gradually dropped to a stiff breeze with scattered rain squalls, which continued to keep the seas boiling round us as we tumbled on westward with a good sailing wind. To obtain accurate wind measurements down among the towering seas Herman had, whenever possible, to make his way up to the swaying masthead, where it was all he could do to hold on.

When the weather moderated, it was as though the big fish around us had become completely infuriated. The water round the raft was full of sharks, tunnies, dolphins, and a few dazed bonitos, all wriggling about close under the timber of the raft and in the waves nearest to it. It was a ceaseless life-and-death struggle; the backs of big fishes arched themselves over the water and shot off like rockets, one chasing another in pairs, while the water round the raft was repeatedly tinged with thick blood. The combatants were mainly tunnies and dolphins, and the dolphins came in big shoals which moved much more quickly and alertly than usual. The tunnies were the assailants; often a fish of 150 to 200 pounds would leap high into the air holding a dolphin's bloody head in its mouth. But, even if individual dolphins dashed off with tunnies hard on their heels, the actual shoal of dolphins did not give ground, although there were often several wriggling round with big gaping wounds in their necks. Now and again the sharks, too, seemed to become blind with rage, and we saw them catch and fight with big tunnies, which met in the shark a superior enemy.

Not one single peaceful little pilot fish was to be seen. They had been devoured by the furious tunnies, or they had hidden in the chinks under the raft or fled far away from the battlefield. We dared not put our heads down into the water to see.

I had a nasty shock—and could not help laughing afterward at my own complete bewilderment—when I was aft, obeying a call of nature. We were accustomed to a bit of a swell in the water closet, but it seemed contrary to all reasonable probabilities when I quite unexpectedly received a violent punch astern from something large and cold and very heavy, which came butting up against me like a shark's head in the sea. I was actually on my way up the mast stay, with a feeling that I had a shark hanging on to my hindquarters, before I collected myself. Herman, who was hanging over the steering oar doubled up with laughter, was able to tell me that a huge tunny had delivered a sideways smack at my nakedness with his 160 pounds or so of cold fish. Afterward, when Herman and then Torstein were on watch, the same fish tried to jump on board with the seas from astern, and twice the big fellow was right up on the end of the logs, but each time it flung itself overboard again before we could get a grip of the slippery body.

After that a stout bewildered bonito came right on board with a sea, and with that, and a tunny caught the day before, we decided to fish, to bring order into the sanguinary chaos that surrounded us.

Our diary says:

—*A six-foot shark was hooked first and hauled on board. As soon as the hook was out again, it was swallowed by an eight-foot shark, and we hauled that on board. When the hook came out again, we got a fresh six-foot shark and had hauled it over the edge of the raft when it broke lose and dived. The hook went out again at once, and an eight-foot shark came on to it and gave us a hard tussle. We had its head over the logs when all four steel lines were cut through and the shark dived into the depths. New hook out, and a seven-foot shark was hauled on board. It was now dangerous to stand on the slippery logs aft fishing, because the three sharks kept on throwing up their heads and snapping, long after one would have thought they were dead. We dragged the sharks forward by the tail into a heap on the foredeck, and soon afterward a big tunny was hooked and gave us more of a fight than any shark before we got it on board. It was so fat and heavy that none of us could lift it by the tail.*

The sea was just as full of furious fish backs. Another shark was hooked but broke away just when it was being pulled on board. But then we got a six-foot shark safely on board. After that a five-foot shark, which also came on board. Then we caught yet another six-foot shark and hauled it up. When the hook came out again, we hauled in a seven-foot shark.

Wherever we walked on deck, there were big sharks lying in the way, beating their tails convulsively on the deck or thrashing against the bamboo cabin as they snapped around them. Already tired and worn out when we began to fish after the storm, we became completely befuddled as to which sharks were quite dead, which were still snapping convulsively if we went near them, and which were quite alive and were lying in ambush for us with their green cat's eyes. When we had nine big sharks lying round us in every direction, we were so weary of hauling on heavy lines and fighting with the twisting and snapping giants that we gave up after five hours' toil.

Next day there were fewer dolphins and tunnies but just as many sharks. We began to fish and haul them in again but soon stopped when we perceived that all the fresh shark's blood that ran off the raft only attracted still more sharks. We threw all the dead sharks overboard and washed the whole deck clean of blood. The bamboo mats were torn by shark teeth and rough sharkskin, and we threw the bloodiest and most torn of them overboard and replaced them with new golden-yellow bamboo mats, several layers of which were lashed fast on the foredeck.

When we turned in on these evenings in our mind's eye we saw greedy, open shark jaws and blood. And the smell of shark meat stuck in our nostrils. We could eat shark—it tasted like haddock if we got the ammonia out of the pieces by putting them in sea water for twenty-four hours—but bonito and tunny were infinitely better.

That evening, for the first time, I heard one of the fellows say that it would soon be pleasant to be able to stretch oneself out comfortably on the green grass on a palm island; he would be glad to see something other than cold fish and rough sea.

The weather had become quite quiet again, but it was never as constant and dependable as before. Incalculable, violent gusts of wind from time to time brought with them heavy showers, which we were glad to see because a large part of our water supply had begun to go bad and tasted like evil-smelling marsh water. When it was pouring the hardest, we collected water from the cabin roof and stood on deck naked, thoroughly to enjoy the luxury of having the salt washed off with fresh water.

The pilot fish were wriggling along again in their usual places, but whether they were the same old ones which had returned after the blood bath, or whether they were new followers taken over in the heat of the battle, we could not say.

On July 21 the wind suddenly died away again. It was oppressive and absolutely still, and we knew from previous experience what this might mean. And, right enough, after a few violent gusts from east and west and south, the wind freshened up to a breeze from southward, where black, threatening clouds had again rushed up over the horizon. Herman was out with his anemometer all the time, measuring already fifty feet and more per second, when suddenly Torstein's sleeping bag went overboard. And what happened in the next few seconds took a much shorter time than it takes to tell it.

Herman tried to catch the bag as it went, took a rash step, and fell overboard. We heard a faint cry for help amid the noise of the waves, and saw Herman's head and a waving arm as well as some vague green object twirling about in the water near him. He was struggling for life to get back to the raft through the high seas which had lifted him out from the port side. Torstein, who was at the steering oar aft, and I myself, up in the bow, were the first to perceive him, and we went cold with fear. We bellowed "Man overboard!" at the top of our lungs as we rushed to the nearest life-saving gear. The others had not heard Herman's cry because of the noise of the sea, but in a trice there was life and bustle on deck. Herman was an excellent swimmer, and, though we realized at once that his life was at stake, we had a fair hope that he would manage to crawl back to the edge of the raft before it was too late.

Torstein, who was nearest, seized the bamboo drum round which was the line we used for the lifeboat, for this was within his reach. It was the only time on the whole voyage that this line got caught up. Herman was now on a level with the stern of the raft but a few yards away, and his last hope was to crawl to the blade of the steering oar and hang on to it. As he missed the end of the logs, he reached out for the oar blade, but it slipped away from him. And there he lay, just where experience had shown we could get nothing back. While Bengt and I launched the dinghy, Knut and Erik threw out the life belt. Carrying a long line, it hung ready for use on the corner of the cabin roof, but today the wind was so strong that when it was thrown it was simply blown back to the raft. After a few unsuccessful throws Herman was already far astern of the steering oar, swimming desperately to keep up with the raft, while the distance increased with each gust of wind. He realized that henceforth the gap would simply go on increasing, but he set a faint hope on the dinghy which we had now got into the water. Without the line, which acted as a brake, it would perhaps be possible to drive the rubber raft to meet the swimming man, but whether the rubber raft would ever get back to the *Kon-Tiki* was another matter. Nevertheless, three men in a rubber dinghy had some chance; one man in the sea had none.

Then we suddenly saw Knut take off and plunge headfirst into the sea. He had the life belt in one hand and was heaving himself along. Every time Herman's head appeared on a wave back Knut was gone, and every time Knut came up Herman was not there. But then we saw both heads at once; they had swum to meet each other and both were hanging on to the life belt. Knut waved his arm, and, as the rubber raft had meanwhile been hauled on board, all four of us took hold of the line of the life belt and hauled for dear life, with our eyes fixed on the great dark object which was visible just behind the two men. This same mysterious beast in the water was pushing a big greenish-black triangle up above the wave crests; it almost gave Knut a shock when he was on his way over to Herman. Only Herman knew then that the triangle did not belong to a shark or any other sea monster. It was an inflated corner of Torstein's watertight sleeping bag. But the sleeping bag did not remain floating for long after we had hauled the two men safe and sound on board. Whatever dragged the sleeping bag down into the depths had just missed a better prey.

"Glad I wasn't in it," said Torstein and took hold of the steering oar where he had let it go.

But otherwise there were not many wisecracks that evening. We all felt a chill running through nerve and bone for a long time afterward. But the cold shivers were mingled with a warm thankfulness that there were still six of us on board.

We had a lot of nice things to say to Knut that day—Herman and the rest of us, too.

But there was not much time to think about what had already happened, for as the sky grew black over our heads the gusts of wind increased in strength, and before night a new storm was upon us. We finally got the life belt to hang astern of the raft on a long line, so that we had something behind the steering oar toward which to swim if one of us should fall overboard again in a squall. Then it grew pitch dark around us as night fell and hid the raft and the sea. Bouncing wildly up and down in the darkness, we only heard and felt the gale howling in masts and guy ropes, while the gusts pressed with smashing force against the springy bamboo cabin till we thought it would fly overboard. But it was covered with canvas and well guyed. And we felt the *Kon-Tiki* tossing with the foaming seas, while the logs moved up and down with the movement of the waves like the keys of an instrument. We were astonished that cascades of water did not gush up through the wide chinks in the floor, but they only acted as a regular bellows through which damp air rushed up and down.

For five whole days the weather varied between full storm and light gale; the sea was dug up into wide valleys filled with the smoke from foaming gray-blue seas, which seemed to have their backs pressed out long and flat under the onset of the wind. Then on the fifth day the heavens split to show a glimpse of blue, and the malignant, black cloud cover gave place to the ever victorious blue sky as the storm passed on. We had come through the gale with the steering oar smashed and the sail rent; the centerboards hung loose and banged about like crowbars among the logs, because all the ropes which had tightened them up under water were worn through. But we ourselves and the cargo were completely undamaged.

After the two storms the *Kon-Tiki* had become a good deal weaker in the joints. The strain of working over the steep wave backs had stretched all the ropes, and the continuously working logs had made the ropes eat into the balsa wood. We thanked Providence that we had followed the Incas' custom and had not used wire ropes, which would simply have sawed the whole raft into matchwood in the gale. And, if we had used bone-dry, high-floating balsa at the start, the raft would long ago have sunk into the sea under us, saturated with sea water. It was the sap in the fresh logs which served as an impregnation and prevented the water from filtering in through the porous balsa wood.

But now the ropes had become so loose that it was dangerous to let one's foot slip down between two logs, for it could be crushed when they came together violently. Forward and aft, where there was no bamboo deck, we had to give at the knees when we stood with our feet wide apart on two logs at the same time. The logs aft were as slippery as banana leaves with wet seaweed, and, even though we had made a regular path through the greenery where we usually walked and had laid down a broad plank for the steering watch to stand on, it was not easy to keep one's foothold when a sea struck the raft. On the port side one of the nine giants bumped and banged against the crossbeams with dull, wet thuds both by night and by day. There came also new and fearful creakings from the ropes which held the two sloping masts together at the masthead, for the steps of the masts worked about independently of each other, because they rested on two different logs.

We got the steering oar spliced and lashed with long billets of mangrove wood, as hard as iron, and with Erik and Bengt as sailmakers Kon-Tiki soon raised his head again and swelled his breast in a stiff bulge toward Polynesia, while the steering oar danced behind in seas which the fine weather had made soft and gentle. But the centerboards never again became quite what they had been; they did not meet the pressure of the water with their full strength but gave way and hung, dangling loose and unguyed, under the raft. It was useless to try to inspect the ropes on the underside, for they were completely overgrown with seaweed. On taking up the whole bamboo deck we found only three of the main ropes broken; they had been lying crooked and pressed against the cargo, which had worn them away. It was evident that the logs had absorbed a great weight of water but, since the cargo had been lightened, this was roughly canceled out. Most of our provisions and drinking water were already used up, likewise the radio operators' dry batteries.

Nevertheless, after the last storm it was clear enough that we should both float and hold together for the short distance that separated us from the islands ahead. Now quite another problem came into the foreground—how would the voyage end?

The *Kon-Tiki* would slog on inexorably westward until she ran her bow into a solid rock or some other fixed object which would stop her drifting. But our voyage would not be ended until all hands had landed safe and sound on one of the numerous Polynesian islands ahead.

When we came through the last storm, it was quite uncertain where the raft would end up. We were at an equal distance from the Marquesas Islands and the Tuamotu group, and in a position which meant that we could very easily pass right between the two groups of islands without having a glimpse of one of them. The nearest island in the Marquesas group lay 300 sea miles northwest, and the nearest island in the Tuamotu group lay 300 sea miles southwest, while wind and current were uncertain, with their general direction westerly and toward the wide ocean gap between the two island groups.

The island which lay nearest to the northwest was no other than Fatu Hiva, the little jungle-clad mountainous island where I had lived in a hut built on piles on the beach and heard the old man's vivid stories of the ancestral hero Tiki. If the *Kon-Tiki* stood in to that same beach, I should meet many acquaintances, but hardly the old man himself. He must have departed long ago, with a fair hope of meeting the real Tiki again. If the raft headed in toward the mountain ranges of the Marquesas group, I knew the few islands in the group were a long way apart and the sea thundered unchecked against perpendicular cliffs where we should have to keep our eyes open while steering for the mouths of the few valleys, which always ended in narrow strips of beach.

If, on the contrary, she headed down toward the coral reefs of the Tuamotu group, there the numerous islands lay close together and covered a wide space of sea. But this group of islands is also known as the Low or Dangerous Archipelago, because the whole formation has been built up entirely by coral polyps and consists of treacherous submerged reefs and palm-clad atolls which rise only six or ten feet above the surface of the sea. Dangerous ring-shaped reefs fling themselves protectingly round every single atoll and are a menace to shipping throughout the area. But, even if coral polyps built the Tuamotu atolls while the Marquesas Islands are remains of extinct volcanoes, both groups are inhabited by the same Polynesian race, and the royal families in both regard Tiki as their primeval ancestor.

As early as July 3, when we were still 1,000 sea miles from Polynesia, Nature herself was able to tell us, as she was able to tell the primitive raftsmen from Peru in their time, that there really was land ahead somewhere out in the sea. Until we were a good thousand sea miles out from the coast of Peru we had noted small flocks of frigate birds. They disappeared at about 100° west, and after that we saw only small petrels which have their home on the sea. But on July 3 the frigate birds reappeared, at 125° west, and from now onward small flocks of frigate birds were often to be seen, either high up in the sky or shooting down over the wave crests, where they snapped up flying fish which had taken to the air to escape from dolphins. As these birds did not come from America astern of us, they must have their homes in another country ahead.

On July 16 Nature betrayed herself still more obviously. On that day we hauled up a nine-foot shark, which threw up from its stomach a large undigested starfish which it had recently brought from some coast out here in the ocean.

And the very next day we had the first definite visitor straight from the islands of Polynesia.

It was a great moment on board when two large boobies were spotted above the horizon to westward and soon afterward came sailing in over our mast, flying low. With a wingspread of five feet they circled round us many times, then folded their wings and settled on the sea alongside us. Dolphins rushed to the spot at once and wriggled inquisitively round the great swimming birds, but neither party touched the other. These were the first living messengers that came to bid us welcome to Polynesia. They did not go back in the evening but rested on the sea, and after midnight we still heard them flying in circles round the mast, uttering hoarse cries.

The flying fish which came on board were now of another and much larger species; I recognized them from fishing trips I had taken with the natives along the coast of Fatu Hiva.

For three days and nights we made straight toward Fatu Hiva, but then a strong northeast wind came on and sent us down in the direction of the Tuamotu atolls. We were now blown out of the real South Equatorial Current, and the ocean currents were no longer behaving dependably. One day they were there; another day they were gone. The currents could run like invisible rivers branching out all over the sea. If the current was swift, there was usually more swell and the temperature of the water usually fell one degree. It showed its direction and strength every day by the difference between Erik's calculated and his measured position.

On the threshold of Polynesia the wind said "Pass," having handed us over to a weak branch of the current which, to our alarm, had its course in the direction of the Antarctic. The wind did not become absolutely still—we never experienced that throughout the voyage—and when it was feeble we hoisted every rag we had to collect what little there was. There was not one day on which we moved backward toward America, and our smallest distance in twenty-four hours was 9 sea miles, while our average run for the voyage as a whole was 42½ sea miles in twenty-four hours.

The trade wind, after all, had not the heart to fail us right in the last lap. It reported for duty again and pushed and shoved at the ramshackle craft which was preparing her entry into a new and strange part of the world.

With each day that passed, larger flocks of sea birds came and circled over us aimlessly in all directions. One evening, when the sun was about to sink into the sea, we noticed that the birds had received a violent impetus. They were flying away in a westerly direction without paying any attention to us or the flying fish beneath them. From the masthead we could see that, as they came over, they all flew straight on on exactly the same course. Perhaps they saw something from up above which we did not see. Perhaps they were flying by instinct. In any case they were flying with a plan, straight home to the nearest island, their breeding place.

We twisted the steering oar and set our course exactly in the direction in which the birds had disappeared. Even after it was dark, we heard the cries of stragglers flying over us against the starry sky on exactly the same course as that which we were now following. It was a wonderful night; the moon was nearly full for the third time in the course of the *Kon-Tiki*'s voyage.

Next day there were still more birds over us, but we did not need to wait for them to show us our way again in the evening. This time we had detected a curious stationary cloud above the horizon. The other clouds were small feathery wisps of wool which came up in the south and passed across the vault of the sky with the trade wind till they disappeared over the horizon in the west. So I had once come to know the drifting trade-wind clouds on Fatu Hiva, and so we had seen them over us night and day on board the *Kon-Tiki*. But the lonely cloud on the horizon to the southwest did not move; it just rose like a motionless column of smoke while the trade-wind clouds drifted by. The Polynesians knew land lay under such clouds. For, when the tropical sun bakes the hot sand, a stream of warm air is created which rises up and causes its vapor content to condense up in the colder strata of air.

We steered on the cloud till it disappeared after sunset. The wind was steady, and with the steering oar lashed tight the *Kon-Tiki* kept to her course unaided. The steering watch's job was now to sit on the plank at the masthead, shiny with wear, and keep a lookout for anything that indicated land.

There was a deafening screaming of birds over us all that night. And the moon was nearly full.

Something Lost

BY JACK SCHAEFER

Even though he wrote many great novels and short stories set in the early American West, Jack Schaefer will no doubt always be best remembered for his classic *Shane*. And while it is Schaefer's prose that makes *Shane* a great read even today, it was director George Steven's film genius that made *Shane* a western movie still without peer, a name to be remembered by generations.

"Something Lost" is Jack Schaefer at his word-slinging best, in a story of survival and adventure set in the natural splendor of the Rocky Mountain high country, where many a man has journeyed to find himself only to find "something lost."

The story is from the splendid book *The Collected Stories of Jack Schaefer*, edited by Winfield Townley Scott, published by Arbor House, New York, in 1966.

★　★　★　★　★

June

This was far up in the mountains and still the great peaks climbed, thrusting up and thinning to the bare bones of rock above the timberline. The high upland valley was lost among them, an irregular pocket caught in the soaring immensity, rimmed by the timeless rock, its glints of meadow green shading into the darker green of forest where it broke into the downward slopes. The figure of the man by the stream near the upper end of the valley, where the water slowed from its rush down the rocks, was unbelievably small in the vastness. He stood stooped by a sandbar where the riffles swung and died in a pool and the slant sunlight flashed on the worn tin in his hands and his shoulders rocked as his arms moved in a circular motion.

The motion stopped and the man bent his head farther to peer into the pan in his hands and the full gleaming of the flakes there was reflected in the pale hazel irises of his eyes. He straightened and nodded his head in slow satisfaction. He studied the sandbar and the pool where the water slipped into apparent stillness and the silt of years had settled to the bottom. He raised his head and looked at the untouched wilderness about him. The valley lay open around him, a half-mile wide and a mile long, its level floor cut by the swinging course of the stream. At its head the mountain wall rose steeply in huge broken steps that the stream took in rushes and falls as it drove down from the endless snow in the far upper reaches of rock. Along the valley sides the slopes climbed, tree-dotted and thicket-entangled, to stop against the enduring stone, on the near side against a high sharp ridge, on the opposite side against a vast rock buttress towering out to tremendous cliff edge. Between the ridge and the buttress the valley entrance swept out to open parkland that dropped abruptly into jack pine forest covering the downward slopes and divided by the deepening gorge of the stream as it sought the lower levels. And beyond the ground rose again, rising in ridge upon ridge to the high eastward mountain barrier.

The man nodded his head again in slow satisfaction and the sun shone warm on the broad flat planes of his face beneath the wide squared brim of his hat. He took a leather pouch from a pocket and eased the flakes into it. He strode across the carpet of wild flowers bordering the stream and bent to pick up the trailing lead rope of the grazing burro. By the slope of the near valley-side, where a thickening stand of spruce and juniper fringed the valley floor, he stopped and pulled the rifle and ax and short shovel from under the tie ropes and unfastened the pack and picketed the burro on a twenty-foot rope length. He selected a fallen tree, angling up, the upper end wedged in a crotch of another tree. Using this as his ridgepole, he began building his shelter. He shed his jacket and sweat darkened the faded brown of his shirt as his short broad body swung in steady rhythm and the ax blade bit into the springy wood.

Across the meadow green, across the wild-flower carpet and the stream, half a mile across the stretching expanse of valley floor and two hundred yards up the opposite slope where bare rock jutted over a flat ledge, the great bear lay and watched the man. It lay limp on the ledge in the warm slant sun, hind legs sprawled back, front legs stretched forward with the big head, broad and dished to the muzzle, resting on the rock between them. A light breeze ruffled through the short brown fur made ragged by the remaining long still unshed hairs touched with silver on the tips. Its small farsighted eyes followed the man's every move among the distant trees.

Eighty-odd miles away, over the mountain barrier to the east, where a ragged collection of rude log cabins and tents straggled along the side of an almost dry stream bed, men worked at their wooden cradles and sluice boxes and grumbled to themselves and each other. The showings of color that had drawn them there to stake their claims were dwindling. In the oblong tarpaulin-roofed shack that served as store and bar other men spoke of the one who had left, quietly, speaking to no one, abandoning his slow half-worked claim to disappear with his burro into the high distances to the west. Their talk was tainted with envious wondering. They argued with each other in edged monotones. Unrest and disappointment crawled through the mining camp.

Far up in his valley, as the midnight stars wheeled in their slow course, the man stirred on his bed of spruce boughs and sat up, suddenly alert. The embers of the fire outside the open end of his shelter had faded to a dull glow that meant nothing to the moonless dark under the trees. He heard the burro moving restlessly on its shortened picket rope. In the following silence he felt a familiar prickling on the back of his neck as the short hairs there stiffened in response to some instinct beyond reach of the mind. His right hand moved and took the rifle and he was leaning forward to rise when he heard the burro scream and lunge to the end of the rope. He leaped to his feet and stood in the open end of the shelter, baffled by the unrelenting blackness of the night. Gradually he could make out the darker shapes of the trees. He went cautiously toward the burro and found it half choked by the taut rope. He spoke softly and it pushed against him and together they stood in a silence that lived and breathed around them. There was not a single separate discernible sound, yet the prickling persisted on his neck and the flesh of the burro quivered against him. The prickling died and the burro quieted and they stood in an empty silence. The man returned to the fire and piled wood on it and kneeled to blow until flames sprang and a circle of firelight fought back the dark. He shifted the burro closer to the circle before he lay again on his spruce bed.

In the morning the man found the tracks. Those of the forefeet were nearly seven inches wide and nine long, those of the hind feet eight inches wide and fourteen long. The claw marks of all five toes on each were plain. Apprehension crept along the man's spine. His hands tightened on the rifle. The tracks led in a circle around his camp and close in by the shelter and again by the place where the burro had first been picketed. He crawled inside his shelter to the low diminishing end where his meager supplies, depleted by weeks of wandering, were cached behind a barrier of short logs. He took a handful of cartridges and dropped them into a jacket pocket. Outside again, he strode off, steady and unhurried, following the tracks away.

They led him across the stream below the pool and across the level of the valley. He lost them on the edge of a field of slide rock near the lower end of the valley. He skirted the field and could find no further trace. He turned back and began a thorough circuit of the valley.

He found signs in many places, old tracks caked where the ground had dried and fresher tracks in soft ground. He found three rubbing trees with bark worn thin and high up, higher than he could reach, gashes where the bark had been torn open crosswise by big gripping jaws. He found the trail angling up the far slope to the ledge. It was hard-packed by years of use by generations of animals reaching back into the dim past, so packed that the imprints of the big claws were all but invisible scratches on the hard surface. Approaching the ledge, he saw the wide and narrowing crevice behind it leading back to blackness under the overhanging rock. No light could penetrate the inner dark depth. He dropped silently back down the trail fifty yards and crouched behind a big stone and shouted and there was no response except the jeering call of a jay. He shouted again and waited. At last he strode down the trail and across the valley. In a few moments he was stooped by the pool, his arms moving in circular motion as the sun glinted on the pan in his hands. But now he looked up at regular intervals and scanned the expanse all around him and the rifle lay within quick reach not more than a yard from his steady hands.

Out of the valley, eight miles around the jagged sweep of the vast rock buttress that towered above the opposite slope, out where the forest of jack pine below the edging parkland flowed unbroken down to the shore of a small lake, the great bear lay in a patch of sunlight on the soft needle carpet. Already it had forgotten the man and the burro. They were new sights, new scents, never before known, tucked away now in the reservoir of experience and would remain untouched until a fresh encounter summoned remembrance into being. They had been seen and smelled and investigated in the caution of the night and dismissed. There was no challenge in them for the bear to understand.

A marten drifted down the trunk of a nearby tree, stretching its small pointed head outward to stare intently at the bear. The scritch of the small claws in the bark was barely audible a few feet away, yet the bear's head rose.

The marten scurried back up the tree. The big head dropped and the bear, full-fed and lazy, drowsed in the sunlight. The tree shadows moved slowly and crept to engulf the bear and it rose and padded softly on through the forest. It was obeying its own instinctive calendar of habit, moving on the periodic four-day feeding march that took it out of the valley on a wide swing and return through the thirty-seven miles of its mountain-bound range.

July

The man strode up the stretch of parkland that edged the forest and led to the valley entrance. The late afternoon sun was full in his face. Behind him the burro trotted obediently, weighted by the big pack, whose new canvas covering gleamed white in the sunlight. Where the parkland leveled to enter the valley he stopped and turned to look back the way he had come, down the long rolling forested slope sliced by the stream gorge and up and over the first high ridge beyond. Satisfied at last that no one followed, he turned again and led the burro up the valley and across the green carpet to his camp in the spruce and juniper fringe. Everything there was as he had left it eight days before. But in the soft ground by the pool he found the big five-toed tracks crossing the stream toward his camp and going back again. He looked across the valley and up. The steep sideslope curving to the high rock buttress was splendid in the late sunlight and the overhanging rock and the ledge two hundred yards above the valley floor shone rust-red and gray against the green around them. A hawk floated in the air above the scattered clinging trees. There was no other sign of life. He strode back to his camp and began unpacking the burro.

Far to the eastward, over the mountain barrier, where the rude cabins and tents marred the bank of the stream bed, men talked to the keeper of the tarpaulined store and bar, worrying again the worn questions of four days about the one who had returned with his burro and bought supplies and shaken bright flakes out of a leather pouch in payment and disappeared again into the western heights. Already the legend was growing. He had made a rich strike. He was scooping dust out of rich silt pockets by the handful. He had unlimited wealth in dust and nuggets cached in his mountain hideout. The voice of a lean man with narrow hatchet face gashed by a thin-lipped mouth was tinged with bitterness as he told of his failure in following the boot and hoofmark traces into the mountains. A trail that well hidden must have been deliberately cloaked to cover its destination. The talk warmed and eyes glittered and the storekeeper did good business over his hewn-log bar.

Twice in the night the man woke, alert and rising to sitting position on his bed of boughs. There was no sound beyond the barrier of logs with which he had closed the open end of his shelter except an occasional soft movement of the burro in the narrow high-poled enclosure he had built for it. In the morning there were no new tracks. It was the same the next night and the next and early during the night after that thunder echoed through the mountains and lightning laced down through the peaks and enough rain fell in the valley to dampen the ground and renew it for fresh writing by any living thing that walked it. In the morning the man took the rifle and made another thorough circuit of the valley. He found no fresh signs, no five-toed tracks except what remained of the old after the erasing action of the rain. But in the moist sand by the stream where it eddied around rolled rocks well below the pool, he found other tracks, split-hooved, deeply indented. He studied these a long moment. He followed them along the stream and when they faded into the firm sod he kept on down the valley. His stride, long for the length of his legs, gnawed steadily into distance.

Half an hour later he was skirting the vast rock buttress, pausing often to scan the sweep of slope opening below him. He was well around, out of sight of the valley entrance, when he saw the elk, three of them, more than a mile away, on the edge of the parkland that slipped abruptly into the jack pine forest. Patient and steady, he began the long approach, angling down the slope to put the light wind directly in his face.

Far ahead where the forest dipped into a deep ravine, a thin column of smoke floated upward from the inside hollow of the shattered stump of a long dead pine. The slow fire, legacy of the lightning, glowed faintly as it ate into the punklike wood. It edged through a split in the old bark and little flames began to flicker along the side of the stump. It worked down and began to creep through the carpet of brown needles. It crept to the tiny outstretched dried twigs of the branch ends of a fallen tree and moved hungrily along them, reaching for the more solid wood.

The man was on his hands and knees, lifting the rifle carefully and setting it down gently with each forward movement of his right hand. He crawled to the top of a slight rise and lay flat to peer over. He was within rifle-shot of the elk. He eased the gun forward and let the sights sink down on the closest of the three. It stood quartering away from him and he aimed a bit behind and below the high foreshoulder and squeezed the trigger. He saw his elk leap a fraction of a second before the others and the three of them swirl and melt like sudden swift shifting shadows into the forest. He rose and went forward and followed. He was well in among the trees when he found the first blood drops, spattered and dark from internal bleeding. He lengthened his stride to follow the trace deeper into the forest. Forty minutes later, winded from climbing over and around down timber, he jumped the wounded elk out of a bushed hollow and his bullet, fired almost without aiming in the instant reflex of long experience, broke the animal's neck as it strove with flagging strength to leap away.

Down the slope, farther into the thick of the forest, the great bear prowled, sniffing for rotted logs among a tangle of fallen trees. It heard the second shot, faint yet distinct, a sound foreign and unknown. The big body stopped moving and the big head, unacquainted with fear in any form, rose and turned toward the sound. The bear waited, listening, then the head lowered and the long straight foreclaws sank into the outer shell of a log and, seeming without effort, ripped it open. The tongue, surprisingly small in the big mouth, licked quickly at the scurrying insects and slowed to take the sluggish wriggling white grubs.

The man worked steadily with his knife, quartering the elk carcass. He had already bled and dressed it. He lifted one of the forequarters, testing the weight, and set it aside. He began to cut poles on which to hang the remaining quarters until he could return with the burro. The small of his back ached from bending over and he straightened to rest it, and as his head came up he caught the first faint tang in the air. His body stiffened and the tiny premonitions running through him tightened into awareness. Smoke. Smoke drifting over the forest ceiling and filtering down fine tendrils that could elude the eyes but not the nose.

The man stood motionless, testing the breeze. It stirred gently, barely whispering through the branches above him. Disregarding the rest of the meat, he hoisted the one forequarter to a shoulder and steadied it with one hand and took the rifle with the other. He started at a right angle to the direction of the breeze, straight up the slope, the shortest path to the edge of the forest and the open parkland. Steadily he hammered on and the breeze freshened and talked in the branches and smoke began weaving among the tree trunks from the left. He angled toward the right, still climbing, and the smoke thickened, seeming to come from ahead as well as from the left, and at last he stopped, listening between the labored rush of his own breathing. The breeze strengthened and was a wind sighing high overhead and faint and far he could hear, not so much heard as sensed, the sullen roar of the racing fire. Around him he could fairly feel the hurrying of panic, the small life of the forest moving, unseen but known, past him down the slope. A deer bounded out of the smoke and saw him and swerved and was gone. He lowered his shoulder and the meat slid to the ground and without hesitation he turned and struck down the slope.

The smoke thickened and the light dimmed strangely and the roar rose until it was clearly audible and a high crackling breaking over it, and in a short while he was running, using his free hand to help him vault fallen logs, stumbling often and driving downward. The ground leveled and the trees ended and he broke through bushes and tripped full length into the shallow shore waters of a lake. The rifle leaped from his hand and disappeared beneath the surface and he scrambled for it. But the water deepened suddenly a few feet out and he floundered, with his chest heaving for air. He struggled back to the shallow edge and stood quietly while his lungs eased their frantic labor. Smoke rolled around him and he kneeled to keep his head close to the water and the layer of clear air just above it. Fire flared on the rim of the forest to the right and moved toward him and the heat grew until it drove him into the deeper water. He stood stretched upward with his head alone above the surface and looked out over the lake through the rolling smoke clouds. Fifty yards from shore a huge rock showed, humping out of the water like the low ridged back of some vast immobile beast. He swam slowly to it, fighting the drag of his clothes and boots, and crawled up on it and lay flat, while his tired muscles jumped and knotted and relaxed to rest.

The man lay on the rock and watched the fire work its way along the shore. He saw flames spire swiftly up one tree and leap to the next and sometimes, driven by the surge of their own tremendous draft, lunge to engulf several trees at once. The roar of the burning drowned all possible other sound. It was nothing heard, little more than a slight prickling on the back of his neck, that turned his eyes to the water past the other end of the rock. Only the broad head showed, with the muzzle cutting the water, as the great bear swam toward the rock. Quietly the man slipped into the water, stretching out in it with one hand holding to the stone while the other took the knife from its sheath on his belt. Silent in the water, he saw the bear's head rise over the rock opposite him, not more than twenty feet away, the forepaws stretch for footing, the massive shoulders emerge into view. He watched the bear turn broadside and shake and send the drops spattering clear across the rock. He watched it settle on its haunches, facing the flaming shoreline, and let its forepaws slide forward until the broad belly rested on the rock and the big head sank on them. He moved cautiously to look out over the rest of the lake. Through the clear area just over the surface he saw that it was almost ringed with fire and there was no other haven showing above water. He turned his head back to the rock and his body stiffened. The bear was looking at him. Its head was raised and swung toward him and the small eyes watched. His knees began to flex under him for a swift thrust outward from the rock but the bear remained motionless and while he waited, taut in tenseness, he saw the big mouth open and stretch in a yawn and the white of the great teeth and the lips drawing lazily back and the muzzle crinkling. The jaws closed and the head swung away and dropped on the forepaws again.

The hot air, uncomfortable but not unendurable, beat against the man's face and the chill of the water sank into his body. Cautiously he reached and put the knife between his teeth and placed both hands on the rock and began to draw himself forward and up on it. The bear's head rose and swung toward him and the small eyes watched. He waited and the bear did not move and he inched forward until at last he was on his hands and knees on the rock. Slowly he shifted position until he was sitting cross-legged, ready for an instant scrambling push striking into the water. The bear watched and when he was settled the big head swung straight again and sank down. Gradually the man's muscles softened and the instant alertness eased out of them. The hot air dried his clothes, and the fingers holding the knife now in his right hand relaxed. The smoke clouds rolled and made a strange unnatural dusk and the fire roared through it along the shore. The man's back and buttocks ached with the strain of his position on the hard rock. Slowly he shifted again until he was stretched full length on his side with his face toward the bear and his head pillowed on his left arm. The bear's ears twitched upright but the big head did not move and in a moment the ears eased limp again. The heat in the air lessened slightly and the fire roared dwindling along the shore. Far off it reached the edge of the gorge of the stream running out of the valley and sought to leap across and failed and fell back and was content with the timber it had taken, held now within the limits of the ravine where it had started behind this and the open parkland above and the gorge cutting down the long slope ahead of it and the beginnings of the open rocky climb below where the first ridge of the eastward mountain barrier thrust upward in the new ascent.

The sun, hidden behind the smoke clouds, dropped behind the westward heights and the remaining flames around the lake sent weird lights dancing in the murky dark over the water. The man's eyes closed and opened abruptly and closed again and at last remained closed. The wind died and the smoke trailed away in wisps and the high stars wheeled in the clearing sky above the two silent figures pinpointed together on their rock in the heart of the soaring immensity of the timeless mountains.

The man woke suddenly in the gray dawn of the light before sunrise. He had rolled over in his sleep on his back and the knife had slipped from his opened hand. As awareness flooded him he fought the stiffness in his muscles to turn quickly on his side and fumble for the knife handle. The seeking fingers halted before they found it. The rock stretched away from him empty and open to the sky. The bear was gone. He pushed to his feet and stooped to take the knife and stood straight. The sound of splashing water turned his head toward the near shore. The bear was emerging from the lake onto a short sandy spit. Against the background of rising slope with charred trunks above blackened floor and thin wisps of smoke still spiraling lazily, it was a miracle of enduring life, enormous and indomitable in the half-light in defiance of the barren desolation. It started inland and drew back with quick mincing steps. There were hot embers under the ashes and flames ready to break forth flickering strong in many places at the push of any breeze. It started to the right along the shore, picking its way in the shallow water. It moved along the shoreline three hundred yards and more and turned inland and disappeared almost in the instant of turning.

The man slipped into the water and swam to the sandy spit. Working from there he made systematic forays into the deeper water until he found the rifle. He washed away the bottom muck and broke it open to blow the barrel and firing chamber clean. Shivering in the first rays of the sun, he moved along the shoreline as the bear had done, stepping slowly but swinging his arms vigorously to warm his muscles. Where the bear had turned he came on a narrow gorge that sliced down the slope to the lake edge with rocky walls guarding a small stream. The fire had done little damage here because there was little to burn and it had leaped over to race on around the lake. The man started the climb, still traveling slowly, and he nodded to himself when he came on the big tracks in soft spots among the bottom stones.

Hidden in an aspen thicket a short way out on the parkland above the stricken forest, the great bear stood over the carcass of a whitetail doe that had fallen in the flight of fear into the upper gorge and broken its neck. The bear had dragged the carcass to the open of the parkland and into the thicket. The big head lifted and the small eyes peered through the thicket. The man was passing, sixty yards away. A low rumble sounded in the bear's throat, soft and deep, not audible to the man and not meant to be. He strode on with the tireless stride of a man long used to the mountains. The bear watched him, its head turning slowly to follow his passing, and when his figure grew small in the distance the big head dropped to feed again.

August

In the clear light of early morning the man stood by the pool and looked at the shallow pan in his hands. The bottom of it was almost covered with the dull gleaming flakes. The pool silt had become richer as he worked deeper into it. He took the leather pouch from a pocket and shook the flakes into it. This was his third panning of the morning and already the pouch was full. He went to his camp and behind it among the trees and stopped by a flat stone. He heaved at the stone to raise one side and braced it against one leg while he set a piece of stout branch to prop it up. In a hollow underneath lay a five-pound salt bag filled to plumpness and another partly filled. He emptied the pouch into the second bag and lowered the stone into place. He went back by the pool and stood slapping the pan gently against his thigh while he looked over the valley. The air was fresh on his face and mystic cloud shadows wandered on the mountain wall at the head of the valley. He dropped the pan on the sandbar and took the rifle from the grassbank and strode off down the valley with the sun warm in his face. He was close to the valley entrance, where the big boulders of an ancient rockslide had rolled out to become bedded in the ageless sod, when he met the bear, suddenly, coming toward him around one of the rocks.

The bear stopped and the man stopped, thirty feet apart. Slowly the man swung up the rifle so that his left hand could grip the barrel and his right forefinger slipped around the trigger. The bear watched him and the low rumble, soft and deep, formed in its throat. Slowly the man stepped to the left, moving in a half-circle, always facing the bear, yielding the right of way. The bear watched him, turning its head to follow him until its neck was arched around. When he completed the half-circle the man turned, deliberately turned from the bear, and his will clamped hard on his muscles to hold them to a steady walk away. When he had traveled some forty feet he looked back. The bear had gone forward on its own way and its big, ridiculously tiny-tailed rump was toward him as it overturned scattered stones and sniffed for the scuttling insects.

Five hours later, in the early afternoon, the man returned to his camp, back-packing the dressed carcass of a small whitetail buck. Across the valley the great bear lay on the ledge and watched him. He could see it there, a dark shape on the stone, while he skinned the deer and pegged out the hide for drying. He built a big fire of dry wood and while he waited for it to burn down to glowing embers he began cutting the meat into strips. He looked across the valley and saw the bear rise and disappear into the dark recess of the crevice and he nodded to himself. He knew its habits now. Always when it was in this part of its range it fed at night and in the early morning hours. By mid-morning it was lying on the ledge. When the sun was high overhead, sliding into the afternoon slant, it sought the cool darkness of the rock depth.

The man raised his poles in a rack over the fire and hung the strips of meat on it. He piled green wood on the fire and retreated from the smoke and sat resting with his back against a tree looking out across the valley. The dropping sun glinted on the pan lying on the sandbar but the man remained still against his tree, rising at long intervals to replenish his fire.

The stream gathered speed as it left the valley and skipped in stony steps down past the edge of the burned-out forest where new green was beginning to rise above the blackened ground. It dropped, gaining momentum, into the deepening gorge that took it farther down and where it raced and whirled in rock pools and raced on. The man stood on the low cliff edge overlooking the gorge. Thirty-five feet below him the great bear lay beside the stream. Its new coat was lengthening and a pale silvery cast was beginning to touch the tips of the thick-grown hairs. It lay limp and relaxed on the pebble strand. Suddenly a forepaw darted and flipped a fat trout flashing through the air and the bear leaped from its lying position to seize the fish as it landed flopping a dozen feet away. Lazily the bear fed, then wandered up the stream to where a smooth rock slanted straight into the water. Standing at the top of the slant, it gave a small bounce and went forward on its belly on the rock with legs outstretched and slid splashing into the stream. The man leaned over the cliff to watch and a soundless chuckle shook him. Lazily the bear climbed again to the top of the smooth rock and rolled over on its back and slid down, tail first, thick legs waving. Its rump struck the water with a spattering smack and the chuckle in the man grew into sound. The bear whirled and rose in the water and looked up. It looked away and inspected the opposite bank in plain pretense that the man was not there. Its head dropped and it shuffled away down the gorge and out of sight around the first turn.

Farther to the eastward, far over the mountain barrier, only a few men worked by the shallow pools that were all that remained of the stream flowing there in the spring and early summer. Most of the cabins were sinking into ruins and only a few tents remained. Under the tarpaulin roof of the store and bar several men argued the failure of prospecting trips into the surrounding country. The storekeeper, short and thick with deep burnt-out eyes in a round bullet head, stood at one end of his bar listening to the low voice of the hatchet-faced man with the thin-lipped mouth. He looked about at his scantily stocked shelves and shrugged his shoulders. Greed and bitterness and discouragement crawled through the mining camp.

Quiet against the sky the man stood on the first ridge outside the valley and saw, small in the vast panorama below him, the great bear stalking an elk. It slipped upwind along a dry gulch and crept out to the shelter of a scrub thicket. The elk grazed closer and the bear broke from the thicket. The elk wheeled into flight, legs driving with the strength of terror. But the bear overtook it and was alongside and reared and a paw flashed in a blur of motion beyond vision and struck the elk's head sideways and snapped the neck like a twig breaking. There had been stillness, a flash of movement, then stillness again, the motionless body of the elk on the grass and the bear standing beside it. The man watched the bear feed slowly then drag the carcass into the gulch and scoop a hole in the soft shale and pull the carcass into this and begin covering it. A small grim smile touched his lips. He turned and started down the other side of the ridge to hunt in another part of the wilderness empire he shared with the great bear.

The chill of the night lingered, gradually giving way to the sun's warmth. The morning air was crystal in its distinct clarity. The man stood by the pool and looked at the pan in his hands. There were only a few scattered flakes in it. The pool was almost worked out. He started to walk along the stream, studying its flow and occasional silt banks. His steps slowed and at last stopped and he looked out over the valley. New color was showing on the clumps of low bushes that dotted the valley floor. Berries were ripening there and along the climbing sides of the valley. Far by the opposite slope he saw the bear rise out of the bushes, settling back on its haunches like a big sitting squirrel, stripping berries into its mouth with its long foreclaws. He strode back to his camp and tossed the pan to one side and lifted the flat stone. Three full salt bags lay there now and a fourth partly filled. He emptied the leather pouch into the fourth bag and lowered the stone in place. Rifle in hand he wandered out through his side of the valley, tasting berries along the way.

September

The green of the valley was changing, darker with a brown cast in barely discernible splotches. The thin cutting edge of fall was invading the air. Among the trees behind the man's camp the flat stone lay undisturbed with grass blades curling over it. The camp itself was neat and orderly. Firewood was stacked in a long pile. A little to one side the pan lay, no longer glinting bright, spotted with dirt and rust. Where the tree fringe abutted the open of the valley the man sat, cross-legged in the sun. Across his lap was a deerskin, tanned with lye from wood ashes and worked to fairly smooth flexibility. Carefully he sliced into the leather, cutting doubled patterns for moccasins to replace his worn boots.

Across the valley, working along the base of the slope and up a short way, the great bear was digging for ground squirrels, ripping into the soil several feet with half a dozen powerful strokes and lying flat on its belly for the final reaching, scraping thrust. The increasing richness of the fur with its silver tipping shone in the clear light. Alternately the man bent to his cutting and raised his head to watch the bear. Suddenly, with the suddenness of decision, he rose and strode back among the spruce and juniper and about, until he found a level space between the trees to his liking. Here he laid out a rough rectangle, scratching the lines with his boot heel. He marked off space inside for a bunk and another rectangle, small and against one end, for a fireplace. He studied his design and nodded to himself and looked around, estimating the standing timber close by. He strode to his shelter and crawled to the low end to inspect what remained of his staple supplies. He came out carrying a small pack and closed the open end of the shelter with its log barrier. He strode to the flat stone and filled the leather pouch from one of the bags. A few moments later he was striding eastward out of the valley with the rifle in one hand, the lead rope of the burro in the other.

A cool wind whipped down the valley, whispering of the winter still hidden far up in the soaring peaks. It moved over the changing green that was darker with the brown splotches plainer and spreading. It moved out the valley entrance and down the rolling slope where the man strode steadily forward, facing straight into it. He was leading a loaded packhorse now and the burdened burro trotted behind. At the crest of the slope he stopped and searched his back trail for long minutes. His head rose higher and his stride lengthened as he passed through the valley entrance and the horse and the burro followed.

Three miles away on the ridge overlooking the last slope, ten feet back in the timber that topped the ridge, two men stood in the tree shadows and watched the three figures entering the valley. The taller of the two, lean even in his thick mackinaw jacket, had a narrow hatchet face gashed by a thin-lipped mouth. The other, shorter but bulking thick from shoulders to hips, had burnt-out eyes in a round bullet head. The thin-lipped one snapped his fingers and nodded to the other. Together they went back deeper into the timber and mounted the two horses there and rode out and down the ridge, circling to the right toward the high shoulder of climbing rock that would give them a view out over the valley.

Restless on its rock ledge, the great bear lay on the stone and watched the empty camp across the valley. Its ears twitched and the big head rose and swung to the right. It saw the man entering the valley and the horse and burro following. It saw the man stop and look toward it and wave his arms and start forward again. The low rumbling, soft and deep, rolled out from the ledge and died away in the afternoon wind. Quietly the bear watched the man stride toward his camp and begin untying the packs. Quietly it rose and padded on the stone into the darkness of the crevice.

Vigor flowed through the man. The afternoon air of his valley flooded his muscles with strength. His ax leaped in his hands and he felled four trees of the right foundation size and lopped away the branches and cut the logs to the lengths he wanted and notched them. Using the ax handle for a measure he took three pieces of rope and used the three-four-five rule to square the corners as he fitted the logs together. As he straightened from checking the fourth joint he saw first the heavy boots, and as his eyes swept upward he saw the small wicked muzzle of the rifle bearing on his belly and the thin-lipped gash of a mouth in the narrow face.

The two men wasted no time. They asked their questions and when he did not answer they roped him to a thick tree. They searched through his camp and came back by him and built a fire and when this was blazing strong they took his rifle and emptied the magazine and laid it with the barrel reaching into the flames and waited for the metal to heat.

The man stood tight against the tree and the pale hazel of his eyes was startling against the dead bloodless brown of his broad wind-burned face. He stared out over the valley and his gaze moved upward and stopped two hundred yards up the opposite slope, and the beginning of living color crept into his face. The muscles along his jaw were ridged hard and he waited, cautious in his cunning, until the hot steel was close to his flesh before he spoke. He spoke quickly and bobbed his head toward the far slope. The two others turned. They saw the ledge and the uneven dark outline of the crevice. They spoke briefly together and the burnt-eyed one swung abruptly and started across the valley and the thin-lipped one sat hump-kneed on the ground and picked up his rifle and set it across his lap.

The man tight against the tree and the thin-lipped one hump-kneed on the ground watched the other move out and across the valley floor. They saw him stop at the base of the opposite side and look around for the trail and find it. They saw him start up, hurrying now, and reach the ledge almost running and disappear into the crevice.

Time passed and they watched, each in his own intentness, and nothing moved across the way. The ledge under its overhanging rock slept in its own quietness in the afternoon sun. The thin-lipped one rose and unloosened the rope holding the man to the tree and ordered him ahead and prodded him in the small of the back with the rifle. The man led and the thin-lipped one followed and they started across the valley floor.

Deep in the crevice darkness the great bear stood over the crumpled body. The big head with the small eyes, red-rimmed now, swung slowly from side to side. The sound of running steps had brought it from sleep into instant alertness. The forward leap out of the inner darkness into the dimness near the crevice entrance and the incredibly swift slashing stroke of forepaw had been instinctive reactions to the challenging affront of invasion. Silently it had dragged the body back into the protective darkness and stepped over it, facing the entrance. The scent of the body, familiar yet unfamiliar, rose in its nostrils and caution at an experience never before known held it waiting in the darkness, listening for further sound out beyond the rock opening.

Striding steadily, the man led the way up the trail. His face was a fixed mask and his muscles bunched in tight tension. When the bear broke from the crevice, red-rimmed eyes blinking for swift focus in the sunlight, the man leaped sideways off the trail and down the steep slope, falling and rolling over the sharp rocks and hard against the trunk of a sturdy spruce. He scrambled to his feet and jumped for the first limb and swung his legs in to the trunk and began climbing.

Above him on the trail the thin-lipped one swung up the rifle and fired and the bullet thudded into the bear's left shoulder and scraped the bone and bore back along the side under the skin. In a silent rush the great bear drove down the trail and the thin-lipped one screamed and turned to run and a crashing forepaw crushed his spine forward into his breastbone and raked tearing down through the muscles of his back. The big jaws closed on the already lifeless body and shook it and flung it twenty feet away.

Close against the trunk, the man peered through the thick branches of the spruce. Below him the great bear quartered the ground like a huge dog on a hunt, moving with a silent flowing deadliness, raising its head often to test the wind. It limped slightly, favoring its left foreleg, and the recurrent pain from the flesh wound in the shoulder swelled the steady rage within and brightened the reddened rims of the eyes. It worked back along the trail near the valley floor and looked across at the man's camp. Abruptly it swung and with steady purpose went up the trail to the ledge and passed along the slopeside and faded into the tangled growth near the head of the valley.

Safe in his spruce, the man watched it go and disappear from his sight. He waited. At last he climbed to the ground and scrambled up to the trail and grabbed the rifle there. Quickly he ejected the spent cartridge shell and pumped another cartridge into the firing chamber. Quickly he checked the magazine and saw it was almost full. Cautious and alert he slipped down and started across the valley.

The packhorse and burro grazed by the camp, quiet now after the brief startling from the single shot across the way. In the fringe of trees behind them and around the camp nothing stirred except the wind whispering its endless murmur through the evergreen branches. As the man approached, downwind, he stopped often to peer forward and swing his head to scan the whole long fringe of trees, searching with his eyes every possible cover. It was the drumming of the horse's hooves as it pounded to the length of its picket rope and jerked around, strangling, that whirled him toward the sound. The great bear streaked toward him out of thicket shadow and he fired in the instant, instinctively—aiming as rapidly as he could pump the gun. The first shot bored into the junction of neck and right shoulder and shattered the bone there and the second smashed into the massive breast and ripped back through the lungs. The great bear drove ahead, uneven in bounding stride with a deep coughing tearing its throat, and the third shot struck through the mouth and back into the spine. The man leaped aside and the bear's rush took it past and it crumpled forward to the ground. The man stood by the bear's body and stared down. It was smaller with the life gone. The muscles of the man's shoulders shook a little and he swung his head slowly from one side to the other and the flat planes of his face were hard as the rock formations ringing the valley.

He stood by the rectangle of notched logs a long time. Quietly he turned and went to the flat stone and took the plump salt bags from under it and carried them over by his shelter and began to prepare his packs. Half an hour later he strode across the valley floor and the packhorse and the burro followed. The sun, dropping below the far peaks, was behind him. The chill rising wind beat against his back. Unbelievably small in the vastness he strode out of the valley, and with him went a new loneliness and a sense of something lost.

Eiger Dreams

From Eiger Dreams

BY JON KRAKAUER

Before his name became a more-or-less permanent fixture on bestseller lists with books such as *Into the Wild* and *Into Thin Air*, Jon Krakauer did a wonderful collection of articles for The Lyons Press based on his early mountain-climbing experiences around the world. "Eiger Dreams," the title piece of the book, is based on the notorious Alpine peak that has challenged climbers like Krakauer for decades—and killed many of them. Even though he does not take us as high as he did in *Into Thin Air* when he carried us to the top of Everest, this trip with Jon Krakauer will convince you that being an "armchair mountaineer" isn't such a bad deal after all.

★   ★   ★   ★   ★

In the early moments of *The Eiger Sanction,* Clint Eastwood saunters into the dimly lit headquarters of C-2 to find out who he is supposed to assassinate next. Dragon, the evil albino who runs the CIA-like organization, tells Eastwood that although the agency does not yet have the target's name, they have discovered that "our man will be involved in a climb in the Alps this summer. And we know which mountain he will climb: the Eiger."

Eastwood has no trouble guessing which route—"The North Face, of course"—and allows that he is familiar with that particular alpine wall: "I tried to climb it twice, it tried to kill me twice . . . Look, if the target's trying to climb the Eiger, chances are my work will be done for me."

The problem with climbing the North Face of the Eiger is that in addition to getting up 6,000 vertical feet of crumbling limestone and black ice, one must climb over some formidable mythology. The trickiest moves on any climb

184

are the mental ones, the psychological gymnastics that keep terror in check, and the Eiger's grim aura is intimidating enough to rattle anyone's poise. The epics that have taken place on the Nordwand have been welded into the world's collective unconscious in grisly detail by more than two thousand newspaper and magazine articles. The dust jackets of books with titles such as *Eiger: Wall of Death,* remind us that the Nordwand "has defeated hundreds and killed forty-four . . . Those who fell were found—sometimes years later—dessicated and dismembered. The body of one Italian mountaineer hung from its rope, unreachable but visible to the curious below, for three years, alternately sealed into the ice sheath of the wall and swaying in the winds of summer."

The history of the mountain resonates with the struggles of such larger-than-life figures as Buhl, Bonatti, Messner, Rebuffat, Terray, Haston, and Harlin, not to mention Eastwood. The names of the landmarks on the face—the Hinterstoisser Traverse, the Ice Hose, the Death Bivouac, the White Spider—are household words among both active and armchair alpinists from Tokyo to Buenos Aires; the very mention of these places is enough to make any climber's hands turn clammy. The rockfall and avalanches that rain continuously down the Nordwand are legendary. So is the heavy weather: Even when the skies over the rest of Europe are cloudless, violent storms brew over the Eiger, like those dark clouds that hover eternally above Transylvanian castles in vampire movies.

Needless to say, all this makes the Eiger North Face one of the most widely coveted climbs in the world.

The Nordwand was first climbed in 1938, and since then it has had more than 150 ascents, among them a solo climb in 1983 that took all of five and a half hours, but don't try to tell Staff Sergeant Carlos J. Ragone, U.S.A.F., that the Eiger has become a scenic cruise. Last fall, Marc Twight and I were sitting outside our tents above Kleine Scheidegg, the cluster of hotels and restaurants at the foot of the Eiger, when Ragone strolled into camp under a bulging pack and announced that he had come to climb the Nordwand. In the discussion that ensued, we learned that he was AWOL from an air base in England. His commanding officer had refused to grant Ragone a leave when the C.O. learned what Ragone intended to do with it, but Ragone had left anyway. "Trying this climb will probably cost me my stripes," he said, "but on the other hand, if I get up the mother they might promote me."

Unfortunately, Ragone didn't get up the mother. September had gone down in the Swiss record books as the wettest since 1864, and the face was in atrocious condition, worse even than usual, plastered with rime and loaded with unstable snow. The weather forecast was for continuing snow and high wind. Two partners who were supposed to rendezvous with Ragone backed out because of the nasty conditions. Ragone, however, was not about to be deterred by the mere lack of company. On October 3 he started up the climb by himself. On the lower reaches of the face, near the top of a buttress known as the First Pillar, he made a misstep. His ice axes and crampons sheared out of the rotten ice, and Ragone found himself airborne. Five hundred vertical feet later he hit the ground.

Incredibly, his landing was cushioned by the accumulation of powder snow at the base of the wall, and Ragone was able to walk away from the fall with no more damage than bruises and a crimp in his back. He hobbled out of the blizzard into the *Bahnhof buffet,* asked for a room, went upstairs, and fell asleep. At some point during his tumble to the bottom of the wall he had lost an ice axe and his wallet, which contained all his identification and money. In the morning, when it was time to settle his room bill, all Ragone could offer for payment was his remaining ice axe. The *Bahnhof* manager was not amused. Before slinking out of Scheidegg, Ragone stopped by our camp to ask if we were interested in buying what was left of his climbing gear. We told him that we'd like to help him out, but we happened to be a little strapped for cash ourselves. In that case, Ragone, seeing as he didn't think he was going to feel like climbing again for a while, said he'd just give the stuff to us. "That mountain is a bastard," he spat, glancing up at the Nordwand one last time. With that, he limped off through the snow toward England to face the wrath of his C.O.

Like Ragone, Marc and I had come to Switzerland to climb the Nordwand. Marc, eight years my junior, sports two earrings in his left ear and a purple haircut that would do a punk rocker proud. He is also a red-hot climber. One of the differences between us was that Marc wanted very badly to climb the Eiger, while I wanted very badly only to have climbed the Eiger. Marc, understand, is at that age when the pituitary secretes an overabundance of those hormones that mask the subtler emotions, such as fear. He tends to confuse things like life-or-death climbing with fun. As a friendly gesture, I planned to let Marc lead all the most fun pitches on the Nordwand.

Unlike Ragone, Marc and I were not willing to go up on the wall until conditions improved. Due to the Nordwand's concave architecture, whenever it snows, few places on the wall are not exposed to avalanches. In summer, if things go well, it will typically take a strong party two days, maybe three, to climb the Nordwand. In the fall, with the shorter days and icier conditions, three to four days is the norm. To maximize our chances of getting up and down the Eiger without unpleasant incident, we figured we needed at least four consecutive days of good weather: one day to allow the buildup of new snow to avalanche off, and three to climb the face and descend the mountain's west flank.

Each morning during our stay at Scheidegg we would crawl out of our tents, plow down through the snowdrifts to the *Bahnhof,* and phone Geneva and Zurich to get a four-day weather forecast. Day after day, the word was the same: Continuing unsettled weather, with rain in the valleys and snow in the mountains. We could do nothing but curse and wait, and the waiting was awful. The Eiger's mythic weight bore down especially hard during the idle days, and it was easy to think too much.

One afternoon, for diversion, we took a ride on the train up to the *Jungfraujoch,* a cog railroad that runs from Kleine Scheidegg to a saddle high on the Eiger-Jungfrau massif. This turned out to be a mistake. The railway traverses the bowels of the Eiger by way of a tunnel that was blasted through the mountain in 1912. Midway up the tracks there is an intermediate station with a series of huge windows that look out from the vertical expanse of the Nordwand.

The view from these windows is so vertiginous that barf bags—the same kind they put in airplane seat-pockets—had been placed on the windowsills. Clouds swirled just beyond the glass. The black rock of the Nord-wand, sheathed in frost feathers and sprouting icicles in the places where it overhung, fell away dizzyingly into the mists below. Small avalanches hissed past. If our route turned out to be anything like what we were seeing, we were going to find ourselves in serious trouble. Climbing in such conditions would be desperate if not impossible.

On the Eiger, constructions of the imagination have a way of blurring with reality, and the Eigerwand station was a little too much like a scene from a recurring dream I've been having for years in which I'm fighting for my life in a storm on some endless climb when I come upon a door set into the mountainside. The doorway leads into a warm room with a fireplace and tables of steaming food and a comfortable bed. Usually, in this dream, the door is locked.

A quarter-mile down the tunnel from the big windows of the midway station there is in fact a small wooden door—always unlocked—that opens out onto the Nordwand. The standard route up the wall passes very near this door, and more than one climber has used it to escape from a storm.

Such an escape, however, poses hazards of its own. In 1981, Mugs Stump, one of America's most accomplished alpinists, popped in through the door after a storm forced him to abort a solo attempt on the wall and started walking toward the tunnel entrance, about a mile away. Before he could reach daylight, he met a train coming up the tracks. The guts of the Eiger are hard black limestone that makes for tough tunneling, and when the tunnel was constructed the builders didn't make it any wider than they had to. It quickly became evident to Stump that the space between the cars and the tunnel walls was maybe a foot, give or take a few inches. The Swiss take great pride in making their trains run on time, and it also became evident that this particular engineer was not about to foul up his schedule simply because some damn climber was on the tracks. All Stump could do was suck in his breath, press up against the rock, and try to make his head thin. He survived the train's passing, but the experience was as harrowing as any of the close scrapes he'd had on the outside of the mountain.

During our third week of waiting for the weather to break, Marc and I rode the train down into Wengen and Lauterbrunnen to find relief from the snow. After a pleasant day of taking in the sights and sipping *Rugenbrau,* we managed to miss the last train up to Scheidegg and were faced with a long walk back to the tents. Marc set out at a blistering pace to try to make camp before dark, but I decided I was in no hurry to get back under the shadow of the Eiger and into the snow zone, and that another beer or two would make the hike easier to endure.

It was dark by the time I left Wengen, but the Oberland trails, though steep (the Swiss, it seems, do not believe in switchbacks) are wide, well maintained, and easy to follow. More important, on this path there were none of the electrified gates that Marc and I had encountered on a rainy night the week before (after missing another train) while walking from Grindelwald to Scheidegg. Such gates are installed to curtail bovine trespassers and are impossible to see in the dark after a few beers. They strike a five-foot nine-inch body at an uncommonly sensitive point precisely six inches below the belt, and with one's feet clad in soggy Nikes they deliver a jolt of sufficient voltage to bring forth confessions to crimes not yet committed.

The walk from Wengen went without incident until I neared the treeline, when I began to hear an intermittent roar that sounded like someone goosing the throttle of a Boeing 747. The first gust of wind hit me when I rounded the shoulder of the Lauberhorn and turned toward Wengernalp. A blast came from out of nowhere and knocked me on my butt. It was the *foehn,* blowing down from the Eiger.

The *foehn* winds of the Bernese Oberland—cousin of the Santa Ana winds that periodically set Southern California on fire and the chinooks that roar down out of the Colorado Rockies—can generate stunning power. They are said to hold a disproportionate number of positive ions, and to make people crazy. "In Switzerland," Joan Didion writes in *Slouching Towards Bethlehem,* "the suicide rate goes up during the *foehn,* and in the courts of some Swiss cantons the wind is considered a mitigating circumstance for crime." The *foehn* figures prominently in Eiger lore. It is a dry, relatively warm wind, and as it melts the snow and ice on the Eiger it brings down terrible avalanches. Typically, immediately following a *foehnsturm* there will be a sharp freeze, glazing the wall with treacherous verglas. Many of the disasters on the Nordwand can be attributed directly to the *foehn;* in *The Eiger Sanction* it is a *foehn* that almost does Eastwood in.

It was all I could do to handle the *foehn* on the trail through the cow pastures. I shuddered to think what it would be like to be hit by one up on the Nordwand. The wind filled my eyes with grit and blew me off my feet over and over again. Several times I simply had to get down on my knees and wait for lulls between gusts. When I finally lurched through the door of the *Bahnhof* at Scheidegg, I found the place packed with railroad workers, cooks, maids, waitresses, and tourists who had become marooned by the storm. The gale raging outside had infected everybody in Scheidegg with some kind of weird, manic energy, and a riotous party was in full swing. In one corner people were dancing to a screaming jukebox, in another they were standing on the tables belting out German drinking songs; everywhere people were calling the waiter for more beer and schnapps.

I was about to join the fun when I spied Marc approaching with a wild look in his eyes. "Jon," he blurted out, "the tents are gone!"

"Hey, I don't really want to deal with it right now," I replied, trying to signal the waiter. "Let's just rent beds upstairs tonight and repitch the tents in the morning."

"No, no, you don't understand. They didn't just get knocked down, they fucking blew away. I found the yellow one about fifty yards away from where it had been, but the brown one is gone, man. I looked but I couldn't find it anywhere. It's probably down in Grindelwald by now."

The tents had been tied down to logs, cement blocks, and an ice screw driven securely into frozen turf. There had been at least two hundred pounds of food and gear inside them. It seemed impossible that they could have been carried away by the wind, but they had. The one that was missing had contained our sleeping bags, clothing, my climbing boots, the stove and pots, some food, God only knew what else. If we didn't find it, the weeks of waiting to climb the Nordwand were going to be in vain, so I zipped up my jacket and headed back out into the *foehnsturm.*

By sheer chance I found the tent a quarter-mile from where it had been pitched—drifted over, lying in the middle of the train tracks to Grindelwald. It was a tangled mess of shredded nylon and broken, twisted poles. After wrestling it back to the *Bahnhof,* we discovered that the stove had sprayed butane over everything, and a dozen eggs had coated our clothing and sleeping bags with a nasty, sulphurous slime, but it appeared that no important gear had been lost during the tent's tour of Scheidegg. We threw everything in a corner and returned to the party to celebrate.

The winds at Scheidegg that night were clocked at 170 kilometers per hour. In addition to laying waste to our camp, they knocked down the big telescope on the gift-shop balcony and blew a ski-lift gondola as big as a truck onto the tracks in front of the *Bahnhof.* At midnight, though, the gale petered out. The temperature plummeted, and by morning a foot of fresh powder had replaced the snowpack melted by the *foehn.* Nevertheless, when we called the weather station in Geneva, we were shocked to hear that an extended period of good weather would be arriving in a couple of days. "Sweet Jesus," I thought. "We're actually going to have to go up on the wall."

The sunshine came on October 8, along with a promise from the meteorologists that there would be no precipitation for at least five days. We gave the Nordwand the morning to slough off the post-*foehn* accumulation of snow, then hiked through crotch-deep drifts over to the base of the route, where we set up a hastily patched-together tent. We were in our sleeping bags early, but I was too scared to even pretend to sleep.

At 3 A.M., the appointed hour to start up the wall, it was raining and some major ice and rockfall was strafing the face. The climb was off. Secretly relieved, I went back to bed and immediately sank into a deep slumber. I awoke at 9 A.M. to the sound of birds chirping. The weather had turned perfect once again. Hurriedly, we threw our packs together. As we started up the Nordwand my stomach felt like a dog had been chewing on it all night.

We had been told by friends who had climbed the Nordwand that the first third of the standard route up the face is "way casual." It isn't, at least not under the conditions we found it. Although there were few moves that were technically difficult, the climbing was continuously insecure. A thin crust of ice lay over deep, unstable powder snow. It was easy to see how Ragone had fallen; it felt as though at any moment the snow underfoot was going to collapse. In places where the wall steepened, the snow cover thinned and our ice axes would ricochet off rock a few inches beneath the crust. It was impossible to find anchors of any kind in or under the rotting snow and ice, so for the first two thousand feet of the climb we simply left the ropes in the packs and "soloed" together.

Our packs were cumbersome and threatened to pull us over backward whenever we would lean back to search out the route above. We had made an effort to pare our loads down to the essentials, but Eiger terror had moved us to throw in extra food, fuel, and clothing in case we got pinned down by a storm, and enough climbing hardware to sink a ship. It had been difficult to decide what to take and what to leave behind. Marc eventually elected to bring along a Walkman and his two favorite tapes instead of a sleeping bag, reasoning that when the going got desperate, the peace of mind to be had by listening to the Dead Kennedys and the Angry Samoans would prove more valuable than staying warm at night.

At 4 P.M., when we reached the overhanging slab called the Rote Fluh, we were finally able to place some solid anchors, the first ones of the climb. The overhang offered protection from the unidentified falling objects that occasionally hummed past, so we decided to stop and bivouac even though there was more than an hour of daylight left. By digging out a long, narrow platform where the snow slope met the rock, we could lie in relative comfort, head-to-head, with the stove between us.

The next morning we got up at three and were away from our little ledge an hour before dawn, climbing by headlamp. A rope-length beyond the bivouac, Marc started leading up a pitch that had a difficulty rating of 5.4. Marc is a 5.12 climber, so I was alarmed when he began to mutter and his progress came to a halt. He tried moving left, and then right, but an eggshell-thin layer of crumbly ice over the vertical rock obscured whatever holds there might have been. Agonizingly slowly, he balanced his way upward a few inches at a time by hooking his crampon points and the picks of his axes on unseen limestone nubbins underneath the patina of rime. Five times he slipped, but caught himself each time after falling only a few feet.

Two hours passed while Marc thrashed around above me. The sun came up. I grew impatient. "Marc," I yelled, "if you don't want to lead this one, come on down and I'll take a shot at it." The bluff worked: Marc attacked the pitch with renewed determination and was soon over it. When I joined him at his belay stance, though, I was worried. It had taken us nearly three hours to climb eighty feet. There is more than eight thousand feet of climbing on the Nordwand (when all the traversing is taken into consideration), and much of it was going to be a lot harder than those eighty feet.

The next pitch was the infamous Hinterstoisser Traverse, a 140-foot end run around some unclimbable overhangs, and the key to gaining the upper part of the Nordwand. It was first climbed in 1936 by Andreas Hinterstoisser, whose lead across its polished slabs was a brilliant piece of climbing. But above the pitch he and his three companions were caught by a storm and forced to retreat. The storm, however, had glazed the traverse with verglas, and the climbers were unable to reverse its delicate moves. All four men perished. Since that disaster, climbers have always taken pains to leave a rope fixed across the traverse to ensure return passage.

We found the slabs of the Hinterstoisser covered with two inches of ice. Thin though it was, it was solid enough to hold our ice axes if we swung them gently. Additionally, an old, frayed fixed rope emerged intermittently from the glazing. By crabbing gingerly across the ice on our front points and shamelessly grabbing the old rope whenever possible, we got across the traverse without a hitch.

Above the Hinterstoisser, the route went straight up, past landmarks that had been the stuff of my nightmares since I was ten: the Swallow's Nest, the First Icefield, the Ice Hose. The climbing never again got as difficult as the pitch Marc had led just before the Hinterstoisser, but we were seldom able to get in any anchors. A slip by either of us would send us both to the bottom of the wall.

As the day wore on, I could feel my nerves beginning to unravel. At one point, while leading over crusty, crumbly vertical ice on the Ice Hose, I suddenly became overwhelmed by the fact that the only things preventing me from flying off into space were two thin steel picks sunk half an inch into a medium that resembled the inside of my freezer when it needs to be defrosted. I looked down at the ground more than three thousand feet below and felt dizzy, as if I were about to faint. I had to close my eyes and take a dozen deep breaths before I could resume climbing.

One 165-foot pitch past the Ice Hose brought us to the bottom of the Second Ice Field, a point slightly more than halfway up the wall. Above, the first protected place to spend the night would be the Death Bivouac, the ledge where Max Sedlmayer and Karl Mehringer had expired in a storm during the first attempt on the Nordwand in 1935. Despite its grim name, the Death Bivouac is probably the safest and most comfortable bivouac site on the face. To get to it, however, we still had to make an eighteen-hundred-foot rising traverse across the Second Ice Field, and then ascend several hundred devious feet more to the top of a buttress called the Flatiron.

It was 1 P.M. We had climbed only about fourteen hundred feet in the eight hours since we'd left our bivouac at the Rote Fluh. Even though the Second Ice Field looked easy, the Flatiron beyond it did not, and I had serious doubts that we could make the Death Bivouac—more than two thousand feet away—in the five hours of daylight that remained. If darkness fell before we reached the Death Bivouac, we would be forced to spend the night without a ledge, in a place that would be completely exposed to the avalanches and rocks that spilled down from the most notorious feature on the Nordwand: the ice field called the White Spider.

"Marc," I said, "we should go down."

"What?!" he replied, shocked. "Why?"

I outlined my reasons: our slow pace, the distance to the Death Bivouac, the poor condition the wall was in, the increasing avalanche hazard as the day warmed up. While we talked, small spindrift avalanches showered down over us from the Spider. After fifteen minutes, Marc reluctantly agreed that I was right, and we began our descent.

Wherever we could find anchors, we rappelled; where we couldn't, we down-climbed. At sunset, below a pitch called the Difficult Crack, Marc found a cave for us to bivouac in. By then we were already second-guessing the decision to retreat, and we spent the evening saying little to each other.

At dawn, just after resuming the descent, we heard voices coming from the face below. Two climbers soon appeared, a man and a woman, moving rapidly up the steps we had kicked two days before. It was obvious from their fluid, easy movements that they were both very, very good climbers. The man turned out to be Christophe Profit, a famous French alpinist. He thanked us for kicking all the steps, then the two of them sped off toward the Difficult Crack at an astonishing clip.

A day after we had wimped-out because the face was "out of condition," it appeared as though two French climbers were going to cruise up the climb as if it were a Sunday stroll. I glanced over at Marc and it looked like he was about to burst into tears. At that point we split up and continued the nerve-wracking descent by separate routes.

Two hours later I stepped down onto the snow at the foot of the wall. Waves of relief swept over me. The vise that had been squeezing my temples and gut was suddenly gone. By God, I had survived! I sat down in the snow and began to laugh.

Marc was a few hundred yards away, sitting on a rock. When I reached him I saw that he was crying, and not out of joy. In Marc's estimation, simply surviving the Nordwand did not cut it. "Hey," I heard myself telling him, "if the Frogs get up the sucker, we can always go into Wengen and buy more food, and then go for it again." Marc perked up immediately at this suggestion, and before I could retract my words he was sprinting off to the tent to monitor the French climbers' progress through binoculars.

At this point, however, my luck with the Nordwand finally took a turn for the better: Christophe Profit and his partner only got as far as the Rote Fluh, the site of our first bivouac, before a large avalanche shot past and scared them into coming down, too. A day later, before my Eiger luck could turn again, I was on a jet home.

Love of Life

From *To Build a Fire and Other Stories*

BY JACK LONDON

Like many Jack London tales, including the classic "To Build a Fire," this short story is set in the Yukon during the Gold Rush, which furnished a treasure trove of story material for London.

Jack London (1876–1916) was an extraordinary man, whose life has always reminded me of a shooting star, brilliant, irresistible, suddenly gone. Not only did he write volumes of wonderful prose created from his seafaring and wilderness trail adventures, he was also a true champion of the weak and the poor, the abused people of his time. What a man he was. And what a writer!

★   ★   ★   ★   ★

"This out of all will remain—
  They have lived and have tossed;
So much of the game will be gain,
  Though the gold of the dice has been lost."

They limped painfully down the bank, and once the foremost of the two men staggered among the rough-strewn rocks. They were tired and weak, and their faces had the drawn expression of patience which comes of hardship long endured. They were heavily burdened with blanket packs which were strapped to their shoulders. Head-straps, passing across the forehead, helped support these packs. Each man carried a rifle. They walked in a stooped posture, the shoulders well forward, the head still farther forward, the eyes bent upon the ground.

"I wish we had just about two of them cartridges that's layin' in that cache of ourn," said the second man.

His voice was utterly and drearily expressionless. He spoke without enthusiasm; and the first man, limping into the milky stream that foamed over the rocks, vouchsafed no reply.

The other man followed at his heels. They did not remove their foot-gear, though the water was icy cold—so cold that their ankles ached and their feet went numb. In places the water dashed against their knees, and both men staggered for footing.

The man who followed slipped on a smooth boulder, nearly fell, but recovered himself with a violent effort, at the same time uttering a sharp exclamation of pain. He seemed faint and dizzy and put out his free hand while he reeled, as though seeking support against the air. When he had steadied himself he stepped forward, but reeled again and nearly fell. Then he stood still and looked at the other man, who had never turned his head.

The man stood still for fully a minute, as though debating with himself. Then he called out:

"I say, Bill, I've sprained my ankle."

Bill staggered on through the milky water. He did not look around. The man watched him go, and though his face was expressionless as ever, his eyes were like the eyes of a wounded deer.

The other man limped up the farther bank and continued straight on without looking back. The man in the stream watched him. His lips trembled a little, so that the rough thatch of brown hair which covered them was visibly agitated. His tongue even strayed out to moisten them.

"Bill!" he cried out.

It was the pleading cry of a strong man in distress, but Bill's head did not turn. The man watched him go, limping grotesquely and lurching forward with stammering gait up the slow slope toward the soft sky-line of the low-lying hill. He watched him go till he passed over the crest and disappeared. Then he turned his gaze and slowly took in the circle of the world that remained to him now that Bill was gone.

Near the horizon the sun was smouldering dimly, almost obscured by formless mists and vapors, which gave an impression of mass and density without outline or tangibility. The man pulled out his watch, the while resting his weight on one leg. It was four o'clock, and as the season was near the last of July or first of August,—he did not know the precise date within a week or two,—he knew that the sun roughly marked the northwest. He looked to the south and knew that somewhere beyond those bleak hills lay the Great Bear Lake; also, he knew that in that direction the Arctic Circle cut its forbidding way across the Canadian Barrens. This stream in which he stood was a feeder to the Coppermine River, which in turn flowed north and emptied into Coronation Gulf and the Arctic Ocean. He had never been there, but he had seen it, once, on a Hudson Bay Company chart.

Again his gaze completed the circle of the world about him. It was not a heartening spectacle. Everywhere was soft sky-line. The hills were all low-lying. There were no trees, no shrubs, no grasses—naught but a tremendous and terrible desolation that sent fear swiftly dawning into his eyes.

"Bill!" he whispered, once and twice; "Bill!"

He cowered in the midst of the milky water, as though the vastness were pressing in upon him with overwhelming force, brutally crushing him with its complacent awfulness. He began to shake as with an ague-fit, till the gun fell from his hand with a splash. This served to rouse him. He fought with his fear and pulled himself together, groping in the water and recovering the weapon. He hitched his pack farther over on his left shoulder, so as to take a portion of its weight from off the injured ankle. Then he proceeded, slowly and carefully, wincing with pain, to the bank.

He did not stop. With a desperation that was madness, unmindful of the pain, he hurried up the slope to the crest of the hill over which his comrade had disappeared—more grotesque and comical by far than that limping, jerking comrade. But at the crest he saw a shallow valley, empty of life. He fought with his fear again, overcame it, hitched the pack still farther over on his left shoulder, and lurched on down the slope.

The bottom of the valley was soggy with water, which the thick moss held, spongelike, close to the surface. This water squirted out from under his feet at every step, and each time he lifted a foot the action culminated in a sucking sound as the wet moss reluctantly released its grip. He picked his way from muskeg to muskeg, and followed the other man's footsteps along and across the rocky ledges which thrust like islets through the sea of moss.

Though alone, he was not lost. Farther on he knew he would come to where dead spruce and fir, very small and weazened, bordered the shore of a little lake, the *titchin-nichilie,* in the tongue of the country, the "land of little sticks." And into that lake flowed a small stream, the water of which was not milky. There was rush-grass on that stream—this he remembered well—but no timber, and he would follow it till its first trickle ceased at a divide. He would cross this divide to the first trickle of another stream, flowing to the west, which he would follow until it emptied into the river Dease, and here he would find a cache under an upturned canoe and piled over with many rocks. And in this cache would be ammunition for his empty gun, fish-hooks and lines, a small net—all the utilities for the killing and snaring of food. Also, he would find flour,—not much,—a piece of bacon, and some beans.

Bill would be waiting for him there, and they would paddle away south down the Dease to the Great Bear Lake. And south across the lake they would go, ever south, till they gained the Mackenzie. And south, still south, they would go, while the winter raced vainly after them, and the ice formed in the eddies, and the days grew chilly and crisp, south to some warm Hudson Bay Company post, where timber grew tall and generous and there was grub without end.

These were the thoughts of the man as he strove onward. But hard as he strove with his body, he strove equally hard with his mind, trying to think that Bill had not deserted him, that Bill would surely wait for him at the cache. He was compelled to think this thought, or else there would not be any use to strive, and he would have lain down and died. And as the dim ball of the sun sank slowly into the northwest he covered every inch—and many times—of his and Bill's flight south before the downcoming winter. And he conned the grub of the cache and the grub of the Hudson Bay Company post over and over again. He had not eaten for two days; for a far longer time he had not had all he wanted to eat. Often he stooped and picked pale muskeg berries, put them into his mouth, and chewed and swallowed them. A muskeg berry is a bit of seed enclosed in a bit of water. In the mouth the water melts away and the seed chews sharp and bitter. The man knew there was no nourishment in the berries, but he chewed them patiently with a hope greater than knowledge and defying experience.

At nine o'clock he stubbed his toe on a rocky ledge, and from sheer weariness and weakness staggered and fell. He lay for some time, without movement, on his side. Then he slipped out of the pack-straps and clumsily dragged himself into a sitting posture. It was not yet dark, and in the lingering twilight he groped about among the rocks for shreds of dry moss. When he had gathered a heap he built a fire,—a smouldering, smudgy fire,—and put a tin pot of water on to boil.

He unwrapped his pack and the first thing he did was to count his matches. There were sixty-seven. He counted them three times to make sure. He divided them into several portions, wrapping them in oil paper, disposing of one bunch in his empty tobacco pouch, of another bunch in the inside band of his battered hat, of a third bunch under his shirt on the chest. This accomplished, a panic came upon him, and he unwrapped them all and counted them again. There were still sixty-seven.

He dried his wet foot-gear by the fire. The moccasins were in soggy shreds. The blanket socks were worn through in places, and his feet were raw and bleeding. His ankle was throbbing, and he gave it an examination. It had swollen to the size of his knee. He tore a long strip from one of his two blankets and bound the ankle tightly. He tore other strips and bound them about his feet to serve for both moccasins and socks. Then he drank the pot of water, steaming hot, wound his watch, and crawled between his blankets.

He slept like a dead man. The brief darkness around midnight came and went. The sun arose in the northeast—at least the day dawned in that quarter, for the sun was hidden by gray clouds.

At six o'clock he awoke, quietly lying on his back. He gazed straight up into the gray sky and knew that he was hungry. As he rolled over on his elbow he was startled by a loud snort, and saw a bull caribou regarding him with alert curiosity. The animal was not more than fifty feet away, and instantly into the man's mind leaped the vision and the savor of a caribou steak sizzling and frying over a fire. Mechanically he reached for the empty gun, drew a bead, and pulled the trigger. The bull snorted and leaped away, his hoofs rattling and clattering as he fled across the ledges.

The man cursed and flung the empty gun from him. He groaned aloud as he started to drag himself to his feet. It was a slow and arduous task. His joints were like rusty hinges. They worked harshly in their sockets, with much friction, and each bending or unbending was accomplished only through a sheer exertion of will. When he finally gained his feet, another minute or so was consumed in straightening up, so that he could stand erect as a man should stand.

He crawled up a small knoll and surveyed the prospect. There were no trees, no bushes, nothing but a gray sea of moss scarcely diversified by gray rocks, gray lakelets, and gray streamlets. The sky was gray. There was no sun nor hint of sun. He had no idea of north, and he had forgotten the way he had come to this spot the night before. But he was not lost. He knew that. Soon he would come to the land of the little sticks. He felt that it lay off to the left somewhere, not far—possibly just over the next low hill.

He went back to put his pack into shape for traveling. He assured himself of the existence of his three separate parcels of matches, though he did not stop to count them. But he did linger, debating, over a squat moose-hide sack. It was not large. He could hide it under his two hands. He knew that it weighed fifteen pounds,—as much as all the rest of the pack,—and it worried him. He finally set it to one side and proceeded to roll the pack. He paused to gaze at the squat moose-hide sack. He picked it up hastily with a defiant glance about him, as though the desolation were trying to rob him of it; and when he rose to his feet to stagger on into the day, it was included in the pack on his back.

He bore away to the left, stopping now and again to eat muskeg berries. His ankle had stiffened, his limp was more pronounced, but the pain of it was as nothing compared with the pain of his stomach. The hunger pangs were sharp. They gnawed and gnawed until he could not keep his mind steady on the course he must pursue to gain the land of little sticks. The muskeg berries did not allay this gnawing, while they made his tongue and the roof of his mouth sore with their irritating bite.

He came upon a valley where rock ptarmigan rose on whirring wings from the ledges and muskegs. Ker—ker—ker was the cry they made. He threw stones at them, but could not hit them. He placed his pack on the ground and stalked them as a cat stalks a sparrow. The sharp rocks cut through his pants' legs till his knees left a trail of blood; but the hurt was lost in the hurt of his hunger. He squirmed over the wet moss, saturating his clothes and chilling his body; but he was not aware of it, so great was his fever for food. And always the ptarmigan rose, whirring, before him, till their ker—ker—ker became a mock to him, and he cursed them and cried aloud at them with their own cry.

Once he crawled upon one that must have been asleep. He did not see it till it shot up in his face from its rocky nook. He made a clutch as startled as was the rise of the ptarmigan, and there remained in his hand three tail-feathers. As he watched its flight he hated it, as though it had done him some terrible wrong. Then he returned and shouldered his pack.

As the day wore along he came into valleys or swales where game was more plentiful. A band of caribou passed by, twenty and odd animals, tantalizingly within rifle range. He felt a wild desire to run after them, a certitude that he could run them down. A black fox came toward him, carrying a ptarmigan in his mouth. The man shouted. It was a fearful cry, but the fox, leaping away in fright, did not drop the ptarmigan.

Late in the afternoon he followed a stream, milky with lime, which ran through sparse patches of rush-grass. Grasping these rushes firmly near the root, he pulled up what resembled a young onion-sprout no larger than a shingle-nail. It was tender, and his teeth sank into it with a crunch that promised deliciously of food. But its fibers were tough. It was composed of stringy filaments saturated with water, like the berries, and devoid of nourishment. He threw off his pack and went into the rush-grass on hands and knees, crunching and munching, like some bovine creature.

He was very weary and often wished to rest—to lie down and sleep; but he was continually driven on—not so much by his desire to gain the land of little sticks as by his hunger. He searched little ponds for frogs and dug up the earth with his nails for worms, though he knew in spite that neither frogs nor worms existed so far north.

He looked into every pool of water vainly, until, as the long twilight came on, he discovered a solitary fish, the size of a minnow, in such a pool. He plunged his arm in up to the shoulder, but it eluded him. He reached for it with both hands and stirred up the milky mud at the bottom. In his excitement he fell in, wetting himself to the waist. Then the water was too muddy to admit of his seeing the fish, and he was compelled to wait until the sediment had settled.

The pursuit was renewed, till the water was again muddied. But he could not wait. He unstrapped the tin bucket and began to bale the pool. He baled wildly at first, splashing himself and flinging the water so short a distance that it ran back into the pool. He worked more carefully, striving to be cool, though his heart was pounding against his chest and his hands were trembling. At the end of half an hour the pool was nearly dry. Not a cupful of water remained. And there was no fish. He found a hidden crevice among the stones through which it had escaped to the adjoining and larger pool—a pool which he could not empty in a night and a day. Had he known of the crevice, he could have closed it with a rock at the beginning and the fish would have been his.

Thus he thought, and crumpled up and sank down upon the wet earth. At first he cried softly to himself, then he cried loudly to the pitiless desolation that ringed him around; and for a long time after he was shaken by great dry sobs.

He built a fire and warmed himself by drinking quarts of hot water, and made camp on a rocky ledge in the same fashion he had the night before. The last thing he did was to see that his matches were dry and to wind his watch. The blankets were wet and clammy. His ankle pulsed with pain. But he knew only that he was hungry, and through his restless sleep he dreamed of feasts and banquets and of food served and spread in all imaginable ways.

He awoke chilled and sick. There was no sun. The gray of earth and sky had become deeper, more profound. A raw wind was blowing, and the first flurries of snow were whitening the hilltops. The air about him thickened and grew white while he made a fire and boiled more water. It was wet snow, half rain, and the flakes were large and soggy. At first they melted as soon as they came in contact with the earth, but ever more fell, covering the ground, putting out the fire, spoiling his supply of moss-fuel.

This was a signal for him to strap on his pack and stumble onward, he knew not where. He was not concerned with the land of little sticks, nor with Bill and the cache under the upturned canoe by the river Dease. He was mastered by the verb "to eat." He was hunger-mad. He took no heed of the course he pursued, so long as that course led him through the swale bottoms. He felt his way through the wet snow to the watery muskeg berries, and went by feel as he pulled up the rush-grass by the roots. But it was tasteless stuff and did not satisfy. He found a weed that tasted sour and he ate all he could find of it, which was not much, for it was a creeping growth, easily hidden under the several inches of snow.

He had no fire that night, nor hot water, and crawled under his blanket to sleep the broken hunger-sleep. The snow turned into a cold rain. He awakened many times to feel it falling on his upturned face. Day came—a gray day and no sun. It had ceased raining. The keenness of his hunger had departed. Sensibility, as far as concerned the yearning for food, had been exhausted. There was a dull, heavy ache in his stomach, but it did not bother him so much. He was more rational, and once more he was chiefly interested in the land of little sticks and the cache by the river Dease.

He ripped the remnant of one of his blankets into strips and bound his bleeding feet. Also, he recinched the injured ankle and prepared himself for a day of travel. When he came to his pack, he paused long over the squat moose-hide sack, but in the end it went with him.

The snow had melted under the rain, and only the hilltops showed white. The sun came out, and he succeeded in locating the points of the compass, though he knew now that he was lost. Perhaps, in his previous days' wanderings, he had edged away too far to the left. He now bore off to the right to counteract the possible deviation from his true course.

Though the hunger pangs were no longer so exquisite, he realized that he was weak. He was compelled to pause for frequent rests, when he attacked the muskeg berries and rush-grass patches. His tongue felt dry and large, as though covered with a fine hairy growth, and it tasted bitter in his mouth. His heart gave him a great deal of trouble. When he had travelled a few minutes it would begin a remorseless thump, thump, thump, and then leap up and away in a painful flutter of beats that choked him and made him go faint and dizzy.

In the middle of the day he found two minnows in a large pool. It was impossible to bale it, but he was calmer now and managed to catch them in his tin bucket. They were no longer than his little finger, but he was not particularly hungry. The dull ache in his stomach had been growing duller and fainter. It seemed almost that his stomach was dozing. He ate the fish raw, masticating with painstaking care, for the eating was an act of pure reason. While he had no desire to eat, he knew that he must eat to live.

In the evening he caught three more minnows, eating two and saving the third for breakfast. The sun had dried stray shreds of moss, and he was able to warm himself with hot water. He had not covered more than ten miles that day; and the next day, travelling whenever his heart permitted him, he covered no more than five miles. But his stomach did not give him the slightest uneasiness. It had gone to sleep. He was in a strange country, too, and the caribou were growing more plentiful, also the wolves. Often their yelps drifted across the desolation, and once he saw three of them slinking away before his path.

Another night; and in the morning, being more rational, he untied the leather string that fastened the squat moose-hide sack. From its open mouth poured a yellow stream of coarse gold-dust and nuggets. He roughly divided the gold in halves, caching one half on a prominent ledge, wrapped in a piece of blanket, and returning the other half to the sack. He also began to use strips of the one remaining blanket for his feet. He still clung to his gun, for there were cartridges in that cache by the river Dease.

This was a day of fog, and this day hunger awoke in him again. He was very weak and was afflicted with a giddiness which at times blinded him. It was no uncommon thing now for him to stumble and fall; and stumbling once, he fell squarely into a ptarmigan nest. There were four newly hatched chicks, a day old—little specks of pulsating life no more than a mouthful; and he ate them ravenously, thrusting them alive into his mouth and crunching them like egg-shells between his teeth. The mother ptarmigan beat about him with great out-cry. He used his gun as a club with which to knock her over, but she dodged out of reach. He threw stones at her and with one chance shot broke a wing. Then she fluttered away, running, trailing the broken wing, with him in pursuit.

The little chicks had no more than whetted his appetite. He hopped and bobbed clumsily along on his injured ankle, throwing stones and screaming hoarsely at times; at other times hopping and bobbing silently along, picking himself up grimly and patiently when he fell, or rubbing his eyes with his hand when the giddiness threatened to overpower him.

The chase led him across swampy ground in the bottom of the valley, and he came upon footprints in the soggy moss. They were not his own—he could see that. They must be Bill's. But he could not stop, for the mother ptarmigan was running on. He would catch her first, then he would return and investigate.

He exhausted the mother ptarmigan; but he exhausted himself. She lay panting on her side. He lay panting on his side, a dozen feet away, unable to crawl to her. And as he recovered she recovered, fluttering out of reach as his hungry hand went out to her. The chase was resumed. Night settled down and she escaped. He stumbled from weakness and pitched head foremost on his face, cutting his cheek, his pack upon his back. He did not move for a long while; then he rolled over on his side, wound his watch, and lay there until morning.

Another day of fog. Half of his last blanket had gone into foot-wrappings. He failed to pick up Bill's trail. It did not matter. His hunger was driving him too compellingly—only—only he wondered if Bill, too, were lost. By midday the irk of his pack became too oppressive. Again he divided the gold, this time merely spilling half of it on the ground. In the afternoon he threw the rest of it away, there remaining to him only the half-blanket, the tin bucket, and the rifle.

An hallucination began to trouble him. He felt confident that one cartridge remained to him. It was in the chamber of the rifle and he had overlooked it. On the other hand, he knew all the time that the chamber was empty. But the hallucination persisted. He fought it off for hours, then threw his rifle open and was confronted with emptiness. The disappointment was as bitter as though he had really expected to find the cartridge.

He plodded on for half an hour, when the hallucination arose again. Again he fought it, and still it persisted, till for very relief he opened his rifle to unconvince himself. At times his mind wandered farther afield, and he plodded on, a mere automaton, strange conceits and whimsicalities gnawing at his brain like worms. But these excursions out of the real were of brief duration, for ever the pangs of the hunger-bite called him back. He was jerked back abruptly once from such an excursion by a sight that caused him nearly to faint. He reeled and swayed, doddering like a drunken man to keep from falling. Before him stood a horse. A horse! He could not believe his eyes. A thick mist was in them, intershot with sparkling points of light. He rubbed his eyes savagely to clear his vision, and beheld, not a horse, but a great brown bear. The animal was studying him with bellicose curiosity.

The man had brought his gun halfway to his shoulder before he realized. He lowered it and drew his hunting-knife from its beaded sheath at his hip. Before him was meat and life. He ran his thumb along the edge of his knife. It was sharp. The point was sharp. He would fling himself upon the bear and kill it. But his heart began its warning thump, thump, thump. Then followed the wild upward leap and tattoo of flutters, the pressing as of an iron band about his forehead, the creeping of the dizziness into his brain.

His desperate courage was evicted by a great surge of fear. In his weakness, what if the animal attacked him? He drew himself up to his most imposing stature, gripping the knife and staring hard at the bear. The bear advanced clumsily a couple of steps, reared up, and gave vent to a tentative growl. If the man ran, he would run after him; but the man did not run. He was animated now with the courage of fear. He, too, growled, savagely, terribly, voicing the fear that is to life germane and that lies twisted about life's deepest roots.

The bear edged away to one side, growling menacingly, himself appalled by this mysterious creature that appeared upright and unafraid. But the man did not move. He stood like a statue till the danger was past, when he yielded to a fit of trembling and sank down into the wet moss.

He pulled himself together and went on, afraid now in a new way. It was not the fear that he should die passively from lack of food, but that he should be destroyed violently before starvation had exhausted the last particle of the endeavor in him that made toward surviving. There were the wolves. Back and forth across the desolation drifted their howls, weaving the very air into a fabric of menace that was so tangible that he found himself, arms in the air, pressing it back from him as it might be the walls of a wind-blown tent.

Now and again the wolves, in packs of two and three, crossed his path. But they sheered clear of him. They were not in sufficient numbers, and besides they were hunting the caribou, which did not battle, while this strange creature that walked erect might scratch and bite.

In the late afternoon he came upon scattered bones where the wolves had made a kill. The débris had been a caribou calf an hour before, squawking and running and very much alive. He contemplated the bones, clean-picked and polished, pink with the cell-life in them which had not yet died. Could it possibly be that he might be that ere the day was done! Such was life, eh? A vain and fleeting thing. It was only life that pained. There was no hurt in death. To die was to sleep. It meant cessation, rest. Then why was he not content to die?

But he did not moralize long. He was squatting in the moss, a bone in his mouth, sucking at the shreds of life that still dyed it faintly pink. The sweet meaty taste, thin and elusive almost as a memory, maddened him. He closed his jaws on the bones and crunched. Sometimes it was the bone that broke, sometimes his teeth. Then he crushed the bones between rocks, pounded them to a pulp, and swallowed them. He pounded his fingers, too, in his haste, and yet found a moment in which to feel surprise at the fact that his fingers did not hurt much when caught under the descending rock.

Came frightful days of snow and rain. He did not know when he made camp, when he broke camp. He travelled in the night as much as in the day. He rested wherever he fell, crawled on whenever the dying life in him flickered up and burned less dimly. He, as a man, no longer strove. It was the life in him, unwilling to die, that drove him on. He did not suffer. His nerves had become blunted, numb, while his mind was filled with weird visions and delicious dreams.

But ever he sucked and chewed on the crushed bones of the caribou calf, the least remnants of which he had gathered up and carried with him. He crossed no more hills or divides, but automatically followed a large stream which flowed through a wide and shallow valley. He did not see this stream nor this valley. He saw nothing save visions. Soul and body walked or crawled side by side, yet apart, so slender was the thread that bound them.

He awoke in his right mind, lying on his back on a rocky ledge. The sun was shining bright and warm. Afar off he heard the squawking of caribou calves. He was aware of vague memories of rain and wind and snow, but whether he had been beaten by the storm for two days or two weeks he did not know.

For some time he lay without movement, the genial sunshine pouring upon him and saturating his miserable body with its warmth. A fine day, he thought. Perhaps he could manage to locate himself. By a painful effort he rolled over on his side. Below him flowed a wide and sluggish river. Its unfamiliarity puzzled him. Slowly he followed it with his eyes, winding in wide sweeps among the bleak, bare hills, bleaker and barer and lower-lying than any hills he had yet encountered. Slowly, deliberately, without excitement or more than the most casual interest, he followed the course of the strange stream toward the sky-line and saw it emptying into a bright and shining sea. He was still unexcited. Most unusual, he thought, a vision or a mirage—more likely a vision, a trick of his disordered mind. He was confirmed in this by sight of a ship lying at anchor in the midst of the shining sea. He closed his eyes for a while, then opened them. Strange how the vision persisted! Yet not strange. He knew there were no seas or ships in the heart of the barren lands, just as he had known there was no cartridge in the empty rifle.

He heard a snuffle behind him—a half-choking gasp or cough. Very slowly, because of his exceeding weakness and stiffness, he rolled over on his other side. He could see nothing near at hand, but he waited patiently. Again came the snuffle and cough, and outlined between two jagged rocks not a score of feet away he made out the gray head of a wolf. The sharp ears were not pricked so sharply as he had seen them on other wolves; the eyes were bleared and bloodshot, the head seemed to droop limply and forlornly. The animal blinked continually in the sunshine. It seemed sick. As he looked it snuffled and coughed again.

This, at least, was real, he thought, and turned on the other side so that he might see the reality of the world which had been veiled from him before by the vision. But the sea still shone in the distance and the ship was plainly discernible. Was it reality, after all? He closed his eyes for a long while and thought, and then it came to him. He had been making north by east, away from the Dease Divide and into the Coppermine Valley. This wide and sluggish river was the Coppermine. That shining sea was the Arctic Ocean. That ship was a whaler, strayed east, far east, from the mouth of the Mackenzie, and it was lying at anchor in Coronation Gulf. He remembered the Hudson Bay Company chart he had seen long ago, and it was all clear and reasonable to him.

He sat up and turned his attention to immediate affairs. He had worn through the blanket-wrappings, and his feet were shapeless lumps of raw meat. His last blanket was gone. Rifle and knife were both missing. He had lost his hat somewhere, with the bunch of matches in the band, but the matches against his chest were safe and dry inside the tobacco pouch and oil paper. He looked at his watch. It marked eleven o'clock and was still running. Evidently he had kept it wound.

He was calm and collected. Though extremely weak, he had no sensation of pain. He was not hungry. The thought of food was not even pleasant to him, and whatever he did was done by reason alone. He ripped off his pants' legs to the knees and bound them about his feet. Somehow he had succeeded in retaining the tin bucket. He would have some hot water before he began what he foresaw was to be a terrible journey to the ship.

His movements were slow. He shook as with a palsy. When he started to collect dry moss, he found he could not rise to his feet. He tried again and again, then contented himself with crawling about on hands and knees. Once he crawled near to the sick wolf. The animal dragged itself reluctantly out of his way, licking its chops with a tongue which seemed hardly to have the strength to curl. The man noticed that the tongue was not the customary healthy red. It was a yellowish brown and seemed coated with a rough and half-dry mucus.

After he had drunk a quart of hot water the man found he was able to stand, and even to walk as well as a dying man might be supposed to walk. Every minute or so he was compelled to rest. His steps were feeble and uncertain, just as the wolf's that trailed him were feeble and uncertain; and that night, when the shining sea was blotted out by blackness, he knew he was nearer to it by no more than four miles.

Throughout the night he heard the cough of the sick wolf, and now and then the squawking of the caribou calves. There was life all around him, but it was strong life, very much alive and well, and he knew the sick wolf clung to the sick man's trail in the hope that the man would die first. In the morning, on opening his eyes, he beheld it regarding him with a wistful and hungry stare. It stood crouched, with tail between its legs, like a miserable and woe-begone dog. It shivered in the chill morning wind, and grinned dispiritedly when the man spoke to it in a voice that achieved no more than a hoarse whisper.

The sun rose brightly, and all morning the man tottered and fell toward the ship on the shining sea. The weather was perfect. It was the brief Indian Summer of the high latitudes. It might last a week. To-morrow or next day it might be gone.

In the afternoon the man came upon a trail. It was of another man, who did not walk, but who dragged himself on all fours. The man thought it might be Bill, but he thought in a dull, uninterested way. He had no curiosity. In fact, sensation and emotion had left him. He was no longer susceptible to pain. Stomach and nerves had gone to sleep. Yet the life that was in him drove him on. He was very weary, but it refused to die. It was because it refused to die that he still ate muskeg berries and minnows, drank his hot water, and kept a wary eye on the sick wolf.

He followed the trail of the other man who dragged himself along, and soon came to the end of it—a few fresh-picked bones where the soggy moss was marked by the foot-pads of many wolves. He saw a squat moose-hide sack, mate to his own, which had been torn by sharp teeth. He picked it up, though its weight was almost too much for his feeble fingers. Bill had carried it to the last. Ha! ha! He would have the laugh on Bill. He would survive and carry it to the ship in the shining sea. His mirth was hoarse and ghastly, like a raven's croak, and the sick wolf joined him, howling lugubriously. The man ceased suddenly. How could he have the laugh on Bill if that were Bill; if those bones, so pinky-white and clean, were Bill?

He turned away. Well, Bill had deserted him; but he would not take the gold, nor would he suck Bill's bones. Bill would have, though, had it been the other way around, he mused as he staggered on.

He came to a pool of water. Stooping over in quest of minnows, he jerked his head back as though he had been stung. He had caught sight of his reflected face. So horrible was it that sensibility awoke long enough to be shocked. There were three minnows in the pool, which was too large to drain; and after several ineffectual attempts to catch them in the tin bucket he forbore. He was afraid, because of his great weakness, that he might fall in and drown. It was for this reason that he did not trust himself to the river astride one of the many drift-logs which lined its sand-spits.

That day he decreased the distance between him and the ship by three miles; the next day by two—for he was crawling now as Bill had crawled; and the end of the fifth day found the ship still seven miles away and him unable to make even a mile a day. Still the Indian Summer held on, and he continued to crawl and faint, turn and turn about; and ever the sick wolf coughed and wheezed at his heels. His knees had become raw meat like his feet, and though he padded them with the shirt from his back it was a red track he left behind him on the moss and stones. Once, glancing back, he saw the wolf licking hungrily his bleeding trail, and he saw sharply what his own end might be—unless—unless he could get the wolf. Then began as grim a tragedy of existence as was ever played—a sick man that crawled, a sick wolf that limped, two creatures dragging their dying carcasses across the desolation and hunting each other's lives.

Had it been a well wolf, it would not have mattered so much to the man; but the thought of going to feed the maw of that loathsome and all but dead thing was repugnant to him. He was finicky. His mind had begun to wander again, and to be perplexed by hallucinations, while his lucid intervals grew rarer and shorter.

He was awakened once from a faint by a wheeze close in his ear. The wolf leaped lamely back, losing its footing and falling in its weakness. It was ludicrous, but he was not amused. Nor was he even afraid. He was too far gone for that. But his mind was for the moment clear, and he lay and considered. The ship was no more than four miles away. He could see it quite distinctly when he rubbed the mists out of his eyes, and he could see the white sail of a small boat cutting the water of the shining sea. But he could never crawl those four miles. He knew that, and was very calm in the knowledge. He knew that he could not crawl half a mile. And yet he wanted to live. It was unreasonable that he should die after all he had undergone. Fate asked too much of him. And, dying, he declined to die. It was stark madness, perhaps, but in the very grip of Death he defied Death and refused to die.

He closed his eyes and composed himself with infinite precaution. He steeled himself to keep above the suffocating languor that lapped like a rising tide through all the wells of his being. It was very like a sea, this deadly languor, that rose and rose and drowned his consciousness bit by bit. Sometimes he was all but submerged, swimming through oblivion with a faltering stroke; and again, by some strange alchemy of soul, he would find another shred of will and strike out more strongly.

Without movement he lay on his back, and he could hear, slowly drawing near and nearer, the wheezing intake and output of the sick wolf's breath. It drew closer, ever closer, through an infinitude of time, and he did not move. It was at his ear. The harsh dry tongue grated like sandpaper against his cheek. His hands shot out—or at least he willed them to shoot out. The fingers were curved like talons, but they closed on empty air. Swiftness and certitude require strength, and the man had not this strength.

The patience of the wolf was terrible. The man's patience was no less terrible. For half a day he lay motionless, fighting off unconsciousness and waiting for the thing that was to feed upon him and upon which he wished to feed. Sometimes the languid sea rose over him and he dreamed long dreams; but ever through it all, waking and dreaming, he waited for the wheezing breath and the harsh caress of the tongue.

He did not hear the breath, and he slipped slowly from some dream to the feel of the tongue along his hand. He waited. The fangs pressed softly; the pressure increased; the wolf was exerting its last strength in an effort to sink teeth in the food for which it had waited so long. But the man had waited long, and the lacerated hand closed on the jaw. Slowly, while the wolf struggled feebly and the hand clutched feebly, the other hand crept across to a grip. Five minutes later the whole weight of the man's body was on top of the wolf. The hands had not sufficient strength to choke the wolf, but the face of the man was pressed close to the throat of the wolf and the mouth of the man was full of hair. At the end of half an hour the man was aware of a warm trickle in his throat. It was not pleasant. It was like molten lead being forced into his stomach, and it was forced by his will alone. Later the man rolled over on his back and slept.

There were some members of a scientific expedition on the whale-ship *Bedford*. From the deck they remarked a strange object on the shore. It was moving down the beach toward the water. They were unable to classify it, and, being scientific men, they climbed into the whale-boat alongside and went ashore to see. And they saw something that was alive but which could hardly be called a man. It was blind, unconscious. It squirmed along the ground like some monstrous worm. Most of its efforts were ineffectual, but it was persistent, and it writhed and twisted and went ahead perhaps a score of feet an hour.

Three weeks afterward the man lay in a bunk on the whale-ship *Bedford,* and with tears streaming down his wasted cheeks told who he was and what he had undergone. He also babbled incoherently of his mother, of sunny Southern California, and a home among the orange groves and flowers.

The days were not many after that when he sat at table with the scientific men and ship's officers. He gloated over the spectacle of so much food, watching it anxiously as it went into the mouths of others. With the disappearance of each mouthful an expression of deep regret came into his eyes. He was quite sane, yet he hated those men at meal-time. He was haunted by a fear that the food would not last. He inquired of the cook, the cabin-boy, the captain, concerning the food stores. They reassured him countless times; but he could not believe them, and pried cunningly about the lazarette to see with his own eyes.

It was noticed that the man was getting fat. He grew stouter with each day. The scientific men shook their heads and theorized. They limited the man at his meals, but still his girth increased and he swelled prodigiously under his shirt.

The sailors grinned. They knew. And when the scientific men set a watch on the man, they knew too. They saw him slouch for'ard after breakfast, and, like a mendicant, with outstretched palm, accost a sailor. The sailor grinned and passed him a fragment of sea biscuit. He clutched it avariciously, looked at it as a miser looks at gold, and thrust it into his shirt bosom. Similar were the donations from other grinning sailors.

The scientific men were discreet. They let him alone. But they privily examined his bunk. It was lined with hardtack; the mattress was stuffed with hardtack; every nook and cranny was filled with hardtack. Yet he was sane. He was taking precautions against another possible famine—that was all. He would recover from it, the scientific men said, and he did, ere the *Bedford*'s anchor rumbled down in San Francisco Bay.

The Elements

From *Airman's Odyssey*

BY ANTOINE DE SAINT-EXUPERY

He was an aviation pioneer, flying in open cockpits with the wind whistling in the rigging as he groped through mountain passes and over deserts where few men had ever flown.

Antoine de Saint-Exupéry (1900–1944) is perhaps best known as the author of *The Little Prince*. But Saint-Exupery's aviation experiences pioneering South American–European mail routes inspired both fiction and nonfiction accounts that rank among the classics of the world's aviation literature. *Night Flight* is a novel vivid and compelling, while *Wind, Sand and Stars* and *Flight to Arras* are memoirs written with feeling, grace, and illuminating observations seldom seen in the prose of famous pilots.

Wind, Sand and Stars, from which this selection is taken, is a book of adventure, beauty, and inspiration, an unusual combination. *Flight to Arras*, Saint-Exupéry's final book, portrays the bravery of French pilots flying in the face of certain defeat in the fall of France at the beginning of World War II. All three of his flying books can still be obtained and are available in a single collection, *Airman's Odyssey*, published by Harcourt Brace & Company.

In 1944, while World War II was raging toward its eventual climax in the next year, Saint-Exupéry took off on a reconnaissance mission over the Mediterranean. He never returned.

★   ★   ★   ★   ★

When Joseph Conrad described a typhoon he said very little about towering waves, or darkness, or the whistling of the wind in the shrouds. He knew better. Instead, he took his reader down into the hold of the vessel, packed with emigrant coolies, where the rolling and the pitching of the ship had ripped up and scattered their bags and bundles, burst open their boxes, and flung their humble belongings into a crazy heap. Family treasures painfully collected in a lifetime of poverty, pitiful mementoes so alike that nobody but their owners could have told them apart, had lost their identity and lapsed into chaos, into anonymity, into an amorphous magma. It was this human drama that Conrad described when he painted a typhoon.

Every airline pilot has flown through cyclonic storms, has returned out of them to the fold—to the little restaurant in Toulouse where we sat in peace under the watchful eye of the waitress—and there, recognizing his powerlessness to convey what he has been through, has given up the idea of describing hell. His descriptions, his gestures, his big words would have made the rest of us smile as if we were listening to a little boy bragging. And necessarily so. The cyclone of which I am about to speak was, physically, much the most brutal and overwhelming experience I ever underwent; and yet beyond a certain point I do not know how to convey its violence except by piling one adjective on another, so that in the end I should convey no impression at all—unless perhaps that of an embarrassing taste for exaggeration.

It took me some time to grasp the fundamental reason for this powerlessness, which is simply that I should be trying to describe a catastrophe that never took place. The reason why writers fail when they attempt to evoke horror is that horror is something invented after the fact, when one is re-creating the experience over again in the memory. Horror does not manifest itself in the world of reality. And so, in beginning my story of a revolt of the elements which I myself lived through I have no feeling that I shall write something which you will find dramatic.

I had taken off from the field at Trelew and was flying down to Comodoro-Rivadavia, in the Patagonian Argentine. Here the crust of the earth is as dented as an old boiler. The high-pressure regions over the Pacific send the winds past a gap in the Andes into a corridor fifty miles wide through which they rush to the Atlantic in a strangled and accelerated buffeting that scrapes the surface of everything in their path. The sole vegetation visible in this barren landscape is a plantation of oil derricks looking like the after-effects of a forest fire. Towering over the round hills on which the winds have left a residue of stony gravel, there rises a chain of prow-shaped, saw-toothed, razor-edged mountains stripped by the elements down to the bare rock.

For three months of the year the speed of these winds at ground level is up to a hundred miles an hour. We who flew the route knew that once we had crossed the marshes of Trelew and had reached the threshold of the zone they swept, we should recognize the winds from afar by a grey-blue tint in the atmosphere at the sight of which we would tighten our belts and shoulder-straps in preparation for what was coming. From then on we had an hour of stiff fighting and of stumbling again and again into invisible ditches of air. This was manual labor, and our muscles felt it pretty much as if we had been carrying a longshoreman's load. But it lasted only an hour. Our machines stood up under it. We had no fear of wings suddenly dropping off. Visibility was generally good, and not a problem. This section of the line was a stint, yes; it was certainly not a drama.

But on this particular day I did not like the color of the sky.

The sky was blue. Pure blue. Too pure. A hard blue sky that shone over the scraped and barren world while the fleshless vertebrae of the mountain chain flashed in the sunlight. Not a cloud. The blue sky glittered like a new-honed knife. I felt in advance the vague distaste that accompanies the prospect of physical exertion. The purity of the sky upset me. Give me a good black storm in which the enemy is plainly visible. I can measure its extent and prepare myself for its attack. I can get my hands on my adversary. But when you are flying very high in clear weather the shock of a blue storm is as disturbing as if something collapsed that had been holding up your ship in the air. It is the only time when a pilot feels that there is a gulf beneath his ship.

Another thing bothered me. I could see on a level with the mountain peaks not a haze, not a mist, not a sandy fog, but a sort of ash-colored streamer in the sky. I did not like the look of that scarf of filings scraped off the surface of the earth and borne out to sea by the wind. I tightened my leather harness as far as it would go and I steered the ship with one hand while with the other I hung on to the longéron that ran alongside my seat. I was still flying in remarkably calm air.

Very soon came a slight tremor. As every pilot knows, there are secret little quiverings that foretell your real storm. No rolling, no pitching. No swing to speak of. The flight continues horizontal and rectilinear. But you have felt a warning drum on the wings of your plane, little intermittent rappings scarcely audible and infinitely brief, little cracklings from time to time as if there were traces of gunpowder in the air.

And then everything round me blew up.

Concerning the next couple of minutes I have nothing to say. All that I can find in my memory is a few rudimentary notions, fragments of thoughts, direct observations. I cannot compose them into a dramatic recital because there was no drama. The best I can do is to line them up in a kind of chronological order.

In the first place, I was standing still. Having banked right in order to correct a sudden drift, I saw the landscape freeze abruptly where it was and remain jiggling on the same spot. I was making no headway. My wings had ceased to nibble into the outline of the earth. I could see the earth buckle, pivot—but it stayed put. The plane was skidding as if on a toothless cogwheel.

Meanwhile I had the absurd feeling that I had exposed myself completely to the enemy. All those peaks, those crests, those teeth that were cutting into the wind and unleashing its gusts in my direction, seemed to me so many guns pointed straight at my defenseless person. I was slow to think, but the thought did come to me that I ought to give up altitude and make for one of the neighboring valleys where I might take shelter against a mountainside. As a matter of fact, whether I liked it or not I was being helplessly sucked down towards the earth.

Trapped this way in the first breaking waves of a cyclone about which I learned, twenty minutes later, that at sea level it was blowing at the fantastic rate of one hundred and fifty miles an hour, I certainly had no impression of tragedy. Now, as I write, if I shut my eyes, if I forget the plane and the flight and try to express the plain truth about what was happening to me, I find that I felt weighed down, I felt like a porter carrying a slippery load, grabbing one object in a jerky movement that sent another slithering down, so that, overcome by exasperation, the porter is tempted to let the whole load drop. There is a kind of law of the shortest distance to the image, a psychological law by which the event to which one is subjected is visualized in a symbol that represents its swiftest summing up: I was a man who, carrying a pile of plates, had slipped on a waxed floor and let his scaffolding of porcelain crash.

I found myself imprisoned in a valley. My discomfort was not less, it was greater. I grant you that a down current has never killed anybody, that the expression "flattened out by a down current" belongs to journalism and not to the language of flyers. How could air possibly pierce the ground? But here I was in a valley at the wheel of a ship that was three-quarters out of my control. Ahead of me a rocky prow swung to left and right, rose suddenly high in the air for a second like a wave over my head, and then plunged down below my horizon.

Horizon? There was no longer a horizon. I was in the wings of a theatre cluttered up with bits of scenery. Vertical, oblique, horizontal, all of plane geometry was awhirl. A hundred transversal valleys were muddled in a jumble of perspectives. Whenever I seemed about to take my bearings a new eruption would swing me round in a circle or send me tumbling wing over wing and I would have to try all over again to get clear of all this rubbish. Two ideas came into my mind. One was a discovery: for the first time I understood the cause of certain accidents in the mountains when no fog was present to explain them. For a single second, in a waltzing landscape like this, the flyer had been unable to distinguish between vertical mountainsides and horizontal planes. The other idea was a fixation: The sea is flat: I shall not hook anything out at sea.

I banked—or should I use that word to indicate a vague and stubborn jockeying through the east-west valleys? Still nothing pathetic to report. I was wrestling with chaos, was wearing myself out in a battle with chaos, struggling to keep in the air a gigantic house of cards that kept collapsing despite all I could do. Scarcely the faintest twinge of fear went through me when one of the walls of my prison rose suddenly like a tidal wave over my head. My heart hardly skipped a beat when I was tripped up by one of the whirling eddies of air that the sharp ridge darted into my ship. If I felt anything unmistakably in the haze of confused feelings and notions that came over me each time one of these powder magazines blew up, it was a feeling of respect. I respected that sharp-toothed ridge. I respected that peak. I respected that dome. I respected that transversal valley opening out into my valley and about to toss me God knew how violently as soon as its torrent of wind flowed into the one on which I was being borne along.

What I was struggling against, I discovered, was not the wind but the ridge itself, the crest, the rocky peak. Despite my distance from it, it was the wall of rock I was fighting with. By some trick of invisible prolongation, by the play of a secret set of muscles, this was what was pummeling me. It was against this that I was butting my head. Before me on the right I recognized the peak of Salamanca, a perfect cone which, I knew, dominated the sea. It cheered me to think I was about to escape out to sea. But first I should have to wrestle with the gale off that peak, try to avoid its down-crushing blow. The peak of Salamanca was a giant. I was filled with respect for the peak of Salamanca.

There had been granted me one second of respite. Two seconds. Something was collecting itself into a knot, coiling itself up, growing taut. I sat amazed. I opened astonished eyes. My whole plane seemed to be shivering, spreading outward, swelling up. Horizontal and stationary it was, yet lifted before I knew it fifteen hundred feet straight into the air in a kind of apotheosis. I who for forty minutes had not been able to climb higher than two hundred feet off the ground was suddenly able to look down on the enemy. The plane quivered as if in boiling water. I could see the wide waters of the ocean. The valley opened out into this ocean, this salvation.—And at that very moment, without any warning whatever, half a mile from Salamanca, I was suddenly struck straight in the midriff by the gale off that peak and sent hurtling out to sea.

There I was, throttle wide open, facing the coast. At right angles to the coast and facing it. A lot had happened in a single minute. In the first place, I had not flown out to sea. I had been spat out to sea by a monstrous cough, vomited out of my valley as from the mouth of a howitzer. When, what seemed to me instantly, I banked in order to put myself where I wanted to be in respect of the coast-line, I saw that the coast-line was a mere blur, a characterless strip of blue; and I was five miles out to sea. The mountain range stood up like a crenelated fortress against the pure sky while the cyclone crushed me down to the surface of the waters. How hard that wind was blowing I found out as soon as I tried to climb, as soon as I became conscious of my disastrous mistake: throttle wide open, engines running at my maximum, which was one hundred and fifty miles an hour, my plane hanging sixty feet over the water, I was unable to budge. When a wind like this one attacks a tropical forest it swirls through the branches like a flame, twists them into corkscrews, and uproots giant trees as if they were radishes. Here, bounding off the mountain range, it was leveling out to sea.

Hanging on with all the power in my engines, face to the coast, face to that wind where each gap in the teeth of the range sent forth a stream of air like a long reptile, I felt as if I were clinging to the tip of a monstrous whip that was cracking over the sea.

In this latitude the South American continent is narrow and the Andes are not far from the Atlantic. I was struggling not merely against the whirling winds that blew off the east-coast range, but more likely also against a whole sky blown down upon me off the peaks of the Andean chain. For the first time in four years of airline flying I began to worry about the strength of my wings. Also, I was fearful of bumping the sea—not because of the down currents which, at sea level, would necessarily provide me with a horizontal air mattress, but because of the helplessly acrobatic positions in which this wind was buffeting me. Each time that I was tossed I became afraid that I might be unable to straighten out. Besides, there was a chance that I should find myself out of fuel and simply drown. I kept expecting the gasoline pumps to stop priming, and indeed the plane was so violently shaken up that in the half-filled tanks as well as in the gas lines the gasoline was sloshing round, not coming through, and the engines, instead of their steady roar, were sputtering in a sort of dot-and-dash series of uncertain growls.

I hung on, meanwhile, to the controls of my heavy transport plane, my attention monopolized by the physical struggle and my mind occupied by the very simplest thoughts. I was feeling practically nothing as I stared down at the imprint made by the wind on the sea. I saw a series of great white puddles, each perhaps eight hundred yards in extent. They were running towards me at a speed of one hundred and fifty miles an hour where the down-surging wind-spouts broke against the surface of the sea in a succession of horizontal explosions. The sea was white and it was green—white with the whiteness of crushed sugar and green in puddles the color of emeralds. In this tumult one wave was indistinguishable from another. Torrents of air were pouring down upon the sea. The winds were sweeping past in giant gusts as when, before the autumn harvests, they blow a great flowing change of color over a wheatfield. Now and again the water went incongruously transparent between the white pools, and I could see a green and black sea-bottom. And then the great glass of the sea would be shattered anew into a thousand glittering fragments.

It seemed hopeless. In twenty minutes of struggle I had not moved forward a hundred yards. What was more, with flying as hard as it was out here five miles from the coast, I wondered how I could possibly buck the winds along the shore, assuming I was able to fight my way in. I was a perfect target for the enemy there on shore. Fear, however, was out of the question. I was incapable of thinking. I was emptied of everything except the vision of a very simple act. I must straighten out. Straighten out. Straighten out.

There were moments of respite, nevertheless. I dare say those moments themselves were equal to the worst storms I had hitherto met, but by comparison with the cyclone they were moments of relaxation. The urgency of fighting off the wind was not quite so great. And I could tell when these intervals were coming. It was not I who moved towards those zones of relative calm, those almost green oases clearly painted on the sea, but they that flowed towards me. I could read clearly in the waters the advertisement of a habitable province. And with each interval of repose the power to feel and to think was restored to me. Then, in those moments, I began to feel I was doomed. Then was the time that little by little I began to tremble for myself. So much so that each time I saw the unfurling of a new wave of the white offensive I was seized by a brief spasm of panic which lasted until the exact instant when, on the edge of that bubbling caldron, I bumped into the invisible wall of wind. That restored me to numbness again.

Up! I wanted to be higher up. The next time I saw one of those green zones of calm it seemed to me deeper than before and I began to be hopeful of getting out. If I could climb high enough, I thought, I would find other currents in which I could make some headway. I took advantage of the truce to essay a swift climb. It was hard. The enemy had not weakened. Three hundred feet. Six hundred feet. If I could get up to three thousand feet I was safe, I said to myself. But there on the horizon I saw again that white pack unleashed in my direction. I gave it up. I did not want them at my throat again; I did not want to be caught off balance. But it was too late. The first blow sent me rolling over and over and the sky became a slippery dome on which I could not find a footing.

One has a pair of hands and they obey. How are one's orders transmitted to one's hands?

I had made a discovery that horrified me: my hands were numb. My hands were dead. They sent me no message. Probably they had been numb a long time and I had not noticed it. The pity was that I had noticed it, had raised the question. That was serious.

Lashed by the wind, the wings of the plane had been dragging and jerking at the cables by which they were controlled from the wheel, and the wheel in my hands had not ceased jerking a single second. I had been gripping the wheel with all my might for forty minutes, fearful lest the strain snap the cables. So desperate had been my grip that now I could not feel my hands.

What a discovery! My hands were not my own. I looked at them and decided to lift a finger: it obeyed me. I looked away and issued the same order: now I could not feel whether the finger had obeyed or not. No message had reached me. I thought: "Suppose my hands were to open: how would I know it?" I swung my head round and looked again: my hands were still locked round the wheel. Nevertheless, I was afraid. How can a man tell the difference between the sight of a hand opening and the decision to open that hand, when there is no longer an exchange of sensations between the hand and the brain? How can one tell the difference between an image and an act of the will? Better stop thinking of the picture of open hands. Hands live a life of their own. Better not offer them this monstrous temptation. And I began to chant a silly litany which went on uninterruptedly until this flight was over. A single thought. A single image. A single phrase tirelessly chanted over and over again: "I shut my hands. I shut my hands. I shut my hands." All of me was condensed into that phrase and for me the white sea, the whirling eddies, the saw-toothed range ceased to exist. There was only "I shut my hands." There was no danger, no cyclone, no land unattained. Somewhere there was a pair of rubber hands which, once they let go the wheel, could not possibly come alive in time to recover from the tumbling drop into the sea.

I had no thoughts. I had no feelings except the feeling of being emptied out. My strength was draining out of me and so was my impulse to go on fighting. The engines continued their dot-and-dash sputterings, their little crashing noises that were like the intermittent cracklings of a ripping canvas. Whenever they were silent longer than a second I felt as if a heart had stopped beating. There! that's the end. No, they've started up again.

The thermometer on the wing, I happened to see, stood at twenty below zero, but I was bathed in sweat from head to foot. My face was running with perspiration. What a dance! Later I was to discover that my storage batteries had been jerked out of their steel flanges and hurtled up through the roof of the plane. I did not know then, either, that the ribs on my wings had come unglued and that certain of my steel cables had been sawed down to the last thread. And I continued to feel strength and will oozing out of me. Any minute now I should be overcome by the indifference born of utter weariness and by the mortal yearning to take my rest.

What can I say about this? Nothing. My shoulders ached. Very painfully. As if I had been carrying too many sacks too heavy for me. I leaned forward. Through a green transparency I saw sea-bottom so close that I could make out all the details. Then the wind's hand brushed the picture away.

In an hour and twenty minutes I had succeeded in climbing to nine hundred feet. A little to the south—that is, on my left—I could see a long trail on the surface of the sea, a sort of blue stream. I decided to let myself drift as far down as that stream. Here where I was, facing west, I was as good as motionless, unable either to advance or retreat. If I could reach that blue pathway, which must be lying in the shelter of something not the cyclone, I might be able to move in slowly to the coast. So I let myself drift to the left. I had the feeling, meanwhile, that the wind's violence had perhaps slackened.

It took me an hour to cover the five miles to shore. There in the shelter of a long cliff I was able to finish my journey south. Thereafter I succeeded in keeping enough altitude to fly inland to the field that was my destination. I was able to stay up at nine hundred feet. It was very stormy, but nothing like the cyclone I had come out of. That was over.

On the ground I saw a platoon of soldiers. They had been sent down to watch for me. I landed near by and we were a whole hour getting the plane into the hangar. I climbed out of the cockpit and walked off. There was nothing to say. I was very sleepy. I kept moving my fingers, but they stayed numb. I could not collect my thoughts enough to decide whether or not I had been afraid. Had I been afraid? I couldn't say. I had witnessed a strange sight. What strange sight? I couldn't say. The sky was blue and the sea was white. I felt I ought to tell someone about it since I was back from so far away! But I had no grip on what I had been through. "Imagine a white sea . . . very white . . . whiter still." You cannot convey things to people by piling up adjectives, by stammering.

You cannot convey anything because there is nothing to convey. My shoulders were aching. My insides felt as if they had been crushed in by a terrible weight. You cannot make drama out of that, or out of the cone-shaped peak of Salamanca. That peak was charged like a powder magazine; but if I said so people would laugh. I would myself. I respected the peak of Salamanca. That is my story. And it is not a story.

There is nothing dramatic in the world, nothing pathetic, except in human relations. The day after I landed I might get emotional, might dress up my adventure by imagining that I who was alive and walking on earth was living through the hell of a cyclone. But that would be cheating, for the man who fought tooth and nail against that cyclone had nothing in common with the fortunate man alive the next day. He was far too busy.

I came away with very little booty indeed, with no more than this meagre discovery, this contribution: How can one tell an act of the will from a simple image when there is no transmission of sensation?

I could perhaps succeed in upsetting you if I told you some story of a child unjustly punished. As it is, I have involved you in a cyclone, probably without upsetting you in the least. This is no novel experience for any of us. Every week men sit comfortably at the cinema and look on at the bombardment of some Shanghai or other, some Guernica, and marvel without a trace of horror at the long fringes of ash and soot that twist their slow way into the sky from those man-made volcanoes. Yet we all know that together with the grain in the granaries, with the heritage of generations of men, with the treasures of families, it is the burning flesh of children and their elders that, dissipated in smoke, is slowly fertilizing those black cumuli.

The physical drama itself cannot touch us until some one points out its spiritual sense.

Everest: West Ridge to the Summit

From *Everest: The West Ridge*

BY THOMAS HORNBEIN

Ten years after the first ascent of the highest peak in the world by Edmund Hillary and Sherpa Tenzing Norgay, an American expedition to the mountain was destined to write one of the most compelling chapters in the history of the mountain. Despite losing climber Jake Breitenbach in the treacherous Khumbu Icefall, the American Everest Expedition of 1963 succeeded in reaching the summit by the traditional North Col-Southeast Ridge route, with climber Jim Whittaker and Sherpa Hawang Gombu being the first to the peak. Others were to follow, including one pair of climbers who made history with their ascent.

Thomas Hornbein and William Unsoeld ("Willi") climbed the mountain by the West Ridge, and then descended by the Southeast Ridge. Their feat marked the first traverse of any Himalayan peak, and as can be expected from such an extraordinary effort, there was plenty of high drama on the mountain. Hornbein and Unsoeld were forced to spend the night near the summit and barely escaped with their lives, ultimately losing some fingers and toes from frostbite.

Thomas Hornbein's book *Everest: The West Ridge* chronicles this amazing climb in some of the most gripping and readable mountain-climbing prose ever written. Many readers who are not climbing literature regulars may have missed this great story, which in recent years has been overshadowed by books like Jon Krakauer's best-seller *Into Thin Air*, detailing one of the most infamous modern-day climbing disasters.

As this story begins, Hornbein and Unsoeld are at Camp V West in the early morning of May 22, ready for their summit attempt up the West Ridge.

★ ★ ★ ★ ★

At four the oxygen ran out, a most effective alarm clock. Two well-incubated butane stoves were fished from inside our sleeping bags and soon bouillon was brewing in the kitchen. Climbing into boots was a breathless challenge to balance in our close quarters. Then overboots, and crampons.

"Crampons, in the tent?"

"Sure," I replied. "It's a hell of a lot colder out there."

"But our air mattresses!"

"Just be careful. We may not be back here again, anyway. I hope."

We were clothed in multilayer warmth. The fishnet underwear next to our skin provided tiny air pockets to hold our body heat. It also kept the outer layers at a distance which, considering our weeks without a bath, was respectful. Next came Duofold underwear, a wool shirt, down underwear tops and bottoms, wool climbing pants, and a lightweight wind parka. In spite of the cold our down parkas would be too bulky for difficult climbing, so we used them to insulate two quarts of hot lemonade, hoping they might remain unfrozen long enough to drink during the climb. Inside the felt inner liners of our reindeer-fur boots were innersoles and two pairs of heavy wool socks. Down shells covered a pair of wool mittens. Over our oxygen helmets we wore wool balaclavas and our parka hoods. The down parka-lemonade muff was stuffed into our packs as padding between the two oxygen bottles. With camera, radio, flashlight, and sundry mementos (including the pages from Emerson's diary), our loads came close to forty pounds. For all the prior evening's planning it was more than two hours before we emerged.

I snugged a bowline about my waist, feeling satisfaction at the ease with which the knot fell together beneath heavily mittened hands. This was part of the ritual, experienced innumerable times before. With it came a feeling of security, not from the protection provided by the rope joining Willi and me, but from my being able to relegate these cold gray brooding forbidding walls, so high in such an unknown world, to common reality—to all those times I had ever tied into a rope before: with warm hands while I stood at the base of sun-baked granite walls in the Tetons, with cold hands on a winter night while I prepared to tackle my first steep ice on Longs Peak. This knot tied me to the past, to experiences known, to difficulties faced and overcome. To tie it here in this lonely morning on Everest brought my venture into context with the known, with that which man might do. To weave the knot so smoothly with clumsily mittened hands was to assert my confidence, to assert some competence in the face of the waiting rock, to accept the challenge.

Hooking our masks in place we bade a slightly regretful goodbye to our tent, sleeping bags, and the extra supply of food we hadn't been able to eat. Willi was at the edge of the ledge looking up the narrow gully when I joined him.

"My oxygen's hissing, Tom, even with the regulator turned off."

For the next twenty minutes we screwed and unscrewed regulators, checked valves for ice, to no avail. The hiss continued. We guessed it must be in the valve, and thought of going back to the tent for the spare bottle, but the impatient feeling that time was more important kept us from retracing those forty feet.

"It doesn't sound too bad," I said. "Let's just keep an eye on the pressure. Besides if you run out we can hook up the sleeping T and extra tubing and both climb on one bottle." Willi envisioned the two of us climbing Everest in lockstep, wed by six feet of rubber hose.

We turned to the climb. It was ten minutes to seven. Willi led off. Three years before in a tent high on Masherbrum he had expounded on the importance of knee-to-toe distance for step-kicking up steep snow. Now his anatomical advantage determined the order of things as he put his theory to the test. Right away we found it was going to be difficult. The Couloir, as it cut through the Yellow Band, narrowed to ten or fifteen feet and steepened to fifty degrees. The snow was hard, too hard to kick steps in, but not hard enough to hold crampons; they slid disconcertingly down through this wind-sheltered, granular stuff. There was nothing for it but to cut steps, zigzagging back and forth across the gully, occasionally finding a bit of rock along the side up which we could scramble. We were forced to climb one at a time with psychological belays from axes thrust a few inches into the snow. Our regulators were set to deliver two liters of oxygen per minute, half the optimal flow for this altitude. We turned them off when we were belaying to conserve the precious gas, though we knew that the belayer should always be at peak alertness in case of a fall.

We crept along. My God, I thought, we'll never get there at this rate. But that's as far as the thought ever got. Willi's leads were meticulous, painstakingly slow and steady. He plugged tirelessly on, deluging me with showers of ice as his ax carved each step. When he ran out the hundred feet of rope he jammed his ax into the snow to belay me. I turned my oxygen on to "2" and moved up as fast as I could, hoping to save a few moments of critical time. By the time I joined him I was completely winded, gasping for air, and sorely puzzled about why. Only late in the afternoon, when my first oxygen bottle was still going strong, did I realize what a low flow of gas my regulator was actually delivering.

Up the tongue of snow we climbed, squeezing through a passage where the walls of the Yellow Band closed in, narrowing the Couloir to shoulder width.

In four hours we had climbed only four hundred feet. It was 11 A.M. A rotten bit of vertical wall forced us to the right onto the open face. To regain the Couloir it would be necessary to climb this sixty-foot cliff, composed of two pitches split by a broken snow-covered step.

"You like to lead this one?" Willi asked.

With my oxygen off I failed to think before I replied, "Sure, I'll try it."

The rock sloped malevolently outward like shingles on a roof—rotten shingles. The covering of snow was no better than the rock. It would pretend to hold for a moment, then suddenly shatter and peel, cascading down on Willi. He sank a piton into the base of the step to anchor his belay.

I started up around the corner to the left, crampon points grating on rusty limestone. Then it became a snowplowing procedure as I searched for some sort of purchase beneath. The pick of my ax found a crack. Using the shaft for gentle leverage, I moved carefully onto the broken strata of the step. I went left again, loose debris rolling under my crampons, to the base of the final vertical rise, about eight feet high. For all its steepness, this bit was a singularly poor plastering job, nothing but wobbly rubble. I searched about for a crack, unclipped a big angle piton from my sling, and whomped it in with the hammer. It sank smoothly, as if penetrating soft butter. A gentle lift easily extracted it.

"Hmmm. Not too good," I mumbled through my mask. On the fourth try the piton gripped a bit more solidly. Deciding not to loosen it by testing, I turned to the final wall. Its steepness threw my weight out from the rock, and my pack became a downright hindrance. There was an unlimited selection of handholds, mostly portable. I shed my mittens. For a few seconds the rock felt comfortably reassuring, but cold. Then not cold any more. My eyes tried to direct sensationless fingers. Flakes peeled out beneath my crampons. I leaned out from the rock to move upward, panting like a steam engine. Damn it, it'll go; I know it will, T, I thought. But my grip was gone. I hadn't thought to turn my oxygen up.

"No soap," I called down. "Can't make it now. Too pooped."

"Come on down. There may be a way to the right."

I descended, half rappelling from the piton, which held. I had spent the better part of an hour up there. A hundred feet out we looked back. Clearly we had been on the right route, for above that last little step the gully opened out. A hundred feet higher the Yellow Band met the gray of the summit limestone. It had to get easier.

"You'd better take it, Willi. I've wasted enough time already."

"Hell, if you couldn't make it, I'm not going to be able to do any better."

"Yes you will. It's really not that hard. I was just worn out from putting that piton in. Turn your regulator clear open, though."

Willi headed up around the corner, moving well. In ten minutes his rope was snapped through the high piton. Discarding a few unsavory holds, he gripped the rotten edge with his unmittened hands. He leaned out for the final move. His pack pulled. Crampons scraped, loosing a shower of rock from beneath his feet. He was over. He leaned against the rock, fighting for breath.

"Man, that's work. But it looks better above."

Belayed, I followed, retrieved the first piton, moved up, and went to work on the second. It wouldn't come. "Guess it's better than I thought," I shouted. "I'm going to leave it." I turned my oxygen to four liters, leaned out from the wall, and scrambled up. The extra oxygen helped, but it was surprising how breathless such a brief effort left me.

"Good lead," I panted. "That wasn't easy."

"Thanks. Let's roll."

Another rope length and we stopped. After six hours of hiss Willi's first bottle was empty. There was still a long way to go, but at least he could travel ten pounds lighter without the extra cylinder. Our altimeter read 27,900. We called Base on the walkie-talkie.

Willi: West Ridge to Base. West Ridge to Base. Over.

Base (Jim Whittaker, excitedly): This is Base here, Willi. How are you? How are things going? What's the word up there? Over.

Willi: Man, this is a real bearcat! We are nearing the top of the Yellow Band and it's mighty tough. It's too damned tough to try to go back. It would be too dangerous.

Base (Jim): I'm sure you're considering all about your exits. Why don't you leave yourself an opening? If it's not going to pan out, you can always start working your way down. I think there is always a way to come back.

Willi: Roger, Jim. We're counting on a further consultation in about two or three hundred feet. It should ease up by then! Goddammit, if we can't start moving together, we'll have to move back down. But it should be easier once the Yellow Band is passed. Over.

Base (Jim): Don't work yourself up into a bottleneck, Willi. How about rappelling? Is that possible, or don't you have any *reepschnur* or anything? Over.

Willi: There are no rappel points, Jim, absolutely no rappel points. There's nothing to secure a rope to. So it's up and over for us today . . .

While the import of his words settled upon those listening 10,000 feet below, Willi went right on:

Willi (continuing): . . . and we'll probably be getting in pretty late, maybe as late as seven or eight o'clock tonight.

As Willi talked, I looked at the mountain above. The slopes looked reasonable, as far as I could see, which wasn't very far. We sat at the base of a big, wide-open amphitheater. It looked like summits all over the place. I looked down. Descent was totally unappetizing. The rotten rock, the softening snow, the absence of even tolerable piton cracks only added to our desire to go on. Too much labor, too many sleepless nights, and too many dreams had been invested to bring us this far. We couldn't come back for another try next weekend. To go down now, even if we could have, would be descending to a future marked by one huge question: what might have been? It would not be a matter of living with our fellow man, but simply living with ourselves, with the knowledge that we had had more to give.

I listened, only mildly absorbed in Willi's conversation with Base, and looked past him at the convexity of rock cutting off our view of the gully we had ascended. Above—a snowfield, gray walls, then blue-black sky. We were committed. An invisible barrier sliced through the mountain beneath our feet, cutting us off from the world below. Though we could see through, all we saw was infinitely remote. The ethereal link provided by our radio only intensified our separation. My wife and children seemed suddenly close. Yet home, life itself, lay only over the top of Everest and down the other side. Suppose we fail? The thought brought no remorse, no fear. Once entertained, it hardly seemed even interesting. What now mattered most was right here: Willi and I, tied together on a rope, and the mountain, its summit not inaccessibly far above. The reason we had come was within our grasp. We belonged to the mountain and it to us. There was anxiety, to be sure, but it was all but lost in a feeling of calm, of pleasure at the joy of climbing. That we couldn't go down only made easier that which we really wanted to do. That we might not get there was scarcely conceivable.

Willi was still talking.

Willi: Any news of Barry and Lute? Over.

Jim: I haven't heard a word from them. Over.

Willi: How about Dingman?

Jim: No word from Dingman. We've heard nothing, nothing at all.

Willi: Well, listen, if you do get hold of Dingman, tell him to put a light in the window because we're headed for the summit, Jim. We can't possibly get back to our camp now. Over.

I stuffed the radio back in Willi's pack. It was 1 P.M. From here we could both climb at the same time, moving across the last of the yellow slabs. Another hundred feet and the Yellow Band was below us. A steep tongue of snow flared wide, penetrating the gray strata that capped the mountain. The snow was hard, almost ice-hard in places. We had only to bend our ankles, firmly plant all twelve crampon points, and walk uphill. At last, we were moving, though it would have appeared painfully slow to a distant bystander.

As we climbed out of the Couloir the pieces of the puzzle fell into place. That snow rib ahead on the left skyline should lead us to the Summit Snowfield, a patch of perpetual white clinging to the North Face at the base of Everest's final pyramid. By three we were on the Snowfield. We had been climbing for eight hours and knew we needed to take time to refuel. At a shaly outcrop of rock we stopped for lunch. There was a decision to be made. We could either cut straight up to the northeast ridge and follow it west to the summit, or we could traverse the face and regain the West Ridge. From where we sat, the Ridge looked easier. Besides, it was the route we'd intended in the first place.

We split a quart of lemonade that was slushy with ice. In spite of its down parka wrapping, the other bottle was already frozen solid, as were the kippered snacks. They were almost tasteless but we downed them more with dutiful thoughts of calories than with pleasure.

To save time we moved together, diagonaling upward across downsloping slabs of rotten shale. There were no possible stances from which to belay each other. Then snow again, and Willi kicked steps, fastidiously picking a route between the outcropping rocks. Though still carting my full load of oxygen bottles, I was beginning to feel quite strong. With this excess energy came impatience, and an unconscious anxiety over the high stakes for which we were playing and the lateness of the day. Why the hell is Willi going so damned slow? I thought. And a little later: He should cut over to the Ridge now; it'll be a lot easier.

I shouted into the wind. "Hold up, Willi!" He pretended not to hear me as he started up the rock. It seemed terribly important to tell him to go to the right. I tugged on the rope. "Damn it, wait up, Willi!" Stopped by a taut rope and an unyielding Hornbein, he turned, and with some irritation anchored his ax while I hastened to join him. He was perched, through no choice of his own, in rather cramped, precarious quarters. I sheepishly apologized.

We were on rock now. One rope length, crampons scraping, brought us to the crest of the West Ridge for the first time since we'd left camp 4W yesterday morning. The South Face fell eight thousand feet to the tiny tents of

Advance Base. Lhotse, straight across the face, was below us now. And near at hand, a hundred and fifty feet higher, the South Summit of Everest shone in the afternoon sun. We were within four hundred feet of the top! The wind whipped across the ridge from the north at nearly sixty miles an hour. Far below, peak shadows reached long across the cloud-filled valleys. Above, the Ridge rose, a twisting, rocky spine.

We shed crampons and overboots to tackle this next rocky bit with the comforting grip of cleated rubber soles. Here I unloaded my first oxygen bottle through it was not quite empty. It had lasted ten hours, which obviously meant I'd been getting a lower flow than indicated by the regulator. Resisting Willi's suggestion to drop the cylinder off the South Face, I left it for some unknown posterity. When I resaddled ten pounds lighter, I felt I could float to the top.

The rock was firm, at least in comparison with our fare thus far. Climbing one at a time, we experienced the joy of delicate moves on tiny holds. The going was a wonderful pleasure, almost like a day in the Rockies. With the sheer drop to the Cwm beneath us, we measured off another four rope lengths. Solid rock gave way to crud, then snow. A thin, firm, knife-edge of white pointed gently toward the sky. Buffeted by the wind, we laced our crampons on, racing each other with rapidly numbing fingers. It took nearly twenty minutes. Then we were off again, squandering oxygen at three liters per minute since time seemed the shorter commodity at the moment. We moved together, Willi in front. It seemed almost as if we were cheating, using oxygen; we could nearly run this final bit.

Ahead the North and South Ridges converged to a point. Surely the summit wasn't that near? It must be off behind. Willi stopped. What's he waiting for, I wondered as I moved to join him. With a feeling of disbelief I looked up. Forty feet ahead tattered and whipped by the wind was the flag Jim had left three weeks before. It was 6:15. The sun's rays sheered horizontally across the summit. We hugged each other as tears welled up, ran down across our oxygen masks, and turned to ice.

★   ★   ★   ★   ★

Just rock, a dome of snow, the deep blue sky, and a hunk of orange-painted metal from which a shredded American flag cracked in the wind. Nothing more. Except two tiny figures walking together those last few feet to the top of the earth.

For twenty minutes we stayed there. The last brilliance of the day cast the shadow of our summit on the cloud plain a hundred miles to the east. Valleys were filled with the indistinct purple haze of evening, concealing the dwellings of man we knew were there. The chill roar of wind made speaking difficult, heightening our feeling of remoteness. The flag left there seemed a feeble gesture of man that had no purpose but to accentuate the isolation. The two of us who had dreamed months before of sharing this moment were linked by a thin line of rope, joined in the intensity of companionship to those inaccessibly far below, Al and Barry and Dick—and Jake.

From a pitch of intense emotional and physical drive it was only partly possible to become suddenly, completely the philosopher of a balmy afternoon. The head of steam was too great, and the demands on it still remained. We have a long way to go to get down, I thought. But the prospect of descent of an unknown side of the mountain in the dark caused me less anxiety than many other occasions had. I had a blind, fatalistic faith that, having succeeded in coming this far, we could not fail to get down. The moment became an end in itself.

There were many things savored in this brief time. Even with our oxygen turned off we had no problem performing those summit obeisances, photographing the fading day (it's a wonderful place to be for sunset photographs), smiling behind our masks for the inevitable "I was there" picture. Willi wrapped the kata given him by Ang Dorje about the flag pole and planted Andy Bakewell's crucifix alongside it in the snow; Lhotse and Makalu, below us, were a contrast of sun-blazed snow etched against the darkness of evening shadow. We felt the lonely beauty of the evening, the immense roaring silence of the wind, the tenuousness of our tie to all below. There was a hint of fear, not for our lives, but of a vast unknown which pressed in upon us. A fleeting feeling of disappointment—that after all those dreams and questions this was only a mountaintop—gave way to the suspicion that maybe there was something more, something beyond the three-dimensional form of the moment. If only it could be perceived.

But it was late. The memories had to be stored, the meanings taken down. The question of why we had come was not now to be answered, yet something up here must yield an answer, something only dimly felt, comprehended by senses reaching farther yet than the point on which we stood; reaching for understanding, which hovered but a few steps higher. The answers lay not on the summit of Everest, nor in the sky above it, but in the world to which we belonged and must now return.

Footprints in the snow told that Lute and Barrel had been here. We'd have a path to follow as long as light remained.

"Want to go first?" Willi asked. He began to coil the rope.

Looking down the corniced edge, I thought of the added protection of a rope from above. "Doesn't matter, Willi. Either way."

"O.K. Why don't I go first then?" he said, handing me the coil. Paying out the rope as he disappeared below me I wondered, Is Unsoeld tired? It was hard to believe. Still he'd worked hard; he had a right to be weary. Starting sluggishly, I'd felt stronger as we climbed. So now we would reverse roles. Going up had been pretty much Willi's show; going down would be mine. I dropped the last coil and started after him.

Fifty feet from the top we stopped at a patch of exposed rock. Only the summit of Everest, shining pink, remained above the shadow sea. Willi radioed to Maynard Miller at Advance Base that we were headed for the South Col. It was 6:35 P.M.

We almost ran along the crest, trusting Lute and Barrel's track to keep us a safe distance from the cornice edge. Have to reach the South Summit before dark, I thought, or we'll never find the way. The sun dropped below the jagged horizon. We didn't need goggles any more. There was a loud hiss as I banged my oxygen bottle against the ice wall. Damn! Something's broken. I reached back and turned off the valve. Without oxygen, I tried to keep pace with the rope disappearing over the edge ahead. Vision dimmed, the ground began to move. I stopped till things cleared, waved my arms and shouted into the wind for Willi to hold up. The taut rope finally stopped him. I tightened the regulator, then turned the oxygen on. No hiss! To my relief it had only been jarred loose. On oxygen again, I could move rapidly. Up twenty feet, and we were on the South Summit. It was 7:15.

Thank God for the footprints. Without them, we'd have had a tough time deciding which way to go. We hurried on, facing outward, driving our heels into the steep snow. By 7:30 it was dark. We took out the flashlight and resumed the descent. The batteries, dregs of the Expedition, had not been helped by our session with Emerson's diary the night before; they quickly faded. There was pitiful humor as Willi probed, holding the light a few inches off the snow to catch some sign of tracks. You could order your eyes to see, but nothing in the blackness complied.

We moved slowly now. Willi was only a voice and an occasional faint flicker of light to point the way. No fear, no worry, no strangeness, just complete absorption. The drive which had carried us to a nebulous goal was replaced by simple desire for survival. There was no time to dwell on the uniqueness of our situation. We climbed carefully, from years of habit. At a rock outcrop we paused. Which way? Willi groped to the right along a corniced edge. In my imagination, I filled in the void.

"No tracks over here," Willi called.

"Maybe we should dig in here for the night."

"I don't know. Dave and Girmi should be at 6."

We shouted into the night, and the wind engulfed our call. A lull. Again we shouted. "Helloooo," the wind answered. Or was it the wind?

"Hellooo," we called once more.

"Hellooo," came back faintly. That wasn't the wind!

"To the left, Willi."

"O.K., go ahead."

In the blackness I couldn't see my feet. Each foot groped cautiously, feeling its way down, trusting to the pattern set by its predecessor. Slowly left, right, left, crampons biting into the snow, right, left, . . .

"*Willeeee!*" I yelled as I somersaulted into space. The rope came taut, and with a soft thud I landed.

"Seems to be a cornice there," I called from beneath the wall. "I'll belay you from here."

Willi sleepwalked down to the edge. The dim outline of his foot wavered until it met my guiding hand. His arrival lacked the flair of my descent. It was well that the one of lighter weight had gone first.

Gusts buffeted from all directions, threatening to dislodge us from the slope. Above a cliff we paused, untied, cut the rope in half, and tied in again. It didn't help; even five feet behind I couldn't see Willi. Sometimes the snow was good, sometimes it was soft, sometimes it lay shallow over rocks so we could only drive our axes in an inch or two. With these psychological belays, we wandered slowly down, closer to the answering shouts. The wind was dying, and so was the flashlight, now no more than an orange glow illuminating nothing. The stars, brilliant above, cast no light on the snow. Willi's oxygen ran out. He slowed, suddenly feeling much wearier.

The voices were close now. Were they coming from those two black shapes on the snow? Or were those rocks?

"Shine your light down here," a voice called.

"Where? Shine yours up here," I answered.

"Don't have one," came the reply.

Then we were with them—not Dave and Girmi, but Lute and Barrel. They were near exhaustion, shivering lumps curled on the snow. Barrel in particular was far gone. Anxious hungering for air through the previous night, and the near catastrophe when their tent caught fire in the morning, had left him tired before they even started. Determination got him to the top, but now he no longer cared. He only wanted to be left alone. Lute was also tired. Because of Barrel's condition he'd had to bear the brunt of the climbing labor. His eyes were painfully burned, perhaps by the fire, perhaps by the sun and wind. From sheer fatigue they had stopped thinking. Their oxygen was gone, except for a bit Lute had saved for Barrel; but they were too weak to make the change.

At 9:30 we were still a thousand feet above Camp 6. Willi sat down on the snow, and I walked over to get Lute's oxygen for Barrel. As I unscrewed Lute's regulator from the bottle, he explained why they were still there. Because of the stove fire that had sent them diving from the tent, they were an hour late in starting. It was 3:30 P.M. when they reached the summit. Seeing no sign of movement down the west side, they figured no one would be any later than they were. At 4:15 they started down. Fatigue slowed their descent. Just after dark they had stopped to rest and were preparing to move when they heard shouts. Dave and Girmi, they thought. No—the sounds seemed to be coming from above. Willi and Tom! So they waited, shivering.

I removed Barrel's regulator from his empty bottle and screwed it into Lute's. We were together now, sharing the support so vigorously debated a week before. Lute would know the way back to their camp, even in the dark. All we had to do was help them down. Fumbling with unfeeling fingers, I tried to attach Barrel's oxygen hose to the regulator. Damn! Can't make the connection. My fingers scraped uncoördinately against the cold metal. Try again. There it goes. Then, quickly, numb fingers clumsy, back into mittens. Feeling slowly returned, and pain. Then, the pain went and the fingers were warm again.

Willi remembered the Dexedrine I had dropped into my shirt pocket the evening before. I fished out two pills—one for Barrel and one for Lute. Barrel was better with oxygen, but why I had balked at his communal use of Lute's regulator, I cannot say. Lack of oxygen? Fatigue? It was fifteen hours since we'd started our climb. Or was it that my thoughts were too busy with another problem? We had to keep moving or freeze.

I led off. Lute followed in my footsteps to point out the route. Lost in the darkness sixty feet back on our ropes, Willi and Barrel followed. The track was more sensed than seen, but it was easier now, not so steep. My eyes watered from searching for the black holes punched in the snow by Lute's and Barrel's axes during their ascent. We walked to the left of the crest, three feet down, ramming our axes into the narrow edge. Thirty feet, and the rope came taut as Barrel collapsed in the snow, bringing the entire caravan to a halt. Lute sat down behind me. Got to keep moving. We'll never get there.

We had almost no contact with the back of the line. When the rope came taut, we stopped, when it loosened we moved on. Somewhere my oxygen ran out, but we were going too slow for me to notice the difference. Ought to dump the empty bottle, I thought, but it was too much trouble to take off my pack.

Heat lightning flashed along the plains to the east, too distant to light our way. Rocks that showed in the snow below seemed to get no closer as the hours passed. Follow the ax holes. Where'd they go? Not sure. There's another.

"Now where, Lute?"

"Can't see, Tom," Lute said. "Can't see a damn thing. We've got to turn down a gully between some rocks."

"Which gully? There's two or three."

"Don't know, Tom."

"Think, Lute. Try to remember. We've got to get to 6."

"I don't know. I just can't see."

Again and again I questioned, badgering, trying to extract some hint. But half blind and weary, Lute had no answer. We plodded on. The rocks came slowly closer.

Once the rope jerked tight, nearly pulling me off balance. Damn! What's going on? I turned and looked at Lute's dim form lying on the snow a few feet further down the Kangshung Face. His fall had been effectively if uncomfortably arrested when his neck snagged the rope between Willi and me.

We turned off the crest, toward the rocks. Tongues of snow pierced the cliffs below. But which one? It was too dangerous to plunge on. After midnight we reached the rocks. It had taken nearly three hours to descend four hundred feet, maybe fifteen minutes' worth by daylight.

Tired. No hope of finding camp in the darkness. No choice but to wait for day. Packs off. Willi and I slipped into our down parkas. In the dark, numb fingers couldn't start the zippers. We settled to the ground, curled as small as possible atop our pack frames. Lute and Barry were somewhere behind, apart, each alone. Willi and I tried hugging each other to salvage warmth, but my uncontrollable shivering made it impossible.

The oxygen was gone, but the mask helped a little for warmth. Feet, cooling, began to hurt. I withdrew my hands from the warmth of my crotch and loosened crampon bindings and boot laces, but my feet stayed cold. Willi offered to rub them. We removed boots and socks and planted both my feet against his stomach. No sensation returned.

Tired by the awkward position, and frustrated by the result, we gave it up. I slid my feet back into socks and boots, but couldn't tie them. I offered to warm Willi's feet. Thinking that his freedom from pain was due to a high tolerance of cold, he declined. We were too weary to realize the reason for his comfort.

The night was overpoweringly empty. Stars shed cold unshimmering light. The heat lightning dancing along the plains spoke of a world of warmth and flatness. The black silhouette of Lhotse lurked half sensed, half seen, still below. Only the ridge on which we were rose higher, disappearing into the night, a last lonely outpost of the world.

Mostly there was nothing. We hung suspended in a timeless void. The wind died, and there was silence. Even without wind it was cold. I could reach back and touch Lute or Barrel lying head to toe above me. They seemed miles away.

Unsignaled, unembellished, the hours passed. Intense cold penetrated, carrying with it the realization that each of us was completely alone. Nothing Willi could do for me or I for him. No team now, just each of us, imprisoned with his own discomfort, his own thoughts, his own will to survive.

Yet for me, survival was hardly a conscious thought. Nothing to plan, nothing to push for, nothing to do but shiver and wait for the sun to rise. I floated in a dreamlike eternity, devoid of plans, fears, regrets. The heat lightning, Lhotse, my companions, discomfort, all were there—yet not there. Death had no meaning, nor, for that matter, did life. Survival was no concern, no issue. Only a dulled impatience for the sun to rise tied my formless thoughts to the future.

About 4:00 the sky began to lighten along the eastern rim, baring the bulk of Kangchenjunga. The sun was slow in following, interminably slow. Not till after 5:00 did it finally come, its light streaming through the South Col, blazing yellow across the Nuptse Wall, then onto the white wave crest of peaks far below. We watched as if our own life was being born again. Then as the cold yellow light touched us, we rose. There were still miles to go.

★   ★   ★   ★   ★

The rest is like a photograph with little depth of field, the focused moments crystal sharp against a blurred background of fatigue. We descended the gully I had been unable to find in the dark. Round the corner, Dave and Girmi were coming toward us. They thought they heard shouts in the night and had started up, but their own calls were followed only by silence. Now, as they came in search of the bodies of Lute and Barry they saw people coming down—not just two, but four. Dave puzzled a moment before he understood.

The tents at Camp 6—and we were home from the mountain. Nima Dorje brought tea. We shed boots. I stared blankly at the marble-white soles of Willi's feet. They were cold and hard as ice. We filled in Emerson's diary for the last time, then started down.

With wind tearing snow from its rocky plain, the South Col was as desolate and uninviting as it had always been described. We sought shelter in the tents at Camp 5 for lunch, then emerged into the gale. Across the Geneva Spur, out of the wind, onto the open sweep of the Lhotse Face we plodded in somber procession. Dave led gently, patiently; the four behind rocked along, feet apart to keep from falling. Only for Willi and me was this side of the mountain new. Like tourists we looked around, forgetting fatigue for the moment.

At Camp 4 we stopped to melt water, then continued with the setting sun, walking through dusk into darkness as Dave guided us among crevasses, down the Cwm. It was a mystery to me how he found the way. I walked along at the back, following the flashlight. Sometimes Willi stopped and I would nearly bump into him. We waited while Dave searched, then moved on. No one complained.

At 10:30 P.M. we arrived at Advance Base. Dick, Barry, and Al were down from the Ridge, waiting. Frozen feet and Barrel's hands were thawed in warm water. Finally to bed, after almost two days. Short a sleeping bag, Willi and I shared one as best we could.

May 24 we were late starting, tired. Lute, Willi, and Barrel walked on thawed feet. It was too dangerous to carry them down through the Icefall. Willi, ahead of me on the rope, heeled down like an awkward clown. The codeine wasn't enough to prevent cries of pain when he stubbed his toes against the snow. I cried as I walked behind, unharmed.

At Camp 1 Maynard nursed us like a mother hen, serving us water laboriously melted from ice samples drilled from the glacier for analysis. Then down through the Icefall, past Jake's grave—and a feeling of finality. It's all done. The dream's finished.

No rest. The next day, a grim gray one, we departed Base. From low-hanging clouds wet snow fell. Willi, Barrel, and Lute were loaded aboard porters to be carried down over the rocky moraine. It was easier walking.

At Gorak Shep we paused. On a huge boulder a Sherpa craftsman had patiently carved:

IN MEMORY OF JOHN E. BREITENBACH,
AMERICAN MOUNT EVEREST EXPEDITION, 1963.

Clouds concealed the mountain that was Jake's grave.

As we descended, the falling snow gave way to a fine drizzle. There was nothing to see; just one foot, then another. But slowly a change came, something that no matter how many times experienced, is always new, like life. It *was* life. From ice and snow and rock, we descended to a world of living things, of green—grass and trees and bushes. There was no taking it for granted. Spring had come, and even the gray drizzle imparted a wet sheen to all that grew. At Pheriche flowers bloomed in the meadows.

Lying in bed, Willi and I listened to a sound that wasn't identifiable, so foreign was it to the place—the chopping whir as a helicopter circled, searching for a place to light. In a flurry of activity Willi and Barrel were loaded aboard. The helicopter rose from the hilltop above the village and dipped into the distance. The chop-chop-chop of the blades faded, until finally the craft itself was lost in the massive backdrop. The departure was too unreal, too much a part of another world, to be really comprehended. Less than five days after they had stood on the summit of Everest, Barrel and Willi were back in Kathmandu. For them the Expedition was ended. Now all that remained was weeks in bed, sitting, rocking in pain, waiting for toes to mummify to the time for amputation.

Up over barren passes made forbidding by mist and a chill wind, we traveled. Hard work. Then down through forests of rain-drenched rhododendrons, blossoming pastels of pink and lavender. Toes hurt. Two weeks to Kathmandu. Feet slipped on the muddy path. Everything was wet.

We were finished. Everest was climbed; nothing to push for now. Existence knew only the instant, counting steps, falling asleep each time we stopped to rest beside the trail. Lester, Emerson, and I talked about motivation; for me it was all gone. It was a time of relaxation, a time when senses were tuned to perceive, but nothing was left to give.

Pleasure lay half-hidden beneath discomfort, fatigue, loneliness. Willi was gone. The gap where he had been was filled with a question: Why hadn't I known that his feet were numb? Surely I could have done something, if only . . . I was too weary to know the question couldn't be resolved. Half of me seemed to have gone with him; the other half was isolated from my companions by an experience I couldn't share and by the feeling that something was ending that had come to mean too much. Talk of home, of the first evening in the Yak and Yeti Bar, of the reception that waited, was it really so important? Did it warrant the rush?

We'd climbed Everest. What good was it to Jake? To Willi, to Barrel? To Norman, with Everest all done now? And to the rest of us? What waits? What price less tangible than toes? There must be something more to it than toiling over the top of another, albeit expensive, mountain. Perhaps there was something of the nobility-that-is-man in it somewhere, but it was hard to be sure.

Yes, it satisfied in a way. Not just climbing the mountain, but the entire effort—the creating something, the few of us molding it from the beginning. With a lot of luck we'd succeeded. But what had we proved?

Existence on a mountain is simple. Seldom in life does it come any simpler: survival, plus the striving toward a summit. The goal is solidly, three-dimensionally there—you can see it, touch it, stand upon it—the way to reach it well defined, the energy of all directed toward its achievement. It is this simplicity that strips the veneer off civilization and makes that which is meaningful easier to come by—the pleasure of deep companionship, moments of uninhibited humor, the tasting of hardship, sorrow, beauty, joy. But it is this very simplicity that may prevent finding answers to the questions I had asked as we approached the mountain.

Then I had been unsure that I could survive and function in a world so foreign to my normal existence. Now I felt at home here, no longer overly afraid. Each step toward Kathmandu carried me back toward the known, yet toward many things terribly unknown, toward goals unclear, to be reached by paths undefined.

Beneath fatigue lurked the suspicion that the answers I sought were not to be found on a mountain. What possible difference could climbing Everest make? Certainly the mountain hadn't been changed. Even now wind and falling snow would have obliterated most signs of our having been there. Was I any greater for having stood on the highest place on earth? Within the wasted figure that stumbled weary and fearful back toward home there was no question about the answer to that one.

It had been a wonderful dream, but now all that lingered was the memory. The dream was ended.

Everest must join the realities of my existence, commonplace and otherwise. The goal, unattainable, had been attained. Or had it? The questions, many of them, remained. And the answers? It is strange how when a dream is fulfilled there is little left but doubt.

Rounding Cape Horn

From *Gipsy Moth Circles the World*

BY SIR FRANCIS CHICHESTER

If you wanted to make a list of the greatest seagoing tales ever written, two similar works would be unanimous qualifiers: Joshua Slocum's *Sailing Alone Around the World* (1900) and Sir Francis Chichester's *Gipsy Moth Circles the World* (1967).

Slocum was the first to sail alone around the world, in a voyage that took three years. After writing *Sailing Alone Around the World* about that experience, he tried to duplicate the feat again, starting in 1909. He disappeared, never to be heard from again.

When Chichester set sail from England, he was 64. When he returned, successful, he was a national hero. Here we are with him on the portion of the voyage when he encounters the infamous Cape Horn waves and weather at the southernmost tip of South America.

★   ★   ★   ★   ★

When I was researching in records and old logs in preparation for my voyage it was soon apparent that the seas around Cape Horn had a reputation unique among all the oceans of the world; more, they have had this reputation for as long as man has known them, ever since Drake deduced that there was the passage that bears his name between Cape Horn and the South Shetland Islands off Antarctica—Drake Strait.

Cape Horn is an island, or rather the tip of an island, a massive cliff some 1,400 feet high that stands where the Pacific and Atlantic oceans meet, at the southerly end of the South American continent. Why has it such an evil reputation? I tried to answer this question in my book *Along the Clipper Way.*

"The prevailing winds in the Forties and Fifties, between 40°S. and 60°S., are westerly and pretty fresh on the average. For instance, off the Horn there are gales of Force 8 or more on one day in four in the spring and one day in eight in the summer. Winds have a lazy nature in that they refuse to climb over a mountain range if they can sweep past the end of it. South America has one of the greatest mountain ranges of the world, the Andes, which blocks the westerlies along a front of 1,200 miles from 35°S. right down to Cape Horn. All this powerful wind is crowding through Drake's Strait between Cape Horn and the South Shetland Islands, 500 miles to the south. The normal westerlies pouring through this gap are interfered with by the turbulent, vicious little cyclones rolling off the Andes. The same process occurs in reverse with the easterly winds which, though more rare than the westerlies, blow when a depression is passing north of the Horn.

"As for the waves, the prevailing westerlies set up a current flowing eastwards round the world at a mean rate of 10 to 20 miles per day. This current flows in all directions at times due to the passing storms, but the result of all the different currents is this 10 to 20 miles per day flowing eastwards. As the easterly may check this current or even reverse it for a while, the prevailing stream flowing eastwards may sometimes amount to as much as 50 miles a day. As with the winds, this great ocean river is forced to pass between South America and the South Shetland Islands. This in itself tends to make the stream turbulent.

"But there is another factor which greatly increases the turbulence. The bottom of the ocean shelves between the Horn and the Shetland Islands and this induces the huge seas to break. It is like a sea breaking on the beach at Bournemouth in a gale, except that the waves, instead of being 4 feet high, are likely to be 60 feet high.

"There is yet another factor to make things worse. Anyone who has sailed out past the Needles from the Solent when the outgoing tide is opposing a Force 6 wind knows what a hateful short steep sea can result. A yacht will seem to be alternately standing on its stem and its stern with a lot of water coming inboard. The same thing happens at the Horn on a gigantic scale if there is an easterly gale blowing against the current flowing past the Horn.

"What size are these notorious waves? No one yet has measured them accurately in the Southern Ocean, but the oceanographers have been measuring waves in the North Atlantic for some years. The British Institute of Oceanography have invented a wave measuring instrument which they use at the weather ships stationed in the Atlantic. Recently one instrument with a 60-foot scale recorded a wave of which the trace went off the scale. This wave was estimated at 69 feet in height, higher than our five storey house in London. An American steamship in the South Pacific is said to have encountered a wave 112 feet high. Brian Grundy who used to sail with me in *Gipsy Moth II* told me that when he was in the Southern Ocean in a big whaling steamer he reckoned that one wave was 120 feet high. L. Draper of the Institute of Oceanography says that, according to *Statistics of a Stationary Random Process,* if a sea of average height 30 feet is running, then one wave out of every 300,000 can be expected to be four times that height, i.e. 120 feet."

I do not think that Drake himself ever saw Cape Horn. We have two accounts of his passage, one by his chaplain in the *Golden Hind,* Francis Fletcher, the other by a Portuguese pilot, Nuno da Silva, whom Drake had captured with a ship he took off the Cape Verde Islands earlier in his voyage. Apparently da Silva accompanied Drake quite willingly for the sheer interest of adventuring into the unknown South Sea, for when Drake freed his other captives da Silva stayed with him. Piecing together Fletcher's and da Silva's accounts, and deducing Drake's navigation from them, I am convinced that Drake never rounded Cape Horn. He was driven west-south-west for 14 or 21 days (the accounts are indefinite about the length of time), he then sailed back over his track for 7 days as soon as the north-east gale had blown out. He fetched up at the Diego Ramirez Islands, where he anchored in 20 fathoms at the range of a big gun from the land. According to the *Admiralty Pilot* there is an anchorage close eastward of the middle of one island in a depth of 16 fathoms with a sandy bottom. I am convinced that Drake never saw Cape Horn, but discovered the Diego Ramirez Islands and correctly deduced, because of the big swell that rolled in from the Atlantic when the north-easterly gale was blowing, that there was a passage between the Atlantic and Pacific Oceans there.

I aimed to pass between the Diego Ramirez group and the Ildefonso Islands, and to round Cape Horn between 40 and 50 miles south of it. I wanted to give the Horn a good clearance, because it is a bit like Portland Bill in the English Channel—the closer to the Bill you pass, the more turbulent the sea, especially with wind against tide. The water diverted by the Bill has to accelerate to get past it, and, in addition, the bottom shelves, so that the current is accelerated again because of the same amount of water having to get through where there is only half the depth. It is exactly the same case with the Horn, only the rough water extends 40 miles south of it instead of 6 miles and where a 40-knot wind would bring a turbulent, 6-foot sea by the Bill, it will be an 80-knot wind with a 60-foot sea off the Horn.

At midnight on Saturday–Sunday, March 18–19, I was approaching land. I was 134 miles from the Ildefonso Islands and 157 miles from the Diego

Ramirez Islands. The nearest land was at the entrance to the Cockburn Channel, which Joshua Slocum had made famous. That was only 75 miles to the NE by N. The barometer had been dropping steadily for forty hours now. I got up and went into the cockpit, to find out what chance I might have of sighting land ahead. It was raining steadily. The big breaking seas showed up dazzling white with phosphorescence, I would say up to 100 yards away. The falling-off, seething bow waves were brilliant white. The keel was leaving a weaving tail like a comet 50–100 feet long, and under the surface. I thought that one would be lucky to sight land 300 yards ahead. This would pose a nutty problem for me next night if I didn't sight any land during the day. If the weather continued I should be lucky to get a fix, and with the strong currents known to be there, my fix of the day before would not reassure me much. I was uneasy about fixes with no checks since Sydney Heads: suppose I had been making a systematic error in my sights . . . But it was no good thinking like that. I realised that I must trust my navigation as I had done before.

I was lucky, and I got a sun fix at 09.22 next morning. That put me about 40 miles south-west of the nearest rocks off Tierra del Fuego. I was 77 miles due west of the Ildefonso Islands, and 148½ miles from Cape Horn.

There was a massive bank of cloud, nearly black at the bottom, away to the north, and I supposed that it was lying on the Darwin Mountains of Tierra del Fuego. There was no land in sight, although the nearest land was only 50 miles off. I now had a big problem to solve—where should I head? My then heading of 78° would lead me to Duff Bay and Morton Island, 15 miles north of the Ildefonsos. But I could gybe at any time, because the wind had backed to west by north. My main problem was this: if I kept headed for the Ildefonso Islands and Cape Horn, which was nearly in line with them, I should reach the islands in eleven hours' time, i.e. at 22.00 that night, which was three and a half hours after dark. This was too risky, because if it rained or snowed I should be unable to see the islands close to. The trouble was that if I bore away from the Ildefonsos, I should then have to cope with the Diego Ramirez Group. The bearing of that batch of rocky islets was only 22° (2 points) to starboard of the Ildefonsos. These islands have no lights, and are inhabited only for part of the year.

It was clear that I should not reach the islands until after dark. The currents were strong here in the neighbourhood of the Horn, running up to 22 miles per day in any direction in fine weather, and up to 50 miles a day in stormy weather. My fix of 09.30 that morning seemed a good one, but at the back of my mind was still the gnawing doubt about my sun navigation, with no check since Sydney Heads, 6,575 miles back. (It was unfortunate that I had made that blunder in my sun fix earlier, on the day before I appeared to have made the big 217 miles day's run.) I could avoid both groups of islands by gybing and heading south-east till dawn; that was safe tactics, but it meant quite a big detour, which I resented. I tried to puzzle out a dog's leg route which would take me between the islands in safety.

At noon the wind shifted, veering suddenly, which put me on a heading of north-east, so I gybed. Then the sun showed through the heavy clouds, and I got a sextant sight. This checked my latitude, for which I was very grateful. I had just finished plotting the result, and had decided on my best heading, when the wind backed in a few seconds from north-west to south. In a matter of minutes it was blowing up to a strong gale, Force 9. I dropped the mainsail, the jib and the genny staysail in turn. I set the spitfire, and found that was enough sail. "I wish," I logged, "that this famous visibility following a wind shift would prove itself! I should just love to get a glimpse of those islands." Until then I had been heading straight for the Ildefonso Islands, and now I decided that the time had come to change course and head midway between the two groups of islands. This put the wind slightly forward of the beam, so I hoisted a storm staysail with the spitfire jib. The barometer had suddenly risen 6½ millibars in the past hour or two. I hoped that the wind would not go on backing into the south-east, which would make it very awkward for me. By 21.00 that night the wind had eased to 15 knots at times, but with periodic bursts of up to 36 knots. I hoisted a bigger stay-sail, but with only the two headsails set the speed was down to 4 knots between the squalls. I decided to put up with this until I had got away from the proximity of that rugged land, so notorious for williwaws.

By midnight the barometer had risen 9½ millibars in the past 7 hours. It was a little less dark out: I could tell the difference between sea and sky.

If my navigation was all right, I should be now passing 18 miles south of the Ildefonso Islands, and at dawn I should be passing 12 miles north of the Diego Ramirez group. It was so dark that I did not think it worth keeping a watch, so I set the off-course alarm to warn me if there was a big wind shift, and I also set an alarm clock to wake me at daybreak. Then I put my trust in my navigation and turned in for a sleep. For a while I lay in the dark with the boat rushing into black night. I used to think I would be better off going head first into danger (in *Gipsy Moth III* I lay feet forward); but I still had the same fear. What would it be like if she hit? Would she crack with a stunning shock and start smashing against the rocks in the breakers? If I could reach the life-raft amidships could I get it untied in the dark, then find the cylinder to inflate it? In the end I slept, and soundly too.

Daybreak was at 05.00. It was a cold, grey morning. The wind had veered right round again to west by south, and the barometer was steady. There was nothing in sight anywhere, which was as it should be. The sea was pretty calm, so I decided to head directly for Cape Horn, instead of passing 40 miles to the south of it as I had planned earlier, in order to avoid the turbulent seas to be expected if closer to the Horn, and if a gale blew up. I decided to hoist the trysail and went on up to do so. I was excited about changing course to east by north after setting the trysail, because changing course northwards there meant changing course for home. I was then 40 miles from the Horn.

When I stepped into the cockpit I was astounded to see a ship near by, about a half-mile off. I had a feeling that if there was one place in the world where I would not see a ship it was off Cape Horn. As soon as I recovered from the shock I realised that because of its drab overall colour it must be a warship, and therefore was likely to be HMS *Protector*. On first sighting it, it had seemed like magic, but on thinking it over I realised that if they had picked up my radio message to Buenos Aires of the night before relating how I was aiming to pass midway between the two groups of islands sailing blind during the night, the warship had only to place herself half-way between the two groups, and if my navigation was correct I should sail straight up to her. I went below and called up HMS *Protector* on 2,182 kcs. She answered immediately. I said I would speak to her again as soon as I had set my trysail.

After setting the trysail I went down below for quite a while. I talked to *Protector,* and that used more time than it should have done, because I had great difficulty in hearing what her operator was saying. This was tantalising because I could clearly hear some land stations up to 7,000 miles away if I wanted to. After that I had my breakfast, and did not hurry over it, then wrote up the log, studied the chart and decided on my tactics, etc. While I was breakfasting a big wave swept over the boat and filled the cockpit half full. It took more than fifteen minutes to drain. By the time I had finished breakfast the wind had risen to 40 knots. At 09.00 I went on deck, and dropped both the trysail and the genoa staysail, leaving only the spitfire set. As I was finishing the deckwork a big wave took *Gipsy Moth* and slewed her round broadside on; in other words she broached to. It was lucky that I was on deck to free the self-steering gear, and to bring her round on to course again. I stood on the cockpit seat to do this so as to keep my legs out of the water in the cockpit. I looked round and there was the Horn, quite plain to see. It stood up out of the sea like a black ice-cream cone. Hermite Island, north-west of it, was grey and outlined against the sky.

At 10.43 I logged:

"I reckon I am east of Old Horn, but I can't get a bearing without going into the cockpit. Perhaps I had better, as I have kept all my oilskins on. Still gusting over 50 knots."

At 11.15 I took a bearing of the Horn and was then definitely past it. As I had made good 39 miles in the past five and a quarter hours, a speed of 7.4

knots, I must have passed the Horn at 11.07½ o'clock. I had no time or inclination at that moment, however, for such niceties of navigation. Before I reached the Horn the familiar quiet roar of wind was beginning; it was blowing up, and the sea was roughing up fast. I dare say that a lot of this was due to being only 7½ miles south of the Horn when I passed it. I was beginning to feel seasick, and had the usual lethargic reluctance to do anything. I just wanted to be left alone, by things and especially by people. I cursed the *Protector* for hanging about, especially as I noted that she looked steady enough to play a game of billiards on her deck.★

Just then I'm damned if an aircraft didn't buzz into sight. I cursed it. If there was one place in the world where I expected to be alone it was off Cape Horn; besides which this aircraft made me apprehensive. I couldn't say exactly why, but I think that an old flier has a perception which amounts almost to instinct about an aeroplane in flight. I thought this one would come down and crash into the water. How the devil was I going to attempt the rescue of its occupants in that sea? I tried to figure out a drill for rescue. Queasiness made it hard to think, and I was greatly relieved when if finally cleared off.★★

★Apparently it was not as smooth aboard her as it appeared. A Reuter staff man, Michael Hayes, was aboard and recorded the following (published in a special issue of *Football Monthly*). "As I stood on the pitching and tossing deck of the Royal Navy Ice Patrol ship H.M.S. *Protector* 400 yards off, the sight was awesome. The translucent, bottle-green seas were moving mountains and valleys of water, rearing, rolling and subsiding with a fearful brute force. The 50-mile an hour wind slashed at the waves, slicing off foaming white crests and sending icy spume flying. Lead-grey clouds, blotting out the weak sun on the horizon, rolled across the sky, so low that it seemed I could reach up and touch them. The thermometer said the temperature was 43° F, but the numbing wind cut through my lined, Antarctic clothing like a knife, and salt spray swelled up and crashed against the face with stinging fury."
★★This was the aircraft, a Piper Apache, in which Murray Sayle of the *Sunday Times,* Clifford Luton and Peter Beggin of the BBC came out to look for *Gipsy Moth*. It was piloted by Captain Rodolfo Fuenzalida, formerly of the Chilean Air Force. Murray Sayle wrote in *The Times* of March 21:

"The flight out to find and photograph him at the most dangerous point of his voyage was a magnificent and terrifying experience. I flew from Puerto Williams, the tiny Chilean naval base which is the southernmost inhabited spot in the Americas.

"As my aircraft rose to find a cleft in the mountains of Hoste Island, the biggest of the Horn group, I was confronted with a superb sight. Green glaciers tumbling from the high snow-blanketed Darwin ranges into the Southern Ocean. As I flew by Cape Horn Island, its grey pyramid could be seen lashed by heavy seas and rimmed by breaking seas which appeared from time to time through the driving rain.

"South of the Horn the waves were driving eastward in long ridges of white and grey-green. Overhead were black driving clouds driven by the gale and a mile or two ahead the clouds were joined to the sea by rain in a black, impenetrable barrier towards the south and the pole.

"I picked up H.M.S. *Protector* first, wallowing in the heavy seas as she kept company with the yacht. Then I picked out the salt grimed hull of *Gipsy Moth* lurching forward as the seas passed
(footnote continued next page)

Ten minutes after noon I logged: "I tried to be too clever (as so often, I regret). I went out to try to coax *Gipsy Moth* to sail more across the wind; the motive being to get north into the lee of land." I thought that if only I could make some northing, I would get protection in the lee of Horn Island, and the islands to the north of it. However, the seas did not like it when I started sailing across them, and a souser filled the cockpit half full when I was in it. As a result, I had to change all my clothes, and also put *Gipsy Moth* back on to her original heading. That kept me just on the edge of the wind shadow from Cape Horn, and that might have made for more turbulence.

However, the wind was backing slowly, so that I steadily approached the heading I wanted to Staten Island. Unfortunately, with the wind shifting into the south-west, I got no protection whatever from the land, and after *Protector* left (one and a half hours after noon) the seas built up to some of the most vicious I had experienced on the voyage.

When *Protector* forged ahead, turned round ahead of *Gipsy Moth* and went away, she left me with a forlorn, empty feeling of desolation. I think it is a far greater strain to have a brief sight of a ship full of people in such conditions than it is to be quite alone: it emphasises the isolation, because it makes one realise the impossibility of being helped should one require help. The odd thing was that I had not only no feeling of achievement whatever at having passed the Horn, but I had no more feeling about it than if I had been passing landmarks all the way from Australia.

It had certainly been a rough sea before *Protector* left; the cockpit had been filled five times up to then. It was an extraordinary sight to see the gear lever throttle control, and instruments of the motor which were placed half-way up the side of the cockpit, all under water. But that sea was kid's stuff compared to what was running three hours later. The biggest wind registered by the anemometer that I noticed was 55 knots. I was doubtful of the accuracy of this instrument in high winds, but even if it was only 55 knots that, added to the 8 knots of speed which *Gipsy Moth* was making, totted up to a 63-knot

under her. My Chilean pilot, Captain Rodolfo Fuenzalida, gamely took us down to 60 ft where spume torn from the seas lashed across the aircraft's windscreen. But I had time to pick out Chichester in his cockpit, apparently nonchalantly preparing for his change of course and the long voyage home.

"When my pilot waggled his wings in salute we were rewarded by a wave of greeting. 'Muy hombre,' said the pilot, which I freely translate as 'What a man'.

"On the flight home we had severe turbulence as we threaded our way back through the mountains, and we lost an engine over the Strait of Magellan. It was a flight I am not too anxious to repeat, but the sight of *Gipsy Moth* ploughing bravely through this wilderness of rain and sea was well worth it."

wind—Force 11. The seas were far more vicious than I should have expected from such a wind and they were frightening.

The self-steering gear seemed unable to control the heading so I went aft to inspect the gear. I found that the connection between the wind vane and the steering oar had come out of its socket again. I tried to replace its proper pin, but could not get it in by hand, so I fetched an ordinary split pin and used that.

I think that this particularly turbulent sea was due to being on the edge of soundings; a few miles to port the depth was only 50 fathoms, and a few miles to starboard it was 2,300 fathoms.

By 16.30, however, there had been one or two lulls, which cheered me enormously. I had been thinking that I should have to stay all night holding the self-steering control lines in my hands. These were the emergency lines which I had led into the cabin, so that I could help out the self-steering gear when it was unable to cope with a broaching of the boat.

At 17.37 I logged:

"A definite lull, with wind not roaring or screaming, and wind speeds down to 25–30 knots. Long may it last! The trouble with these gales is that I lose my appetite just when plenty of food is needed, I am sure. There were some wonderful pictures of big seas this afternoon after *Protector* left, but I just cannot face photographing them. Photography seems so paltry beside the tremendous display of force by nature."

I was headed north-east for the east point of Staten Island. *Gipsy Moth* was travelling fast, although she had only the storm jib set, and that was reefed so that the total area was only 60 square feet, which is not much for an 18-ton boat. The wind had swung round to south-west and I heard later that some-one aboard *Protector* had said the wind was 100 miles an hour when she left *Gipsy Moth*. I think that was a misquote, but six hours later I was in an angry storm, as if the Horn was letting me know what it could do if it tried. The anemometer only reads to 60 knots which, with the boat speed of 6 knots, amounted to at least 66 knots, but I would say it was gusting up to 75 knots and perhaps occasionally 85 knots or 100 mph. Powerful seas roared past, and breaking tops came rolling down on to me from the stern. I thanked God that I could run before it. My only fear was that the wind would continue to back, and make the land a lee shore. There was far more power in this sea than in the one that had capsized *Gipsy Moth* off Australia, and if I had had to stop running and lie ahull—well, it couldn't have been done. The worst time was at nightfall. In the increasing darkness the seas were just terrific. I admit I was frightened for a while.★

However, fear does not last. I turned in and went to sleep. I slept for about two hours, until an hour after midnight. I found that the speedometer batteries had run down and I changed them. Unfortunately I did not allow for the distance run being under-registered. This might have had serious consequences. I logged:

"The rolling is frightful. It is very difficult to stand in the cabin. The wind is pretty strong still, 23–33 knots in the quieter periods."

The barometer had steadied. I ought to have realised that there was something wrong with the mileometer, because it registered only 8.8 miles run in three hours. All the morning I had been making good about 8 miles in one hour. I had run up the dead reckoning position at 22.00 using the distance recorded by the mileometer. I was on a heading of NE by E to pass close east of Staten Island. There seemed a good open space before me on the chart, with the east cape of Staten Island 85 miles ahead by the dead reckoning. The navigation looked so easy that I did not pay much attention to it.

At 04.40 in the morning I gybed, because *Gipsy Moth* had been forced up to a heading of NNE by the backing wind. I logged: "My hands are numb and I have difficulty in hanging up my coat or in writing." There was a strong wind still blowing, over 60 knots. I found that the long-suffering wind vane was catching up in the mizzen backstay, and I used a length of cord to prevent the backstay from fouling it. No wonder the self-steering gear had been eccentric in the gale! I had a hot rum to warm me up and wrote in the log:

"I now feel as tight as a coot, though I don't know how a coot could be tight. It was very good rum though. When we are going dead before the wind it seems as quiet as a church at times when the boat is not rolling. I think I am short of food—I have had only two square meals in two days, supplemented by snacks, mostly liquid like chocolate or honey and lemon. I am not sure that the paraffin stove is not upsetting me with carbon monoxide. Big

---

★Clements, in *A Gypsy of the Horn,* writes: "A winter's gale on a lee shore is a nerve-racking experience. Not so a Cape Horn sea. One merely triumphs in the exhibition of such stupendous power and sublimity. Death itself would be a small thing in such surroundings." I think that things like this must be written in peace and security, weeks after actually experiencing Cape Horn seas.

wash-outs on the deck send a spurt of salt water down the stove pipe and the flames burn yellow instead of blue for a while. I have had a nagging headache for a day and have been wondering if the stove causes it. It is difficult to make the cowl work because of eddies from the gale blowing on to it from astern. The fumes are pushed back into the cabin."

There was nothing in sight at 05.30 and I had seen nothing while working for quite a while on the stern at daybreak. I felt hungry and started preparing breakfast. I chanced to look out of the window in the doghouse on the port side and I felt as if the roots of my hair all over my body had turned red. I was startled to the bone, when, on looking out of the hatch, I saw a vast craggy bulk of land less than 10 miles away, and we had nearly passed it. I expected Staten Island to be still 35 miles ahead. Had I been pushed in by the tide to close Tierra del Fuego in the night? If so I must be bearing down on Staten Island ahead as a lee shore in winds up to 40 knots. I took three bearings of a cape that *Gipsy Moth* was passing, from which I reckoned that we were 7 miles off it, and that the ground speed was 8.8 knots. As soon as I had sighted the land I had prised myself up in the companion and peered over the top of the hood above it. I was headed to pass a headland, leaving it 5 miles to port. I must establish my position. My breakfast, of course, had gone for a burton. Fortunately, the sun had risen nearly dead ahead; a sun observation would give me a position line which would decide how far up the coast I was. I hurriedly fished out the sextant and set to work. Meanwhile, the headland was rushing up fast. The hilly land rising to mountainous country behind it was moving up as fast as if I was passing in a train. I think I have seldom taken and worked out a sight quicker. At the same time I was taking it steadily, set on not making a mistake. I plotted the resultant position line. I was passing the East Cape of Staten Island. I could hardly believe it. I checked my working again—there was no mistake.

Although I could hardly believe it at the time, when I came to look at the chart and study the dead reckoning navigation, it all became simple. From my noon position near Cape Horn I had worked out the heading which would take me 5 miles past the easternmost cape of Staten Island. In fact, I passed 7 miles off it. The distance was 140 miles, and if I had worked out the time at the morning's ground speed of 7.4 knots my estimated time of arrival at the Cape would have been nineteen hours after leaving the noon position, i.e. at 07.00 on the Tuesday morning. In fact, I arrived there at one and a half minutes past 8. It took me longer, because the wind eased during the night, and *Gipsy Moth*, still with only the 60-foot spitfire set, slowed down. What I had forgotten to take into account was the fact that the speedometer batteries had run down, and had undoubtedly been under-registering; therefore I thought I was going much slower than in fact I was. That I overlooked this is understandable to myself; I got agitated and disturbed by the presence of the warship, and having to talk to her, and also by the arrival of the aircraft, and being anxious that she was going to ditch. I felt tired, strained and extremely lonely when they all cleared off. On top of that I was seasick, and later in a Cape Horn grey-bearder storm, and so I neglected to take account of the mileometer under-reading.

Now Staten Island had rushed past, and already it was disappearing in the haze. At last I felt I had rounded the Horn properly, and was headed into the middle of the wide waters of the South Atlantic. As I left Staten Island, I had an immense feeling of relief. It was the same feeling as the clipper sailors record, of feeling that they were home when they rounded the Horn. Gradually this fades and vanishes, and is forgotten as the 8,000-mile voyage up the Atlantic proceeds. Those oceans turn out to be no lily ponds, as they seem to be after turning the Horn.

My log takes up the tale:

"March 21, 11.56. There is still a very rough sea. Thank God we are going downwind. When the boat is slewed round broadside to the seas, she gets a pounding straight away. The problem now is whether to change course to the north to pass west of the Falkland Islands, or head north-east as at present to pass east of the Falkland Isles. Considering the wind is sure to swing to the west after this, and that north-east is the downwind course we are on at present, the eastward passage is the obvious one. If I keep to this heading I can relax till tomorrow morning, when I must start cocking an eye for Beauchene Island. Meanwhile, what I must do is tighten up the wind vane, which now slips every time a good-sized wave hits the stern. I feel tired to the bone; this gale stuff goes on and on. The noise, the incessant effort to hold on, or balance, and avoid being thrown, the nervous strain of waiting for a socker wave, loss of appetite due to the movement, disturbed sleep. Put clocks forward one hour.

"14.20. I found that the bolt holding the wind vane to its shaft had sheered. With difficulty I replaced it with a new bolt without losing the vane in the Force 6 wind. I expect that one end of this bolt had sheered through some time ago, which is why I was so worried about the vane's erratic behaviour during the night. I think it is a miracle that it survives a big blow and rough seas. I got a sun sight. I hoisted the storm staysail and set the spitfire higher up its stay by using the tack pennant. We are jogging along quietly at 5 knots with those two sails only, and I think I will leave it so till the sea, which is still very rough by normal standards, goes down. I started the motor for charging. I used the heat starter which I seldom have to do normally. Now here is another seeming miracle—that the motor starts right away. After watching the instrument panel, the throttle and gear lever all under sea water for nearly a quarter of an hour, and considering that they have had several similar submersions, it is just like a miracle that it starts with no trouble. Now for some lunch.

"18.05. That blow is over: it is fine mild weather. It makes me feel I have rounded the Horn at last, and in a few minutes I am going to crack a bottle of champagne to celebrate. After that I want a big sleep. The boat is undercanvassed but that must wait. By the way, as I passed the Horn at 16.07½ GMT March 20 I won my race with the sun; but only just—by 15.275 miles, the distance which the sun was still south of the Line.

"March 22, 01.20. Another proper piece of Charleyism: I went off into a deep sleep at 7 p.m., and woke just before midnight to find we were headed *south* and going well! The wind had veered and I wondered when? I hope I woke when it happened, but doubt it, I was so tired. At least it was taking me away from danger, the Falkland group. If only I had set the off-course alarm! I must plot the DR from Staten Island. To show how I feel, I have not plotted the DR up from the Horn yet, or totted up the day's run. [It was 160½ miles noon to noon all under the spitfire only.] Meanwhile, I will run the DR up to the present and work out two positions, according to whether the ship changed heading when I started to sleep, or when I finished sleeping. Anyway I gybed as soon as I woke and so got close to the right heading. I avoided any blunders on deck, though still thick-headed with drowsiness. I tried to finish the job without a safety-belt on, but had forgotten the levered shrouds. So I had to don harness in the middle of the gybe to go forward and handle the shrouds. How I would relish 12 hours' solid sleep. I was thinking it was that warship and all the telephoning which fagged me. After 50 days plodding across the Southern Ocean alone, I needed the Horn to myself, somehow. This must sound daft, but 50 days' solitude is strong medicine."

Having written that, which, I think, truly reflected my feelings in the early hours of that morning, I decided to leave the yacht as she was going for the moment and go back to sleep. I stayed in my bunk until nine o'clock, when I got up and unreefed the spitfire jib, thinking that a scrap more sail would steady the boat. It did, and also increased her speed a little. Then I thought about breakfast, and was annoyed to find that I couldn't have any wholemeal toast because I had run out of bread. I breakfasted instead on Ryvita and butter and marmalade, which I enjoyed, but I like my wholemeal bread, so after breakfast I baked another batch. I had to give the albatrosses the rest of Lorna's cake (a splendid cake, given to me by Lorna Anderson in Sydney). I had spun it out too long, and the fat in it had turned rancid. There were seven albatrosses following *Gipsy Moth,* and they certainly did love that cake. They kept swooping close to the boat, only 20–30 feet away, obviously asking for more, but I had no more to give them.

It rained pretty consistently, with visibility down to a mile or so, and with no chance of a sight to check direction. But I reckoned that I was giving Beauchene Island a wide enough berth. That afternoon I figured that I must have passed over the edge of the Burdwood Bank (minimum depth 25 fathoms). The yacht had a rough time of it, with several waves breaking on her, and big, sweeping troughs with the waves. After this rough patch, the sea was comparatively smooth, with no considerable troughs. Later, after studying my dead reckoning I figured that we must have been on the edge of the bank around noon, and then sailed along the edge until we left it. That would tally exactly with the sea's suddenly becoming flatter and milder.

I was now headed out into the South Atlantic on a north-easterly course. My track was roughly parallel with the coast of South America and about 850 miles off it. Abeam to starboard was the island of South Georgia, 500 miles away. After that there was a big wide open space ahead in the South Atlantic for 1,600 miles, when I was due to pass Ilha da Trinidade, leaving it 500 miles to port. It was a great relief not to have to worry about running on to lee coasts in stormy weather; also I had a feeling of peace on getting away from the Horn area which had seemed decidedly overcrowded. I could relax.

I turned in early, and spent seven and a half hours in my bunk—a good sleep, but bad for navigation. I was awakened by that irresistible arouser, cramp, and got up just before 5 a.m. The barometer kept on falling and I logged that I wished I were well to the north in case it meant a big storm. The US Pilot Chart showed that there was not a considerable drop in gale percentage until I was north of 45° S. Between 50 and 45° S, 12 per cent of the winds recorded there were gales compared with 9 per cent in the lee of the Falklands and 26 per cent off the Horn. I reckoned, however, that I must be getting some protection from the Falklands, about 80 miles to windward.

Instead of a storm, the weather cleared up during the morning (March 23), and I had all plain sail set again, for the first time for ages. The wind had become a gentle breeze of about 14 knots, the sun shone, the sea was blue, and the barometer began to rise. I was heartened to go on deck to set the mizzen without adding any deck clothes, but this was a mistake, for that gentle wind was biting cold, even through my thick woollen sweater.

That day ended with a lovely starry night, a nearly full moon, and not a cloud in the sky. I turned in trying to think when I last saw such a sky, and couldn't remember one on the whole of this passage. Alas, my joyous looking forward to a sunny, quiet sail went awry. I went to sleep pondering about bringing out my big genoa to keep the yacht going in light airs, and woke to a north-westerly gale. I had to strip all sail off the yacht, except the working jib. The sun was shining, though, which was heartening. But it was bitterly cold, and my hands got so cold that I had difficulty in writing up my log.

On coming below after taking in sail I hung my deck trousers, soaked with spray, just inside the companion, where I thought that the water running off them would make less mess than in the cabin. Unfortunately, a souser wave overran the boat, and the bit that came through the hatch emptied straight into my trousers. You just can't do right in rough weather.

The sea that day (March 24) gave me a good pounding but it was not a high, or steep sea. Nor did the barometer drop a great deal. I figured that I was on the north-east quarter of a depression going through. By afternoon the wind had lost that roaring whistle which tells you that it is too strong for peace of mind, and changed to a sort of low, moaning roar. The sea remained very rough, and I waited until evening before setting the genoa staysail. I had a good supper of two Caroni rums, hot, two onions fried with a tin of baked beans, and a tin of pineapple. After supper I felt that more sail was needed, and my conscience told me that I ought to set the main. But I was reluctant to tackle it after my good supper, and wondered if the mizzen would do until dawn. Setting that would be only a tenth of the effort of hoisting the main. In the end, the mizzen seemed the job, and it changed the yacht's tempo at once. She began scuttling instead of lurching. After the gale it was a lovely moonlit night, and it was thrilling to be on deck in the moonlight with the lively sea, and the boat going well.

I put my thoughts into a radio message that night:

"At last," I reported, "I feel as though I am waking from a nightmare of sailing through that Southern Ocean. There is something nightmarishly frightening about those big breaking seas and screaming wind. They give a feeling of helplessness before their irresistible, remorseless power rolling down on top of one, and it all has ten times the impact when alone. Till yesterday I still felt I was in the wind shadow of the Horn. It was still wet, cold and grey and the wind still blowing hard. The seas were not so threatening but I shall be glad to get north of 50° S. without another big blow."

The off-course alarm shook me out of a heavy sleep at six o'clock next morning. I turned it off but cramp made me get up. It was a fine dawn, but very cold. I altered course downwind. Really I could have done with a poled-out jib, but the wind as I was going was near gybing point, so I left things as they were and waited for the gybe.

Doing my navigation that morning (March 25) I found that I had crossed the parallel of 50° S about midnight. The clipper captains, especially of the California clippers, considered this point very important, and always compared their times round the Horn from 50° S to 50° S. I crossed the 50th parallel west of the Horn in the Pacific at zero hours on March 12, and crossed it in the Atlantic at zero hours on March 25. That made thirteen days.

My mileage tally for the week that saw me round the Horn was 1,106½, an average of 158 miles a day, or 6.58 knots. This was the fifth week in succession that *Gipsy Moth* had sailed over 1,000 miles in the week; 5,230½ miles in 35 days, an average of 149.4 miles per day. These distances, of course, are run over straight lines between noon positions, and do not include tacks or digressions.

On the Oregon Trail

From *The Oregon Trail*

BY FRANCIS PARKMAN

If any mellow old classic deserves a second look, this one certainly lives up to that distinction. Perhaps you first encountered *The Oregon Trail* as required reading as a school kid. That's fine, but you're really cheating yourself if you don't give it another go. Parkman (1823–1893) showed us the way west as few have captured it in prose and will continue to deserve readers for generations to come.

★   ★   ★   ★   ★

The country before us was now thronged with buffalo, and a sketch of the manner of hunting them will not be out of place. There are two methods commonly practised, "running" and "approaching." The chase on horseback, which goes by the name of "running," is the more violent and dashing mode of the two, that is to say, when the buffalo are in one of their wild moods; for otherwise it is tame enough. A practised and skilful hunter, well mounted, will sometimes kill five or six cows in a single chase, loading his gun again and again as his horse rushes through the tumult. In attacking a small band of buffalo, or in separating a single animal from the herd and assailing it apart from the rest, there is less excitement and less danger. In fact, the animals are at times so stupid and lethargic that there is little sport in killing them. With a bold and well-trained horse the hunter may ride so close to the buffalo that as they gallop side by side he may touch him with his hand; nor is there much danger in this as long as the buffalo's strength and breath continue unabated; but when he becomes tired and can no longer run with ease, with his tongue lolls out and the foam flies from his jaws, then the hunter had better keep a more respectful distance; the distressed brute may turn upon him at any instant; and especially at the moment when he fires his gun. The horse then leaps aside, and the hunter has need of a tenacious seat in the saddle, for if he is thrown to the ground there is no hope for him. When he sees his attack defeated, the buffalo resumes his flight, but if the shot is well directed he soon stops; for a few moments he stands still, then totters and falls heavily upon the prairie.

The chief difficulty in running buffalo, as it seems to me, is that of loading the gun or pistol at full gallop. Many hunters for convenience's sake carry three or four bullets in the mouth; the powder is poured down the muzzle of the piece, the bullet dropped in after it, the stock struck hard upon the pommel of the saddle, and the work is done. The danger of this is obvious. Should the blow on the pommel fail to send the bullet home, or should the bullet, in the act of aiming, start from its place and roll towards the muzzle, the gun would probably burst in discharging. Many a shattered hand and worse casualties besides have been the result of such an accident. To obviate it, some hunters make use of a ramrod, usually hung by a string from the neck, but this materially increases the difficulty of loading. The bows and arrows which the Indians use in running buffalo have many advantages over firearms, and even white men occasionally employ them.

The danger of the chase arises not so much from the onset of the wounded animal as from the nature of the ground which the hunter must ride over. The prairie does not always present a smooth, level, and uniform surface; very often it is broken with hills and hollows, intersected by ravines, and in the remoter parts studded by the stiff wild-sage bushes. The most formidable obstructions, however, are the burrows of wild animals, wolves, badgers, and particularly prairie-dogs, with whose holes the ground for a very great extent is frequently honeycombed. In the blindness of the chase the hunter rushes over it unconscious of danger; his horse, at full career, thrusts his leg deep into one of the burrows; the bone snaps, the rider is hurled forward to the ground and probably killed. Yet accidents in buffalo running happen less frequently than one would suppose; in the recklessness of the chase, the hunter enjoys all the impunity of a drunken man, and may ride in safety over gullies and declivities, where, should he attempt to pass in his sober senses, he would infallibly break his neck.

The method of "approaching," being practised on foot, has many advantages over that of "running"; in the former, one neither breaks down his horse nor endangers his own life; he must be cool, collected, and watchful; must understand the buffalo, observe the features of the country and the course of the wind, and be well skilled in using the rifle. The buffalo are strange animals; sometimes they are so stupid and infatuated that a man may walk up to them in full sight on the open prairie, and even shoot several of their number before the rest will think it necessary to retreat. At another moment they will be so shy and wary that in order to approach them the utmost skill, experience, and judgment are necessary. Kit Carson, I believe, stands preeminent in running buffalo; in approaching, no man living can bear away the palm from Henry Chatillon.

After Tête Rouge had alarmed the camp, no further disturbance occurred during the night. The Arapahoes did not attempt mischief, or if they did the wakefulness of the party deterred them from effecting their purpose. The next day was one of activity and excitement, for about ten o'clock the man in advance shouted the gladdening cry of *buffalo, buffalo!* and in the hollow of the prairie just below us, a band of bulls was grazing. The temptation was irresistible, and Shaw and I rode down upon them. We were badly mounted on our travelling horses, but by hard lashing we overtook them, and Shaw, running alongside a bull, shot into him both balls of his double-barreled gun. Looking round as I galloped by, I saw the bull in his mortal fury rushing again and again upon his antagonist, whose horse constantly leaped aside, and avoided the onset. My chase was more protracted, but at length I ran close to the bull and killed him with my pistols. Cutting off the tails of our victims by way of trophy, we rejoined the party in about a quarter of an hour after we had left it. Again and again that morning rang out the same welcome cry of *buffalo, buffalo!* Every few moments, in the broad meadows along the river, we saw bands of bulls, who, raising their shaggy heads, would gaze in stupid amazement at the approaching horsemen, and then breaking into a clumsy gallop, file off in a long line across the trail in front, towards the rising prairie on the left. At noon, the plain before us was alive with thousands of buffalo,—bulls, cows, and calves,—all moving rapidly as we drew near; and far off beyond the river the swelling prairie was darkened with them to the very horizon. The party was in gayer spirits than ever. We stopped for a nooning near a grove of trees by the river.

"Tongues and hump-ribs tomorrow," said Shaw, looking with contempt at the venison steaks which Deslauriers placed before us. Our meal finished, we lay down to sleep. A shout from Henry Chatillon aroused us, and we saw him standing on the cart-wheel, stretching his tall figure to its full height, while he looked towards the prairie beyond the river. Following the direction of his eyes, we could clearly distinguish a large, dark object, like the black shadow of a cloud, passing rapidly over swell after swell of the distant plain; behind it followed another of similar appearance, though smaller, moving more rapidly, and drawing closer and closer to the first. It was the hunters of the Arapahoe camp chasing a band of buffalo. Shaw and I caught and saddled our best horses, and went plunging through sand and water to the farther bank. We were too late. The hunters had already mingled with the herd, and the work of slaughter was nearly over. When we reached the ground we found it strewn far and near with numberless carcasses, while the remnants of the herd, scattered in all directions, were flying away in terror, and the Indians still rushing in pursuit. Many of the hunters, however, remained upon the spot, and among the rest was our yesterday's acquaintance, the chief of the village. He had alighted by the side of a cow, into which he had shot five or six arrows, and his squaw, who had followed him on horseback to the hunt, was giving him a draught of water from a canteen, purchased or plundered from some volunteer soldier. Recrossing the river, we overtook the party, who were already on their way.

We had gone scarcely a mile when we saw an imposing spectacle. From the river-bank on the right, away over the swelling prairie on the left, and in front as far as the eye could reach, was one vast host of buffalo. The outskirts of the herd were within a quarter of a mile. In many parts they were crowded so densely together that in the distance their rounded backs presented a surface of uniform blackness; but elsewhere they were more scattered, and from amid the multitude rose little columns of dust where some of them were rolling on the ground. Here and there a battle was going forward among the bulls. We could distinctly see them rushing against each other, and hear the clattering of their horns and their hoarse bellowing. Shaw was riding at some distance in advance, with Henry Chatillon; I saw him stop and draw the leather covering from his gun. With such a sight before us, but one thing could be thought of. That morning I had used pistols in the chase. I had now a mind to try the virtue of a gun. Deslauriers had one, and I rode up to the side of the cart; there he sat under the white covering, biting his pipe between his teeth and grinning with excitement.

"Lend me your gun, Deslauriers."

"*Oui, Monsieur, oui,*" said Deslauriers, tugging with might and main to stop the mule, which seemed obstinately bent on going forward. Then everything but his moccasons disappeared as he crawled into the cart and pulled at the gun to extricate it.

"Is it loaded?" I asked.

"*Oui, bien chargé;* you'll kill, *mon bourgeois;* yes, you'll kill—*c'est um bon fusil.*"

I handed him my rifle and rode forward to Shaw.

"Are you ready?" he asked.

"Come on," said I.

"Keep down that hollow," said Henry, "and then they won't see you till you get close to them."

The hollow was a kind of wide ravine; it ran obliquely towards the buffalo, and we rode at a canter along the bottom until it became too shallow; then we bent close to our horses' necks, and, at last, finding that it could no longer conceal us, came out of it and rode directly towards the herd. It was within gunshot; before its outskirts, numerous grizzly old bulls were scattered, holding guard over their females. They glared at us in anger and astonishment, walked towards us a few yards, and then turning slowly round, retreated at a trot which afterwards broke into a clumsy gallop. In an instant the main body caught the alarm. The buffalo began to crowd away from the point towards which we were approaching, and a gap was opened in the side of the herd. We entered it, still restraining our excited horses. Every instant the tumult was thickening. The buffalo, pressing together in large bodies, crowded away from us on every hand. In front and on either side we could see dark columns and masses, half hidden by clouds of dust, rushing along in terror and confusion, and hear the tramp and clattering of ten thousand hoofs. That countless multitude of powerful brutes, ignorant of their own strength, were flying in a panic from the approach of two feeble horsemen. To remain quiet longer was impossible.

"Take that band on the left," said Shaw; "I'll take these in front."

He sprang off, and I saw no more of him. A heavy Indian whip was fastened by a band to my wrist; I swung it into the air and lashed my horse's flank with all the strength of my arm. Away she darted, stretching close to the ground. I could see nothing but a cloud of dust before me, but I knew that it concealed a band of many hundreds of buffalo. In a moment I was in the midst of the cloud, half suffocated by the dust and stunned by the trampling of the flying herd; but I was drunk with the chase and cared for nothing but the buffalo. Very soon a long dark mass became visible, looming through the dust; then I could distinguish each bulky carcass, the hoofs flying out beneath, the short tails held rigidly erect. In a moment I was so close that I could have touched them with my gun. Suddenly, to my amazement, the hoofs were jerked upwards, the tails flourished in the air, and amid a cloud of dust the buffalo seemed to sink into the earth before me. One vivid impression of that instant remains upon my mind. I remember looking down upon the backs of several buffalo dimly visible through the dust. We had run unawares upon a ravine. At that moment I was not the most accurate judge of depth and width, but when I passed it on my return, I found it about twelve feet deep and not quite twice as wide at the bottom. It was impossible to stop; I would have done so gladly if I could; so, half sliding, half plunging, down went the little mare. She came down on her knees in the loose sand at the bottom; I was pitched forward against her neck and nearly thrown over her head among the buffalo, who amid dust and confusion came tumbling in all around. The mare was on her feet in an instant and scrambling like a cat up the opposite side. I thought for a moment that she would have fallen back and crushed me, but with a violent effort she clambered out and gained the hard prairie above. Glancing back, I saw the huge head of a bull clinging as it were by the forefeet at the edge of the dusty gulf. At length I was fairly among the buffalo. They were less densely crowded than before, and I could see nothing but bulls, who always run at the rear of a herd to protect their females. As I passed among them they would lower their heads, and turning as they ran, try to gore my horse; but as they were already at full speed there was no force in their onset, and as Pauline ran faster than they, they were always thrown behind her in the effort. I soon began to distinguish cows amid the throng. One just in front of me seemed to my liking, and I pushed close to her side. Dropping the reins, I fired, holding the muzzle of the gun within a foot of her shoulder. Quick as lightning she sprang at Pauline; the little mare dodged the attack, and I lost sight of the wounded animal amid the tumult. Immediately after, I selected another, and urging forward Pauline, shot into her both pistols in succession. For a while I kept her in view, but in attempting to load my gun, lost sight of her also in the confusion. Believing her to be mortally wounded and unable to keep up with the herd, I checked my horse. The crowd rushed onwards. The dust and tumult passed away, and on the prairie, far behind the rest, I saw a solitary buffalo galloping heavily. In a moment I and my victim were running side by side. My firearms were all empty, and I had in my pouch nothing but rifle bullets, too large for the pistols and too small for the gun. I loaded the gun, however, but as often as I levelled it to fire, the bullets would roll out of the muzzle and the gun returned only a report like a squib, as the powder harmlessly exploded. I rode in front of the buffalo and tried to turn her back; but her eyes glared, her mane bristled, and lowering her head, she rushed at me with the utmost fierceness and activity. Again and again I rode before her, and again and again she repeated her furious charge. But little Pauline was in her element. She dodged her enemy at every rush, until at length the buffalo stood still, exhausted with her own efforts, her tongue lolling from her jaws.

Riding to a little distance, I dismounted, thinking to gather a handful of dry grass to serve the purpose of wadding, and load the gun at my leisure. No sooner were my feet on the ground than the buffalo came bounding in such a rage towards me that I jumped back again into the saddle and with all possible despatch. After waiting a few minutes more, I made an attempt to ride up and stab her with my knife; but Pauline was near being gored in the attempt. At length, bethinking me of the fringes at the seams of my buckskin trousers, I jerked off a few of them, and, reloading the gun, forced them down the barrel to keep the bullet in its place; then approaching, I shot the wounded buffalo through the heart. Sinking to her knees, she rolled over lifeless on the prairie. To my astonishment, I found that, instead of a cow, I had been slaughtering a stout yearling bull. No longer wondering at his fierceness, I opened his throat, and cutting out his tongue, tied it at the back of my saddle. My mistake was one which a more experienced eye than mine might easily make in the dust and confusion of such a chase.

Then for the first time I had leisure to look at the scene around me. The prairie in front was darkened with the retreating multitude, and on either hand the buffalo came filing up in endless columns from the low plains upon the river. The Arkansas was three or four miles distant. I turned and moved slowly towards it. A long time passed before, far in the distance, I distinguished the white covering of the cart and the little black specks of horsemen before and behind it. Drawing near, I recognized Shaw's elegant tunic, the red flannel shirt, conspicuous far off. I overtook the party, and asked him what success he had had. He had assailed a fat cow, shot her with two bullets, and mortally wounded her. But neither of us was prepared for the chase that afternoon, and Shaw, like myself, had no spare bullets in his pouch; so he abandoned the disabled animal to Henry Chatillon, who followed, despatched her with his rifle, and loaded his horse with the meat.

We encamped close to the river. The night was dark, and as we lay down we could hear, mingled with the howling of wolves, the hoarse bellowing of the buffalo, like the ocean beating upon a distant coast.

★   ★   ★   ★   ★

No one in the camp was more active than Jim Gurney, and no one half so lazy as Ellis. Between these two there was a great antipathy. Ellis never stirred in the morning until he was compelled, but Jim was always on his feet before daybreak; and this morning as usual the sound of his voice awakened the party.

"Get up, you booby! up with you now, you're fit for nothing but eating and sleeping. Stop your grumbling and come out of that buffalo-robe, or I'll pull it off for you."

Jim's words were interspersed with numerous expletives, which gave them great additional effect. Ellis drawled out something in a nasal tone from among the folds of his buffalo-robe; then slowly disengaged himself, rose into a sitting posture, stretched his long arms, yawned hideously, and, finally raising his tall person erect, stood staring about him to all the four quarters of the horizon. Deslauriers' fire was soon blazing, and the horses and mules, loosened from their pickets, were feeding on the neighboring meadow. When we sat down to breakfast the prairie was still in the dusky light of morning; and as the sun rose we were mounted and on our way again.

"A white buffalo!" exclaimed Munroe.

"I'll have that fellow," said Shaw, "if I run my horse to death after him."

He threw the cover of his gun to Deslauriers and galloped out upon the prairie.

"Stop, Mr. Shaw, stop!" called out Henry Chatillon, "you'll run down your horse for nothing; it's only a white ox."

But Shaw was already out of hearing. The ox, which had no doubt strayed away from some of the government wagon trains, was standing beneath some low hills which bounded the plain in the distance. Not far from him a band of veritable buffalo bulls were grazing; and startled at Shaw's approach, they all broke into a run, and went scrambling up the hillsides to gain the high prairie above. One of them in his haste and terror involved himself in a fatal catastrophe. Along the foot of the hills was a narrow strip of deep marshy soil, into which the bull plunged and hopelessly entangled himself. We all rode to the spot. The huge carcass was half sunk in the mud, which flowed to his very chin, and his shaggy mane was outspread upon the surface. As we came near, the bull began to struggle with convulsive strength; he writhed to and fro, and in the energy of his fright and desperation would lift himself for a moment half out of the slough, while the reluctant mire returned a sucking sound as he strained to drag his limbs from its tenacious depths. We stimulated his exertions by getting behind him and twisting his tail; nothing would do. There was clearly no hope for him. After every effort his heaving sides were more deeply embedded, and the mire almost overflowed his nostrils; he lay still at length, and looking round at us with a furious eye, seemed to resign himself to fate. Ellis slowly dismounted, and, levelling his boasted yager, shot the old bull through the heart; then lazily climbed back again to his seat, pluming himself no doubt on having actually killed a buffalo. That day the invincible yager drew blood for the first and last time during the whole journey.

The morning was a bright and gay one, and the air so clear that on the farthest horizon the outline of the pale blue prairie was sharply drawn against the sky. Shaw was in the mood for hunting; he rode in advance of the party, and before long we saw a file of bulls galloping at full speed upon a green swell of the prairie at some distance in front. Shaw came scouring along behind them, arrayed in his red shirt, which looked very well in the distance; he gained fast on the fugitives, and as the foremost bull was disappearing behind the summit of the swell, we saw him in the act of assailing the hindmost; a smoke sprang from the muzzle of his gun and floated away before the wind like a little white cloud; the bull turned upon him, and just then the rising ground concealed them both from view.

We were moving forward until about noon, when we stopped by the side of the Arkansas. At that moment Shaw appeared riding slowly down the side of a distant hill; his horse was tired and jaded, and when he threw his saddle upon the ground, I observed that the tails of two bulls were dangling behind it. No sooner were the horses turned loose to feed than Henry, asking Munroe to go with him, took his rifle and walked quietly away. Shaw, Tête Rouge, and I sat down by the side of the cart to discuss the dinner which Deslauriers placed before us, and we had scarcely finished when we saw Munroe walking towards us along the river-bank. Henry, he said, had killed four fat cows, and had sent him back for horses to bring in the meat. Shaw took a horse for himself and another for Henry, and he and Munroe left the camp together. After a short absence all three of them came back, their horses loaded with the choicest parts of the meat. We kept two of the cows for ourselves, and gave the others to Munroe and his companions. Deslauriers seated himself on the grass before the pile of meat, and worked industriously for some time to cut it into thin broad sheets for drying, an art in which he had all the skill of an Indian squaw. Long before night, cords of raw hide were stretched around the camp, and the meat was hung upon them to dry in the sunshine and pure air of the prairie. Our California companions were less successful at the work; but they accomplished it after their own fashion, and their side of the camp was soon garnished in the same manner as our own.

We meant to remain at this place long enough to prepare provisions for our journey to the frontier, which, as we supposed, might occupy about a month. Had the distance been twice as great and the party ten times as large, the rifle of Henry Chatillon would have supplied meat enough for the whole within two days; we were obliged to remain, however, until it should be dry enough for transportation; so we pitched our tent and made other arrangements for a permanent camp. The California men, who had no such shelter, contented themselves with arranging their packs on the grass around their fire. In the mean time we had nothing to do but amuse ourselves. Our tent was within a rod of the river, if the broad sand-beds, with a scanty stream of water coursing here and there along their surface, deserve to be dignified with the name of river. The vast flat plains on either side were almost on a level with the sand-beds, and they were bounded in the distance by low, monotonous hills, parallel to the course of the stream. All was one expanse of grass; there was no wood in view, except some trees and stunted bushes upon two islands which rose from the wet sands of the river. Yet far from being dull and tame, the scene was often a wild and animated one; for twice a day, at sunrise and at noon, the buffalo came issuing from the hills, slowly advancing in their grave processions to drink at the river. All our amusements were to be at their expense. An old buffalo bull is a brute of unparalleled ugliness. At first sight of him every feeling of pity vanishes. The cows are much smaller and of a gentler appearance, as becomes their sex. While in this camp we forbore to attack them, leaving to Henry Chatillon, who could better judge their quality, the task of killing such as we wanted for use; but against the bulls we waged an unrelenting war. Thousands of them might be slaughtered without causing any detriment to the species, for their numbers greatly exceed those of the cows; it is the hides of the latter alone which are used for the purposes of commerce and for making the lodges of the Indians; and the destruction among them is therefore greatly disproportionate.

Our horses were tired, and we now usually hunted on foot. While we were lying on the grass after dinner, smoking, talking, or laughing at Tête Rouge, one of us would look up and observe, far out on the plains beyond the river, certain black objects slowly approaching. He would inhale a parting whiff from the pipe, then rising lazily, take his rifle, which leaned against the cart, throw over his shoulder the strap of his pouch and powder-horn, and with his moccasons in his hand, walk across the sand towards the opposite side of the river. This was very easy; for though the sands were about a quarter of a mile wide, the water was nowhere more than two feet deep. The farther bank was about four or five feet high, and quite perpendicular, being cut away by the water in spring. Tall grass grew along its edge. Putting it aside with his hand, and cautiously looking through it, the hunter can discern the huge shaggy back of the bull slowly swaying to and fro, as, with his clumsy, swinging gait, he advances towards the river. The buffalo have regular paths by which they come down to drink. Seeing at a glance along which of these his intended victim is moving, the hunter crouches under the bank within fifteen or twenty yards, it may be, of the point where the path enters the river. Here he sits down quietly on the sand. Listening intently, he hears the heavy, monotonous tread of the approaching bull. The moment after, he sees a motion among the long weeds and grass just at the spot where the path is channelled through the bank. An enormous black head is thrust out, the horns just visible amid the mass of tangled mane. Half sliding, half plunging, down comes the buffalo upon the river-bed below. He steps out in full sight upon the sands. Just before him a runnel of water is gliding, and he bends his head to drink. You may hear the water as it gurgles down his capacious throat. He raises his head, and the drops trickle from his wet beard. He stands with an air of stupid abstraction, unconscious of the lurking danger. Noiselessly the hunter cocks his rifle. As he sits upon the sand, his knee is raised, and his elbow rests upon it, that he may level his heavy weapon with a steadier aim. The stock is at his shoulder; his eye ranges along the barrel. Still he is in no haste to fire. The bull, with slow deliberation, begins his march over the sands to the other side. He advances his foreleg, and exposes to view a small spot, denuded of hair, just behind the point of his shoulder; upon this the hunter brings the sight of his rifle to bear; lightly and delicately his finger presses the hair-trigger. The spiteful crack of the rifle responds to his touch, and instantly in the middle of the bare spot appears a small red dot. The buffalo shivers; death has overtaken him, he cannot tell from whence; still he does not fall, but walks heavily forward, as if nothing had happened. Yet before he has gone far out upon the sand, you see him stop; he totters; his knees bend under him, and his head sinks forward to the ground. Then his whole vast bulk sways to one side; he rolls over on the sand, and dies with a scarcely perceptible struggle.

Waylaying the buffalo in this manner, and shooting them as they come to water, is the easiest method of hunting them. They may also be approached by crawling up ravines or behind hills, or even over the open prairie. This is often surprisingly easy; but at other times it requires the utmost skill of the most experienced hunter. Henry Chatillon was a man of extraordinary strength and hardihood; but I have seen him return to camp quite exhausted with his efforts, his limbs scratched and wounded, and his buckskin dress stuck full of the thorns of the prickly-pear, among which he had been crawling. Sometimes he would lie flat upon his face, and drag himself along in this position for many rods together.

On the second day of our stay at this place, Henry went out for an afternoon hunt. Shaw and I remained in camp, until, observing some bulls approaching the water upon the other side of the river, we crossed over to attack them. They were so near, however, that before we could get under cover of the bank our appearance as we walked over the sands alarmed them. Turning round before coming within gun-shot, they began to move off to the right in a direction parallel to the river. I climbed up the bank and ran after them. They were walking swiftly, and before I could come within gun-shot distance they slowly wheeled about and faced me. Before they had turned far enough to see me I had fallen flat on my face. For a moment they stood and stared at the strange object upon the grass; then turning away, again they walked on as before; and I, rising immediately, ran once more in pursuit. Again they wheeled about, and again I fell prostrate. Repeating this three or four times, I came at length within a hundred yards of the fugitives, and as I saw them turning again, I sat down and levelled my rifle. The one in the centre was the largest I had ever seen. I shot him behind the shoulder. His two companions ran off. He attempted to follow, but soon came to a stand, and at length lay down as quietly as an ox chewing the cud. Cautiously approaching him, I saw by his dull and jelly-like eye that he was dead.

When I began the chase, the prairie was almost tenantless; but a great multitude of buffalo had suddenly thronged upon it, and looking up I saw within fifty rods a heavy, dark column stretching to the right and left as far as I could see. I walked towards them. My approach did not alarm them in the least. The column itself consisted almost entirely of cows and calves, but a great many old bulls were ranging about the prairie on its flank, and as I drew near they faced towards me with such a grim and ferocious look that I thought it best to proceed no farther. Indeed, I was already within close rifle-shot of the column, and I sat down on the ground to watch their movements. Sometimes the whole would stand still, their heads all one way; then they would trot forward, as if by a common impulse, their hoofs and horns clattering together as they moved. I soon began to hear at a distance on the left the sharp reports of a rifle, again and again repeated; and not long after, dull and heavy sounds succeeded, which I recognized as the familiar voice of Shaw's double-barreled gun. When Henry's rifle was at work there was always meat to be brought in. I went back across the river for a horse, and, returning, reached the spot where the hunters were standing. The buffalo were visible on the distant prairie. The living had retreated from the ground, but ten or twelve carcasses were scattered in various directions. Henry, knife in hand, was stooping over a dead cow, cutting away the best and fattest of the meat.

When Shaw left me he had walked down for some distance under the river-bank to find another bull. At length he saw the plains covered with the host of buffalo, and soon after heard the crack of Henry's rifle. Ascending the bank, he crawled through the grass, which for a rod or two from the river was very high and rank. He had not crawled far before to his astonishment he saw Henry standing erect upon the prairie, almost surrounded by the buffalo. Henry was in his element. Quite unconscious that any one was looking at him, he stood at the full height of his tall figure, one hand resting upon his side, and the other arm leaning carelessly on the muzzle of his rifle. His eye was ranging over the singular assemblage around him. Now and then he would select such a cow as suited him, level his rifle, and shoot her dead; then quietly reloading, he would resume his former position. The buffalo seemed no more to regard his presence than if he were one of themselves; the bulls were bellowing and butting at each other, or rolling about in the dust. A group of buffalo would gather about the carcass of a dead cow, snuffing at her wounds; and sometimes they would come behind those that had not yet fallen, and endeavor to push them from the spot. Now and then some old bull would face towards Henry with an air of stupid amazement, but none seemed inclined to attack or fly from him. For some time Shaw lay among the grass, looking in surprise at this extraordinary sight; at length he crawled cautiously forward, and spoke in a low voice to Henry, who told him to rise and come on. Still the buffalo showed no sign of fear; they remained gathered about their dead companions. Henry had already killed as many cows as he wanted for use, and Shaw, kneeling behind one of the carcasses, shot five bulls before the rest thought it necessary to disperse.

The frequent stupidity and infatuation of the buffalo seems the more remarkable from the contrast it offers to their wildness and wariness at other times. Henry knew all their peculiarities; he had studied them as a scholar studies his books, and derived quite as much pleasure from the occupation. The buffalo were in a sense companions to him, and, as he said, he never felt alone when they were about him. He took great pride in his skill in hunting. He was one of the most modest of men; yet in the simplicity and frankness of his character, it was clear that he looked upon his pre-eminence in this respect as a thing too palpable and well established to be disputed. But whatever may have been his estimate of his own skill, it was rather below than above that which others placed upon it. The only time that I ever saw a shade of scorn darken his face was when two volunteer soldiers, who had just killed a buffalo for the first time, undertook to instruct him as to the best method of "approaching." Henry always seemed to think that he had a sort of prescriptive right to the buffalo, and to look upon them as something belonging to himself. Nothing excited his indignation so much as any wanton destruction committed among the cows, and in his view shooting a calf was a cardinal sin.

Henry Chatillon and Tête Rouge were of the same age; that is, about thirty. Henry was twice as large, and about six times as strong as Tête Rouge. Henry's face was roughened by winds and storms; Tête Rouge's was bloated by sherry-cobblers and brandy-toddy. Henry talked of Indians and buffalo; Tête Rouge of theatres and oyster-cellars. Henry had led a life of hardship and privation; Tête Rouge never had a whim which he would not gratify at the first moment he was able. Henry moreover was the most disinterested man I ever saw; while Tête Rouge, though equally good natured in his way, cared for nobody but himself. Yet we would not have lost him on any account; he served the purpose of a jester in a feudal castle; our camp would have been lifeless without him. For the past week he had fattened in a most amazing manner; and, indeed, this was not at all surprising, since his appetite was inordinate. He was eating from morning till night; half the time he would be at work cooking some private repast for himself, and he paid a visit to the coffee-pot eight or ten times a day. His rueful and disconsolate face became jovial and rubicund, his eyes stood out like a lobster's, and his spirits, which before were sunk to the depths of despondency, were now elated in proportion; all day he was singing, whistling, laughing, and telling stories. Being mortally afraid of Jim Gurney, he kept close in the neighborhood of our tent. As he had seen an abundance of low fast life, and had a considerable fund of humor, his anecdotes were extremely amusing, especially since he never hesitated to place himself in a ludicrous point of view, provided he could raise a laugh by doing so. Tête Rouge, however, was sometimes rather troublesome; he had an inveterate habit of pilfering provisions at all times of the day. He set ridicule at defiance, and would never have given over his tricks, even if they had drawn upon him the scorn of the whole party. Now and then, indeed, something worse than laughter fell to his share; on these occasions he would exhibit much contrition, but half an hour after we would generally observe him stealing round to the box at the back of the cart, and slyly making off with the provisions which Deslauriers had laid by for supper. He was fond of smoking; but having no tobacco of his own, we used to provide him with as much as he wanted, a small piece at a time. At first we gave him half a pound together; but this experiment proved an entire failure, for he invariably lost not only the tobacco, but the knife intrusted to him for cutting it, and a few minutes after he would come to us with many apologies and beg for more.

We had been two days at this camp, and some of the meat was nearly fit for transportation, when a storm came suddenly upon us. About sunset the whole sky grew as black as ink, and the long grass at the edge of the river bent and rose mournfully with the first gusts of the approaching hurricane. Munroe and his two companions brought their guns and placed them under cover of our tent. Having no shelter for themselves, they built a fire of driftwood that might have defied a cataract, and, wrapped in their buffalo-robes, sat on the ground around it to bide the fury of the storm. Deslauriers esconced himself under the cover of the cart. Shaw and I, together with Henry and Tête Rouge, crowded into the little tent; but first of all the dried meat was piled together, and well protected by buffalo-robes pinned firmly to the ground. About nine o'clock the storm broke amid absolute darkness; it blew a gale, and torrents of rain roared over the boundless expanse of open prairie. Our tent was filled with mist and spray beating through the canvas, and saturating everything within. We could only distinguish each other at short intervals by the dazzling flashes of lightning, which displayed the whole waste around us with its momentary glare. We had our fears for the tent; but for an hour or two it stood fast, until at length the cap gave way before a furious blast; the pole tore through the top, and in an instant we were half suffocated by the cold and dripping folds of the canvas, which fell down upon us. Seizing upon our guns, we placed them erect, in order to lift the saturated cloth above our heads. In this agreeable situation, involved among wet blankets and buffalo-robes, we spent several hours of the night, during which the storm would not abate for a moment, but pelted down with merciless fury. Before long the water gathered beneath us in a pool two or three inches deep; so that for a considerable part of the night we were partially immersed in a cold bath. In spite of all this, Tête Rouge's flow of spirits did not fail him; he laughed, whistled, and sang in defiance of the storm, and that night paid off the long arrears of ridicule which he owed us. While we lay in silence, enduring the infliction with what philosophy we could muster, Tête Rouge, who was intoxicated with animal spirits, cracked jokes at our expense by the hour together. At about three o'clock in the morning, preferring "the tyranny of the open night" to such a wretched shelter, we crawled out from beneath the fallen canvas. The wind had abated, but the rain fell steadily. The fire of the California men still blazed amid the darkness, and we joined them as they sat around it. We made ready some hot coffee by way of refreshment; but when some of the party sought to replenish their cups, it was found that Tête Rouge, having disposed of his own share, had privately abstracted the coffee-pot and drunk the rest of the contents out of the spout.

In the morning, to our great joy, an unclouded sun rose upon the prairie. We presented a rather laughable appearance, for the cold and clammy buck-skin, saturated with water, clung fast to our limbs. The light wind and warm sunshine soon dried it again, and then we were all encased in armor of intolerable stiffness. Roaming all day over the prairie and shooting two or three bulls, were scarcely enough to restore the stiffened leather to its usual pliancy.

Besides Henry Chatillon, Shaw and I were the only hunters in the party. Munroe this morning made an attempt to run a buffalo, but his horse could not come up to the game. Shaw went out with him, and being better mounted, soon found himself in the midst of the herd. Seeing nothing but cows and calves around him, he checked his horse. An old bull came galloping on the open prairie at some distance behind, and turning, Shaw rode across his path, levelling his gun as he passed, and shooting him through the shoulder into the heart.

A great flock of buzzards was usually soaring about a few trees that stood on the island just below our camp. Throughout the whole of yesterday we had noticed an eagle among them; today he was still there; and Tête Rouge, declaring that he would kill the bird of America, borrowed Deslauriers's gun and set out on his unpatriotic mission. As might have been expected, the eagle suffered no harm at his hands. He soon returned, saying that he could not find him, but had shot a buzzard instead. Being required to produce the bird in proof of his assertion, he said he believed that he was not quite dead, but he must be hurt, from the swiftness with which he flew off.

"If you want," said Tête Rouge, "I'll go and get one of his feathers; I knocked off plenty of them when I shot him."

Just opposite our camp, was another island covered with bushes, and behind it was a deep pool of water, while two or three considerable streams coursed over the sand not far off. I was bathing at this place in the afternoon when a white wolf, larger than the largest Newfoundland dog, ran out from behind the point of the island, and galloped leisurely over the sand not half a stone's-throw distant. I could plainly see his red eyes and the bristles about his snout; he was an ugly scoundrel, with a bushy tail, a large head, and a most repulsive countenance. Having neither rifle to shoot nor stone to pelt him with, I was looking after some missile for his benefit, when the report of a gun came from the camp, and the ball threw up the sand just beyond him; at this he gave a slight jump, and stretched away so swiftly that he soon dwindled into a mere speck on the distant sand-beds. The number of carcasses that by this time were lying about the neighboring prairie summoned the wolves from every quarter; the spot where Shaw and Henry had hunted together soon became their favorite resort, for here about a dozen dead buffalo were fermenting under the hot sun. I used often to go over the river and watch them at their meal. By lying under the bank it was easy to get a full view of them. There were three different kinds: the white wolves and the gray wolves, both very large, and besides these the small prairie wolves, not much bigger than spaniels. They would howl and fight in a crowd around a single carcass, yet they were so watchful, and their senses so acute, that I never was able to crawl within a fair shooting distance; whenever I attempted it, they would all scatter at once and glide silently away through the tall grass. The air above this spot was always full of turkey-buzzards or black vultures; whenever the wolves left a carcass they would descend upon it, and cover it so densely that a rifle bullet shot at random among the gormandizing crowd would generally strike down two or three of them. These birds would often sail by scores just above our camp, their broad black wings seeming half transparent as they expanded them against the bright sky. The wolves and the buzzards thickened about us every hour, and two or three eagles also came to the feast. I killed a bull within rifle-shot of the camp; that night the wolves made a fearful howling close at hand, and in the morning the carcass was completely hollowed out by these voracious feeders.

After remaining four days at this camp we prepared to leave it. We had for our own part about five hundred pounds of dried meat, and the California men had prepared some three hundred more; this consisted of the fattest and choicest parts of eight or nine cows, a small quantity only being taken from each, and the rest abandoned to the wolves. The pack animals were laden, the horses saddled, and the mules harnessed to the cart. Even Tête Rouge was ready at last, and slowly moving from the ground, we resumed our journey eastward. When we had advanced about a mile, Shaw missed a valuable hunting-knife, and turned back in search of it, thinking that he had left it at the camp. The day was dark and gloomy. The ashes of the fires were still smoking by the river-side; the grass around them was trampled down by men and horses, and strewn with all the litter of a camp. Our departure had been a gathering signal to the birds and beasts of prey. Scores of wolves were prowling about the smouldering fires, while multitudes were roaming over the neighboring prairie; they all fled as Shaw approached, some running over the sand-beds and some over the grassy plains. The vultures in great clouds were soaring overhead, and the dead bull near the camp was completely blackened by the flock that had alighted upon it; they flapped their broad wings, and stretched upwards their crested heads and long skinny necks, fearing to remain, yet reluctant to leave their disgusting feast. As he searched about the fires he saw the wolves seated on the hills waiting for his departure. Having looked in vain for his knife, he mounted again, and left the wolves and the vultures to banquet undisturbed.

Typhoon

From *Typhoon*

BY JOSEPH CONRAD

Perhaps he was the most talented seafaring writer ever. Joseph Conrad (1857–1924) wrote so many wonderful novels and short stories set in the vast Pacific region that I often wonder why he is not taught more in universities and colleges. *Lord Jim, Typhoon, Heart of Darkness, The Secret Sharer* . . . the list could go on and on.

My personal favorite is *Typhoon*, to me still the greatest story ever written about a lonely ship and a brutal and massive storm at sea. While this excerpt cannot possibly replace the pleasures of reading the complete original novella, it provides a superb portrait of the storm's approach and the first hours of surviving in its fearful wake. The interaction between Captain MacWhirr and the Chief Mate, Mr. Jukes, is sheer storytelling genius as Conrad lays the groundwork for the looming disaster. Captain MacWhirr is a man just asking for trouble. And he gets all he can handle!

★　　★　　★　　★　　★

Captain MacWhirr, of the steamer *Nan-Shan,* had a physiognomy that, in the order of material appearances, was the exact counterpart of his mind: it presented no marked characteristics of firmness or stupidity; it had no pronounced characteristics whatever; it was simply ordinary, irresponsive, and unruffled.

The only thing his aspect might have been said to suggest, at times, was bashfulness; because he would sit, in business offices ashore, sunburnt and smiling faintly, with downcast eyes. When he raised them, they were perceived to be direct in their glance and of blue colour. His hair was fair and extremely fine, clasping from temple to temple the bald dome of his skull in a clamp as of fluffy

271

silk. The hair of his face, on the contrary, carroty and flaming, resembled a growth of copper wire clipped short to the line of the lip; while, no matter how close he shaved, fiery metallic gleams passed, when he moved his head, over the surface of his cheeks. He was rather below the medium height, a bit round-shouldered, and so sturdy of limb that his clothes always looked a shade too tight for his arms and legs. As if unable to grasp what is due to the difference of latitudes, he wore a brown bowler hat, a complete suit of a brownish hue, and clumsy black boots. These harbour togs gave to his thick figure an air of stiff and uncouth smartness. A thin silver watch-chain looped his waistcoat, and he never left his ship for the shore without clutching in his powerful, hairy fist an elegant umbrella of the very best quality, but generally unrolled. Young Jukes, the chief mate, attending his commander to the gangway, would sometimes venture to say, with the greatest gentleness, "Allow me, sir"—and possessing himself of the umbrella deferentially, would elevate the ferule, shake the folds, twirl a neat furl in a jiffy, and hand it back; going through the performance with a face of such portentous gravity, that Mr. Solomon Rout, the chief engineer, smoking his morning cigar over the skylight, would turn away his head in order to hide a smile. "Oh! aye! The blessed gamp. . . . Thank 'ee, Jukes, thank 'ee," would mutter Captain MacWhirr, heartily, without looking up.

Having just enough imagination to carry him through each successive day, and no more, he was tranquilly sure of himself; and from the very same cause he was not in the least conceited. It is your imaginative superior who is touchy, overbearing, and difficult to please; but every ship Captain MacWhirr commanded was the floating abode of harmony and peace. It was, in truth, as impossible for him to take a flight of fancy as it would be for a watchmaker to put together a chronometer with nothing except a two-pound hammer and a whip-saw in the way of tools. Yet the uninteresting lives of men so entirely given to the actuality of the bare existence have their mysterious side. It was impossible in Captain MacWhirr's case, for instance, to understand what under heaven could have induced that perfectly satisfactory son of a petty grocer in Belfast to run away to sea. And yet he had done that very thing at the age of fifteen. It was enough, when you thought it over, to give you the idea of an immense, potent, and invisible hand thrust into the ant-heap of the earth, laying hold of shoulders, knocking heads together, and setting the unconscious faces of the multitude towards inconceivable goals and in undreamt-of directions.

His father never really forgave him for this undutiful stupidity. "We could have got on without him," he used to say later on, "but there's the business. And he an only son, too!" His mother wept very much after his disappearance. As it had never occurred to him to leave word behind, he was mourned over for dead till, after eight months, his first letter arrived from Talcahuano. It was short, and contained the statement: "We had very fine weather on our passage out." But evidently, in the writer's mind, the only important intelligence was to the effect that his captain had, on the very day of writing, entered him regularly on the ship's articles as Ordinary Seaman. "Because I can do the work," he explained. The mother again wept copiously, while the remark, "Tom's an ass," expressed the emotions of the father. He was a corpulent man, with a gift for sly chaffing, which to the end of his life he exercised in his intercourse with his son, a little pityingly, as if upon a half-witted person.

MacWhirr's visits to his home were necessarily rare, and in the course of years he despatched other letters to his parents, informing them of his successive promotions and of his movements upon the vast earth. In these missives could be found sentences like this: "The heat here is very great." Or: "On Christmas day at 4 P.M. we fell in with some icebergs." The old people ultimately became acquainted with a good many names of ships, and with the names of the skippers who commanded them—with the names of Scots and English shipowners—with the names of seas, oceans, straits, promontories—with outlandish names of lumber-ports, of rice-ports, of cotton-ports—with the names of islands—with the name of their son's young woman. She was called Lucy. It did not suggest itself to him to mention whether he thought the name pretty. And then they died.

The great day of MacWhirr's marriage came in due course, following shortly upon the great day when he got his first command.

All these events had taken place many years before the morning when, in the chart-room of the steamer *Nan-Shan,* he stood confronted by the fall of a barometer he had no reason to distrust. The fall—taking into account the excellence of the instrument, the time of the year, and the ship's position on the terrestrial globe—was of a nature ominously prophetic; but the red face of the man betrayed no sort of inward disturbance. Omens were as nothing to him, and he was unable to discover the message of a prophecy till the fulfilment had brought it home to his very door. "That's a fall, and no mistake," he thought. "There must be some uncommonly dirty weather knocking about."

The *Nan-Shan* was on her way from the southward to the treaty port of Fu-chau, with some cargo in her lower holds, and two hundred Chinese coolies returning to their village homes in the province of Fo-kien, after a few years of work in various tropical colonies. The morning was fine, the oily sea heaved without a sparkle, and there was a queer white misty patch in the sky like a halo of the sun. The fore-deck, packed with Chinamen, was full of sombre clothing, yellow faces, and pigtails, sprinkled over with a good many naked shoulders, for there was no wind, and the heat was close. The coolies lounged, talked, smoked, or stared over the rail; some, drawing water over the side, sluiced each other; a few slept on hatches, while several small parties of six sat on their heels surrounding iron trays with plates of rice and tiny teacups; and every single Celestial of them was carrying with him all he had in the world—a wooden chest with a ringing lock and brass on the corners, containing the savings of his labours: some clothes of ceremony, sticks of incense, a little opium maybe, bits of nameless rubbish of conventional value, and a small hoard of silver dollars, toiled for in coal lighters, won in gambling-houses or in petty trading, grubbed out of earth, sweated out in mines, on railway lines, in deadly jungle, under heavy burdens—amassed patiently, guarded with care, cherished fiercely.

A cross swell had set in from the direction of Formosa Channel about ten o'clock, without disturbing these passengers much, because the *Nan-Shan,* with her flat bottom, rolling chocks on bilges, and great breadth of beam, had the reputation of an exceptionally steady ship in a sea-way. Mr. Jukes, in moments of expansion on shore, would proclaim loudly that the "old girl was as good as she was pretty." It would never have occurred to Captain MacWhirr to express his favourable opinion so loud or in terms so fanciful.

★　★　★　★　★

Observing the steady fall of the barometer, Captain MacWhirr thought, "There's some dirty weather knocking about." This is precisely what he thought. He had had an experience of moderately dirty weather—the term dirty as applied to the weather implying only moderate discomfort to the sea-man. Had he been informed by an indisputable authority that the end of the world was to be finally accomplished by a catastrophic disturbance of the atmosphere, he would have assimilated the information under the simple idea of dirty weather, and no other, because he had no experience of cataclysms, and belief does not necessarily imply comprehension. The wisdom of his country had pronounced by means of an Act of Parliament that before he could be considered as fit to take charge of a ship he should be able to answer certain simple questions on the subject of circular storms such as hurricanes, cyclones, typhoons; and apparently he had answered them, since he was now in command of the *Nan-Shan* in the China seas during the season of typhoons. But if he had answered he remembered nothing of it. He was, however, conscious of being made uncomfortable by the clammy heat. He came out on the bridge, and found no relief to this oppression. The air seemed thick. He gasped like a fish, and began to believe himself greatly out of sorts.

The *Nan-Shan* was ploughing a vanishing furrow upon the circle of the sea that had the surface and the shimmer of an undulating piece of gray silk. The sun, pale and without rays, poured down leaden heat in a strangely indecisive light, and the Chinamen were lying prostrate about the decks. Their bloodless, pinched, yellow faces were like the faces of bilious invalids. Captain MacWhirr noticed two of them especially, stretched out on their backs below the bridge. As soon as they had closed their eyes they seemed dead. Three others, however, were quarrelling barbarously away forward; and one big fellow, half naked, with herculean shoulders, was hanging limply over a winch; another, sitting on the deck, his knees up and his head drooping sideways in a girlish attitude, was plaiting his pigtail with infinite languor depicted in his whole person and in the very movement of his fingers. The smoke struggled with difficulty out of the funnel, and instead of streaming away spread itself out like an infernal sort of cloud, smelling of sulphur and raining soot all over the decks.

"What the devil are you doing there, Mr. Jukes?" asked Captain MacWhirr.

This unusual form of address, though mumbled rather than spoken, caused the body of Mr. Jukes to start as though it had been prodded under the fifth rib. He had had a low bench brought on the bridge, and sitting on it, with a length of rope curled about his feet and a piece of canvas stretched over his knees, was pushing a sail-needle vigorously. He looked up, and his surprise gave to his eyes an expression of innocence and candour.

"I am only roping some of that new set of bags we made last trip for whipping up coals," he remonstrated, gently. "We shall want them for the next coaling, sir."

"What became of the others?"

"Why, worn out of course, sir."

Captain MacWhirr, after glaring down irresolutely at his chief mate, disclosed the gloomy and cynical conviction that more than half of them had been lost overboard, "if only the truth was known," and retired to the other end of the bridge. Jukes, exasperated by this unprovoked attack, broke the needle at the second stitch, and dropping his work got up and cursed the heat in a violent undertone.

The propeller thumped, the three Chinamen forward had given up squabbling very suddenly, and the one who had been plaiting his tail clasped his legs and stared dejectedly over his knees. The lurid sunshine cast faint and sickly shadows. The swell ran higher and swifter every moment, and the ship lurched heavily in the smooth, deep hollows of the sea.

"I wonder where that beastly swell comes from," said Jukes aloud, recovering himself after a stagger.

"North-east," grunted the literal MacWhirr, from his side of the bridge. "There's some dirty weather knocking about. Go and look at the glass."

When Jukes came out of the chart-room, the cast of his countenance had changed to thoughtfulness and concern. He caught hold of the bridge-rail and stared ahead.

The temperature in the engine-room had gone up to a hundred and seventeen degrees. Irritated voices were ascending through the skylight and through the fiddle of the stokehold in a harsh and resonant uproar, mingled with angry clangs and scrapes of metal, as if men with limbs of iron and throats of bronze had been quarrelling down there. The second engineer was falling foul of the stokers for letting the steam go down. He was a man with arms like a blacksmith, and generally feared; but that afternoon the stokers were answering him back recklessly, and slammed the furnace doors with the fury of despair. Then the noise ceased suddenly, and the second engineer appeared, emerging out of the stokehold streaked with grime and soaking wet like a chimney-sweep coming out of a well. As soon as his head was clear of the fiddle he began to scold Jukes for not trimming properly the stokehold ventilators; and in answer Jukes made with his hands deprecatory soothing signs meaning: No wind—can't be helped—you can see for yourself. But the other wouldn't hear reason. His teeth flashed angrily in his dirty face. He didn't mind, he said, the trouble of punching their blanked heads down there, blank his soul, but did the condemned sailors think you could keep steam up in the God-forsaken boilers simply by knocking the blanked stokers about? No, by George! You had to get some draught, too—may he be everlastingly blanked for a swab-headed deck-hand if you didn't! And the chief, too, rampaging before the steam-gauge and carrying on like a lunatic up and down the engine-room ever since noon. What did Jukes think he was stuck up there for, if he couldn't get one of his decayed, good-for-nothing deck-cripples to turn the ventilators to the wind?

The relations of the "engine-room" and the "deck" of the *Nan-Shan* were, as is known, of a brotherly nature; therefore Jukes leaned over and begged the other in a restrained tone not to make a disgusting ass of himself; the skipper was on the other side of the bridge. But the second declared mutinously that he didn't care a rap who was on the other side of the bridge, and Jukes, passing in a flash from lofty disapproval into a state of exaltation, invited him in unflattering terms to come up and twist the beastly things to please himself, and catch such wind as a donkey of his sort could find. The second rushed up to the fray. He flung himself at the port ventilator as though he meant to tear it out bodily and toss it overboard. All he did was to move the cowl round a few inches, with an enormous expenditure of force, and seemed spent in the effort. He leaned against the back of the wheelhouse, and Jukes walked up to him.

"Oh, Heavens!" ejaculated the engineer in a feeble voice. He lifted his eyes to the sky, and then let his glassy stare descend to meet the horizon that, tilting up to an angle of forty degrees, seemed to hang on a slant for a while and settled down slowly. "Heavens! Phew! What's up, anyhow?"

Jukes, straddling his long legs like a pair of compasses, put on an air of superiority. "We're going to catch it this time," he said. "The barometer is tumbling down like anything, Harry. And you trying to kick up that silly row. . . ."

The word "barometer" seemed to revive the second engineer's mad animosity. Collecting afresh all his energies, he directed Jukes in a low and brutal tone to shove the unmentionable instrument down his gory throat. Who cared for his crimson barometer? It was the steam—the steam—that was going down; and what between the firemen going faint and the chief going silly, it was worse than a dog's life for him; he didn't care a tinker's curse how soon the whole show was blown out of the water. He seemed on the point of having a cry, but after regaining his breath he muttered darkly, "I'll faint them," and dashed off. He stopped upon the fiddle long enough to shake his fist at the unnatural daylight, and dropped into the dark hole with a whoop.

When Jukes turned, his eyes fell upon the rounded back and the big red ears of Captain MacWhirr, who had come across. He did not look at his chief officer, but said at once, "That's a very violent man, that second engineer."

"Jolly good second, anyhow," grunted Jukes. "They can't keep up steam," he added, rapidly, and made a grab at the rail against the coming lurch.

Captain MacWhirr, unprepared, took a run and brought himself up with a jerk by an awning stanchion.

"A profane man," he said, obstinately. "If this goes on, I'll have to get rid of him the first chance."

"It's the heat," said Jukes. "The weather's awful. It would make a saint swear. Even up here I feel exactly as if I had my head tied up in a woollen blanket."

Captain MacWhirr looked up. "D'ye mean to say, Mr. Jukes, you ever had your head tied up in a blanket? What was that for?"

"It's a manner of speaking, sir," said Jukes, stolidly.

"Some of you fellows do go on! What's that about saints swearing? I wish you wouldn't talk so wild. What sort of saint would that be that would swear? No more saint than yourself, I expect. And what's a blanket got to do with

it—or the weather either. . . . The heat does not make me swear—does it? It's
filthy bad temper. That's what it is. And what's the good of your talking like this?"

Thus Captain MacWhirr expostulated against the use of images in
speech, and at the end electrified Jukes by a contemptuous snort, followed by
words of passion and resentment: "Damme! I'll fire him out of the ship if he
don't look out."

And Jukes, incorrigible, thought: "Goodness me! Somebody's put a
new inside to my old man. Here's temper, if you like. Of course it's the
weather; what else? It would make an angel quarrelsome—let alone a saint."

All the Chinamen on deck appeared at their last gasp.

At its setting the sun had a diminished diameter and an expiring
brown, rayless glow, as if millions of centuries elapsing since the morning had
brought it near its end. A dense bank of cloud became visible to the northward;
it had a sinister dark olive tint, and lay low and motionless upon the sea, resembling a solid obstacle in the path of the ship. She went floundering towards it like
an exhausted creature driven to its death. The coppery twilight retired slowly,
and the darkness brought out overhead a swarm of unsteady, big stars, that, as if
blown upon, flickered exceedingly and seemed to hang very near the earth. At
eight o'clock Jukes went into the chart-room to write up the ship's log.

He copied neatly out of the rough-book the number of miles, the
course of the ship, and in the column for "wind" scrawled the word "calm"
from top to bottom of the eight hours since noon. He was exasperated by the
continuous, monotonous rolling of the ship. The heavy inkstand would slide
away in a manner that suggested perverse intelligence in dodging the pen.
Having written in the large space under the head of "Remarks" "Heat very
oppressive," he stuck the end of the pen-holder in his teeth, pipe fashion, and
mopped his face carefully.

"Ship rolling heavily in a high cross swell," he began again, and com-
mented to himself, "Heavily is no word for it." Then he wrote: "Sunset threatening, with a low bank of clouds to N. and E. Sky clear overhead."

Sprawling over the table with arrested pen, he glanced out of the door,
and in that frame of his vision he saw all the stars flying upwards between the
teakwood jambs on a black sky. The whole lot took flight together and
disappeared, leaving only a blackness flecked with white flashes, for the sea was
as black as the sky and speckled with foam afar. The stars that had flown to the
roll came back on the return swing of the ship, rushing downwards in their
glittering multitude, not of fiery points, but enlarged to tiny discs brilliant with
a clear wet sheen.

Jukes watched the flying big stars for a moment, and then wrote: "8 P.M. Swell increasing. Ship labouring and taking water on her decks. Battened down the coolies for the night. Barometer still falling." He paused, and thought to himself, "Perhaps nothing whatever'll come of it." And then he closed resolutely his entries: "Every appearance of a typhoon coming on."

On going out he had to stand aside, and Captain MacWhirr strode over the doorstep without saying a word or making a sign.

"Shut the door, Mr. Jukes, will you?" he cried from within.

Jukes turned back to do so, muttering ironically: "Afraid to catch cold, I suppose." It was his watch below, but he yearned for communion with his kind; and he remarked cheerily to the second mate: "Doesn't look so bad, after all—does it?"

The second mate was marching to and fro on the bridge, tripping down with small steps one moment, and the next climbing with difficulty the shifting slope of the deck. At the sound of Jukes' voice he stood still, facing forward, but made no reply.

"Hallo! That's a heavy one," said Jukes, swaying to meet the long roll till his lowered hand touched the planks. This time the second mate made in his throat a noise of an unfriendly nature.

He was an oldish, shabby little fellow, with bad teeth and no hair on his face. He had been shipped in a hurry in Shanghai, that trip when the second officer brought from home had delayed the ship three hours in port by contriving (in some manner Captain MacWhirr could never understand) to fall overboard into an empty coal-lighter lying alongside, and had to be sent ashore to the hospital with concussion of the brain and a broken limb or two.

Jukes was not discouraged by the unsympathetic sound. "The China-men must be having a lovely time of it down there," he said. "It's lucky for them the old girl has the easiest roll of any ship I've ever been in. There now! This one wasn't so bad."

"You wait," snarled the second mate.

With his sharp nose, red at the tip, and his thin pinched lips, he always looked as though he were raging inwardly; and he was concise in his speech to the point of rudeness. All his time off duty he spent in his cabin with the door shut, keeping so still in there that he was supposed to fall asleep as soon as he had disappeared; but the man who came in to wake him for his watch on deck would invariably find him with his eyes wide open, flat on his back in the bunk, and glaring irritably from a soiled pillow. He never wrote any letters, did not seem to hope for news from anywhere; and though he had been heard once to mention West Hartlepool, it was with extreme bitterness, and only in connection with the extortionate charges of a boarding-house. He was one of those men who are picked up at need in the ports of the world. They are competent enough, appear hopelessly hard up, show no evidence of any sort of vice, and carry about them all the signs of manifest failure. They come aboard on an emergency, care for no ship afloat, live in their own atmosphere of casual connection amongst their shipmates who know nothing of them, and make up their minds to leave at inconvenient times. They clear out with no words of leave-taking in some God-forsaken port other men would fear to be stranded in, and go ashore in company of a shabby sea-chest, corded like a treasure-box, and with an air of shaking the ship's dust off their feet.

"You wait," he repeated, balanced in great swings with his back to Jukes, motionless and implacable.

"Do you mean to say we are going to catch it hot?" asked Jukes with boyish interest.

"Say? . . . I say nothing. You don't catch me," snapped the little second mate, with a mixture of pride, scorn, and cunning, as if Jukes' question had been a trap cleverly detected. "Oh, no! None of you here shall make a fool of me if I know it," he mumbled to himself.

Jukes reflected rapidly that this second mate was a mean little beast, and in his heart he wished poor Jack Allen had never smashed himself up in the coal-lighter. The far-off blackness ahead of the ship was like another night seen through the starry night of the earth—the starless night of the immensities beyond the created universe, revealed in its appalling stillness through a low fissure in the glittering sphere of which the earth is the kernel.

"Whatever there might be about," said Jukes, "we are steaming straight into it."

"*You've* said it," caught up the second mate, always with his back to Jukes. "You've said it, mind—not I."

"Oh, go to Jericho!" said Jukes, frankly; and the other emitted a triumphant little chuckle.

"You've said it," he repeated.

"And what of that?"

"I've known some real good men get into trouble with their skippers for saying a dam' sight less," answered the second mate feverishly. "Oh, no! You don't catch me."

"You seem deucedly anxious not to give yourself away," said Jukes, completely soured by such absurdity. "I wouldn't be afraid to say what I think."

"Aye, to me. That's no great trick. I am nobody, and well I know it."

The ship, after a pause of comparative steadiness, started upon a series of rolls, one worse than the other, and for a time Jukes, preserving his equilibrium, was too busy to open his mouth. As soon as the violent swinging had quieted down somewhat, he said: "This is a bit too much of a good thing. Whether anything is coming or not I think she ought to be put head on to that swell. The old man is just gone in to lie down. Hang me if I don't speak to him."

But when he opened the door of the chart-room he saw his captain reading a book. Captain MacWhirr was not lying down: he was standing up with one hand grasping the edge of the bookshelf and the other holding open before his face a thick volume. The lamp wriggled in the gimbals, the loosened books toppled from side to side on the shelf, the long barometer swung in jerky circles, the table altered its slant every moment. In the midst of all this stir and movement Captain MacWhirr, holding on, showed his eyes above the upper edge, and asked, "What's the matter?"

"Swell getting worse, sir."

"Noticed that in here," muttered Captain MacWhirr. "Anything wrong?"

Jukes, inwardly disconcerted by the seriousness of the eyes looking at him over the top of the book, produced an embarrassed grin.

"Rolling like old boots," he said, sheepishly.

"Aye! Very heavy—very heavy. What do you want?"

At this Jukes lost his footing and began to flounder.

"I was thinking of our passengers," he said, in the manner of a man clutching at a straw.

"Passengers?" wondered the Captain, gravely. "What passengers?"

"Why, the Chinamen, sir," explained Jukes, very sick of this conversation.

"The Chinamen! Why don't you speak plainly? Couldn't tell what you meant. Never heard a lot of coolies spoken of as passengers before. Passengers, indeed! What's come to you?"

Captain MacWhirr, closing the book on his forefinger, lowered his arm and looked completely mystified. "Why are you thinking of the Chinamen, Mr. Jukes?" he inquired.

Jukes took a plunge, like a man driven to it. "She's rolling her decks full of water, sir. Thought you might put her head on perhaps—for a while. Till this goes down a bit—very soon, I dare say. Head to the eastward. I never knew a ship roll like this."

He held on in the doorway, and Captain MacWhirr, feeling his grip on the shelf inadequate, made up his mind to let go in a hurry, and fell heavily on the couch.

"Head to the eastward?" he said, struggling to sit up. "That's more than four points off her course."

"Yes, sir. Fifty degrees. . . . Would just bring her head far enough round to meet this. . . ."

Captain MacWhirr was now sitting up. He had not dropped the book, and he had not lost his place.

"To the eastward?" he repeated, with dawning astonishment. "To the . . . Where do you think we are bound to? You want me to haul a full-powered steamship four points off her course to make the Chinamen comfortable! Now, I've heard more than enough of mad things done in the world— but this. . . . If I didn't know you, Jukes, I would think you were in liquor. Steer four points off. . . . And what afterwards? Steer four points over the other way, I suppose, to make the course good. What put it into your head that I would start to tack a steamer as if she were a sailing-ship?"

"Jolly good thing she isn't," threw in Jukes, with bitter readiness. "She would have rolled every blessed stick out of her this afternoon."

"Aye! And you just would have had to stand and see them go," said Captain MacWhirr, showing a certain animation. "It's a dead calm, isn't it?"

"It is, sir. But there's something out of the common coming, for sure."

"Maybe. I suppose you have a notion I should be getting out of the way of that dirt," said Captain MacWhirr, speaking with the utmost simplicity of manner and tone, and fixing the oilcloth on the floor with a heavy stare. Thus he noticed neither Jukes' discomfiture nor the mixture of vexation and astonished respect on his face.

"Now, here's this book," he continued with deliberation, slapping his thigh with the closed volume. "I've been reading the chapter on the storms there."

This was true. He had been reading the chapter on the storms. When he had entered the chart-room, it was with no intention of taking the book down. Some influence in the air—the same influence, probably, that caused the steward to bring without orders the Captain's sea-boots and oilskin coat up to the chart-room—had as it were guided his hand to the shelf; and without taking the time to sit down he had waded with a conscious effort into the terminology of the subject. He lost himself amongst advancing semi-circles, left- and right-hand quadrants, the curves of the tracks, the probable bearing of the centre, the shifts of wind and the readings of barometer. He tried to bring all these things into a definite relation to himself, and ended by becoming contemptuously angry with such a lot of words and with so much advice, all headwork and supposition, without a glimmer of certitude.

"It's the damnedest thing, Jukes," he said. "If a fellow was to believe all that's in there, he would be running most of his time all over the sea trying to get behind the weather."

Again he slapped his leg with the book; and Jukes opened his mouth, but said nothing.

"Running to get behind the weather! Do you understand that, Mr. Jukes? It's the maddest thing!" ejaculated Captain MacWhirr, with pauses, gazing at the floor profoundly. "You would think an old woman had been writing this. It passes me. If that thing means anything useful, then it means that I should at once alter the course away, away to the devil somewhere, and come booming down on Fu-chau from the northward at the tail of this dirty weather that's supposed to be knocking about in our way. From the north! Do you understand, Mr. Jukes? Three hundred extra miles to the distance, and a pretty coal bill to show. I couldn't bring myself to do that if every word in there was gospel truth, Mr. Jukes. Don't you expect me. . . ."

And Jukes, silent, marvelled at this display of feeling and loquacity.

"But the truth is that you don't know if the fellow is right, anyhow. How can you tell what a gale is made of till you get it? He isn't aboard here, is he? Very well. Here he says that the centre of them things bears eight points off the wind; but we haven't got any wind, for all the barometer falling. Where's his centre now?"

"We will get the wind presently," mumbled Jukes.

"Let it come, then," said Captain MacWhirr, with dignified indignation. "It's only to let you see, Mr. Jukes, that you don't find everything in books. All these rules for dodging breezes and circumventing the winds of heaven, Mr. Jukes, seem to me the maddest thing, when you come to look at it sensibly."

He raised his eyes, saw Jukes gazing at him dubiously, and tried to illustrate his meaning.

"About as queer as your extraordinary notion of dodging the ship head to sea, for I don't know how long, to make the Chinamen comfortable; whereas all we've got to do is to take them to Fu-chau, being timed to get there before noon on Friday. If the weather delays me—very well. There's your log-book to talk straight about the weather. But suppose I went swinging off my course and came in two days late, and they asked me: 'Where have you been all that time, Captain?' What could I say to that? 'Went around to dodge the bad weather,' I would say. 'It must've been dam' bad,' they would say. 'Don't know,' I would have to say, 'I've dodged clear of it.' See that, Jukes? I have been thinking it all out this afternoon."

He looked up again in his unseeing, unimaginative way. No one had ever heard him say so much at one time. Jukes, with his arms open in the doorway, was like a man invited to behold a miracle. Unbounded wonder was the intellectual meaning of his eye, while incredulity was seated in his whole countenance.

"A gale is a gale, Mr. Jukes," resumed the Captain, "and a full-powered steam-ship has got to face it. There's just so much dirty weather knocking about the world, and the proper thing is to go through it with none of what old Captain Wilson of the *Melita* calls 'storm strategy.' The other day ashore I heard him hold forth about it to a lot of shipmasters who came in and sat at a table next to mine. It seemed to me the greatest nonsense. He was telling them how he outmanœuvred, I think he said, a terrific gale, so that it never came nearer than fifty miles to him. A neat piece of head-work he called it. How he knew there was a terrific gale fifty miles off beats me altogether. It was like listening to a crazy man. I would have thought Captain Wilson was old enough to know better."

Captain MacWhirr ceased for a moment, then said, "It's your watch below, Mr. Jukes?"

Jukes came to himself with a start. "Yes, sir."

"Leave orders to call me at the slightest change," said the Captain. He reached up to put the book away, and tucked his legs upon the couch. "Shut the door so that it don't fly open, will you? I can't stand a door banging. They've put a lot of rubbishy locks into this ship, I must say."

Captain MacWhirr closed his eyes.

He did so to rest himself. He was tired, and he experienced that state of mental vacuity which comes at the end of an exhaustive discussion that had liberated some belief matured in the course of meditative years. He had indeed been making his confession of faith, had he only known it; and its effect was to make Jukes, on the other side of the door, stand scratching his head for a good while.

Captain MacWhirr opened his eyes.

He thought he must have been asleep. What was that loud noise? Wind? Why had he not been called? The lamp wriggled in its gimbals, the barometer swung in circles, the table altered its slant every moment; a pair of limp sea-boots with collapsed tops went sliding past the couch. He put out his hand instantly, and captured one.

Jukes' face appeared in a crack of the door: only his face, very red, with staring eyes. The flame of the lamp leaped, a piece of paper flew up, a rush of air enveloped Captain MacWhirr. Beginning to draw on the boot, he directed an expectant gaze at Jukes' swollen, excited features.

"Came on like this," shouted Jukes, "five minutes ago . . . all of a sudden."

The head disappeared with a bang, and a heavy splash and patter of drops swept past the closed door as if a pailful of melted lead had been flung against the house. A whistling could be heard now upon the deep vibrating noise outside. The stuffy chart-room seemed as full of draughts as a shed. Captain MacWhirr collared the other sea-boot on its violent passage along the floor. He was not flustered, but he could not find at once the opening for inserting his foot. The shoes he had flung off were scurrying from end to end of the cabin, gambolling playfully over each other like puppies. As soon as he stood up he kicked at them viciously, but without effect.

He threw himself into the attitude of a lunging fencer, to reach after his oilskin coat; and afterwards he staggered all over the confined space while he jerked himself into it. Very grave, straddling his legs far apart, and stretching his neck, he started to tie deliberately the strings of his sou'-wester under his chin, with thick fingers that trembled slightly. He went through all the movements of a woman putting on her bonnet before a glass, with a strained, listening attention, as though he had expected every moment to hear the shout of his name in the confused clamour that had suddenly beset his ship. Its increase filled his ears while he was getting ready to go out and confront whatever it might mean. It was tumultuous and very loud—made up of the rush of the wind, the crashes of the sea, with that prolonged deep vibration of the air, like the roll of an immense and remote drum beating the charge of the gale.

He stood for a moment in the light of the lamp, thick, clumsy, shapeless in his panoply of combat, vigilant and red-faced.

"There's a lot of weight in this," he muttered.

As soon as he attempted to open the door the wind caught it. Clinging to the handle, he was dragged out over the doorstep, and at once found himself engaged with the wind in a sort of personal scuffle whose object was the shutting of that door. At the last moment a tongue of air scurried in and licked out the flames of the lamp.

Ahead of the ship he perceived a great darkness lying upon a multitude of white flashes; on the starboard beam a few amazing stars drooped, dim and fitful, above an immense waste of broken seas, as if seen through a mad drift of smoke.

On the bridge a knot of men, indistinct and toiling, were making great efforts in the light of the wheelhouse windows that shone mistily on their heads and backs. Suddenly darkness closed upon one pane, then on another. The voices of the lost group reached him after the manner of men's voices in a gale, in shreds and fragments of forlorn shouting snatched past the ear. All at once Jukes appeared at his side, yelling, with his head down.

"Watch—put in—wheelhouse shutters—glass—afraid—blow in."

Jukes heard his commander upbraiding.

"This—come—anything—warning—call me."

He tried to explain, with the uproar pressing on his lips.

"Light air—remained—bridge—sudden—north-east—could turn—thought—you—sure—hear."

They had gained the shelter of the weather-cloth, and could converse with raised voices, as people quarrel.

"I got the hands along to cover up all the ventilators. Good job I had remained on deck. I didn't think you would be asleep, and so . . . What did you say, sir? What?"

"Nothing," cried Captain MacWhirr. "I said—all right."

"By all the powers! We've got it this time," observed Jukes in a howl.

"You haven't altered her course?" inquired Captain MacWhirr, straining his voice.

"No, sir. Certainly not. Wind came out right ahead. And here comes the head sea."

A plunge of the ship ended in a shock as if she had landed her forefoot upon something solid. After a moment of stillness a lofty flight of sprays drove hard with the wind upon their faces.

"Keep her at it as long as we can," shouted Captain MacWhirr.

Before Jukes had squeezed the salt water out of his eyes all the stars had disappeared.

★   ★   ★   ★   ★

Jukes was as ready a man as any half-dozen young mates that may be caught by casting a net upon the waters; and though he had been somewhat taken aback by the startling viciousness of the first squall, he had pulled himself together on the instant, had called out the hands and had rushed them along to secure such openings about the deck as had not been already battened down earlier in the evening. Shouting in his fresh, stentorian voice, "Jump, boys, and bear a hand!" he led in the work, telling himself the while that he had "just expected this."

But at the same time he was growing aware that this was rather more than he had expected. From the first stir of the air felt on his cheek the gale seemed to take upon itself the accumulated impetus of an avalanche. Heavy sprays enveloped the *Nan-Shan* from stem to stern, and instantly in the midst of her regular rolling she began to jerk and plunge as though she had gone mad with fright.

Jukes thought, "This is no joke." While he was exchanging explanatory yells with his captain, a sudden lowering of the darkness came upon the night, falling before their vision like something palpable. It was as if the masked lights of the world had been turned down. Jukes was uncritically glad to have his captain at hand. It relieved him as though that man had, by simply coming on deck, taken most of the gale's weight upon his shoulders. Such is the prestige, the privilege, and the burden of command.

Captain MacWhirr could expect no relief of that sort from any one on earth. Such is the loneliness of command. He was trying to see, with that watchful manner of a seaman who stares into the wind's eye as if into the eye of an adversary, to penetrate the hidden intention and guess the aim and force of the thrust. The strong wind swept at him out of a vast obscurity; he felt under his feet the uneasiness of his ship, and he could not even discern the shadow of her shape. He wished it were not so; and very still he waited, feeling stricken by a blind man's helplessness.

To be silent was natural to him, dark or shine. Jukes, at his elbow, made himself heard yelling cheerily in the gusts, "We must have got the worst of it at once, sir." A faint burst of lightning quivered all round, as if flashed into a cavern—into a black and secret chamber of the sea, with a floor of foaming crests.

It unveiled for a sinister, fluttering moment a ragged mass of clouds hanging low, the lurch of the long outlines of the ship, the black figures of men caught on the bridge, heads forward, as if petrified in the act of butting. The darkness palpitated down upon all this, and then the real thing came at last.

It was something formidable and swift, like the sudden smashing of a vial of wrath. It seemed to explode all round the ship with an overpowering concussion and a rush of great waters, as if an immense dam had been blown up to windward. In an instant the men lost touch of each other. This is the disintegrating power of a great wind: it isolates one from one's kind. An earthquake, a landslip, an avalanche, overtake a man incidentally, as it were—without passion. A furious gale attacks him like a personal enemy, tries to grasp his limbs, fastens upon his mind, seeks to rout his very spirit out of him.

Jukes was driven away from his commander. He fancied himself whirled a great distance through the air. Everything disappeared—even, for a moment, his power of thinking; but his hand had found one of the rail-stanchions. His distress was by no means alleviated by an inclination to disbelieve the reality of this experience. Though young, he had seen some bad weather, and had never doubted his ability to imagine the worst; but this was so much beyond his powers of fancy that it appeared incompatible with the existence of any ship whatever. He would have been incredulous about himself in the same way, perhaps, had he not been so harassed by the necessity of exerting a wrestling effort against a force trying to tear him away from his hold. Moreover, the conviction of not being utterly destroyed returned to him through the sensations of being half-drowned, bestially shake, and partly choked.

It seemed to him he remained there precariously alone with the stanchion for a long, long time. The rain poured on him, flowed, drove in sheets. He breathed in gasps; and sometimes the water he swallowed was fresh and sometimes it was salt. For the most part he kept his eyes shut tight, as if suspecting his sight might be destroyed in the immense flurry of the elements. When he ventured to blink hastily, he derived some moral support from the green gleam of the starboard light shining feebly upon the flight of rain and sprays. He was actually looking at it when its ray fell upon the uprearing sea which put it out. He saw the head of the wave topple over, adding the mite of its crash to the tremendous uproar raging around him, and almost at the same instant the stanchion was wrenched away from his embracing arms. After a crushing thump on his back he found himself suddenly afloat and borne upwards. His first irresistible notion was that the whole China Sea had climbed on the bridge. Then, more sanely, he concluded himself gone overboard. All the time he was being tossed, flung, and rolled in great volumes of water, he kept on repeating mentally, with the utmost precipitation, the words: "My God! My God! My God! My God!"

All at once, in a revolt of misery and despair, he formed the crazy resolution to get out of that. And he began to thresh about with his arms and legs. But as soon as he commenced his wretched struggles he discovered that he had become somehow mixed up with a face, an oilskin coat, somebody's boots. He clawed ferociously all these things in turn, lost them, found them again, lost them once more, and finally was himself caught in the firm clasp of a pair of stout arms. He returned the embrace closely round a thick solid body. He had found his captain.

They tumbled over and over, tightening their hug. Suddenly the water let them down with a brutal bang; and, stranded against the side of the wheelhouse, out of breath and bruised, they were left to stagger up in the wind and hold on where they could.

Jukes came out of it rather horrified, as though he had escaped some unparalleled outrage directed at his feelings. It weakened his faith in himself. He started shouting aimlessly to the man he could feel near him in that fiendish blackness, "Is it you, sir? Is it you, sir?" till his temples seemed ready to burst. And he heard in answer a voice, as if crying far away, as if screaming to him fretfully from a very great distance, the one word "Yes!" Other seas swept again over the bridge. He received them defencelessly right over his bare head, with both his hands engaged in holding.

The motion of the ship was extravagant. Her lurches had an appalling helplessness: she pitched as if taking a header into a void, and seemed to find a wall to hit every time. When she rolled she fell on her side headlong, and she would be righted back by such a demolishing blow that Jukes felt her reeling as a clubbed man reels before he collapses. The gale howled and scuffled about gigantically in the darkness, as though the entire world were one black gully. At certain moments the air streamed against the ship as if sucked through a tunnel with a concentrated solid force of impact that seemed to lift her clean out of the water and keep her up for an instant with only a quiver running through her from end to end. And then she would begin her tumbling again as if dropped back into a boiling cauldron. Jukes tried hard to compose his mind and judge things coolly.

The sea, flattened down in the heavier gusts, would uprise and over-whelm both ends of the *Nan-Shan* in snowy rushes of foam, expanding wide, beyond both rails, into the night. And on this dazzling sheet, spread under the blackness of the clouds and emitting a bluish glow, Captain MacWhirr could catch a desolate glimpse of a few tiny specks black as ebony, the tops of the hatches, the battened companions, the heads of the covered winches, the foot of a mast. This was all he could see of his ship. Her middle structure, covered by the bridge which bore him, his mate, the closed wheelhouse where a man was steering shut up with the fear of being swept overboard together with the whole thing in one great crash—her middle structure was like a half-tide rock awash upon a coast. It was like an outlying rock with the water boiling up, streaming over, pouring off, beating round—like a rock in the surf to which shipwrecked people cling before they let go—only it rose, it sank, it rolled continuously, without respite and rest, like a rock that should have miraculously struck adrift from a coast and gone wallowing upon the sea.

The *Nan-Shan* was being looted by the storm with a senseless, de-structive fury: trysails torn out of the extra gaskets, double-lashed awnings blown away, bridge swept clean, weather-cloths burst, rails twisted, light-screens smashed—and two of the boats had gone already. They had gone un-heard and unseen, melting, as it were, in the shock and smother of the wave. It was only later, when upon the white flash of another high sea hurling itself amidships, Jukes had a vision of two pairs of davits leaping black and empty out of the solid blackness, with one overhauled fall flying and an iron-bound block capering in the air, that he became aware of what had happened within about three yards of his back.

He poked his head forward, groping for the ear of his commander. His lips touched it—big, fleshy, very wet. He cried in an agitated tone, "Our boats are going now, sir."

And again he heard that voice, forced and ringing feebly, but with a penetrating effect of quietness in the enormous discord of noises, as if sent out from some remote spot of peace beyond the black wastes of the gale; again he heard a man's voice—the frail and indomitable sound that can be made to carry an infinity of thought, resolution and purpose, that shall be pronouncing confident words on the last day, when heavens fall, and justice is done—again he heard it, and it was crying to him, as if from very, very far—"All right."

He thought he had not managed to make himself understood. "Our boats—I say boats—the boats, sir! Two gone!"

The same voice, within a foot of him and yet so remote, yelled sensibly, "Can't be helped."

Captain MacWhirr had never turned his face, but Jukes caught some more words on the wind.

"What can—expect—when hammering through—such— Bound to leave—something behind—stands to reason."

Watchfully Jukes listened for more. No more came. This was all Captain MacWhirr had to say; and Jukes could picture to himself rather than see the broad squat back before him. An impenetrable obscurity pressed down upon the ghostly glimmers of the sea. A dull conviction seized upon Jukes that there was nothing to be done.

If the steering-gear did not give way, if the immense volumes of water did not burst the deck in or smash one of the hatches, if the engines did not give up, if way could be kept on the ship against this terrific wind, and she did not bury herself in one of these awful seas, of whose white crests alone, topping high above her bows, he could now and then get a sickening glimpse—then there was a chance of her coming out of it. Something within him seemed to turn over, bringing uppermost the feeling that the *Nan-Shan* was lost.

"She's done for," he said to himself, with a surprising mental agitation, as though he had discovered an unexpected meaning in this thought. One of these things was bound to happen. Nothing could be prevented now, and nothing could be remedied. The men on board did not count, and the ship could not last. This weather was too impossible.

Jukes felt an arm thrown heavily over his shoulders; and to this overture he responded with great intelligence by catching hold of his captain round the waist.

They stood clasped thus in the blind night, bracing each other against the wind, cheek to cheek and lip to ear, in the manner of two hulks lashed stem to stern together.

And Jukes heard the voice of his commander hardly any louder than before, but nearer, as though, starting to march athwart the prodigious rush of the hurricane, it had approached him, bearing that strange effect of quietness like the serene glow of a halo.

"D'ye know where the hands got to?" it asked, vigorous and evanescent at the same time, overcoming the strength of the wind, and swept away from Jukes instantly.

Jukes didn't know. They were all on the bridge when the real force of the hurricane struck the ship. He had no idea where they had crawled to. Under the circumstances they were nowhere, for all the use that could be made of them. Somehow the Captain's wish to know distressed Jukes.

"Want the hands, sir?" he cried, apprehensively.

"Ought to know," asserted Captain MacWhirr. "Hold hard."

They held hard. An outburst of unchained fury, a vicious rush of the wind absolutely steadied the ship; she rocked only, quick and light like a child's cradle, for a terrific moment of suspense, while the whole atmosphere, as it seemed, streamed furiously past her, roaring away from the tenebrous earth.

It suffocated them, and with eyes shut they tightened their grasp. What from the magnitude of the shock might have been a column of water running upright in the dark, butted against the ship, broke short, and fell on her bridge, crushingly, from on high, with a dead burying weight.

A flying fragment of that collapse, a mere splash, enveloped them in one swirl from their feet over their heads, filling violently their ears, mouths and nostrils with salt water. It knocked out their legs, wrenched in haste at their arms, seethed away swiftly under their chins; and opening their eyes, they saw the piled-up masses of foam dashing to and fro amongst what looked like the fragments of a ship. She had given way as if driven straight in. Their panting hearts yielded, too, before the tremendous blow; and all at once she sprang up again to her desperate plunging, as if trying to scramble out from under the ruins.

The seas in the dark seemed to rush from all sides to keep her back where she might perish. There was hate in the way she was handled, and a ferocity in the blows that fell. She was like a living creature thrown to the rage of a mob: hustled terribly, struck at, borne up, flung down, leaped upon. Captain MacWhirr and Jukes kept hold of each other, deafened by the noise, gagged by the wind; and the great physical tumult beating about their bodies, brought, like an unbridled display of passion, a profound trouble to their souls. One of these wild and appalling shrieks that are heard at times passing mysteriously overhead in the steady roar of a hurricane, swooped, as if borne on wings, upon the ship, and Jukes tried to outscream it.

"Will she live through this?"

The cry was wrenched out of his breast. It was as unintentional as the birth of a thought in the head, and he heard nothing of it himself. It all became extinct at once—thought, intention, effort—and of his cry the inaudible vibration added to the tempest waves of the air.

He expected nothing from it. Nothing at all. For indeed what answer could be made? But after a while he heard with amazement the frail and resisting voice in his ear, the dwarf sound, unconquered in the giant tumult.

"She may!"

It was a dull yell, more difficult to seize than a whisper. And presently the voice returned again, half submerged in the vast crashes, like a ship battling against the waves of an ocean.

"Let's hope so!" it cried—small, lonely and unmoved, a stranger to the visions of hope or fear; and it flickered into disconnected words: "Ship. . . . . This. . . . Never—Anyhow . . . for the best." Jukes gave it up.

Then, as if it had come suddenly upon the one thing fit to withstand the power of a storm, it seemed to gain force and firmness for the last broken shouts:

"Keep on hammering . . . builders . . . good men. . . . . And chance it . . . engines. . . . Rout . . . good man."

Captain MacWhirr removed his arm from Jukes' shoulders, and thereby ceased to exist for his mate, so dark it was; Jukes, after a tense stiffening of every muscle, would let himself go limp all over. The gnawing of profound discomfort existed side by side with an incredible disposition to somnolence, as though he had been buffeted and worried into drowsiness. The wind would get hold of his head and try to shake it off his shoulders; his clothes, full of water, were as heavy as lead, cold and dripping like an armour of melting ice: he shivered—it lasted a long time; and with his hands closed hard on his hold, he was letting himself sink slowly into the depths of bodily misery. His mind became concentrated upon himself in an aimless, idle way, and when something pushed lightly at the back of his knees he nearly, as the saying is, jumped out of his skin.

In the start forward he bumped the back of Captain MacWhirr, who didn't move; and then a hand gripped his thigh. A lull had come, a menacing lull of the wind, the holding of a stormy breath—and he felt himself pawed all over. It was the boatswain. Jukes recognized these hands, so thick and enormous that they seemed to belong to some new species of man.

The boatswain had arrived on the bridge, crawling on all fours against the wind, and had found the chief mate's legs with the top of his head. Immediately he crouched and began to explore Jukes' person upwards with prudent, apologetic touches, as became an inferior.

He was an ill-favoured, undersized, gruff sailor of fifty, coarsely hairy, short-legged, long-armed, resembling an elderly ape. His strength was immense; and in his great lumpy paws, bulging like brown boxing-gloves on the end of furry forearms, the heaviest objects were handled like playthings. Apart from the grizzled pelt on his chest, the menacing demeanour and the hoarse voice, he had none of the classical attributes of his rating. His good nature almost amounted to imbecility: the men did what they liked with him, and he had not an ounce of initiative in his character, which was easy-going and talkative. For these reasons Jukes disliked him; but Captain MacWhirr, to Jukes' scornful disgust, seemed to regard him as a first-rate petty officer.

He pulled himself up by Jukes' coat, taking that liberty with the greatest moderation, and only so far as it was forced upon him by the hurricane.

"What is it, bosun, what is it?" yelled Jukes, impatiently. What could that fraud of a bosun want on the bridge? The typhoon had got on Jukes' nerves. The husky bellowings of the other, though unintelligible, seemed to suggest a state of lively satisfaction. There could be no mistake. The old fool was pleased with something.

The boatswain's other hand had found some other body, for in a changed tone he began to inquire: "Is it you, sir? Is it you, sir?" The wind strangled his howls.

"Yes!" cried Captain MacWhirr.

★   ★   ★   ★   ★

All that the boatswain, out of a superabundance of yells, could make clear to Captain MacWhirr was the bizarre intelligence that "All them Chinamen in the fore 'tween-deck have fetched away, sir."

Jukes to leeward could hear these two shouting within six inches of his face, as you may hear on a still night half a mile away two men conversing across a field. He heard Captain MacWhirr's exasperated "What? What?" and the strained pitch of the other's hoarseness. "In a lump . . . seen them my-self. . . . Awful sight, sir . . . thought . . . tell you."

Jukes remained indifferent, as if rendered irresponsible by the force of the hurricane, which made the very thought of action utterly vain. Besides, being very young, he had found the occupation of keeping his heart com-pletely steeled against the worst so engrossing that he had come to feel an overpowering dislike towards any other form of activity whatever. He was not scared; he knew this because, firmly believing he would never seen another sunrise, he remained calm in that belief.

These are the moments of do-nothing heroics to which even good men surrender at times. Many officers of ships can no doubt recall a case in their experience when just such a trance of confounded stoicism would come all at once over a whole ship's company. Jukes, however, had no wide experi-ence of men or storms. He conceived himself to be calm—inexorably calm; but as a matter of fact he was daunted; not abjectly, but only so far as a decent man may, without becoming loathsome to himself.

It was rather like a forced-on numbness of spirit. The long, long stress of a gale does it; the suspense of the interminably culminating catastrophe; and there is a bodily fatigue in the mere holding on to existence within the exces-sive tumult; a searching and insidious fatigue that penetrates deep into a man's breast to cast down and sadden his heart, which is incorrigible, and of all the gifts of the earth—even before life itself—aspires to peace.

Jukes was benumbed much more than he supposed. He held on—very wet, very cold, stiff in every limb; and in a momentary hallucination of swift visions (it is said that a drowning man thus reviews all his life) he beheld all sorts of memories altogether unconnected with his present situation. He re-membered his father, for instance: a worthy business man, who at an unfortu-nate crisis in his affairs went quietly to bed and died forthwith in a state of resignation. Jukes did not recall these circumstances, of course, but remaining otherwise unconcerned he seemed to see distinctly the poor man's face; a cer-tain game of nap played when quite a boy in Table Bay on board a ship, since lost with all hands; the thick eyebrows of his first skipper; and without any emotion, as he might years ago have walked listlessly into her room and found her sitting there with a book, he remembered his mother—dead, too, now—the resolute woman, left badly off, who had been very firm in his bringing up.

It could not have lasted more than a second, perhaps not so much. A heavy arm had fallen about his shoulders; Captain MacWhirr's voice was speaking his name into his ear.

"Jukes! Jukes!"

He detected the tone of deep concern. The wind had thrown its weight on the ship, trying to pin her down amongst the seas. They made a clean breach over her, as over a deep-swimming log; and the gathered weight of crashes menaced monstrously from afar. The breakers flung out of the night with a ghostly light on their crests—the light of sea-foam that in a ferocious, boiling-up pale flash showed upon the slender body of the ship the toppling rush, the downfall, and the seething mad scurry of each wave. Never for a moment could she shake herself clear of the water; Jukes, rigid, perceived in her motion the ominous sign of haphazard floundering. She was no longer struggling intelligently. It was the beginning of the end; and the note of busy concern in Captain MacWhirr's voice sickened him like an exhibition of blind and pernicious folly.

The spell of the storm had fallen upon Jukes. He was penetrated by it, absorbed by it; he was rooted in it with a rigour of dumb attention. Captain MacWhirr persisted in his cries, but the wind got between them like a solid wedge. He hung round Jukes' neck as heavy as a millstone, and suddenly the sides of their heads knocked together.

"Jukes! Mr. Jukes, I say!"

He had to answer that voice that would not be silenced. He answered in the customary manner: ". . . Yes, sir."

And directly, his heart, corrupted by the storm that breeds a craving for peace, rebelled against the tyranny of training and command.

Captain MacWhirr had his mate's head fixed firm in the crook of his elbow, and pressed it to his yelling lips mysteriously. Sometimes Jukes would break in, admonishing hastily: "Look out, sir!" or Captain MacWhirr would bawl an earnest exhortation to "Hold hard, there!" and the whole black universe seemed to reel together with the ship. They paused. She floated yet. And Captain MacWhirr would resume his shouts. ". . . . Says . . . whole lot . . . fetched away. . . . Ought to see . . . what's the matter."

Directly the full force of the hurricane had struck the ship, every part of her deck became untenable; and the sailors, dazed and dismayed, took shelter in the port alleyway under the bridge. It had a door aft, which they shut; it was very black, cold, and dismal. At each heavy fling of the ship they would groan all together in the dark, and tons of water could be heard scuttling about as if trying to get at them from above. The boatswain had been keeping up a gruff talk, but a more unreasonable lot of men, he said afterwards, he had never been with. They were snug enough there, out of harm's way, and not wanted to do anything, either; and yet they did nothing but grumble and complain peevishly like so many sick kids. Finally, one of them said that if there had been at least some light to see each other's noses by, it wouldn't be so bad. It was making him crazy, he declared, to lie there in the dark waiting for the blamed hooker to sink.

"Why don't you step outside, then, and be done with it at once?" the boatswain turned on him.

This called up a shout of execration. The boatswain found himself overwhelmed with reproaches of all sorts. They seemed to take it ill that a lamp was not instantly created for them out of nothing. They would whine after a light to get drowned by—anyhow! And though the unreason of their revilings was patent—since no one could hope to reach the lamp-room, which was forward—he became greatly distressed. He did not think it was decent of them to be nagging at him like this. He told them so, and was met by general contumely. He sought refuge, therefore, in an embittered silence. At the same time their grumbling and sighing and muttering worried him greatly, but by-and-by it occurred to him that there were six globe lamps hung in the 'tween-deck, and that there could be no harm in depriving the coolies of one of them.

The *Nan-Shan* had an athwartship coal-bunker, which, being at times used as cargo space, communicated by an iron door with the fore 'tween-deck. It was empty then, and its manhole was the foremost one in the alleyway. The boatswain could get in, therefore, without coming out on deck at all; but to his great surprise he found he could induce no one to help him in taking off the manhole cover. He groped for it all the same, but one of the crew lying in his way refused to budge.

"Why, I only want to get you that blamed light you are crying for," he expostulated, almost pitifully.

Somebody told him to go and put his head in a bag. He regretted he could not recognize the voice, and that it was too dark to see, otherwise, as he said, he would have put a head on *that* son of a sea-cook, anyway, sink or swim. Nevertheless, he had made up his mind to show them he could get a light, if he were to die for it.

Through the violence of the ship's rolling, every movement was dangerous. To be lying down seemed labour enough. He nearly broke his neck dropping into the bunker. He fell on his back, and was sent shooting helplessly from side to side in the dangerous company of a heavy iron bar—a coal-trimmer's slice probably—left down there by somebody. This thing made him as nervous as though it had been a wild beast. He could not see it, the inside of the bunker coated with coal-dust being perfectly and impenetrably black; but he heard it sliding and clattering, and striking here and there, always in the neighbourhood of his head. It seemed to make an extraordinary noise, too—to give heavy thumps as though it had been as big as a bridge girder. This was remarkable enough for him to notice while he was flung from port to starboard and back again, and clawing desperately the smooth sides of the bunker in the endeavour to stop himself. The door into the 'tween-deck not fitting quite true, he saw a thread of dim light at the bottom.

Being a sailor, and a still active man, he did not want much of a chance to regain his feet; and as luck would have it, in scrambling up he put his hand on the iron slice, picking it up as he rose. Otherwise he would have been afraid of the thing breaking his legs, or at least knocking him down again. At first he stood still. He felt unsafe in this darkness that seemed to make the ship's motion unfamiliar, unforeseen, and difficult to counteract. He felt so much shaken for a moment that he dared not move for fear of "taking charge again." He had no mind to get battered to pieces in that bunker.

He had struck his head twice; he was dazed a little. He seemed to hear yet so plainly the clatter and bangs of the iron slice flying about his ears that he tightened his grip to prove to himself he had it there safely in his hand. He was vaguely amazed at the plainness with which down there he could hear the gale raging. Its howls and shrieks seemed to take on, in the emptiness of the bunker, something of the human character, of human rage and pain—being not vast but infinitely poignant. And there were, with every roll, thumps, too—profound, ponderous thumps, as if a bulk object of five-ton weight or so had got play in the hold. But there was no such thing in the cargo. Something on deck? Impossible. Or alongside? Couldn't be.

He thought all this quickly, clearly, competently, like a seaman, and in the end remained puzzled. This noise, though, came deadened from outside, together with the washing and pouring of water on deck above his head. Was it the wind? Must be. It made down there a row like the shouting of a big lot of crazed men. And he discovered in himself a desire for a light, too—if only to get drowned by—and a nervous anxiety to get out of that bunker as quickly as possible.

He pulled back the bolt: the heavy iron plate turned on its hinges; and it was as though he had opened the door to the sounds of the tempest. A gust of hoarse yelling met him: the air was still; and the rushing of water overhead was covered by a tumult of strangled, throaty shrieks that produced an effect of desperate confusion. He straddled his legs the whole width of the doorway and stretched his neck. And at first he perceived only what he had come to seek: six small yellow flames swinging violently on the great body of the dusk.

It was stayed like the gallery of a mine, with a row of stanchions in the middle, and cross-beams overhead, penetrating into the gloom ahead—indefinitely. And to port there loomed, like the caving in of one of the sides, a bulky mass with a slanting outline. The whole place, with the shadows and the shapes, moved all the time. The boatswain glared: the ship lurched to starboard, and a great howl came from that mass that had the slant of fallen earth.

Pieces of wood whizzed past. Planks, he thought, inexpressibly startled, and flinging back his head. At his feet a man went sliding over, open-eyed, on his back, straining with uplifted arms for nothing: and another came bounding like a detached stone with his head between his legs and his hands clenched. His pigtail whipped in the air; he made a grab at the boatswain's legs, and from his opened hand a bright white disc rolled against the boatswain's foot. He recognized a silver dollar, and yelled at it with astonishment. With a precipitated sound of trampling and shuffling of bare feet, and with guttural cries, the mound of writhing bodies piled up to port detached itself from the ship's side and sliding, inert and struggling, shifted to starboard, with a dull, brutal thump. The cries ceased. The boatswain heard a long moan through the roar and whistling of the wind; he saw an inextricable confusion of heads and shoulders, naked soles kicking upwards, fists raised, tumbling backs, legs, pigtails, faces.

"Good Lord!" he cried, horrified, and banged-to the iron door upon this vision.

This was what he had come on the bridge to tell. He could not keep it to himself; and on board ship there is only one man to whom it is worth while to unburden yourself. On his passage back the hands in the alleyway swore at him for a fool. Why didn't he bring that lamp? What the devil did the coolies matter to anybody? And when he came out, the extremity of the ship made what went on inside of her appear of little moment.

At first he thought he had left the alleyway in the very moment of her sinking. The bridge ladders had been washed away, but an enormous sea filling the after-deck floated him up. After that he had to lie on his stomach for some time, holding to a ring-bolt, getting his breath now and then, and swallowing salt water. He struggled farther on his hands and knees, too frightened and distracted to turn back. In this way he reached the after-part of the wheelhouse. In that comparatively sheltered spot he found the second mate. The boatswain was pleasantly surprised—his impression being that everybody on deck must have been washed away a long time ago. He asked eagerly where the captain was.

The second mate was lying low, like a malignant little animal under a hedge.

"Captain? Gone overboard, after getting us into this mess." The mate, too, for all he knew or cared. Another fool. Didn't matter. Everybody was going by-and-by.

The boatswain crawled out again into the strength of the wind; not because he much expected to find anybody, he said, but just to get away from "that man." He crawled out as outcasts go to face an inclement world. Hence his great joy at finding Jukes and the Captain. But what was going on in the 'tween-deck was to him a minor matter by that time. Besides, it was difficult to make yourself heard. But he managed to convey the idea that the Chinaman had broken adrift together with their boxes, and that he had come up on purpose to report this. As to the hands, they were all right. Then, appeased, he subsided on the deck in a sitting posture, hugging with his arms and legs the stand of the engine-room telegraph—an iron casting as thick as a post. When that went, why, he expected he would go, too. He gave no more thought to the coolies.

The River of Doubt

From *Through the Brazilian Wilderness*

BY THEODORE ROOSEVELT

Of all the men so casually labeled "larger than life," one who truly lived up to that distinction was Theodore Roosevelt. The twenty-sixth president of the United States was a man unlike any other at his level of influence and authority. He loved the strenuous outdoor life, as a rancher, hunter, naturalist, and explorer.

Roosevelt survived considerable tragedy and heartbreak at a very young age, when, in 1884, his young wife and his mother died within twelve hours of each other. After moving west, he lived the life of an ordinary rancher in the Dakota Territory on the Little Missouri River. He later went on to become the daring "Rough Rider" who led troops up San Juan Hill in the 1898 war against Spain and then to so many national and international achievements that they fill several books. Indeed, a new Roosevelt biography by Edmund Morris, *Theodore Rex*, is a tribute to the man's awesome and exciting personality.

In 1914, with his brother Kermit, Roosevelt ventured down Amazon tributaries such as the *Rio da Duvida*, or River of Doubt, which had never been mapped. Death was a possibility that waited around every bend. Starvation, poisonous snake and insect bites, hostile natives, and dangerous waters were everyday threats. And the threats sometimes took their toll.

★   ★   ★   ★   ★

On February 27, 1914, shortly after midday, we started down the River of Doubt into the unknown. We were quite uncertain whether after a week we should find ourselves in the Gy-Paraná, or after six weeks in the Madeira, or after three months we knew not where. That was why the river was rightly christened the Dúvida.

We had been camped close to the river, where the trail that follows the telegraph-line crosses it by a rough bridge. As our laden dugouts swung into the stream, Amilcar and Miller and all the others of the Gy-Paraná party were on the banks and the bridge to wave farewell and wish us good-by and good luck. It was the height of the rainy season, and the swollen torrent was swift and brown. Our camp was at about 12° 1′ latitude south and 60° 15′ longitude west of Greenwich. Our general course was to be northward toward the equator, by waterway through the vast forest.

We had seven canoes, all of them dugouts. One was small, one was cranky, and two were old, waterlogged, and leaky. The other three were good. The two old canoes were lashed together, and the cranky one was lashed to one of the others. Kermit with two paddlers went in the smallest of the good canoes; Colonel Rondon and Lyra with three other paddlers in the next largest; and the doctor, Cherrie, and I in the largest with three paddlers. The remaining eight camaradas—there were sixteen in all—were equally divided between our two pairs of lashed canoes. Although our personal baggage was cut down to the limit necessary for health and efficiency, yet on such a trip as ours, where scientific work has to be done and where food for twenty-two men for an unknown period of time has to be carried, it is impossible not to take a good deal of stuff; and the seven dugouts were too heavily laden.

The paddlers were a strapping set. They were expert river-men and men of the forest, skilled veterans in wilderness work. They were lithe as panthers and brawny as bears. They swam like water-dogs. They were equally at home with pole and paddle, with axe and machete; and one was a good cook and others were good men around camp. They looked like pirates in the pictures of Howard Pyle or Maxfield Parrish; one or two of them were pirates, and one worse than a pirate; but most of them were hard-working, willing, and cheerful. They were white,—or, rather, the olive of southern Europe,—black, copper-colored, and of all intermediate shades. In my canoe Luiz the steersman, the headman, was a Matto Grosso negro; Julio the bowsman was from Bahia and of pure Portuguese blood; and the third man, Antonio, was a Parecís Indian.

The actual surveying of the river was done by Colonel Rondon and Lyra, with Kermit as their assistant. Kermit went first in his little canoe with the sighting-rod, on which two disks, one red and one white, were placed a metre apart. He selected a place which commanded as long vistas as possible upstream and down, and which therefore might be at the angle of a bend; landed; cut away the branches which obstructed the view; and set up the sighting-pole—incidentally encountering maribundi wasps and swarms of biting and singing ants. Lyra, from his station up-stream, with his telemetre established the distance, while Colonel Rondon with the compass took the direction, and made the records. Then they moved on to the point Kermit had left, and Kermit established a new point within their sight. The first half-day's work was slow. The general course of the stream was a trifle east of north, but at short intervals it bent and curved literally toward every point of the compass. Kermit landed nearly a hundred times, and we made but nine and a third kilometres.

My canoe ran ahead of the surveying canoes. The height of the water made the going easy, for most of the snags and fallen trees were well beneath the surface. Now and then, however, the swift water hurried us toward ripples that marked ugly spikes of sunken timber, or toward uprooted trees that stretched almost across the stream. Then the muscles stood out on the backs and arms of the paddlers as stroke on stroke they urged us away from and past the obstacle. If the leaning or fallen trees were the thorny, slender-stemmed boritana palms, which love the wet, they were often, although plunged beneath the river, in full and vigorous growth, their stems curving upward, and their frond-crowned tops shaken by the rushing water. It was interesting work, for no civilized man, no white man, had ever gone down or up this river or seen the country through which we were passing. The lofty and matted forest rose like a green wall on either hand. The trees were stately and beautiful. The looped and twisted vines hung from them like great ropes. Masses of epiphytes grew both on the dead trees and the living; some had huge leaves like elephants' ears. Now and then fragrant scents were blown to us from flowers on the banks. There were not many birds, and for the most part the forest was silent; rarely we heard strange calls from the depths of the woods, or saw a cormorant or ibis.

My canoe ran only a couple of hours. Then we halted to wait for the others. After a couple of hours more, as the surveyors had not turned up, we landed and made camp at a spot where the bank rose sharply for a hundred yards to a level stretch of ground. Our canoes were moored to trees. The axemen cleared a space for the tents; they were pitched, the baggage was brought up, and fires were kindled. The woods were almost soundless. Through them ran old tapir trails, but there was no fresh sign. Before nightfall the surveyors arrived. There were a few piums and gnats, and a few mosquitoes after dark, but not enough to make us uncomfortable. The small stingless bees, of slightly aromatic odor, swarmed while daylight lasted and crawled over our faces and hands; they were such tame, harmless little things that when they tickled too much I always tried to brush them away without hurting them. But they became a great nuisance after a while. It had been raining at intervals, and the weather was overcast; but after the sun went down the sky cleared. The stars were brilliant overhead, and the new moon hung in the west. It was a pleasant night, the air almost cool, and we slept soundly.

Next morning the two surveying canoes left immediately after break-fast. An hour later the two pairs of lashed canoes pushed off. I kept our canoe to let Cherrie collect, for in the early hours we could hear a number of birds in the woods near by. The most interesting birds he shot were a cotinga, brilliant turquoise-blue with a magenta-purple throat, and a big woodpecker, black above and cinnamon below with an entirely red head and neck. It was almost noon before we started. We saw a few more birds; there were fresh tapir and paca tracks at one point where we landed; once we heard howler monkeys from the depth of the forest, and once we saw a big otter in midstream. As we drifted and paddled down the swirling brown current, through the vivid rain-drenched green of the tropic forest, the trees leaned over the river from both banks. When those that had fallen in the river at some narrow point were very tall, or where it happened that two fell opposite each other, they formed barriers which the men in the leading canoes cleared with their axes. There were many palms, both the burity with its stiff fronds like enormous fans, and a handsome species of ba-caba, with very long, gracefully curving fronds. In places the palms stood close together, towering and slender, their stems a stately colonnade, their fronds an arched fretwork against the sky. Butterflies of many hues fluttered over the river. The day was overcast, with showers of rain. When the sun broke through rifts in the clouds, his shafts turned the forest to gold.

In mid-afternoon we came to the mouth of a big and swift affluent entering from the right. It was undoubtedly the Bandeira, which we had crossed well toward its head, some ten days before, on our road to Bonofacio. The Nhambiquaras had then told Colonel Rondon that it flowed into the Dúvida. After its junction, with the added volume of water, the river widened without losing its depth. It was so high that it had overflowed and stood among the trees on the lower levels. Only the higher stretches were dry. On the sheer banks where we landed we had to push the canoes for yards or rods through the branches of the submerged trees, hacking and hewing. There were occasional bays and ox-bows from which the current had shifted. In these the coarse marsh grass grew tall.

This evening we made camp on a flat of dry ground, densely wooded, of course, directly on the edge of the river and five feet above it. It was fine to see the speed and sinewy ease with which the choppers cleared an open space for the tents. Next morning, when we bathed before sunrise, we dived into deep water right from the shore, and from the moored canoes. This second day we made sixteen and a half kilometres along the course of the river, and nine kilometres in a straight line almost due north.

The following day, March 1, there was much rain—sometimes show-ers, sometimes vertical sheets of water. Our course was somewhat west of north and we made twenty and a half kilometres. We passed signs of Indian habitation. There were abandoned palm-leaf shelters on both banks. On the left bank we came to two or three old Indian fields, grown up with coarse fern and studded with the burned skeletons of trees. At the mouth of a brook which entered from the right some sticks stood in the water, marking the site of an old fish-trap. At one point we found the tough vine hand-rail of an Indian bridge running right across the river, a couple of feet above it. Evidently the bridge had been built at low water. Three stout poles had been driven into the stream-bed in a line at right angles to the current. The bridge had consisted of poles fastened to these supports, leading between them and from the support at each end to the banks. The rope of tough vines had been stretched as a hand-rail, necessary with such precarious footing. The rise of the river had swept away the bridge, but the props and the rope hand-rail remained. In the afternoon, from the boat, Cherrie shot a large dark-gray monkey with a prehensile tail. It was very good eating.

We camped on a dry level space, but a few feet above, and close beside, the river—so that our swimming-bath was handy. The trees were cleared and camp was made with orderly hurry. One of the men almost stepped on a poisonous coral-snake, which would have been a serious thing, as his feet were bare. But I had on stout shoes, and the fangs of these serpents—unlike those of the pit-vipers—are too short to penetrate good leather. I promptly put my foot on him, and he bit my shoe with harmless venom. It has been said that the brilliant hues of the coral-snake when in its native haunts really confer on it a concealing coloration. In the dark and tangled woods, and to an only less extent in the ordinary varied landscape, anything motionless, especially if partially hidden, easily eludes the eye. But against the dark-brown mould of the forest floor on which we found this coral-snake its bright and varied coloration was distinctly revealing; infinitely more so than the duller mottling of the jararaca and other dangerous snakes of the genus lachecis. In the same place, however, we found a striking example of genuine protective or mimetic coloration and shape. A rather large insect larva—at least we judged it to be a larval form, but we were none of us entomologists—bore a resemblance to a partially curled dry leaf which was fairly startling. The tail exactly resembled the stem or continuation of the midrib of the dead leaf. The flattened body was curled up at the sides, and veined and colored precisely like the leaf. The head, colored like the leaf, projected in front.

We were still in the Brazilian highlands. The forest did not teem with life. It was generally rather silent; we did not hear such a chorus of birds and mammals as we had occasionally heard even on our overland journey, when more than once we had been awakened at dawn by the howling, screaming, yelping, and chattering of monkeys, toucans, macaws, parrots, and parakeets. There were, however, from time to time, queer sounds from the forest, and after nightfall different kinds of frogs and insects uttered strange cries and calls. In volume and frequency these seemed to increase until midnight. Then they died away and before dawn everything was silent.

At this camp the carregadores ants completely devoured the doctor's undershirt, and ate holes in his mosquito-net; and they also ate the strap of Lyra's gun-case. The little stingless bees, of many kinds, swarmed in such multitudes, and were so persevering, that we had to wear our head-nets when we wrote or skinned specimens.

The following day was almost without rain. It was delightful to drift and paddle slowly down the beautiful tropical river. Until mid-afternoon the current was not very fast, and the broad, deep, placid stream bent and curved in every direction, although the general course was northwest. The country was flat, and more of the land was under than above water. Continually we found ourselves travelling between stretches of marshy forest where for miles the water stood or ran among the trees. Once we passed a hillock. We saw brilliantly colored parakeets and trogons. At last the slow current quickened. Faster it went, and faster, until it began to run like a mill-race, and we heard the roar of rapids ahead. We pulled to the right bank, moored the canoes, and while most of the men pitched camp two or three of them accompanied us to examine the rapids. We had made twenty kilometres.

We soon found that the rapids were a serious obstacle. There were many curls, and one or two regular falls, perhaps six feet high. It would have been impossible to run them, and they stretched for nearly a mile. The carry, however, which led through woods and over rocks in a nearly straight line, was somewhat shorter. It was not an easy portage over which to carry heavy loads and drag heavy dugout canoes. At the point where the descent was steepest there were great naked flats of friable sandstone and conglomerate. Over parts of these, where there was a surface of fine sand, there was a growth of coarse grass. Other parts were bare and had been worn by the weather into fantastic shapes—one projection looked like an old-fashioned beaver hat upside down. In this place, where the naked flats of rock showed the projection of the ledge through which the river had cut its course, the torrent rushed down a deep, sheer-sided, and extremely narrow channel. At one point it was less than two yards across, and for quite a distance not more than five or six yards. Yet only a mile or two above the rapids the deep, placid river was at least a hundred yards wide. It seemed extraordinary, almost impossible, that so broad a river could in so short a space of time contract its dimensions to the width of the strangled channel through which it now poured its entire volume.

This has for long been a station where the Nhambiquaras at intervals built their ephemeral villages and tilled the soil with the rude and destructive cultivation of savages. There were several abandoned old fields, where the dense growth of rank fern hid the tangle of burnt and fallen logs. Nor had the Nhambiquaras been long absent. In one trail we found what gypsies would have called a "pateran," a couple of branches arranged crosswise, eight leaves to a branch; it had some special significance, belonging to that class of signals, each with some peculiar and often complicated meaning, which are commonly used by many wild peoples. The Indians had thrown a simple bridge, consisting of four long poles, without a hand-rail, across one of the narrowest parts of the rock gorge through which the river foamed in its rapid descent. This sub-tribe of Indians was called the Navaïté; we named the rapids after them, Navaïté Rapids. By observation Lyra found them to be (in close approximation to) latitude 11° 44' south and longitude 60° 18' west from Greenwich.

We spent March 3 and 4 and the morning of the 5th in portaging around the rapids. The first night we camped in the forest beside the spot where we had halted. Next morning we moved the baggage to the foot of the rapids, where we intended to launch the canoes, and pitched our tents on the open sandstone flat. It rained heavily. The little bees were in such swarms as to be a nuisance. Many small stinging bees were with them, which stung badly. We were bitten by huge horse-flies, the size of bumblebees. More serious annoyance was caused by the pium and boroshuda flies during the hours of daylight, and by the polvora, the sand-flies, after dark. There were a few mosquitoes. The boroshudas were the worst pests; they brought the blood at once, and left marks that lasted for weeks. I did my writing in head-net and gauntlets. Fortunately we had with us several bottles of "fly dope"—so named on the label—put up, with the rest of our medicine, by Doctor Alexander Lambert; he had tested it in the north woods and found it excellent. I had never before been forced to use such an ointment, and had been reluctant to take it with me; but now I was glad enough to have it, and we all of us found it exceedingly useful. I would never again go into mosquito or sand-fly country without it. The effect of an application wears off after half an hour or so, and under many conditions, as when one is perspiring freely, it is of no use; but there are times when minute mosquitoes and gnats get through head-nets and under mosquito-bars, and when the ointments occasionally renewed may permit one to get sleep or rest which would otherwise be impossible of attainment. The termites got into our tent on the sand-flat, ate holes in Cherrie's mosquito-net and poncho, and were starting to work at our duffel-bags, when we discovered them.

Packing the loads across was simple. Dragging the heavy dugouts was labor. The biggest of the two water-logged ones was the heaviest. Lyra and Kermit did the job. All the men were employed at it except the cook, and one man who was down with fever. A road was chopped through the forest and a couple of hundred stout six-foot poles, or small logs, were cut as rollers and placed about two yards apart. With block and tackle the seven dugouts were hoisted out of the river up the steep banks, and up the rise of ground until the level was reached. Then the men harnessed themselves two by two on the drag-rope, while one of their number pried behind with a lever, and the canoe, bumping and sliding, was twitched through the woods. Over the sandstone flats there were some ugly ledges, but on the whole the course was downhill and relatively easy. Looking at the way the work was done, at the good-will, the endurance, and the bull-like strength of the camaradas, and at the intelligence and the unwearied efforts of their commanders, one could but wonder at the ignorance of those who do not realize the energy and the power that are so often possessed by, and that may be so readily developed in, the men of the tropics. Another subject of perpetual wonder is the attitude of certain men who stay at home, and still more the attitude of certain men who travel under easy conditions, and who belittle the achievements of the real explorers of, the real adventures in, the great wilderness. The impostors and romancers among explorers or would-be explorers and wilderness wanderers have been unusually prominent in connection with South America (although the conspicuous ones are not South Americans, by the way); and these are fit subjects for condemnation and derision. But the work of the genuine explorer and wilderness wanderer is fraught with fatigue, hardship, and danger. Many of the men of little knowledge talk glibly of portaging as if it were simple and easy. A portage over rough and unknown ground is always a work of difficulty and of some risk to the canoe; and in the untrodden, or even in the unfrequented, wilderness risk to the canoe is a serious matter. This particular portage at Navaïté Rapids was far from being unusually difficult; yet it not only cost two and a half days of severe and incessant labor, but it cost something in damage to the canoes. One in particular, the one in which I had been journeying, was split in a manner which caused us serious uneasiness as to how long, even after being patched, it would last. Where the canoes were launched, the bank was sheer, and one of the water-logged canoes filled and went to the bottom; and there was more work in raising it.

We were still wholly unable to tell where we were going or what lay ahead of us. Round the camp-fire, after supper, we held endless discussions and hazarded all kinds of guesses on both subjects. The river might bend sharply to the west and enter the Gy-Paraná high up or low down, or go north to the

Madeira, or bend eastward and enter the Tapajos, or fall into the Canumá and finally through one of its mouths enter the Amazon direct. Lyra inclined to the first, and Colonel Rondon to the second, of these propositions. We did not know whether we had one hundred or eight hundred kilometres to go, whether the stream would be fairly smooth or whether we would encounter waterfalls, or rapids, or even some big marsh or lake. We could not tell whether or not we would meet hostile Indians, although no one of us ever went ten yards from camp without his rifle. We had no idea how much time the trip would take. We had entered a land of unknown possibilities.

We started down-stream again early in the afternoon of March 5. Our hands and faces were swollen from the bites and stings of the insect pests at the sand-flat camp, and it was a pleasure once more to be in the middle of the river, where they did not come, in any numbers, while we were in motion. The current was swift, but the river was so deep that there were no serious obstructions. Twice we went down over slight riffles, which in the dry season were doubtless rapids; and once we struck a spot where many whirlpools marked the presence underneath of bowlders which would have been above water had not the river been so swollen by the rains. The distance we covered in a day going down-stream would have taken us a week if we had been going up. The course wound hither and thither, sometimes in sigmoid curves; but the general direction was east of north. As usual, it was very beautiful; and we never could tell what might appear around any curve. In the forest that rose on either hand were tall rubber-trees. The surveying canoes, as usual, went first, while I shepherded the two pairs of lashed cargo canoes. I kept them always between me and the surveying canoes—ahead of me until I passed the surveying canoes, then behind me until, after an hour or so, I had chosen a place to camp. There was so much overflowed ground that it took us some little time this afternoon before we found a flat place high enough to be dry. Just before reaching camp Cherrie shot a jacu, a handsome bird somewhat akin to, but much smaller than, a turkey; after Cherrie had taken its skin, its body made an excellent canja. We saw parties of monkeys; and the false bell-birds uttered their ringing whistles in the dense timber around our tents. The giant ants, an inch and a quarter long, were rather too plentiful around this camp; one stung Kermit; it was almost like the sting of a small scorpion, and pained severely for a couple of hours. This half-day we made twelve kilometres.

On the following day we made nineteen kilometres, the river twisting in every direction, but in its general course running a little west of north. Once we stopped at a bee-tree, to get honey. The tree was a towering giant, of the kind called milk-tree, because a thick milky juice runs freely from any cut. Our camaradas eagerly drank the white fluid that flowed from the wounds made by their axes. I tried it. The taste was not unpleasant, but it left a sticky feeling in the mouth. The helmsman of my boat, Luiz, a powerful negro, chopped into the tree, balancing himself with springy ease on a slight scaffolding. The honey was in a hollow, and had been made by medium-sized stingless bees. At the mouth of the hollow they had built a curious entrance of their own, in the shape of a spout of wax about a foot long. At the opening the walls of the spout showed the wax formation, but elsewhere it had become in color and texture indistinguishable from the bark of the tree. The honey was delicious, sweet and yet with a tart flavor. The comb differed much from that of our honey-bees. The honey-cells were very large, and the brood-cells, which were small, were in a single instead of a double row. By this tree I came across an example of genuine concealing coloration. A huge tree-toad, the size of a bullfrog, was seated upright—not squatted flat—on a big rotten limb. It was absolutely motionless; the yellow brown of its back, and its dark sides, exactly harmonized in color with the light and dark patches on the log; the color was as concealing, here in its natural surroundings, as is the color of our common wood-frog among the dead leaves of our woods. When I stirred it up it jumped to a small twig, catching hold with the disks of its finger-tips, and balancing itself with unexpected ease for so big a creature, and then hopped to the ground and again stood motionless. Evidently it trusted for safety to escaping observation. We saw some monkeys and fresh tapir sign, and Kermit shot a jacu for the pot.

At about three o'clock I was in the lead, when the current began to run more quickly. We passed over one or two decided ripples, and then heard the roar of rapids ahead, while the stream began to race. We drove the canoe into the bank, and then went down a tapir trail, which led alongside the river, to reconnoitre. A quarter of a mile's walk showed us that there were big rapids, down which the canoes could not go; and we returned to the landing. All the canoes had gathered there, and Rondon, Lyra, and Kermit started down-stream to explore. They returned in an hour, with the information that the rapids continued for a long distance, with falls and steep pitches of broken water, and that the portage would take several days. We made camp just above the rapids. Ants swarmed, and some of them bit savagely. Our men, in clearing away the forest for our tents, left several very tall and slender accashy palms; the bole of this palm is as straight as an arrow and is crowned with delicate, gracefully curved fronds. We had come along the course of the river almost exactly a hundred kilometres; it had twisted so that we were only about fifty-five kilometres north of our starting-point. The rock was porphyritic.

The 7th, 8th, and 9th we spent in carrying the loads and dragging and floating the dugouts past the series of rapids at whose head we had stopped.

The first day we shifted camp a kilometre and a half to the foot of this series of rapids. This was a charming and picturesque camp. It was at the edge of the river, where there was a little, shallow bay with a beach of firm sand. In the water, at the middle point of the beach, stood a group of three burity palms, their great trunks rising like columns. Round the clearing in which our tents stood were several very big trees; two of them were rubber-trees. Kermit went down-stream five or six kilometres, and returned, having shot a jacu and found that at the point which he had reached there was another rapids, almost a fall, which would necessitate our again dragging the canoes over a portage. Antonio, the Parecís, shot a big monkey; of this I was glad because portaging is hard work, and the men appreciated the meat. So far Cherrie had collected sixty birds on the Dúvida, all of them new to the collection, and some probably new to science. We saw the fresh sign of paca, agouti, and the small peccary, and Kermit with the dogs roused a tapir, which crossed the river right through the rapids; but no one got a shot at it.

Except at one or perhaps two points a very big dugout, lightly loaded, could probably run all these rapids. But even in such a canoe it would be silly to make the attempt on an exploring expedition, where the loss of a canoe or of its contents means disaster; and moreover such a canoe could not be taken, for it would be impossible to drag it over the portages on the occasions when the portages became inevitable. Our canoes would not have lived half a minute in the wild water.

On the second day the canoes and loads were brought down to the foot of the first rapids. Lyra cleared the path and laid the logs for rollers, while Kermit dragged the dugouts up the bank from the water with block and tackle, with strain of rope and muscle. Then they joined forces, as over the uneven ground it needed the united strength of all their men to get the heavy dugouts along. Meanwhile the colonel with one attendant measured the distance, and then went on a long hunt, but saw no game. I strolled down beside the river for a couple of miles, but also saw nothing. In the dense tropical forest of the Amazonian basin hunting is very difficult, especially for men who are trying to pass through the country as rapidly as possible. On such a trip as ours getting game is largely a matter of chance.

On the following day Lyra and Kermit brought down the canoes and loads, with hard labor, to the little beach by the three palms where our tents were pitched. Many pacovas grew round about. The men used their immense leaves, some of which were twelve feet long and two and a half feet broad, to roof the flimsy shelters under which they hung their hammocks. I went into the woods, but in the tangle of vegetation it would have been a mere hazard had I seen any big animal. Generally the woods were silent and empty. Now and then little troops of birds of many kinds passed—wood-hewers, ant-thrushes, tanagers, flycatchers; as in the spring and fall similar troops of warblers, chick-adees, and nuthatches pass through our northern woods. On the rocks and on the great trees by the river grew beautiful white and lilac orchids—the sobralia, of sweet and delicate fragrance. For the moment my own books seemed a trifle heavy, and perhaps I would have found the day tedious if Kermit had not lent me the Oxford Book of French Verse. Eustache Deschamp, Joachim du Bellay, Ronsard, the delightful La Fontaine, the delightful but appalling Villon, Victor Hugo's "Guitare," Madame Desbordes-Valmore's lines on the little girl and her pillow, as dear little verses about a child as ever were written—these and many others comforted me much, as I read them in head-net and gauntlets, sitting on a log by an unknown river in the Amazonian forest.

On the 10th we again embarked and made a kilometre and a half, spending most of the time in getting past two more rapids. Near the first of these we saw a small cayman, a jacaré-tinga. At each set of rapids the canoes were unloaded and the loads borne past on the shoulders of the camaradas; three of the canoes were paddled down by a couple of naked paddlers apiece; and the two sets of double canoes were let down by ropes, one of one couple being swamped but rescued and brought safely to shore on each occasion. One of the men was upset while working in the swift water, and his face was cut against the stones. Lyra and Kermit did the actual work with the camaradas. Kermit, dressed substantially like the camaradas themselves, worked in the water, and, as the overhanging branches were thronged with crowds of biting and stinging ants, he was marked and blistered over his whole body. Indeed, we all suffered more or less from these ants; while the swarms of biting flies grew constantly more numerous. The termites ate holes in my helmet and also in the cover of my cot. Every one else had a hammock. At this camp we had come down the river about 102 kilometres, according to the surveying records, and in height had descended nearly 100 metres, as shown by the aneroid—al-though the figure in this case is only an approximation, as an aneroid cannot be depended on for absolute accuracy of results.

Next morning we found that during the night we had met with a se-rious misfortune. We had halted at the foot of the rapids. The canoes were moored to trees on the bank, at the tail of the broken water. The two old ca-noes, although one of them was our biggest cargo-carrier, were water-logged and heavy, and one of them was leaking. In the night the river rose. The leaky canoe, which at best was too low in the water, must have gradually filled from the wash of the waves. It sank, dragging down the other; they began to roll, bursting their moorings; and in the morning they had disappeared. A canoe was launched to look for them; but, rolling over the bowlders on the rocky bottom, they had at once been riven asunder, and the big fragments that were soon found, floating in eddies, or along the shore, showed that it was useless to look farther. We called these rapids Broken Canoe Rapids.

It was not pleasant to have to stop for some days; thanks to the rapids, we had made slow progress, and with our necessarily limited supply of food, and no knowledge whatever of what was ahead of us, it was important to make good time. But there was no alternative. We had to build either one big canoe or two small ones. It was raining heavily as the men started to explore in different directions for good canoe trees. Three—which ultimately proved not very good for the purpose—were found close to camp; splendid-looking trees, one of them five feet in diameter three feet from the ground. The axemen immediately attacked this one under the superintendence of Colonel Rondon. Lyra and Kermit started in opposite directions to hunt. Lyra killed a jacu for us, and Kermit killed two monkeys for the men. Toward nightfall it cleared. The moon was nearly full, and the foaming river gleamed like silver.

Our men were "regional volunteers," that is, they had enlisted in the service of the Telegraphic Commission especially to do this wilderness work, and were highly paid, as was fitting, in view of the toil, hardship, and hazard to life and health. Two of them had been with Colonel Rondon during his eight months' exploration in 1909, at which time his men were regulars, from his own battalion of engineers. His four aides during the closing months of this trip were Lieutenants Lyra, Amarante, Alencarliense, and Pyrineus. The naturalist Miranda Ribeiro also accompanied him. This was the year when, marching on foot through an absolutely unknown wilderness, the colonel and his party finally reached the Gy-Paraná, which on the maps was then (and on most maps is now) placed in an utterly wrong course, and over a degree out of its real position. When they reached the affluents of the Gy-Paraná a third of the members of the party were so weak with fever that they could hardly crawl. They had no baggage. Their clothes were in tatters, and some of the men were almost naked. For months they had had no food except what little game they shot, and especially the wild fruits and nuts; if it had not been for the great abundance of the Brazil-nuts they would all have died. At the first big stream they encountered they built a canoe, and Alencarliense took command of it and descended to map the course of the river. With him went Ribeiro, the doctor Tanageira, who could no longer walk on account of the ulceration of one foot, three men whom the fever had rendered unable longer to walk, and six men who were as yet well enough to handle the canoe. By the time the remainder of the party came to the next navigable river eleven more fever-stricken men had nearly reached the end of their tether. Here they ran across a poor devil who had for four months been lost in the forest and was dying of slow starvation. He had eaten nothing but Brazil-nuts and the grubs of insects. He could no longer walk, but could sit erect and totter feebly for a few feet. Another canoe was built, and in it Pyrineus started down-stream with the eleven fever patients and the starving wanderer. Colonel Rondon kept up the morale of his men by still carrying out the forms of military discipline. The ragged bugler had his bugle. Lieutenant Pyrineus had lost every particle of his clothing except a hat and a pair of drawers. The half-naked lieutenant drew up his eleven fever patients in line; the bugle sounded; every one came to attention; and the haggard colonel read out the orders of the day. Then the dugout with its load of sick men started down-stream, and Rondon, Lyra, Amarante, and the twelve remaining men resumed their weary march. When a fortnight later they finally struck a camp of rubber-gatherers three of the men were literally and entirely naked. Meanwhile Amilcar had ascended the Jacyparaná a month or two previously with provisions to meet them; for at that time the maps incorrectly treated this river as larger, instead of smaller, than the Gy-Paraná, which they were in fact descending; and Colonel Rondon had supposed that they were going down the former stream. Amilcar returned after himself suffering much hardship and danger. The different parties finally met at the mouth of the Gy-Paraná, where it enters the Madeira. The lost man whom they had found seemed on the road to recovery, and they left him at a ranch, on the Madeira, where he could be cared for; yet after they had left him they heard that he had died.

On the 12th the men were still hard at work hollowing out the hard wood of the big tree, with axe and adze, while watch and ward were kept over them to see that the idlers did not shirk at the expense of the industrious. Kermit and Lyra again hunted; the former shot a curassow, which was welcome, as we were endeavoring in all ways to economize our food supply. We were using the tops of palms also. I spent the day hunting in the woods, for the most part by the river, but saw nothing. In the season of the rains game is away from the river and fish are scarce and turtles absent. Yet it was pleasant to be in the great silent forest. Here and there grew immense trees, and on some of them mighty buttresses sprang from the base. The lianas and vines were of every size and shape. Some were twisted and some were not. Some came down straight and slender from branches a hundred feet above. Others curved like long serpents around the trunks. Others were like knotted cables. In the shadow there was little noise. The wind rarely moved the hot, humid air. There were few flowers or birds. Insects were altogether too abundant, and even when travelling slowly it was impossible always to avoid them—not to speak of our constant companions the bees, mosquitoes, and especially the boroshudas or bloodsucking flies. Now while bursting through a tangle I disturbed a nest of wasps, whose resentment was active; now I heedlessly stepped among the outliers of a small party of the carnivorous foraging ants; now, grasping a branch as I stumbled, I shook down a shower of fire-ants; and among all these my attention was particularly arrested by the bite of one of the giant ants, which stung like a hornet, so that I felt it for three hours. The camaradas generally went barefoot or only wore sandals; and their ankles and feet were swollen and inflamed from the bites of the boroshudas and ants, some being actually incapacitated from work. All of us suffered more or less, our faces and hands swelling slightly from the boroshuda bites; and in spite of our clothes we were bitten all over our bodies, chiefly by ants and the small forest ticks. Because of the rain and the heat our clothes were usually wet when we took them off at night, and just as wet when we put them on again in the morning.

All day on the 13th the men worked at the canoe, making good progress. In rolling and shifting the huge, heavy tree-trunk every one had to assist now and then. The work continued until ten in the evening, as the weather was clear. After nightfall some of the men held candles and the others plied axe or adze, standing within or beside the great, half-hollowed logs, while the flicker of the lights showed the tropic forest rising in the darkness round about. The night air was hot and still and heavy with moisture. The men were stripped to the waist. Olive and copper and ebony, their skins glistened as if oiled, and rippled with the ceaseless play of the thews beneath.

On the morning of the 14th the work was resumed in a torrential tropic downpour. The canoe was finished, dragged down to the water, and launched soon after midday, and another hour or so saw us under way. The descent was marked, and the swollen river raced along. Several times we passed great whirlpools, sometimes shifting, sometimes steady. Half a dozen times we ran over rapids, and, although they were not high enough to have been obstacles to loaded Canadian canoes, two of them were serious to us. Our heavily laden, clumsy dugouts were sunk to within three or four inches of the surface of the river, and, although they were buoyed on each side with bundles of burity-palm branch-stems, they shipped a great deal of water in the rapids. The two biggest rapids we only just made, and after each we had hastily to push ashore in order to bail. In one set of big ripples or waves my canoe was nearly swamped. In a wilderness, where what is ahead is absolutely unknown, alike in terms of time, space, and method—for we had no idea where we would come out, how we would get out, or when we would get out—it is of vital consequence not to lose one's outfit, especially the provisions; and yet it is of only less consequence to go as rapidly as possible lest all the provisions be exhausted and the final stages of the expedition be accomplished by men weakened from semi-starvation, and therefore ripe for disaster. On this occasion, of the two hazards, we felt it necessary to risk running the rapids; for our progress had been so very slow that unless we made up the time, it was probable that we would be short of food before we got where we could expect to procure any more except what little the country in the time of the rains and floods, might yield. We ran until after five, so that the work of pitching camp was finished in the dark. We had made nearly sixteen kilometres in a direction slightly east of north. This evening the air was fresh and cool.

The following morning, the 15th of March, we started in good season. For six kilometres we drifted and paddled down the swift river without incident. At times we saw lofty Brazil-nut trees rising above the rest of the forest on the banks; and back from the river these trees grow to enormous proportions, towering like giants. There were great rubber-trees also, their leaves always in sets of threes. Then the ground on either hand rose into bowlder-strewn, forest-clad hills and the roar of broken water announced that once more our course was checked by dangerous rapids. Round a bend we came on them; a wide descent of white water, with an island in the middle, at the upper edge. Here grave misfortune befell us, and graver misfortune was narrowly escaped.

Kermit, as usual, was leading in his canoe. It was the smallest and least seaworthy of all. He had in it little except a week's supply of our boxed provisions and a few tools; fortunately none of the food for the camaradas. His dog Trigueiro was with him. Besides himself, the crew consisted of two men: João, the helmsman, or pilot, as he is called in Brazil, and Simplicio, the bowsman. Both were negroes and exceptionally good men in every way. Kermit halted his canoe on the left bank, above the rapids, and waited for the colonel's canoe. Then the colonel and Lyra walked down the bank to see what was ahead. Kermit took his canoe across to the island to see whether the descent could be better accomplished on the other side. Having made his investigation, he ordered the men to return to the bank he had left, and the dugout was headed up-stream accordingly. Before they had gone a dozen yards, the paddlers digging their paddles with all their strength into the swift current, one of the shifting whirlpools of which I have spoken came down-stream, whirled them around, and swept them so close to the rapids that no human power could avoid going over them. As they were drifting into them broadside on, Kermit yelled to the steersman to turn her head, so as to take them in the only way that offered any chance whatever of safety. The water came aboard, wave after wave, as they raced down. They reached the bottom with the canoe upright, but so full as barely to float, and the paddlers urged her toward the shore. They had nearly reached the bank when another whirlpool or whirling eddy tore them away and hurried them back to midstream, where the dugout filled and turned over. João, seizing the rope, started to swim ashore; the rope was pulled from his hand, but he reached the bank. Poor Simplicio must have been pulled under at once and his life beaten out on the bowlders beneath the racing torrent. He never rose again, nor did we ever recover his body. Kermit clutched his rifle, his favorite 405 Winchester with which he had done most of his hunting both in Africa and America, and climbed on the bottom of the upset boat. In a minute he was swept into the second series of rapids, and whirled away from the rolling boat, losing his rifle. The water beat his helmet down over his head and face and drove him beneath the surface; and when he rose at last he was almost drowned, his breath and strength almost spent. He was in swift but quiet water, and swam toward an overhanging branch. His jacket hindered him, but he knew he was too nearly gone to be able to get it off, and, thinking with the curious calm one feels when death is but a moment away, he realized that the utmost his failing strength could do was to reach the branch. He reached, and clutched it, and then almost lacked strength to haul himself out on the land. Good Trigueiro had faithfully swum alongside him through the rapids, and now himself scrambled ashore. It was a very narrow escape. Kermit was a great comfort and help to me on the trip; but the fear of some fatal accident befalling him was always a nightmare to me. He was to be married as soon as the trip was over; and it did not seem to me that I could bear to bring bad tidings to his betrothed and to his mother.

Simplicio was unmarried. Later we sent to his mother all the money that would have been his had he lived. The following morning we put on one side of the post erected to mark our camping-spot the following inscription, in Portuguese:

"IN THESE RAPIDS DIED POOR SIMPLICIO."

On an expedition such as ours death is one of the accidents that may at any time occur, and narrow escapes from death are too common to be felt as they would be felt elsewhere. One mourns sincerely, but mourning cannot interfere with labor. We immediately proceeded with the work of the portage. From the head to the tail of this series of rapids the distance was about six hundred yards. A path was cut along the bank, over which the loads were brought. The empty canoes ran the rapids without mishap, each with two skilled paddlers. One of the canoes almost ran into a swimming tapir at the head of the rapids; it went down the rapids, and then climbed out of the river. Kermit accompanied by João, went three or four miles down the river, looking for the body of Simplicio and for the sunk canoe. He found neither. But he found a box of provisions and a paddle, and salvaged both by swimming into midstream after them. He also found that a couple of kilometres below there was another stretch of rapids, and following them on the left-hand bank to the foot he found that they were worse than the ones we had just passed, and impassable for canoes on this left-hand side.

We camped at the foot of the rapids we had just passed. There were many small birds here, but it was extremely difficult to see or shoot them in the lofty tree tops, and to find them in the tangle beneath if they were shot. However, Cherrie got four species new to the collection. One was a tiny hummer, one of the species known as woodstars, with dainty but not brilliant plumage; its kind is never found except in the deep, dark woods, not coming out into the sunshine. Its crop was filled with ants; when shot it was feeding at a cluster of long red flowers. He also got a very handsome trogon and an exquisite little tanager, as brilliant as a cluster of jewels; its throat was lilac, its breast turquoise, its crown and forehead topaz, while above it was glossy purple-black, the lower part of the back ruby-red. This tanager was a female; I can hardly imagine that the male is more brilliantly colored. The fourth bird was a queer hawk of the genus *ibycter,* black, with a white belly, naked red cheeks and throat and red legs and feet. Its crop was filled with the seeds of fruits and a few insect remains; an extraordinary diet for a hawk.

The morning of the 16th was dark and gloomy. Through sheets of blinding rain we left our camp of misfortune for another camp where misfortune also awaited us. Less than half an hour took our dugouts to the head of the rapids below. As Kermit had already explored the left-hand side, Colonel Rondon and Lyra went down the right-hand side and found a channel which led round the worst part, so that they deemed it possible to let down the canoes by ropes from the bank. The distance to the foot of the rapids was about a kilometre. While the loads were being brought down the left bank, Luiz and Antonio Correa, our two best watermen, started to take a canoe down the right side, and Colonel Rondon walked ahead to see anything he could about the river. He was accompanied by one of our three dogs, Lobo. After walking about a kilometre he heard ahead a kind of howling noise, which he thought was made by spider-monkeys. He walked in the direction of the sound and

Lobo ran ahead. In a minute he heard Lobo yell with pain, and then, still yelping, come toward him, while the creature that was howling also approached, evidently in pursuit. In a moment a second yell from Lobo, followed by silence, announced that he was dead; and the sound of the howling when near convinced Rondon that the dog had been killed by an Indian, doubtless with two arrows. Probably the Indian was howling to lure the spider-monkeys toward him. Rondon fired his rifle in the air, to warn off the Indian or Indians, who in all probability had never seen a civilized man, and certainly could not imagine that one was in the neighborhood. He then returned to the foot of the rapids, where the portage was still going on, and, in company with Lyra, Kermit, and Antonio Parecís, the Indian, walked back to where Lobo's body lay. Sure enough he found him, slain by two arrows. One arrow-head was in him, and near by was a strange stick used in the very primitive method of fishing of all these Indians. Antonio recognized its purpose. The Indians, who were apparently two or three in number, had fled. Some beads and trinkets were left on the spot to show that we were not angry and were friendly.

Meanwhile Cherrie stayed at the head and I at the foot of the portage as guards. Luiz and Antonio Correa brought down one canoe safely. The next was the new canoe, which was very large and heavy, being made of wood that would not float. In the rapids the rope broke, and the canoe was lost, Luiz being nearly drowned.

It was a very bad thing to lose the canoe, but it was even worse to lose the rope and pulleys. This meant that it would be physically impossible to hoist big canoes up even small hills or rocky hillocks, such as had been so frequent beside the many rapids we had encountered. It was not wise to spend the four days necessary to build new canoes where we were, in danger of attack from the Indians. Moreover, new rapids might be very near, in which case the new canoes would hamper us. Yet the four remaining canoes would not carry all the loads and all the men, no matter how we cut the loads down; and we intended to cut everything down at once. We had been gone eighteen days. We had used over a third of our food. We had gone only 125 kilometres, and it was probable that we had at least five times, perhaps six or seven times, this distance still to go. We had taken a fortnight to descend rapids amounting in the aggregate to less than seventy yards of fall; a very few yards of fall makes a dangerous rapid when the river is swollen and swift and there are obstructions. We had only one aneroid to determine our altitude, and therefore could make merely a loose approximation to it, but we probably had between two and three times this descent in the aggregate of rapids ahead of us. So far the country had offered little in the way of food except palm-tops. We had lost four canoes and one man. We were in the country of wild Indians, who shot well with their bows. It behooved us to go warily, but also to make all speed possible, if we were to avoid serious trouble.

The best plan seemed to be to march thirteen men down along the bank, while the remaining canoes, lashed two and two, floated down beside them. If after two or three days we found no bad rapids, and there seemed a reasonable chance of going some distance at decent speed, we could then build the new canoes—preferably two small ones, this time, instead of one big one. We left all the baggage we could. We were already down as far as comfort would permit; but we now struck off much of the comfort. Cherrie, Kermit, and I had been sleeping under a very light fly; and there was another small light tent for one person, kept for possible emergencies. The last was given to me for my cot, and all five of the others swung their hammocks under the big fly. This meant that we left two big and heavy tents behind. A box of surveying instruments was also abandoned. Each of us got his personal belongings down to one box or duffel-bag—although there was only a small diminution thus made; because we had so little that the only way to make a serious diminution was to restrict ourselves to the clothes on our backs.

The biting flies and ants were to us a source of discomfort and at times of what could fairly be called torment. But to the camaradas, most of whom went barefoot or only wore sandals—and they never did or would wear shoes—the effect was more serious. They wrapped their legs and feet in pieces of canvas or hide; and the feet of three of them became so swollen that they were crippled and could not walk any distance. The doctor, whose courage and cheerfulness never flagged, took excellent care of them. Thanks to him, there had been among them hitherto but one or two slight cases of fever. He administered to each man daily a half-gram—nearly eight grains—of quinine, and every third or fourth day a double dose.

The following morning Colonel Rondon, Lyra, Kermit, Cherrie, and nine of the camaradas started in single file down the bank, while the doctor and I went in the two double canoes, with six camaradas, three of them the invalids with swollen feet. We halted continually, as we went about three times as fast as the walkers; and we traced the course of the river. After forty minutes' actual going in the boats we came to some rapids; the unloaded canoes ran them without difficulty, while the loads were portaged. In an hour and a half we were again under way, but in ten minutes came to other rapids, where the river ran among islands, and there were several big curls. The clumsy, heavily laden dugouts, lashed in couples, were unwieldy and hard to handle. The rapids came just round a sharp bend, and we got caught in the upper part of the swift water and had to run the first set of rapids in consequence. We in the leading pair of dugouts were within an ace of coming to grief on some big bowlders against which we were swept by a cross current at the turn. All of us paddling hard—scraping and bumping—we got through by the skin of our teeth, and managed to make the bank and moor our dugouts. It was a narrow escape from grave disaster. The second pair of lashed dugouts profited by our experience, and made the run—with risk, but with less risk—and moored beside us. Then all the loads were taken out, and the empty canoes were run down through the least dangerous channels among the islands.

This was a long portage, and we camped at the foot of the rapids, having made nearly seven kilometres. Here a little river, a rapid stream of volume equal to the Dúvida at the point where we first embarked, joined from the west. Colonel Rondon and Kermit came to it first, and the former named it Rio Kermit. There was in it a waterfall about six or eight feet high, just above the junction. Here we found plenty of fish. Lyra caught two pacu, good-sized, deep-bodied fish. They were delicious eating. Antonio the Parecís said that these fish never came up heavy rapids in which there were falls they had to jump. We could only hope that he was correct, as in that case the rapids we would encounter in the future would rarely be so serious as to necessitate our dragging the heavy dugouts overland. Passing the rapids we had hitherto encountered had meant severe labor and some danger. But the event showed that he was mistaken. The worst rapids were ahead of us.

While our course as a whole had been almost due north, and sometimes east of north, yet where there were rapids the river had generally, although not always, turned westward. This seemed to indicate that to the east of us there was a low northward projection of the central plateau across which we had travelled on mule-back. This is the kind of projection that appears on the maps of this region as a sierra. Probably it sent low spurs to the west, and the farthest points of these spurs now and then caused rapids in our course (for the rapids generally came where there were hills) and for the moment deflected the river westward from its general downhill trend to the north. There was no longer any question that the Dúvida was a big river, a river of real importance. It was not a minor affluent of some other affluent. But we were still wholly in the dark as to where it came out. It was still possible, although exceedingly improbable, that it entered the Gy-Paraná, as another river of substantially the same size, near its mouth. It was much more likely, but not probable, that it entered the Tapajos. It was probable, although far from certain, that it entered the Madeira low down, near its point of junction with the Amazon. In this event it was likely, although again far from certain, that its mouth would prove to be the Aripuanan. The Aripuanan does not appear on the maps as a river of any size; on a good standard map of South America which I had with me its name does not appear at all, although a dotted indication of a small river or creek at about the right place probably represents it. Nevertheless, from the report of one of his lieutenants who had examined its mouth, and from the stories of the rubber-gatherers, or seringuerros, Colonel Rondon had come to the conclusion that this was the largest affluent of the Madeira, with such a body of water that it must have a big drainage basin. He thought that the Dúvida was probably one of its head streams—although every existing map represented the lay of the land to be such as to render impossible the existence of such a river system and drainage basin. The rubber-gatherers reported that they had gone many days' journey up the river, to a point where there was a series of heavy rapids with above them the junction-point of two large rivers, one entering from the west. Beyond this they had difficulties because of the hostility of the Indians; and where the junction-point was no one could say. On the chance Colonel Rondon had directed one of his subordinate officers, Lieutenant Pyrineus, to try to meet us, with boats and provisions, by ascending the Aripuanan to the point of entry of its first big affluent. This was the course followed when Amilcar had been directed to try to meet the explorers who in 1909 came down the Gy-Paraná. At that time the effort was a failure, and the two parties never met; but we might have better luck, and in any event the chance was worth taking.

On the morning following our camping by the mouth of the Rio Kermit, Colonel Rondon took a good deal of pains in getting a big post set up at the entry of the smaller river into the Dúvida. Then he summoned me, and all the others, to attend the ceremony of its erection. We found the camaradas drawn up in line, and the colonel preparing to read aloud "the orders of the day." To the post was nailed a board with "Rio Kermit" on it; and the colonel read the orders reciting that by the direction of the Brazilian Government, and inasmuch as the unknown river was evidently a great river, he formally christened it the Rio Roosevelt. This was a complete surprise to me. Both Lauro Müller and Colonel Rondon had spoken to me on the subject, and I had urged, and Kermit had urged, as strongly as possible, that the name be kept as Rio da Dúvida. We felt that the "River of Doubt" was an unusually good name; and it is always well to keep a name of this character. But my kind friends insisted otherwise, and it would have been churlish of me to object longer. I was much touched by their action, and by the ceremony itself. At the conclusion of the reading Colonel Rondon led in cheers for the United States and then for me and for Kermit; and the camaradas cheered with a will. I proposed three cheers for Brazil and then for Colonel Rondon, and Lyra, and the doctor, and then for all the camaradas. Then Lyra said that everybody had been cheered except Cherrie; and so we all gave three cheers for Cherrie, and the meeting broke up in high good humor.

Immediately afterward the walkers set off on their march down-stream, looking for good canoe-trees. In a quarter of an hour we followed with the canoes. As often as we overtook them we halted until they had again gone a good distance ahead. They soon found fresh Indian sign, and actually heard the Indians; but the latter fled in panic. They came on a little Indian fishing village, just abandoned. The three low, oblong huts, of palm-leaves, had each an entrance for a man on all fours, but no other opening. They were dark inside, doubtless as a protection against the swarms of biting flies. On a pole in this village an axe, a knife, and some strings of red beads were left, with the hope that the Indians would return, find the gifts, and realize that we were friendly. We saw further Indian sign on both sides of the river.

After about two hours and a half we came on a little river entering from the east. It was broad but shallow, and at the point of entrance rushed down, green and white, over a sharply inclined sheet of rock. It was a lovely sight and we halted to admire it. Then on we went, until, when we had covered about eight kilometres, we came on a stretch of rapids. The canoes ran them with about a third of the loads, the other loads being carried on the men's shoulders. At the foot of the rapids we camped, as there were several good canoe-trees near, and we had decided to build two rather small canoes. After dark the stars came out; but in the deep forest the glory of the stares in the night of the sky, the serene radiance of the moon, the splendor of sunrise and sunset, are never seen as they are seen on the vast open plains.

The following day, the 19th, the men began work on the canoes. The ill-fated big canoe had been made of wood so hard that it was difficult to work, and so heavy that the chips sank like lead in the water. But these trees were araputangas, with wood which was easier to work, and which floated. Great buttresses, or flanges, jutted out from their trunks at the base, and they bore big hard nuts or fruits which stood erect at the ends of the branches. The first tree felled proved rotten, and moreover it was chopped so that it smashed a number of lesser trees into the kitchen, overthrowing everything, but not in-flicting serious damage. Hard-working, willing, and tough though the cama-radas were, they naturally did not have the skill of northern lumberjacks.

We hoped to finish the two canoes in three days. A space was cleared in the forest for our tents. Among the taller trees grew huge-leafed pacovas, or wild bananas. We bathed and swam in the river, although in it we caught piranhas. Carregadores ants swarmed all around our camp. As many of the nearest of their holes as we could we stopped with fire; but at night some of them got into our tents and ate things we could ill spare. In the early morning a column of foraging ants appeared, and we drove them back, also with fire. When the sky was not overcast the sun was very hot, and we spread out everything to dry. There were many wonderful butterflies round about, but only a few birds. Yet in the early morning and late afternoon there was some attractive bird music in the woods. The two best performers were our old friend the false bell-bird, with its series of ringing whistles, and a shy, attractive ant-thrush. The latter walked much on the ground, with dainty movements, courtesying and raising its tail; and in accent and sequence, although not in tone or time, its song resembled that of our white-throated sparrow.

It was three weeks since we had started down the River of Doubt. We had come along its winding course about 140 kilometres, with a descent of somewhere in the neighborhood of 124 metres. It had been slow progress. We could not tell what physical obstacles were ahead of us, nor whether the Indians would be actively hostile. But a river normally describes in its course a parabola, the steep descent being in the upper part; and we hoped that in the future we should not have to encounter so many and such difficult rapids as we had already encountered, and that therefore we would make better time—a hope destined to failure.

Permissions Acknowledgments